Ageing Women in Literature and Visual Culture

Cathy McGlynn · Margaret O'Neill
Michaela Schrage-Früh
Editors

Ageing Women in Literature and Visual Culture

Reflections, Refractions, Reimaginings

Editors
Cathy McGlynn
Independent Researcher
Limerick, Ireland

Margaret O'Neill
Gender ARC
University of Limerick
Limerick, Ireland

Michaela Schrage-Früh
Languages, Literatures and Cultures
National University of Ireland Galway
Galway, Ireland

ISBN 978-3-319-87593-4 ISBN 978-3-319-63609-2 (eBook)
DOI 10.1007/978-3-319-63609-2

Cover illustration: Geber86, Credit: JPM

Printed on acid-free paper

This Palgrave Macmillan imprint is published by Springer Nature
The registered company is Springer International Publishing AG
The registered company address is: Gewerbestrasse 11, 6330 Cham, Switzerland

Acknowledgements

Some of the chapters in this volume were first presented at the international, interdisciplinary conference "Women and Ageing: New Critical and Cultural Perspectives," which took place at the University of Limerick, Ireland, in May 2015. The editors would like to thank all participants for turning this conference into a vibrant platform for interdisciplinary dialogue and exchange. We also gratefully acknowledge the generous support of the Irish Research Council (New Foundations scheme), Fáilte Ireland, and the University of Limerick, most notably the Faculty of Arts, Humanities and Social Sciences; the School of Culture and Communication; the School of Modern Languages and Applied Linguistics; Gender ARC; and the Centre for German-Irish Studies. Last but not least, we would like to express thanks to our supportive editors at Palgrave Macmillan, notably Martina O'Sullivan and Heloise Harding, as well as two anonymous readers for their invaluable comments and suggestions.

Contents

Editors and Contributors

About the Editors

Cathy McGlynn is an independent researcher and has lectured in the University of Limerick, Ireland, and the Dún Laoghaire Institute of Art, Design and Technology, Ireland. Her research interests include the representation of ageing women in interwar and Modernist fiction by women writers, and women's travel writing. She is a founding member of WARN (Women and Ageing Research Network).

Margaret O'Neill is Gender ARC Project Coordinator at the University of Limerick, Ireland. She researches and publishes in twentieth-century and contemporary Irish women's writing and feminist and psychoanalytic theory. She has taught in the University of Limerick and Maynooth University. She is a founding member of WARN (Women and Ageing Research Network).

Michaela Schrage-Früh is Lecturer in German at the National University of Ireland, Galway, and Lecturer in English at the University of Mainz, Germany. She has previously taught at the University of Limerick, Ireland. She holds a Ph.D. in English from the University of Mainz (2003) and has published widely on contemporary Irish and British poetry and fiction. Her recent monograph is *Philosophy, Dreaming and the Literary Imagination* (Palgrave Macmillan, 2016). She is a founding member of WARN (Women and Ageing Research Network).

Contributors

Eva Adelseck M.A. studied Contemporary German Literature and Media Communication at the Universities of Bonn and Oxford. Her research interests focus on First World War Literature and the depiction of age-related dementia in contemporary literature and film. She is currently working as a DAAD-funded German language tutor at the University of Manchester.

Kate Antosik-Parsons is a contemporary art historian and visual artist with a Ph.D. in Art History from University College Dublin (2012). Kate is a Research Associate of the UCD Humanities Institute. Her interdisciplinary research is concerned with gender, sexuality, embodiment and memory. She has published essays on Irish performance and video artists including Amanda Coogan, Pauline Cummins, Willie Doherty, Jaki Irvine, Alanna O'Kelly and Áine Phillips.

Julia K. Dabbs is Associate Professor at the University of Minnesota, Morris. Her research focuses on women artists, especially of the early modern period, and historical documentation of their lives and careers. This work has resulted in publications such as *Life Stories of Women Artists, 1550–1800* (Ashgate, 2009) and "Vision and Insight: Portraits of the Aged Woman Artist, 1600–1800," *Occasion: Interdisciplinary Studies in the Humanities* (2012).

Saskia Fürst (Ph.D. Phil from the University of Salzburg) is an independent scholar. She holds a B.A. in German and Women & Gender Studies from Rice University (USA) and a Diploma in English and American Studies from the University of Graz (Austria). Her article "The Sexy, Mature Black Woman in US Advertisements" was published in *Racial and Ethnic Identities in the Media* (2016).

Germaine Greer was born in Melbourne and educated in Australia and at Cambridge University. Her first book, *The Female Eunuch* (1969), took the world by storm and remains one of the most influential texts of the feminist movement. Germaine Greer has had a distinguished academic career in Britain and the USA. She makes regular appearances in print and other media as a broadcaster, journalist, columnist and reviewer. Since 2001 she has been involved in rehabilitating 60 hectares of subtropical rainforest in south-east Queensland; in 2011 she set up

Friends of Gondwana Rainforest, a UK charity, to help in financing that and similar projects.

Hannah Grist is Lecturer in Media at the University of Gloucestershire, and postdoctoral researcher at the Centre for Women, Ageing and Media (WAM). Hannah is involved in a number of research projects focused on memory, heritage, identity and representations of older age. She teaches and has published on qualitative research methods, television as heritage, ageing and film noir, and is currently working on a manuscript about the representation of carers and care work in the British media.

Deborah Jermyn is Reader in Film and Television at the University of Roehampton. She has published widely on the matrix of women, feminism and popular culture, most recently with a focus on ageing femininities, including as editor of the collections *Female Celebrity and Ageing: Back In The Spotlight* (2013) and (with Su Holmes) *Women, Celebrity and Cultures of Ageing: Freeze Frame* (2015). Her latest monograph is *Nancy Meyers* (Bloomsbury, 2017).

Ros Jennings is Professor of Ageing, Culture and Media and Director of the Centre for Women, Ageing and Media (WAM) at the University of Gloucestershire, UK. She is co-editor with Abigail Gardner of *Rock On: Women, Ageing and Popular Music* (2013) and author of "Popular Music and Ageing" in Twigg, J. and Martin, W. (eds) *The Handbook of Cultural Gerontology*. She has published numerous articles on women, ageing and media in peer-reviewed journals and collections.

Anne Jerslev is Professor of Film and Media Studies at the University of Copenhagen. She currently researches contemporary processes of celebrification and representations of ageing women. She has published numerous articles and books about contemporary film and television culture, media reception and audience studies and reality television. She has edited a number of journal issues and volumes in English, among these (co-edited with Lúcia Nagib) *Impure Cinema: Intermedial and Intercultural Approaches to Film* (I.B. Tauris, 2014).

Amber Jones received her B.S. in Secondary Education with an M.A. in English in May 2009 from Tennessee Technological University. She is currently Composition and Rhetoric instructor and Program Chair at Ivy Tech Community College in Richmond, Indiana, USA.

Susan Liddy lectures in the Department of Media and Communications in MIC, Limerick. Her research interests and publications relate to the representation of older women in film, gender issues in the script development and production process, creativity and creative practice and the work of Irish female writers/directors.

Bridie Moore is Lecturer in Drama, Theatre and Performance at the University of Huddersfield. She is completing her AHRC funded Ph.D. study on Age and Ageing in Contemporary British Theatre at the University of Sheffield. Passages Theatre, her old women's performance group, was formed in 2012 and has presented age-critical performances in venues and at conferences nationally. Her article "Depth, Significance and Absence: Age-Effects in New British Theatre" was published in the journal *Age, Culture, Humanities* in 2014.

Antoinette Pretorius received a Ph.D. from the University of Pretoria in 2015. She is Lecturer in the Department of English Studies at the University of South Africa. Her current research explores the relationship between notions of culture, gender, identity and food in contemporary South African literature.

EL Putnam is a visual artist, scholar, and writer working predominately in performance art, video, sound and interactive media. Her work draws from multiple themes and sources, including explorations of gender and sexuality, play, materialism and the study of place. Her research focuses on continental aesthetic philosophy, performance studies, digital studies, feminist theory and examining the influence of neoliberalism on artistic production. Originally from the United States, EL currently lives in works in Dublin, Ireland.

Lucinda Rasmussen completed her doctorate degree at the University of Alberta in 2014 where she teaches English and Composition. Her dissertation examines women's illness memoirs. Her teaching and research interests include contemporary women's auto/biography, Indigenous literatures in North America, and postfeminism and popular culture. She has co-edited and contributed to "Auto/Biography in Transit," a special issue of *Biography: An Interdisciplinary Quarterly* (38.1, Winter 2015).

Katherine Whitehurst recently completed her Ph.D. at the University of Stirling under the supervision of Prof. Karen Boyle and Dr. Katharina Linder. She now teaches at the University of Liverpool in the Department of Communication and Media. Her research explores representations of female growth and ageing in Western contemporary filmic, televisual and comic adaptations of "Snow White."

Theresa Wray is an independent scholar and has been involved in community education for many years. Her work on Mary Lavin has been published in *New Hibernia Review* (Summer 2015), *The Irish Short Story: Traditions and Trends* (2015), *Mary Lavin* (2013), *New Voices, Inherited Lines: Literary and Cultural Representations of the Irish Family* (2013), *The Irish Review* (Winter 2013) and *The Politics of Irish Writing* (2010).

List of Figures

CHAPTER 1

Introduction

Cathy McGlynn, Margaret O'Neill and Michaela Schrage-Früh

At the 2016 Billboard Music Awards, on receipt of an award for Woman of the Year, Madonna delivered an emotional speech detailing the misogyny and sexism she has experienced throughout her career. She stated that "the most controversial thing that I've done is to stick around," given that in the entertainment world "to age is a sin. You will be criticized, you will be vilified, and you will definitely not be played on the radio"[1] (Blake 2016). Three days previously, on the British

[1] This reference to radio play is almost certainly related to the BBC Radio 1 controversy in the UK. In 2014, the then head of music at BBC Radio1 and 1Xtra, George Ergatoudis, stated that "The vast majority of people who like Madonna, who like her music now, are

C. McGlynn (✉)
Limerick, Ireland
e-mail: cathymcglynn@gmail.com

M. O'Neill
University of Limerick, Limerick, Ireland
e-mail: Margaret.ONeill@ul.ie

M. Schrage-Früh
National University of Ireland Galway, Galway, Ireland
e-mail: Michaela.Schrage-Frueh@nuigalway.ie

C. McGlynn et al. (eds.), *Ageing Women in Literature and Visual Culture*,
DOI 10.1007/978-3-319-63609-2_1

television show *Good Morning Britain*, Piers Morgan pretended to vomit upon seeing a clip of Madonna twerking on James Corden's popular "Carpool Karaoke" segment for *The Late Late Show*. He claimed, "I loved Madonna when she acted her age [...] you can't be 58 and prancing about." Six weeks later, in his column for the *Mail Online*, Piers Morgan blasted Madonna's version of angry feminism, referring to Madonna as "once the fresh, exciting Material Girl, now the bitter, cynical, ageing Vinegar Girl who can always be relied upon to sour anything she touches" (Morgan 2017). Morgan here constructs the ageing woman[2] according to a strict binary logic that aligns female sexuality and power exclusively with youth: she is no longer "fresh." Madonna's refusal to retreat into silence in middle age and her repeated assertion of an overt sexuality are demonised, especially in the context of a demonstration for women's equality. Loudly proclaiming himself an ardent feminist, Morgan in his article adeptly uses Madonna's repudiation of cultural norms relating to ageing to attack feminism itself. It seems feminism is acceptable only at the expense of the exclusion of ageing women.

The Madonna-Morgan spat is symptomatic of a wider cultural obsession with and marginalisation of the ageing woman. In contemporary celebrity culture, examples abound of women's experience of ageism (see Jermyn and Holmes 2015). In her 2011 memoir *Shockaholic*, Carrie Fisher discussed her casting as Princess Leia in *Star Wars*, and wrote: "What I didn't realise, back when I was this twenty-five-year-old pinup for geeks in that me myself and iconic metal bikini, was that I had

continued over 30 and frankly, we've moved on from Madonna." A year later Madonna's newly released single "Living for Love" was omitted from the station's playlist, leading to accusations of ageism from the singer. See Deardon (2015).

[2]We recognise that "ageing" is a contextual, perspective-based term, which is also often negatively associated with decline and stereotype. When we use this term, rather than substitute it with "older" or "later life," it is in the context of our guiding premise: that the body is embedded in discourse, and confronting and naming categories in the cultural world provides for resisting such forces, to "unveil," as it were, the ageing subject. By using the term "ageing" rather than "older," we also draw attention to the fact that ageing is a life-long process and that signs of ageing affect individual women at different stages in the life-course. Accordingly, while this volume's focus ranges from middle age to the fourth age, some chapters also specifically explore how prevalent cultural notions of ageing, such as the "horror of growing old" (de Beauvoir 1997, 587) or the cult of youth, can impact on younger women's self-perception (see, for instance, Chaps. 7, 11 and 12).

signed an invisible contract to stay looking the exact same way for the next thirty to forty years. Well, clearly I've broken that contract" (Fisher 2011, 27). Four years later, Fisher would take to Twitter to defend herself against accusations of ageing badly in the 2015 *Star Wars: The Force Awakens.* She tweeted: "Please stop debating about whetherOR not [I] aged well.unfortunately it hurts all3 of my feelings.My BODY hasnt aged as well as I have" (Fisher 2015 *sic*). Here Fisher articulates a significant difference between her experience of ageing and its visible manifestation in her body. The physical embodiment of ageing does not, in Fisher's experience, match her corresponding lived experience of ageing and in this way resembles what Jeannette King refers to as "the ideal embodied subject" who "construct[s] an identity for herself that is determined neither by the ageing body nor by the discourses that construct it as 'ageing'" (2013, 173). This complexity is at the root of dominant cultural conceptions of the ageing female body, which tend to conflate biology and experience, identifying the "I"(self) and the ageing body as one and the same, leading to what Margaret Morganroth Gullette refers to as a loss of "selfhood" (1999, 36). Fisher insists on the separation of the subject "I" from the body, thus asserting a robust selfhood in a later tweet: "I identify more w/who I feel myself 2be than what I look like. Either way, Am I obliged 2entertain U w/my appearance?" (Fisher 2015 *sic*).

This obligation to entertain audiences with appearance relates to the broader context of women having less success in their careers as they age. Certainly in the entertainment industry, women's youth is a prized commodity that loses value with age and when the physical signs of youth are no longer visible, the older woman is rendered invisible.[3] In an interview with *The Telegraph* in 2015, Jane Fonda spoke about her experience of invisibility, observing that "We are the fastest-growing demographic in the world, and yet we have no face in the mass media. It is OK for men to get older, because men become more desirable by being powerful. With women, it's all about how we look." The visibility of women in the mass entertainment industry is dependent on making the visible signs of ageing invisible—in Fonda's case, this resulted in plastic surgery. She explained, "I need to work, so I had some plastic surgery [...] I think it probably bought me a decade of work" (Mulkerrins 2015). Fonda's

[3] See Kathleen Woodward, "Introduction," *Figuring Age: Women, Bodies, Generations,* 1999 for a discussion of the invisibility of the ageing woman.

experience demonstrates that, as King notes, "the value of the female body and its talents is dependent on its youthfulness" (2013, 176). Fonda's acknowledgement that an anti-ageing procedure literally increased her earnings is suggestive of the way in which contemporary culture, driven by consumption, transforms women's bodies into products with economic value. Youthful (female) bodies make money.

The ageism experienced by Madonna, Carrie Fisher and Jane Fonda is not atypical in the contemporary entertainment industry, but the issues it raises with regards to the cultural construction of the ageing woman are common across multiple cultural texts and contexts. The sexualised ageing woman as a source of disgust, the commodified female body, the (dis)connection between the ageing body and the ageing subject, the cultural obsession with the visual manifestations of ageing: all these concerns can be discerned in representations of ageing women in popular culture, celebrity culture, literature, film and television, art, performance art and fashion. And yet, the ageing woman's experience is one that has, up until relatively recently, received little critical attention in feminist studies. Simone de Beauvoir's *The Second Sex* (1949) was arguably the first feminist text to overtly address the "horror of growing old" and the "sorry tragedy of the aged woman" (1997, 587, 603). De Beauvoir would, three decades later, publish *La Viellesse* (translated and published in 1972 as *The Coming of Age*), a full-length consideration of the ageing process, but this latter text is curiously devoid of any in-depth consideration of gender in relation to the ageing process.[4] In 1972 Susan Sontag published "The Double Standard of Aging" in *The Saturday Review*, in which she lamented the fact that "there is a double standard of aging that denounces women with special severity. Society is much more permissive about aging in men" (1972, 31). This double standard is still prevalent in contemporary culture—consider for example a recent *Huffington Post* article which describes "30 Celebs who are Aging Gracefully," 23 of whom are women. *Elle* magazine does not bother to include men in its 2015 article "18 Celebrities Who Don't Age and the Anti-Ageing Secrets they Swear by" (Dawson Hoff).

Following Sontag, ageing was a topic largely absent from feminist discourse until the publication of Germaine Greer's *The Change: Women,*

[4]This goes in part to explain why *The Coming of Age* was largely ignored by feminists. For a detailed analysis of the text see King (2013), 67–72.

Ageing and the Menopause in 1991. Greer's critique of the medical establishment's treatment of the menopause was groundbreaking. Unlike her predecessors, Greer does celebrate the onset of old age in women as an avenue of freedom: as a woman's looks recede, she is no longer culturally constructed as a sexual object, and, now "unwanted," the ageing woman can "be free" (1992, 4). This stance partly explains Greer's reaction to reading the *Telegraph* article featuring Jane Fonda's criticism of the entertainment industry's bias against ageing women. A day after the Fonda interview was published, Greer spoke disparagingly at the Hay Festival about Fonda's decision to have plastic surgery for the sake of her career: "I read Jane Fonda today saying men want younger women so we have to try to look young. Jane! Why not say older women want gorgeous boys? Men want younger women? So let them want. There's no shortage out there. You don't have to pretend to be one!" Greer's attack on Fonda's effort to look young was framed by her acknowledgement that "the terror of growing old is worse than it ever was" (Singh 2015). This, in Greer's view, is due in part to anti-ageing products, which don't work and "are marketed by exploiting [...] women's anxiety" (Singh 2015). The "terror of ageing" then is a cultural construction synonymous with the commodification of women's bodies. The rise and success of the anti-ageing beauty product industry since Greer's 1991 book on ageing testifies to the growing need for a sustained critical consideration of prevailing attitudes to the ageing woman's experience in multiple texts and contexts.

Accordingly, with the rise of cultural gerontology as a discipline, more critical attention has been devoted to the cultural construction of the ageing woman. Kathleen Woodward's pioneering essay collection, *Figuring Age: Women, Bodies, Generations* (1999) focuses on making visible "the virtually invisible subject of older women" (x) and arguably spearheaded a new direction in ageing studies, represented by literary critics such as Sally Chivers, Zoe Brennan, Jeanette King and Heike Hartung, and media and visual culture experts such as Ros Jennings, Julia Twigg, Deborah Jermyn and Imelda Whelehan, all of whom link gender to ageing in specific genres or aspects such as popular culture.[5]

[5] Examples for publications on ageing and literature include Chivers (2003), Brennan (2005), King (2013) and Hartung (2016); examples for publications on ageing and celebrity/popular culture include Jennings and Gardner (2012), Whelehan and Gwynne (2014) and Jermyn and Holmes (2015); an example for a study on ageing and fashion is Twigg (2013).

Margaret Cruikshank's *Learning to Be Old: Gender, Culture and Ageing* (2003) concentrates on American women's experiences of ageing, arguing that "ageing is a creation of this time and place, more cultural than biological, determined by social institutions, or, more optimistically, a set of life experiences we can consciously shape, once we see how others are attempting to shape them for us" (2003, 2). The very fact that ageing is largely socially constructed means, in Cruikshank's positive view, that it can be resisted. In her view, "learning to be old requires that we both observe how aging is socially constructed and find ways to resist being molded to its dictates" (2003, 2), and her study details some of the ways in which this might be achieved. However, as recently as 2006, Calasanti, Slevin and King have produced research that demonstrates how ageing studies is still largely marginalised in feminist discourse. They lament the fact that "The number of women's studies scholars engaged in work on later life is still so small that those with any interest in aging can count them" (2006, 13). This essay collection, then, marks a vital contribution to a field still in its relative infancy. In contrast to most recent publications on this topic, which tend to look at ageing in one genre, such as literature, or one aspect, such as popular culture, this book seeks to put diverse genres and media into conversation, acknowledging that conceptions of the ageing woman are constructed across different visual and verbal media.

As our initial examples taken from celebrity culture illustrate, visuality plays a dominant role in discourses on women and ageing. However, while it is true that we live in "a culture saturated by images" (Woodward 1999, xix) and that "age is itself a visual phenomenon" (Twigg and Martin 2015, 5), we argue that such images are created—and can be resisted or reshaped—both visually and verbally. Not only do images and texts often go hand in hand, but literary texts can activate powerful processes of visualisation in the reader. As Margarita Dikovitskaya puts it in *Visual Culture* (2005): "The psychological notions of vision—interior vision, imagining, dreaming, remembering—are activated by both visual and literary means. Thus, the study of visual culture allows all these aspects to come into view: One begins to look at and actually examine the process of visualizing literary texts" (56). While much of the work done in the fields of ageing studies and cultural gerontology has focused on visual culture, it is important to note that what Gullette refers to as "inner storytelling" and "nonvisual memories" (2004, 10) can result in new cultural narratives of ageing that enrich, complicate, counteract and complement the visual image. This is arguably most effectively realised in literary genres, such as life writing or the *Reifungsroman*, which focus on the ageing subject's inner life, often at odds with outward visual appearance. Several contributions in this collection testify to the inextricable interconnections between the visual and the verbal, such as Julia Dabbs's chapter, which focuses on the ways in which contemporary, male-authored biographies and art histories treat (or ignore) early modern women artists and their productivity in old age. Another case in point is performance art. Thus, as Bridie Moore points out in her chapter in this collection, Peggy Shaw's age performances in "gentleman drag" present her audience with the outward image of a gentleman in his thirties while the story she tells is that of "a sixty-plus year old, second-generation Irish, working-class, grand-butch-mother." Other chapters illuminate similar themes, such as prescribed social roles for older women, through the lens of either literature or visual culture, thus complementing and enriching each other.

As the image of the ageing woman is reflected and refracted across cultural texts and media, our collection brings together experts in literature and visual culture to foster a much-needed dialogue across disciplines. In doing so, it analyses the power that these constructions exert over public and private conceptions of age, and explores the ways in which the figure of the ageing woman is reimagined or reinscribed across media, genres and cultures. In acknowledging the diversity of experiences and perspectives, we aim to follow Woodward's invitation, voiced in the preface to *Figuring Age*, "to write about women, bodies, and generations not just in terms of mainstream, middle-class culture, one that is predominantly white, but in a myriad of other cultural and subcultural contexts as well" (1999, xxiii). Thus, section four on "Class, 'Race' and Agency" includes chapters which explore ageing in African American (Fürst), South African (Pretorius) and emigrant Irish (O'Neill) contexts. More generally, the contributors to this volume engage in transnational, multi-disciplinary research methods, including fields of life writing, memory studies, postcolonial and feminist approaches. The collection is deliberately structured to facilitate the imbrication of visual culture and literature so as to arrive at a multifaceted and overtly interdisciplinary analysis of cultural representations of ageing. Our hope is that this intersectional and cross-disciplinary structure will foster a fruitful dialogue across disciplinary and generic boundaries.

Narratives of Ageing

The first thematic section brings together four chapters on narratives of ageing. Narrative has emerged as central to cultural gerontology. Discussing literature and ageing, Sarah Falcus, in her contribution to the *Routledge Handbook of Cultural Gerontology*, notes that "With its insistence on the temporal, narrative is of obvious interest to those exploring age, often based on the idea that we live storied lives" (2015, 57). The analysis of narrative draws on a range of critical approaches. The contributors in this section interweave psychoanalytic, historical, biographic and generic approaches as they explore how older women in biography, biopic, fiction, and performance art confront social expectations. Their readings are further illuminated by theories of narrative and ageing. To expand on such theories, Woodward, for example, has commented on the process of reminiscence in narratives of old age, which involve backward and forward movement, and are both private and social (1997, 3). Heike Hartung has further established age as a literary category with particularly gendered inflections. As she notes, "narratives of ageing are always gendered, differentiating the potential scope for development as well as the possible social and individual roles for men and women" (2016, 3). Such theories shed light on the cultural texts under exploration in this section, as narratives effect a conversation between older and younger generations of women and meander in a manner that nods to psychic time as well as the progression of chronological time. Though they encompass different genres and media, each essay in this section has a biographical leaning. In this context, it is significant that narratives of ageing have been read both in terms of decline and of progress. The decline of the old is so widely and pervasively assumed that it is embedded in narratives of old age (Gullette 1997). Barbara Frey Waxman, however, coined the term *Reifungsroman* to describe progress narratives in which, positively, "We cannot underestimate the political power [...] to effect change in younger people's attitude toward the elderly, in individuals' attitudes toward their own aging, and in notions of appropriate social roles for elders" (1990, 187). The essays in this section illustrate these oppositional attitudes towards the progression of age, as they read stories of decline as well as regeneration. As these contributions testify, periods of later life, however negatively or affirmatively they are depicted, can both reflect as well as interrogate cultural values. Doing so, they open out generative spaces which may be informed by new concepts of ageing.

The first chapter, by Julia K. Dabbs, focuses on the (in)visibility of older women artists in the early modern period. While recent male-authored studies on artists and old age tend to omit or marginalise women artists past the age of 50, Dabbs draws on early modern sources to explore both verbal and visual representations of women artists productive in their later years. Studying these artists' life narratives in light of prominent old-age tropes associated with male artists as well as negative cultural tropes associated with older women, her analysis highlights alternative, more positive representations of the older woman artist in terms of wisdom, creativity and agency.

Following this, Eva Adelseck turns to more recent examples of successful women by examining two biographical films, *Iris* (2001) and *The Iron Lady* (2011), about novelist Iris Murdoch and former Prime Minister Margaret Thatcher, respectively. The two biopics are linked by their focus on Alzheimer's disease, from which both women suffered in their later years. Adelseck explores the representation of the formerly successful and autonomous protagonists' loss of memory, identity and independence in light of psychoanalytical concepts such as othering and the uncanny. In doing so, she argues that ageing women suffering from dementia are doubly othered and that this othering is, in part, perpetuated in the films that narrate their mental decline.

The next chapter focuses on literary narrative. Michaela Schrage-Früh reads Clare Boylan's novel *Beloved Stranger*, a fictionalised account of the relationship between Boylan's parents, as an example of the recently emerged genre of the *Reifungsroman*, or novel of ripening. In her analysis, Schrage-Früh foregrounds the narrative features of this genre, one of whose central aims is to resist the cultural myth of ageing as a narrative of decline, by exploring the seventy-five-year-old protagonist's fictional life review and her difficult journey towards self-discovery, progress and liberation.

In the final chapter in this section, Bridie Moore shifts the focus to performance art and Peggy Shaw's autobiographical age performances in particular. Moore argues that the absence of a linear narrative or a coherent fictional world enables the performance artist, in this case an older, lesbian woman in "gentleman drag," to subvert "the normative age scripts of femininity." As Moore points out, by also performing and engaging with the infirmity of her post-stroke body, Shaw challenges the conventional decline narrative, instead presenting an "old woman" who counters the figure popularly staged as dependent, obsolete or obscene.

Social Roles

Section two explores the ways in which social roles and expectations for ageing women are reflected or reimagined in, or indeed shaped by, different media and genres. As cultural gerontology has established, old age is not solely biological but is also culturally situated, its meaning influenced by wider social structures. The important project of foregrounding age in socio-cultural analysis is exemplified in the research of Julia Twigg, who argues that age, like gender, is "one of the most profound elements that structure the social realm. Age and aging are deeply social" (2004, 70). Furthermore, old age is not only a collective but also an individual experience. An individual's position is informed by physical, psychological as well as cultural and social conditions, and it is always in flux. However, the identities of older people are often airbrushed in and by a culture of youth which asserts the pressure to "pass" as younger. The "invisible" older woman, as King writes in her seminal work *Discourses of Ageing in Fiction and Feminism: The Invisible Woman*, is compelled to disguise herself as younger to become visible (2013). Connectedly, Gullette has famously argued that we are "aged by culture," whereby dominant concepts of age in culture are mapped onto the body, which is then monitored for signs that it is in decline (2004). This phenomenon pervades in contemporary postfeminist culture in which, under the guise that equality has been achieved and within a consumerist society, the figure of the young woman represents an ideal of attainment. Exploring different facets of the histories of this culture, the contributions to this section illuminate the influence that symbols and stereotypes of womanhood, such as the "mothers" created by Jane Austen, still hold today. Recognising the historically and culturally constructed nature of these images and speaking to their present-day endurance, these chapters interrogate the consequences of two-dimensional representations of older women, illustrating how such stereotypes inform and impoverish social status in old age. Doing so, these essays reinforce the importance of diversity and creativity in cultural representation.

The first chapter in section two, by Amber Jones, takes a fresh look at Jane Austen's representation of ageing mothers. Taking into account the lasting popularity of Austen's novels, Jones argues that, while Austen's young and unconventional heroines still appeal to readers today, their ageing female counterparts are harder to identify with, as they tend to be presented as a source of ridicule and conflict. However, as Jones shows,

Austen's largely negative representations of ageing mothers must be read in their historical and cultural context, more specifically in line with the limitations inherent in social and cultural norms which, for ageing mothers, often evolved into literal, physical boundaries.

If Austen's fictions have lastingly impacted readers' negative conceptions of older women, the same can be said of fairy tales, which often depict older female characters as wicked stepmothers or witches. Accordingly, in her chapter on ABC's television programme *Once Upon a Time*, Katherine Whitehurst examines the depiction of the three female leads, Snow White, Snow White's daughter and the Evil Queen, all of whom have been cast within the same age bracket, thus seemingly diverting from generational conflicts and age stereotypes. As Whitehurst shows, however, the programme reiterates the Queen's and Snow White's connection with ageing and youth through their ideological associations with different generations of mothers and feminists, thus ultimately perpetuating narratives that idealise youth and reaffirming the narrative of the evil older woman.

Following this, Cathy McGlynn's chapter shifts the focus from motherhood to spinsterhood. More specifically, McGlynn looks at the representation of ageing women in relation to the construction of spinsterhood in Sylvia Townsend Warner's short fiction, spanning the author's long writing career from the interwar period in the 1930s to her later work in the 1960s. Taking Warner's most famous ageing spinster Lolly Willowes as her starting-point, McGlynn analyses the construction of spinsterhood in a selection of Warner's critically neglected short stories, demonstrating the author's increasingly subversive critique of a youth culture that marginalises the old and unmarried.

The fourth chapter included in this section has a combined focus on the depiction of the ageing mother and widow. In her analysis of Helen Fielding's *Bridget Jones: Mad about The Boy*, Lucinda Rasmussen shows how the third novel about Bridget Jones differs from its predecessors in that the chick-lit heroine is now a fifty-one-year-old widow and single mother rather than a singleton in her mid-thirties. Examining the negative reactions by readers and critics, who shame the older protagonist for her perceived immaturity, Rasmussen discusses the novel in the context of postfeminism, arguing that *Mad about The Boy* allows us to better understand how a now mature postfeminism depends vitally on its continuing suppression of its female subjects as they age.

The Body and Embodiment

The contributions in section three partake in a burgeoning field of work on the body and embodiment in ageing, exploring how the body is aged in and by culture. It is notable that much of previous feminist work has focused on younger bodies. This avoidance comes not only from within feminism but also from within gerontology, as biomedical accounts have been privileged over the social. Essentially, this reflects reluctance in wider culture to address issues of old age (Twigg 2004, 60). However, with the cultural turn in gerontology, renewed considerations of the body have emerged in the humanities and cultural studies, illustrating, as Twigg demonstrates, that "The aging body is thus not natural, is not prediscursive, but fashioned within and by culture" (2004, 60). The cultural in gerontology signifies a movement away from bodies as purely physiological towards thinking of ageing in relation to power, as with gender and sexuality. Furthermore, as Emmanuelle Tulle illustrates in her contribution to the *Routledge Handbook of Cultural Gerontology*, "Gender as well as class (and ethnicity) are inscribed in and on bodies" (2015, 130). The essays in this section starkly illustrate how bodies in culture are created by discourses and regulated by social practices. Individually, they deal with representations of the body and embodiment in film, fiction, television, fashion campaigns and performance art. These essays draw our attention to the mechanisms that operate to construct and control the body, as well as individual subversion of these expectations and stereotypes. Contributors explore discourses that regulate the body according to social standards and expectations of beauty and sexuality in a culture of anti-ageing. In doing so they highlight significant differences in how society perceives the ageing bodies of women and of men, and how this can have an effect on lived experience. As age differentiates older and younger, it also differentiates women and men, particularly when it comes to the appearance of old age. Therefore, old age is a time of commonality and of difference. However, depictions of strategies of resistance to ageist and gendered social expectation may be read across these essays. Together, these contributions illustrate that the position of the aged body in culture is gendered, subjective and open to many variables.

The section starts out with Susan Liddy's chapter on representations of older women and sexuality in film. As Liddy argues, in recent years cinematic films have engaged more overtly with later-life sexuality, thus challenging the cultural myth that sexual passion belongs exclusively to the young. However, analysing the representation of female mature sexuality in three recent films, *Hope Springs*, *Le Week-End* and *45 Years*, Liddy shows that these films still perpetuate some problematic cultural conventions, such as the absence of the ageing female body, which, as Liddy concludes, points to a patriarchal and youth-dominated culture as well as a gendered film industry.

Following this chapter on film, Theresa Wray explores perceptions of the ageing process in Irish fiction. Focusing on a range of diverse texts by Mary Lavin, Bridget O'Connor, Mary Costello and Claire Kilroy, Wray analyses the ways in which their fictional characters struggle with bodily signs of ageing that carry negative cultural connotations and therefore impact adversely on their self-conception. In her analysis, Wray connects these diverse characters' perceptions of ageing to dominant cultural, media and health discourses and emphasises the importance of women's voices to counter prescribed meanings of what it means to grow older.

Ros Jennings' and Hannah Grist's chapter complements Liddy's and Wray's work on film and literature by exploring representations of the older female body in Lena Dunham's comedy television drama *Girls*. The authors show that the programme's representation of older women for the most part perpetuates dominant stereotypes such as the dying grandmother, the powerless disabled older woman or the postmenopausal cougar. Analysing the reasons for the programme's failure to transcend these categories, Jennings and Grist argue that current intergenerational politics of cultural ageism and chronological models of ageing prevent an imaginary where older women can be represented as powerfully complex and diverse. They also suggest that by reimagining ageing and motherhood through a "desire for the postmaternal," the ageing woman might be empowered and a younger generation of women might be provided with alternative cultural narratives.

In the next chapter, Deborah Jermyn and Anne Jerslev examine recent fashion campaigns featuring older women. Analysing the 2015 Céline campaign featuring Joan Didion, and the 2017 Pirelli calendar, they note that at first glance these campaigns increase the visibility of the older woman in popular culture and contribute to forging a positive image of the older woman's body. However, similar to older women's representation in recent film, the older female model ideal in fashion is overwhelmingly white and slim, just like in fashion photography in general.

Exploring the implications of the "cool" image as exemplified by older women in fashion photography, the authors nevertheless conclude that a cool appearance could provide an aesthetic space for older women in which to dissolve and reimagine norms about appearance as an older woman.

The last chapter included in this section, by EL Putnam, focuses on performance art in which the artists use their own bodies in the process of artistic creation. Putnam analyses three different performance acts of experimental artists: Rocio Boliver (Mexico), who holds up a grotesque mirror to the beauty industry and its commodification of youth and beauty; Pauline Cummins and Frances Mezzetti (Ireland), who take on male dress and mannerisms in public contexts to expose how older men and women are treated differently in public space; and Marilyn Arsem (United States), who draws attention to the female, ageing body as the corporeal inscription of time. As Putnam concludes, despite their differences, all of these artists treat experiences of ageing as performative. They do so through the creation of live works that emerge from embodied experiences and that reveal new forms of knowledge situated in the ageing female body.

Class, "Race" and Agency

The essays in the final section of this volume explore the gendered, racial, and class-based nature of old age. Age has come to the fore as a category of analysis that may be situated alongside feminist, postcolonial or queer approaches to understanding cultural texts. Due to different experiences and trajectories of growing older, age differentiates while it collectivises. It can be read as "the last difference, the unspoken but inevitable site of a difference not only *between* subjects but also a difference *within* subjects as they are exiled from their younger selves" (Bazin and White 2006, ii). In ageing, a conversation emerges both internally, between our past and present selves, and externally, as age functions to create distances and barriers between and among social groups. Age also crosses paths with categories of gender, "race,'" class and ethnicity. Intersecting with all, it is a common denominator in that "Each of us has confronted, or will eventually have to confront, the physical, psychological, social, and other changes that happen with time; all of us who live will eventually belong to the 'Othered' category that is old age" (Marshall 2006, vii). Focusing on Irish, South African and American contexts, the essays in this section illustrate that because women have so often been objectified or treated as symbols, and as older women are "invisible," they have to struggle for political and personal agency. Together, these contributions emphasise the material conditions and social factors such as sexism, racism and poverty that influence the experience as well as construction of old age. Following on from our explorations of narratives of ageing, the socially constructed nature of ageing and the regulation of the ageing body in culture, this section further complicates and moves us away from age-related experience as simply biological. Applying theories in cultural gerontology in new ways alongside postcolonial, feminist and psychoanalytic criticism, the essays in this section can contribute to shaping future responses and possibilities for analysing ageing and old age.

The first contribution is Antoinette Pretorius' chapter on J.M. Coetzee's *Age of Iron*, a novel set in the last days of the South African Apartheid regime. Pretorius shows how Coetzee's text subverts the conventional notion of dependency associated with the concepts of childhood, femininity and older age by foregrounding the ageing white female protagonist's body as a marker of transcendence rather than as one of inevitable decline and deterioration. In the context of South Africa's transition to democracy, the elderly female body could thus be seen as representative of the irony underlying the complex and often paradoxical tensions governing societal change. As Pretorius further shows, Coetzee, through his representation of the elderly protagonist's body in pain and her awakening social consciousness and agency, subverts conventional representations of women in relation to land, and to some extent liberates the figure of the ageing woman from socially prescribed meanings.

Moving the focus away from South Africa to North America, the next chapter, by Saskia Fürst, explores how Clarence Major's novel *Such Was the Season* uses African American humour and speech acts to negotiate a mature identity in its protagonist Annie-Eliza. As Fürst points out, until very recently, mainstream print and television culture either ignored African American older women or represented them in stereotypical ways. In contrast, Major's creation of his character Annie-Eliza, inspired by the voices of Major's mother and other female relatives, gives voice, agency and legitimacy to the perspective of an older black woman from a working-/middle-class background in the US. Fürst further shows that Major's use of humour works to criticise mainstream views of mature black womanhood as well as the concept of successful ageing.

The next chapter, by Margaret O'Neill, explores the literary representation of a formerly celebrated Irish actress, who lives a life of loneliness and poverty in 1950s London. O'Neill reads Joseph O'Connor's novel *Ghost Light*, a fictional biography of Molly Allgood, with reference to Freud's concept of the Uncanny. O'Neill shows how, by means of narrative technique, the novel reveals the complexity of the aged protagonist's inner life as she retells and relives her memories of the younger Molly's romance with playwright J.M. Synge, while simultaneously struggling to survive in an environment hostile to the old and the poor. As O'Neill concludes, the novel thus demonstrates the potential for art to reveal the moral failings of a wider community, eventually seen in Molly's bleak death.

This section concludes with Kate Antosik-Parsons' chapter on the visibility of women's ageing and agency in American artist Suzanne Lacy's performance art, particularly her two major participatory works *The Crystal Quilt* (1987) and *Silver Action* (2013). As Antosik-Parsons notes, Lacy defines her work as "new genre public art"; work created in the public realm that is activist in nature, incorporating traditional and non-traditional media to render visible the impact that political, economic and social conditions have on women's lives. She further analyses the ways in which Lacy's participatory works directly challenge viewers to confront their own fears and misconceptions about ageing and reveal the need to approach ageing from multiple points of analyses, accounting for gender, sexuality, "race," class and abilities.

Finally, in her Afterword to this collection, Germaine Greer, twenty-six years after the publication of *The Change: Women, Ageing and the Menopause* (1991), denounces the indignities older women still endure in a youth-obsessed culture that habitually sidelines and humiliates them while perpetuating negative images of old age. In contrast to this, in the second half of her Afterword, she notes the growing number of women writers and artists who are not only productive in their later years but who provide valuable fictional and autobiographical accounts of their own ageing that deserve to be heard and that we ignore at our peril. Many of these women have been relegated to the margins of cultural discourse and Greer's insistence on the need for a recognition of their achievement persuasively signposts possible future avenues for research on women and ageing.

Together, the contributions in this collection reveal new insights into contemporary representations of ageing women, while simultaneously recognising the historically constructed nature of these images. They bring together visual, literary, media and popular culture to explore reflections, refractions and reimaginings of the ageing woman and to consider how these representations shape contemporary society. In the understanding that the ageing body is embedded in, informed by and informs the cultural world, these essays explore and interrogate this relationship. They consider the potential of narrative, as well as its shortcomings; the limits of society, as well as modes of resistance; the ageing body as shaped by discourse, as well as intersections of "race," class, gender and ageing. In concluding with the section on "Class, 'Race' and Agency," we encourage readers to retrospectively consider the many and varied ways in which age intersects with stratified power relations throughout this volume. While the structure serves to highlight specific themes that have emerged as central to critical ageing studies in recent years, in many cases the chapters comprised in a specific section also lend themselves to consideration in light of other sections. For example, Margaret O'Neill's chapter in the "Class, 'Race' and Agency" section may productively be read as an exploration of the process of reminiscence in narratives of ageing. Likewise, Michaela Schrage-Früh's chapter in the "Narratives of Ageing" section might equally be read to illuminate how social roles such as widowhood and motherhood might be reimagined. The chapters by Bridie Moore and Antoinette Pretorius, in the "Narratives of Ageing" and "Class, 'Race' and Agency" sections respectively, both foreground the potential for a focus on bodies and embodiment to destabilise social, cultural and political representations of ageing. As a whole, the contributions in this volume serve to complicate and challenge dominant ideologies of ageing. They testify that, as Leni Marshall notes: "The deconstruction of dichotomies in genders and sexualities, feminist approaches to postmodern selfhood, analyses of the connections between power and economy, and the plethora of works on body-based identity categories: each of these ideas could be brought to bear on the performance and construction of aging" (Marshall 2006, viii). Furthermore, as authors and artists explore these issues, they harness feminist theory that has so often overlooked the figure of the ageing woman, to contribute to and extend an emerging, innovative, vibrant discourse. In doing so, they open out new cultural and critical spaces that enable the creation of alternative futures.

Works Cited

Bazin, Victoria, and Rosie White. 2006. Generations: Women, Age and Difference. *Studies in the Literary Imagination* 39 (2): 1–11.

Beauvoir, Simone de. 1997. *The Second Sex.* London: Vintage.

Blake, Liza. 2016. Madonna praised by James Corden, Jessica Chastain, JoJo & More for Billboard Women in Music Speech. *Billboard*, Dec 14. http://www.billboard.com/articles/events/women-in-music/7624575/madonna-billboard-women-in-music-speech-reaction.

Brennan, Zoe. 2005. *The Older Woman in Recent Fiction.* Jefferson, NC: McFarland & Co.

Calasanti, Toni, Kathleen F. Slevin, and Neal King. 2006. Ageism and Feminism: From 'Et Cetera' to Center. *NWSA Journal* 18 (1) (Spring): 13–30.

Chivers, Sally. 2003. *From Old Woman to Older Women: Contemporary Culture and Women's Narratives.* Columbus: Ohio State University Press.

Cruikshank, Margaret. 2003. *Learning to Be Old: Gender, Culture and Aging.* Lanham, MD: Rowman and Littlefield.

Dearden, Lizzie. 2015. Madonna Urges Music Industry to Deal with Ageism 'Taboo' After Radio 1 Playlist Snub. *The Independent.* http://www.independent.co.uk/arts-entertainment/music/news/madonna-urges-music-industry-to-deal-with-ageism-taboo-after-radio-1-playlist-snub-10106742.html.

Dikovitskaya, Margaret. 2005. *Visual Culture: The Study of the Visual After the Cultural Turn.* Cambridge, MA: MIT Press.

Falcus, Sarah. 2015. Literature and Ageing. In *Routledge Handbook of Cultural Gerontology*, eds. Julia Twigg and Wendy Martin, 53–60. London: Routledge.

Fisher, Carrie. 2011. *Shockaholic.* London: Simon & Schuster.

Fisher, Carrie. 2015. Twitter Post, December 28, 11.26pm, http://twitter.com/carriefisher.

Fisher, Carrie. 2015. Twitter post, December 30, 3:49pm, http://twitter.com/carriefisher.

Greer, Germaine. 1992. *The Change: Women, Ageing and the Menopause.* New York: Penguin.

Gullette, Margaret Morganroth. 1997. *Declining to Decline: Cultural Combat and the Politics of the Midlife.* Charlottesville, VA: University of Virginia Press.

Gullette, Margaret Morganroth. 1999. The Other End of the Fashion Cycle. In *Figuring Age: Women, Bodies, Generations*, ed. Kathleen Woodward, 34–58. Bloomington and Indianapolis: Indiana University Press.

Gullette, Margaret Morganroth. 2004. *Aged by Culture.* Chicago: University of Chicago Press.

Hartung, Heike. 2016. *Ageing, Gender and Illness in Anglophone Literature: Narrating Age in the Bildungsroman.* New York and London: Routledge.

Hoff, Victoria Dawson. 2015. 18 Celebrities Who Don't Age: And the Anti-Aging Secrets they Swear By. *Elle*, June 29. http://www.elle.com/beauty/g26467/celebrity-anti-aging-secrets/.

Jennings, Ros, and Abigail Gardner (eds.). 2012. *'Rock On': Women, Ageing and Popular Music.* Farnha: Ashgate.

Jermyn, Deborah, and Susan Holmes (eds.). 2015. *Women, Celebrity and Cultures of Ageing: Freeze Frame.* Basingstoke: Palgrave Macmillan.

King, Jeanette. 2013. *Discourses of Ageing in Fiction and Feminism: The Invisible Woman.* London: Palgrave Macmillan.

Marshall, Leni. 2006. Aging: A Feminist Issue. *NWSA Journal* 18 (1) (Spring, 2006): vii–xiii.

Morgan, Piers. 2017. Bomb Threats Don't Trump Hate: Piers Morgan on the Day Madonna and a Bunch of Famous, Foul-mouthed Nasty Women Let Down Ladies Everywhere. *Mail Online*, Jan 23. http://www.dailymail.co.uk/news/article-4148206/PIERS-MORGAN-Madonna-Bomb-threats-don-t-Trump-hate.html#ixzz4aLz01YVt.

Mulkerrins, Jane. Jane Fonda: 'Men Want Young Women. For us, it's About Trying to Stay Young. 2015. *The Telegraph*, May 22. http://www.telegraph.co.uk/culture/tvandradio/11623128/Jane-Fonda-Men-want-young-women.-For-us-its-about-trying-to-stay-young.html.

Singh, Anita. 2015. Germaine Greer vs. Jane Fonda: 'Poor old Jane Has a Replacement Hip but Not a Replacement Brain'. *The Telegraph*, May 23. http://www.telegraph.co.uk/culture/hay-festival/11626572/Germaine-Greer-vs-Jane-Fonda-Poor-old-Jane-has-a-replacement-hip-but-not-a-replacement-brain.html.

Sontag, Susan. 1972. The Double Standard of Aging. *The Saturday Review*. Sept 23. *NZ.org: Periodicals, Books and Authors.* http://www.unz.org/Pub/SaturdayRev-1972sep23-00029.

30 Celebs who are Aging Gracefully. 2011. *Huffington Post.* Nov 10. http://www.huffingtonpost.com/2011/11/10/30-celebs-aging-with-grac_n_1082444.html.

Tulle, Emmanuelle. 2015. Theorising Embodiment and Ageing. In *Routledge Handbook of Cultural Gerontology*, ed. Julia Twigg and Wendy Martin, 125132. London: Routledge.

Twigg, Julia. 2004. The Body, Gender, and Age: Feminist Insights in Social Gerontology. *Journal of Aging Studies* 18: 59–73.

Twigg, Julia. 2013. *Fashion and Age: Dress, the Body and Later Life.* London: Bloomsbury Academic.

Twigg, Julia, and Wendy Martin. 2015. Introduction. In *Routledge Handbook of Cultural Gerontology*, ed. Julia Twigg and Wendy Martin, 1–15. London: Routledge.

Waxman, Barbara Frey. 1990. *From The Hearth to the Open Road: A Feminist Study of Aging in Contemporary Literature*. New York: Greenwood Press.

Whelehan, Imelda, and Joel Gwynne (eds.). 2014. *Ageing, Popular Culture and Contemporary Feminism: Harleys and Hormones*. Basingstoke: Palgrave Macmillan.

Woodward, Kathleen M. 1997. *Telling Stories*. With responses by Andrew E. Scharlach and Marilyn Fabe. Occasional papers for the Doreen B. Townsend Center for the Humanities, no. 9.

Woodward, Kathleen M. 1999. Introduction. In *Figuring Age: Women, Bodies, Generations*, ed. Kathleen Woodward, ix–xxix. Bloomington and Indianapolis: Indiana University Press.

PART I

Narratives of Ageing

CHAPTER 2

Making the Invisible Visible: The Presence of Older Women Artists in Early Modern Artistic Biography

Julia K. Dabbs

Introduction

In the early modern period (i.e. from 1400–1800), professional women artists were greatly outnumbered by their male counterparts, given that women were typically deterred from working, training or being educated outside the home. Women were also perceived as lacking the necessary physical strength and the intelligence to succeed as fine artists (Boccaccio 2001, 251). Yet, we do know of successful women artists from this period, such as Artemisia Gentileschi and Sofonisba Anguissola, thanks not only to the scholarly efforts of modern-day art historians, but also the writings of early modern artistic biographers. These authors included life stories of selected remarkable women in their collected "lives of the artists"; that is, biographical compendia that were published throughout Europe following the popular success of Giorgio Vasari's *Le vite de' più eccellenti pittori, scultori, e architettori* (1550). Like their

J.K. Dabbs (✉)
University of Minnesota, Morris, MN, USA
e-mail: dabbsj@morris.umn.edu

C. McGlynn et al. (eds.), *Ageing Women in Literature and Visual Culture*,
DOI 10.1007/978-3-319-63609-2_2

hagiographical antecedents, the characterizations of artists were to a certain extent formulaic in order to fit the mould of what that culture considered an exemplary individual. Thus, the female artist was, regardless of the facts, stereotypically characterized as young, virtuous and beautiful—the three "graces" associated with women of the period.[1]

Did this emphasis on youth and beauty mean, then, that women artists who continued to create art into middle age, or later, were ignored by male biographers? Recent scholarship suggests that this indeed was the case; for example, in her essay on "Old Women in Early Modern Europe," Lynn Botelho writes: "Finally, given the gendered construction of early modern Europe, there were few active women artists, and fewer still whose late life-style could be analysed and consequently our understanding of the artist in old age is overwhelmingly male" (2013, 306). Indeed, a review of the literature to date would reasonably give one that impression, as studies such as Philip Sohm's *The Artist Grows Old: The Aging of Art and Artists in Italy 1500–1800* (2007) or Thomas Dormandy's *Old Masters: Great Artists in Old Age* (2000) only peripherally mention a few women artists who worked into their later years.

However, as I will argue, this absence of the elder woman artist from more recent historical studies of the subject is not because there were few women who continued to work until later in life. Indeed, of the 46 women artists included in my anthology, *Life Stories of Women Artists 1550–1800*, at least one-third are described as creating art past the age of 50.[2] Further research will likely show that this number is just the tip of the iceberg, for at least 52 early modern women artists whose life dates are known with some certainty *lived* beyond 50 years of age. Thus, one intention of this chapter is to reverse the current misapprehension of the longevity of early modern women artists, and render these "invisible"

[1] See Baldesar Castiglione, *The Book of the Courtier*, 1528, trans. George Bull (New York: Penguin, 1967) 211, for the association of women with virtue and beauty; and for the youthful stereotype, it is only necessary to glance through a catalogue on Renaissance portraiture, such as David Alan Brown, *Virtue & Beauty* (Washington D.C.: National Gallery of Art, 2001). The "formula" for female artists was largely set by Vasari, who writes of sculptor Properzia de' Rossi that she was "a young woman" who not only was a talented homemaker and musician, but also "very beautiful," even though the portrait of de' Rossi that accompanies her life story suggests otherwise (in Dabbs 2009, 56).

[2] 50 years of age, according to Botelho (2013, 301), is an approximate number used to mark "cultural old age" in the early modern period, so it is being used here.

elder women creators more visible. Yet, in addition, I will consider how the woman artist was characterized by her biographer in old age, and provide some comparison with literary tropes associated with elder male artists of the period, to see to what extent gender may have factored into cultural perceptions and attitudes towards old age.

Old Age Tropes in the Life Story of the Male Artist

"I am an old man and death has robbed me of the dreams of youth—may those who do not know what old age means bear it with what patience they may when they reach it, because it cannot be imagined beforehand" (Sohm 2007, 3). So wrote Michelangelo Buonarroti in a letter of 1547, when he was 72 years of age. Although Michelangelo's comments may seem especially harsh, they did find echoes in the early modern period. Indeed, old age and its inevitable illnesses were characterized as "fierce, powerful enemies" by the seventeenth-century artistic biographer, Domenico Bernini (Bernini 2011, 231). Another biographer, the former painter Carlo Ridolfi, stated that particularly for the artist, old age "brings great annoyance and infirmity and is unsuitable for working" (in Sohm 2007, 24).

Given this predominantly negative attitude towards old age, it is unsurprising that early modern biographers generally pay little attention to the end of an artist's life, whether the artist be male or female, famous or infamous. To some degree, this is because early modern biographers, whose literary genre was primarily epideictic in nature,[3] likely would have little to praise given the inevitable decline of the artist's abilities and/or physical condition as he or she aged. Indeed, as Campbell and Sohm have affirmed in their studies of older male artists of the early modern period, the end of life experiences are often negatively cast (Campbell 2002, 322; Sohm 2007, 19–35). As Sohm explains, "Art biographers of elderly artists repeated the same story, dismal in its sameness: eyesight fades; reflexes and coordination slacken; the hand trembles" (2007, 4). For the visual artist, dependent on physical action in order to express his or her ideas, this corporeal deterioration was often devastating.

[3] Rubin (1990), 36. Here Rubin discusses the "oratory of praise" or epideictic approach used in Vasari's *Lives of the Artists*, but this rhetorical manner was certainly followed by other biographers of the early modern period.

Should his eyesight become compromised, as was the case for Giovanni Paolo Lomazzo, his ability to create art was finished. Should his hands become arthritic, or overcome by tremors, or his eye-hand coordination lessen, he might still be able to paint, but with diminished skill or ability to delineate detail. For some artists, this decline could lead to a loss of patronage and subsequent impoverishment (Sohm 2007, 26). Even celebrated artists such as the Venetian painter Titian were not immune from criticism when their style changed in old age. Vasari states in his life story of Titian that "it would have been well for him in these his last years not to work save as a pastime, so as not to diminish with works of less excellence the reputation gained in his best years, when his natural powers were not declining and drawing towards imperfection" (1996, II, 798). Or as the seventeenth-century sculptor Gian Lorenzo Bernini put it, upon viewing a later painting by the French master Nicolas Poussin, "there comes a time when one should cease work, for there is a falling off in everyone in old age" (in Sohm 2007, 71).

Of course the problem, then as now, was not being able to admit that one had declining abilities or stamina. For some older artists, as Vasari relates in the life stories of Beccafumi and Pontormo, this could result in death due to overwork at an advanced age (1996, II, 203, 371). However, biographers could put a positive spin on such denials of physical limitations. For example Bernini, at the age of 82, insisted on climbing up and down a ladder himself in order to help fix a structurally unsound building as requested by the Pope; this over-exertion was later blamed for weakening the artist's body, leading shortly thereafter to his death (Bernini 2011, 227, 231). Yet for Bernini, it was a matter of pride—he couldn't refuse the Pope or leave the work to someone potentially less capable. His enactment of what we might call "heroic old age," overcoming or at least not succumbing to physical barriers that would intimidate others his age, thus gave the biographer a climactic chance to gain the reader's sympathy and admiration.[4]

Besides the loss of physical functionality, a pervasive concern regarding ageing in modern times is the demise of intellectual functionality. However, this type of decline rarely surfaces in early modern artistic biography; instead, intellectual competence and acuity in old age are emphasized.

[4]Another example of "heroic old age" can be found in Vasari's *vita* of the early Renaissance master Luca Signorelli, in which he assists with a fresco project at the age of 82, even though hindered by paralysis (1996, I: 613–614).

Teaching or writing about art are often mentioned as compensatory activities for the artist who could no longer physically create art (Campbell 2002, 330; Sohm 2007, 75). In this respect, the biographer was able to draw upon the commonly held positive association between old age and wisdom during the early modern period.[5] A cogent example is found in Bernini's life story, where his son states that his father's clarity of intellect was not obfuscated by old age or illness. Domenico then explains that his father even devised a method of sign language so that he could still communicate with those around him when, close to death, he was no longer able to speak: "for everyone it was now a cause of wonder how well he could communicate with the priest merely by the movement of his left hand and eyes. This was indeed a clear sign of that great liveliness of spirit of his, which not even then, when his life was failing, showed any sign of surrender" (Bernini 2011, 232). Bernini's ability to overcome this disability by means of his intellectual acuity can thus serve as another manifestation of "heroic old age" evidenced in artistic biography.

The passage above concerning Bernini's last days, in addition to additional description by his son Domenico, emphasize two other key concepts associated with biographical descriptions of ageing: the psychological and spiritual conditions of the individual. In the early modern period, the life stage of old age in men was associated with melancholia, given the belief that psychological states were related to one's physiological condition—thus as the body became cold and dry due to ageing, so one's temperament would inevitably tend towards melancholy.[6] For some older artists such as Pontormo, who became overwrought by negative feelings concerning their work, this extreme form of melancholia could be attributed as a cause of death (Vasari 1996, II, 371).

Bernini, in contrast, is shown by his biographer to once again act heroically in the face of death, this time expressed by his emotional

[5] See for example Castiglione's *The Courtier*, in which old men are advised to "make use of the prudence and knowledge they will have acquired through their long experience, act like oracles to whom everyone will turn for advice" (Castiglione 1967, 123). On this point, see also Campbell (2002), 321 and 330.

[6] Sohm (2007), 97–98. For a helpful explanation of humoral theory, especially as it related to melancholia, see Dixon (2013), 11–13.

resoluteness and fervent faith: "In talking of death, he would do so not with the distress and horror that is usual among old people, but with an incomparable steadfastness of spirit, ever reminding himself of its approach so as to prepare to meet it properly" (Bernini 2011, 230). As Sohm notes, there are numerous other examples of older (male) artists who exhibit this kind of heightened spirituality, which might be expressed in their artwork, as well as in their behaviour (2007, 69–71).

In this brief overview, then, we have shown that both positive and negative tropes can be found in the life stories of male artists as they age. The most common negative trope is the inevitable physical decline and its impact on art. However, this physical loss could be countered to some extent by exemplary or heroic reactions to this decline, such as an increased emphasis on intellectual acuity, or emotional or spiritual strength. As will be shown, on occasion this latter trope can also be found in life stories of women artists. Yet we also encounter other themes that occur more uniquely in regards to elder female creators, which demonstrates that there wasn't a standardized biographical approach to writing the artist's life in old age.

Old Age Tropes in the Life Story of the Female Artist

For the early modern artistic biographer, writing about an elder female artist was an inherently more challenging task compared to characterizing an elder male artist. Reasons for this involved the general nature as well as more specific physical and emotional properties associated with older women in this period. First, there was the lingering negative cultural stereotype of the older woman as witch, crone or hag (Botelho 2013, 297, 305). As Botelho states in her survey of the subject, "Given the patriarchal nature of the early modern world, cultural constructions of aged females, particularly those expressed in literature, were heavily weighted towards the negative" (2013, 305). In art of the period, the old woman often performed the role of lower-class servant, whose weather-beaten and desiccated body was used as a point of contrast to the beautiful, ivory-skinned young lady who was the focus of the painting (as seen, for example, in Caravaggio's *Judith Beheading Holofernes*, Rome, Galleria Nazionale d'Arte Antica). Even in the hands of a woman artist, the old woman could be a subject for ridicule and scorn, as we see in Sofonisba Anguissola's drawing of *Old Woman Studying the*

Alphabet with a Laughing Girl (Fig. 2.1). As Perlinghieri has suggested, the older woman was likely a servant of the Anguissola family (1992, 44), and so one purpose of the drawing was for Sofonisba to practise her observational skills, particularly when it came to portraying different ages of women. Yet the artist has chosen to not just portray physical difference, but also intellectual difference as the young woman attempts to teach the elder woman. From a positive perspective, Anguissola does show the old woman trying to become literate; however, the activity seems rather fruitless and farcical, given that the young woman has to literally guide the elder woman's hand over the page, as if she were reading braille. The cultural stereotype of the old woman as simple,

Fig. 2.1 Sofonisba Anguissola, *Old Woman Studying the Alphabet with a Laughing Girl*, 1550s (Florence, Uffizi; Mondadori Portfolio/Art Resource, NY)

unintelligent and physically impaired is ultimately reinforced. Indeed, the old woman stereotype was a difficult hurdle for artists and biographers to overcome.

Another challenge for the early modern artistic biographer in writing about the older woman artist was the stereotypical view of the female creator as young and beautiful, such that she was said to embody the beauty of her creations (Sohm 2007, 20). Some Renaissance men made this connection quite directly; an admirer of Sofonisba Anguissola wrote that "There is nothing that I desire more than the image of the artist herself, so that in a single work I can exhibit two marvels, one the work, the other the artist" (in Chapman 2013, 198). However, as Germaine Greer warned in her groundbreaking book, *The Obstacle Race: The Fortunes of Women Painters and Their Work* (first published in 1979), "Young women grow old; [...] If the female painter shows herself a serious rival to men, committed to advancing her own career and not simply playing, she may expect opposition to harden against her" (2001, 88). One form of opposition was to ridicule the physical appearance of older female subjects. The eighteenth-century pastellist, Rosalba Carriera, was repeatedly derided for her lack of beauty as she aged; for example, Emperor Charles VI of Austria was said to remark to a court artist after being introduced to Carriera, then aged 55, that "She may well be worthy... but she is very ugly" (in Dabbs 2008, 37, note 20). Another eighteenth-century artist, the German painter Anna Dorothea Therbusch, was harshly criticized for her perceived physical and social deficiencies by the influential art writer, Denis Diderot: "It was not charm that she lacked, it was not talent that she lacked in order to create a great sensation in this country, [...] it was youth, it was beauty, it was modesty, it was coquetry..." (in Greer 2001, 89). More often, however, the physical appearance of the older woman artist goes unmentioned in early modern life stories, which is similarly the case for older male artists, thereby allowing for more focus on inner traits and conduct.

In addition to physical appearance, there were also the issues of emotional vulnerability and distress as the woman artist aged. Like their male counterparts, elder women artists were, on occasion, described as suffering from depression or melancholia. However, this depression was not said to derive from a loss of artistic ability or patronage as was often the case for male artists, but instead was invariably linked to the death of a loved one, such as a spouse or child. The late Renaissance painter Lavinia Fontana (1552–1614) is said to have died of heartbreak after the death of her daughter, who had shown talent as an artist (in Dabbs 2009, 82–84). Similarly, the Italian painter Giovanna Fratellini (1666–1731) is described as being inconsolable for two years after the death of her son, who also had been following in his mother's footsteps as an artist (in Dabbs 2009, 316). In a third example, the seventeenth-century Chinese painter Li Yin (1616–1685) is said to have mourned the death of her husband, and the political overthrow of her homeland, for over 30 years, as "with deepest grief, she faced alone a Buddhist eternal lamp night after night" (in Dabbs 2009, 154–156).

In contrast to the biographical emphasis on emotional vulnerability, physical and intellectual decline in old age are generally less emphasized in life stories of early modern women artists, in comparison to those of their male counterparts. In terms of physical decline, this divergence might be explained by the fact that very few women artists undertook the physically laborious work of fresco painting or large-scale sculpture, which was the undoing of numerous male artists as they aged. Thus, within the twenty-four life stories of women artists who lived past the age of 50 that I have gathered to date (Dabbs 2009), only one biographer remarks on a lessening of skill in an artist's advanced age. This occurs in Jan van Gool's life story of Dutch still-life painter Rachel Ruysch (1664–1750), where he notes that a work she had recently executed at 84 years of age "will be less" that what had come before (in Dabbs 2009, 270). Yet, what he was comparing the painting to was a still life created when Ruysch was 80 years old, about which he exclaims: "In her house I saw a piece that she had painted in her eightieth year of her life; I was profoundly amazed, so precisely and elaborately was everything executed" (in Dabbs 2009, 270). Indeed, flower painting was a demanding subject that required careful observation and incredible eye-hand coordination, in order to capture and convey a sense of verisimilitude. That Ruysch was apparently still able to paint so effectively into her 80s was indeed a wonder.

One aspect of physical decline that is mentioned relatively more often for aged women artists compared to male artists, however, is vision loss (Dabbs 2012). In some life stories, women artists are praised as exceptional because their vision was still good in old age: the aforementioned Rachel Ruysch is said by her biographer to have had surprisingly good mental capacities and eyesight even at age 84 (in Dabbs 2009, 270), and Lucia Casalini Torelli (1677–1762) is said to "have always worked vigorously until the end of her days (even to the decrepit age of eighty-five years), always without eyeglasses" (in Dabbs 2009, 395).

In two other cases, however, biographers discuss at more length how women artists faced the consequences of vision loss in their old age. For Rosalba Carriera (1673–1757), vision loss occurred in 1746, when she was in her early 70s but still actively working in pastels. Despite undergoing cataract surgery two times, there was little sustained improvement in Carriera's vision, and by the age of 76, she was completely blind (Mariette 1966, I: 331). One of Carriera's last works of art is her haunting *Self-portrait as Tragedy* (Fig. 2.2), which shows a woman transformed by age, with her hair thinning and a somewhat glassy,

Fig. 2.2 Rosalba Carriera, *Self-portrait as Tragedy*, ca. 1746 (Venice: Accademia; Scala/Art Resource, NY)

unfocused left eye. Carriera seems to know that her artistic career will soon come to an end, and thus she assumes the role of tragedy, given the devastating loss of vision for an artist.[7] Yet, the laurel-leaf wreath and resolute expression suggest that she is not defeated by age, but instead continues to look into the light. One of Carriera's biographers, Francesco Moücke, in fact writes that although she was "deprived of the bodily light [i.e. eyesight], she was just as much enlightened in her mind" (Moücke 1752, IV: 245). In this way, Moücke significantly asserts that Carriera was able to transcend the tragedy of vision loss through her intellective powers, which counters a common perception of the period that women lacked the capacity for intelligence, and in particular the faculty of judgement that was considered crucial to artistic excellence (Huarte 1959, 273, 286; Maclean 1983, 35).

Interestingly, Carriera's intellectual transcendence of vision loss in old age had a precedent in the life of Sofonisba Anguissola (c.1532–1625). A gifted portraitist who, like Carriera, had a successful, international career, Anguissola continued to create art into her old age. Yet, in her 90s the artist went blind, according to her biographer, Raffaele Soprani; significantly, though, he adds that she "at least enjoyed conversing with painters, always discussing the difficulty that they were encountering in art, and offering them very rare and useful documents" (in Dabbs 2009, 117). One artist who confirms that this type of informal instruction took place is Anthony van Dyck, a young Flemish artist who in 1624 had come to Palermo, where Anguissola was then living, due to a portrait commission. Van Dyck's visit to the aged artist was apparently so significant to him that he both visually and verbally recorded what transpired in a sketchbook. He writes that she "has all her memory and is very quick-witted" (in Brown 1983, 82, 84), which indeed must have been amazing to witness in a 96-year-old woman. Even more compelling are van Dyck's comments, later relayed by Soprani in his life story of Anguissola, that "van Dyck used to say that he considered himself very indebted to have conversed with Sofonisba, and confessed to having received much

[7] Carriera herself made the initial connection between this self-portrait and the concept of tragedy, as one biographer states that a few years before her blindness she "made her own portrait with a garland of leaves, and having been asked what she meant to signify with that, she responded, that it was Tragedy, and that Rosalba must end tragically, as it was in real life." Antonio Maria Zanetti, *Della pittura veneziana*, 1771 (Venice: Filippi Editore, 1972) 449.

greater instruction from the words of a blind woman, than from the works of the most esteemed painters" (in Dabbs 2009, 117). This indeed was no faint praise, for van Dyck had studied paintings by such artists as Titian and Rubens, yet here he is crediting a blind old woman with having been the more influential teacher. Was this just rhetorical hyperbole, a not uncommon feature of early modern biographical writing? If so, it is unprecedented in regards to a woman artist; and even if the comment is potentially exaggerated, Soprani's comments demonstrate that it was possible for the woman artist to be seen as a sage mentor who could transcend the career-ending fate of blindness through her active intelligence.

Rosalba Carriera and Sofonisba Anguissola are two women artists whose biographical characterizations, I believe, place them in the exemplary category of "heroic old age" through their inspirational demonstrations of emotional tenacity and intellectual acuity in the face of blindness. My interpretation of their positive exemplarity thus dovetails with more recent research in ageing studies that supports an alternative view of old women in the early modern period in which they are shown to exhibit wisdom, creativity, authority and other forms of agency (Botelho 2013, 306). To demonstrate that this type of positive characterization of the elder woman artist was indeed not an anomaly, I would like to conclude with a slightly later example, that of the American sculptor Patience Wright (1725–1786). Following the death of her husband in 1769, Wright needed to support herself and her four children, and given the lack of art materials and training in the colonies she turned to the domestic medium of wax, which she taught herself to sculpt. Eventually, Wright, along with her sister, established the first travelling waxworks exhibit in America. However, with little art patronage in colonial times, especially for wax busts, Wright and her family moved to London in 1772, where she set up a studio at the age of 47. The astonishing verisimilitude of her figures, as seen in the lone surviving statue of *William Pitt* (London, Westminster Abbey), led to a flurry of patronage, including that of King George III and Queen Charlotte (Sellers 1976). Nevertheless, Wright, who very atypically for a woman was working in the medium of sculpture, was at times portrayed negatively, or at best ambivalently, due to her transgression of normative gender roles in the eighteenth century. This can be seen in an illustration of the artist which accompanied a relatively lengthy life story of Wright published in *The London Magazine* in 1775 (Fig. 2.3). At first glance, we see Wright as a respectably dressed, older matron who is rather regally depicted in profile; but then our gaze

Fig. 2.3 Anonymous, *Portrait of Patience Wright*, from the *London Magazine* (Nov. 1775), p. 557

is disrupted by the puzzling sight of a middle-aged male figure seemingly emanating from Wright's mid-section, and who gazes up at her. This rendering may reference Wright's unusual "birthing" technique for creating her wax portrait busts in which she would partially model the wax between her thighs to maintain its malleability (Dabbs 2009, 424). While the life story's author claims that the illustration is an "exact likeness" of Wright, the inclusion of the male figure results in an image of the elder woman artist that is provocative and potentially scandalous, yet not uncommon in popular print images of "transgressive" women sculptors in the eighteenth century (Dabbs 2009, 424).

However, the life story that accompanies this illustration of Wright is much less provocative, and in fact is an extraordinarily positive characterization of this strong-willed, older woman. Published some 11 years before her death, the anonymous writer approaches his subject from a respectful perspective, given that Wright, now age 50, was in her last stage of life. The biographer not only has high praise for Wright's artistic skills, but also her unblemished character, so as to deflect any rumours of inappropriate behaviour. Yet he particularly emphasizes Wright's intellect, lauding her "sense and argument on public subjects, [such] that the most learned men may draw instruction from the keenness of her observations, and the satire of her language. She is a kind of exotic prodigy, and appears, like Pallas [Athena] to have come forth complete from the head of Jove" (in Dabbs 2009, 428–49). In other passages, the biographer notes Wright's intelligence by referencing her "genius," a trait rarely used in relation to women artists due to their perceived physiological difference from men (Dixon 2013, 13). He visually reinforces this quality by describing Wright, even as an older woman, as having "an eye of that quick and brilliant water, that it penetrates and darts through the person it looks on…" (in Dabbs 2009, 428). Although the biographer's verbiage can seem excessively embellished to the modern reader, his characterization finds a striking echo in a slightly later portrait of Wright (Fig. 2.4). Now approximately 57 years of age, we see the older creator apparently preparing to work as she leans forward, with a modelling apron over her lap. Wright's head is actively turned and her eyes cast upwards, allowing her face to be fully illuminated by an unseen light source, thus effectively suggesting the work of the mind that preceded the work of the hands. Although Wright appears more aged than in Fig. 2.3, we are still presented with an artist who is capable and active, both physically and mentally.

Fig. 2.4 Robert Edge Pine (attrib.), *Portrait of Patience Lovell Wright*, c. 1782 (National Portrait Gallery, Smithsonian Institution)

As these examples of Wright, Anguissola, Carriera and Ruysch have shown, the elder woman artist in the early modern period was in no way invisible; it is only our limited modern vision that has veiled them from view. Not only have art historical studies of older artists minimized the presence of the female creator, but recent books on the history of self-portraits more often depict older male artists in comparison to older female artists.[8] Even books focusing on women artists continue to be

[8] In James Hall's *The Self-Portrait: A Cultural History* (London: Thames & Hudson, 2014), of the approximately 100 self-portraits of men, 19 (or roughly 20%) are of male artists over 50 years of age, while only one out of nine self-portraits of women depict a female over 50. An even greater disparity is found in Laura Cumming's *A Face to the World: On*

predominantly illustrated with portraits of younger, rather than older women; to cite one example, Jordi Vigué's *Great Women Masters of Art* (2002) includes eleven images of older women artists out of a total of 85 portraits.[9] When will "greatness" for the female artist no longer require a youthful, beautiful portrayal? Can it not be evidenced in the abilities of Wright and Ruysch to continue creating works of art into their later years? Or Anguissola's desire to instruct young artists into her 90s? Or Carriera's effort to transcend the loss of her eyesight with courage and fortitude? It is only when we fully investigate the lives of women artists, in the same way as we have for many male artists, that we will recognize that their achievements go far beyond the surface beauty of youth. There is so much more we can learn about, and from, these elder female creators.

Acknowledgement

Support for this project was made possible by an Imagine Fund Award from the University of Minnesota.

Works Cited

Bernini, Domenico. 2011. *The Life of Gian Lorenzo Bernini* [1713], trans. Franco Mormando. University Park, PA: Penn State University Press.

Boccaccio, Giovanni. 2001. *Famous Women* [1374], trans. Virginia Brown. Cambridge and London: Harvard University Press.

Botelho, Lynn. 2013. Old Women in Early Modern Europe. In *The Ashgate Research Companion to Women and Gender in Early Modern Europe*, eds. Allyson M. Poska, Jane Couchman, and Katherine A. McIver, 297–315. Burlington, VT: Ashgate.

Self-Portraits (London: Harper Press, 2009): of the 71 self-portraits by male artists, some 24 are of men over 50, yet of the 11 self-portraits by women, none are over 50 years of age.

[9] In another case, Whitney Chadwick's *Women, Art, and Society* (London: Thames & Hudson, 2012) includes three images of women artists past the age of 50, out of a total of 29 portraits. In compiling these statistics, we continued to use the early modern "threshold" of 50 years of age to identify which portrayals, whether of a male or female artist, might be considered "old." I would like to thank research assistant Sophia Chadbourne for her work on collecting this data.

Brown, Christopher. 1983. *Van Dyck*. Ithaca, NY: Cornell University Press.

Campbell, Erin J. 2002. The Art of Aging Gracefully: The Elderly Artist as Courtier in Early Modern Art Theory and Criticism. *Sixteenth-Century Journal* 33: 321–331.

Castiglione, Baldesar. 1967. *The Book of the Courtier* [1528], trans. George Bull. New York: Penguin.

Chadwick, Whitney. 2012. *Women, Art, and Society*. London: Thames & Hudson.

Chapman, H. Perry. 2013. Self-Portraiture 1400–1700. In *A Companion to Renaissance and Baroque Art*, eds. Babette Bohn and James M. Saslow, 189–209. Hoboken: Wiley.

Cumming, Laura. 2009. *A Face to the World: On Self-Portraits*. London: HarperPress.

Dabbs, Julia K. 2008. Anecdotal Insights: Changing Perceptions of Italian Women Artists in 18th-Century Life Stories. *Eighteenth-Century Women* 5: 29–51.

Dabbs, Julia K. 2009. *Life Stories of Women Artists 1550–1800: An Anthology*. Burlington, VT: Ashgate.

Dabbs, Julia K. 2012. Vision and Insight: Portraits of the Aged Woman Artist, 1600–1800. *Occasion: Interdisciplinary Studies in the Humanities*. Arcade: Stanford University. 4 (May 31 2012). Web. http://arcade.stanford.edu/occasion/vision-and-insight-portraits-aged-woman-artist-1600-1800.

Dixon, Laurinda. 2013. *The Dark Side of Genius: The Melancholic Persona in Art, Ca. 1500–1700*. University Park, PA: The Pennsylvania State University Press.

Greer, Germaine. 2001. *The Obstacle Race: The Fortunes of Women Painters and Their Work*. New York: Tauris Parke.

Hall, James. 2014. *The Self-Portrait: A Cultural History*. London: Thames & Hudson.

Huarte, Juan. 1959. *Examen de ingenios: The Examination of Men's Wits (1594)*, trans. Richard Carew. Gainesville: Scholars' Facsimiles & Reprints.

Maclean, Ian. 1983. *The Renaissance Notion of Woman: A Study in the Fortunes of Scholasticism and Medical Science in European Intellectual Life*. Cambridge: Cambridge University Press.

Mariette, P.J. 1966. *Abecedario* [1851–53]. Paris: F. de Nobele.

Moücke, Francesco. 1752–1762. Rosalba Carriera. In *Serie di ritratti degli eccellenti pittori dipinti di propria mano che esistono nell'Imperial galleria di Firenze*. Florence.

Perlingieri, Ilya. 1992. *Sofonisba Anguissola: The First Great Woman Artist of the Renaissance*. New York: Rizzoli.

Rubin, Patricia. 1990. What Men Saw: Vasari's Life of Leonardo da Vinci and the Image of the Renaissance Artist. *Art History* 13: 34–46.

Sellers, Charles C. 1976. *Patience Wright: American Artist and Spy in George III's London*. Middleton, CT: Wesleyan University Press.

Sohm, Philip L. 2007. *The Artist Grows Old: The Aging of Art and Artists in Italy, 1500–1800.* New Haven/London: Yale University Press.
Vasari, Giorgio. 1996. *Lives of the Painters, Sculptors and Architects* [1568], trans. Gaston du C. de Vere. 2 vols. New York: Knopf.
Vigué, Jordi. 2002. *Great Women Masters of Art.* New York: Watson-Guptill.
Zanetti, Antonio Maria. 1972. *Della pittura veneziana* [1771]. Venice: Filippi Editore.

CHAPTER 3

Losing One's Self: The Depiction of Female Dementia Sufferers in *Iris* (2001) and *The Iron Lady* (2011)

Eva Adelseck

"Inside every older person is a younger person wondering what the hell happened." This quotation is taken from a birthday card found in a random card shop in Manchester. It is obviously intended as a joke, but when I read it, I felt that there was a profound truth to it. I had witnessed this accretive divide in myself, approaching 30; I had listened to my mother telling me stories to this effect, and even more so, it reminded me of my grandmother who suffered from Alzheimer's Disease (AD) in her later years. The more she lost touch with what was happening in the present, the more she believed herself to be her "younger person" within, being absolutely puzzled by the fact that the bizarre "hotel" she stayed in (which was actually a care home) was teeming with old people only, refusing to believe those who tried to tell her that she was just as old as the other residents.

Age-related dementia is one of the most prominent illnesses in media and politics and as such one of the most urgent problems that our ageing

E. Adelseck (✉)
University of Manchester, Manchester, UK
e-mail: eva.adelseck@manchester.ac.uk

C. McGlynn et al. (eds.), *Ageing Women in Literature and Visual Culture*,
DOI 10.1007/978-3-319-63609-2_3

society will have to solve. The number of dementia patients in the UK will increase by 40% in the next twelve years alone.[1] Dementia is widely perceived as a particularly vicious illness which robs its patients of the memories that construe their life stories and make them who they are. This, according to literary scholar Paul John Eakin, is the greatest fear that people have in regard to the disease:

> What would it be like to live without memory? What would it be like to lose one's self every hour, indeed every few seconds? [...] I've never encountered anyone who didn't hope that his or her memory and the sense of life story it supports, would survive intact to the end. [...] Most people fear memory loss and the death of the extended self that follows from it – witness the widespread anxiety about Alzheimer's Disease and aging in the U.S. today. (2006, 185)

With dementia, short-term memories are always lost first, and memories from a patient's youth stay with them the longest. To construe identity, these patients have to rely on old memories, making them seemingly "live" more and more in the past. Thinking back to the phrase on the birthday card, this evokes the question of whether the concept between the "two persons" in the ageing process and the loss of self in dementia are somehow linked. Narrative life accounts, be they literary fiction or autobiographical life stories, might hold the key to this question. I will, therefore, examine the biopics of two extraordinary women who both developed AD in their later lives. The films I have chosen are *Iris* (2001), about novelist Iris Murdoch, and *The Iron Lady* (2011), about former British Prime Minister Margaret Thatcher. *Iris* focuses on the life of British author, philosopher and literary critic Iris Murdoch (1919–1999), who was known for her sharp wit, intellectuality and verbal acuity. *The Iron Lady* focuses on the life of British Prime Minister Margaret Thatcher (1925–2013), who was known for her assertiveness and her indomitability in seeing her agenda through despite critical opposition. Both films depict well-known intellectual but also controversial women and aim to provide conclusive biographies. In both films, AD is used as the focal point of the story and the one decisive motif that

[1] Statistic according to the Alzheimer's Society, released in 2015: https://www.alzheimers.org.uk/site/scripts/documents_info.php?documentID=412.

strings together the plotlines. Regarding the realisation of the two narratives, both films use two different actresses to portray their respective protagonist's young and old version of self. This paper will explore how the dichotomy between the younger and the older self is narrated in the films and how the fact that both protagonists are women and patients of dementia impacts the narration.

Simone de Beauvoir described in *La Vieillesse* (2012, original from 1970) how, during the ageing process, an individual is bound to perceive a divide, almost a conflict within, between a "young self" and an "old self." Usually, this divide is aligned with the divide between body and mind: "Age is a dialectic relation between my being in the eyes of others, as it presents itself objectively, and my own consciousness that I gain through ageing" (364).[2] Whereas individuals do not tend to note the changes ageing makes to their thinking and their selves and can, therefore, remain unaware of having aged, the conspicuous changes in the ageing body manifest the process and make it undeniable. The visibility of those changes to themselves and the outside world is alienating for the individual's self-perception. Strangers start to treat the older person differently because of the age they look. When these perceptions clash, the perceived dichotomy of the two selves within the same person comes into being.

Only recently, in an interview with Gabrielle Donnelly for the Women's Section of the *Daily Mail* entitled Fe-Mail, a marvellously aged Jane Fonda stated that "You could not pay me to be young again. I don't care how much money I was offered, I wouldn't do it" (Donnelly 2016). But contrary to this article's age-promoting headline, "I wouldn't be young again for anything," the reality of discussing the ageing process in the media is different. Women's magazines often reveal a great gap between empowering statements like this and blown-up advertisements for anti-aging serums or various ways to dress, look and feel younger. The fear of old age is very present in our society—even this article with its age-positive headline is no exception. Looking at the article more closely, one realises that its underlying tone is not so much in favour of ageing but rather complimentary of Fonda's good looks and active lifestyle *despite her age*.

[2] My translation from the German edition.

Cultural gerontologists like Margaret Morganroth Gullette have argued that ageing is understood by our society as the signifier of a decline that will ultimately lead to death, when at the same time, this understanding is perpetuated and enforced by society itself. In *Aged by Culture* (2004), she stresses how society promotes "the dominance of decline narrative, early nostalgia, [and] age apprehensiveness" (37). Noticing signs of ageing in familiar people instinctively reminds us of mortality—the mortality of our loved ones as well as our own. Psychoanalytical readings conclude, therefore, that society tries to avoid the subject of ageing to keep its inner stability.[3] This avoidance is, in Freudian and Lacanian terms, a form of disavowal.[4] An aged person is turned into an "other," something that people do not feel comfortable identifying themselves with. They subconsciously deny the possibility of growing old themselves and this results in attempts to distance themselves from their fear. Amelia deFalco adds another psychoanalytical dimension to the unconscious processes behind the "othering" of the aged: uncanniness, which is caused by recognising familiar traits and at the same time being confronted with unfamiliar traits of an individual or oneself:

> The not-yet-old, or more specifically, the not-yet-afflicted-by-age, deny the otherness of human temporality by refusing to accept the cohabitation of continuity and change. By opting for one or the other, they deny the more unsettling possibility of uncanny aging, of subjects, of selves, at once the same and different, familiar and strange. (2010, 80)

Therefore the term "other," as used in this chapter, incorporates not only a different perception of the individual because of their age, but also carries all the uncanny implications of the psychoanalytical otherness that we might react to with forms of disavowal.

---

[3] See deFalco (2010) for a detailed psychoanalytical explanation of society's reaction to the ageing process (9-12).

[4] Freud used the term disavowal (Verleugnung) in early case studies to describe the act of rejecting a perception and dismissing it as inconceivable, mostly in reference to a young boy's disbelief and denial at the discovery that females do not have a penis. Later, in his essay "'Fetischismus"' (1928), he expands the concept also to the general psychological mechanic of dismissing a truth for its perceived inconceivability. Lacan also uses the term disavowal (in French: démenti) in his seminar on Object Relations (1956-1957), emphasising that the perception as such is not erased from memory but only rejected. Thus, the key element of disavowal is that the perception has to be accepted as true and rejected simultaneously.

I argue that the mechanism of "othering" is even stronger when it comes to dementia patients. This can be observed when looking more closely at the kind of metaphors used to address dementia. Susan Sontag has pointed out in *Illness as Metaphor* (1978) that certain illnesses, particularly those whose origins cannot be explained and which cannot be cured, are often referred to in metaphorical terms (see Sontag 1978, 5–7). Numerous metaphors associated with dementia involve the idea of travelling one-way: an Australian documentary was entitled "Journey of No Return."[5] Even more poetic, the German magazine *Der Spiegel* named its lead article on the subject "Journey into the Sunset"[6] and a German TV production on the subject was called "Silent Farewell."[7] There are also a lot of battle metaphors: the Alzheimer's Society UK carries the slogan "Leading the fight against dementia,"[8] US president Barrack Obama's signing of the "National Alzheimer's Project Act" is often referred to in the media as "Obama's war on Alzheimer's"[9] and a German TV drama on the subject was entitled "The Annihilation."[10]

These categories of metaphors show two different aspects to the perception of dementia: "travelling without return" comprises fear of the loss of self, while the battle metaphors suggest fear of the destruction of the self. Depictions of dementia hence represent the ultimate fear of old age—being helpless, useless and completely dependent, mentally and later even physically. It is a much more graphic horror scenario of old age than the idea of "just ageing" without the additional constraints of the disease. Therefore, AD provokes a stronger reaction in society, namely a stronger form of othering and disavowal, which finds expression in the drastic metaphors listed above. The idea of dementia leading to social marginalisation and othering has already been picked up by clinical sociology and feminist thinkers. There have been a number of studies and articles striving to explore the effects and mechanisms

---

[5] ABC, 2006.

[6] *Der Spiegel*, vol. 1 (2010).

[7] ZDF, "Stiller Abschied," 2013.

[8] Homepage of the Alzheimer's Society UK: http://www.alzheimers.org.uk/

[9] For example on the blog "Scientific American" on 31 January 2012. http://blogs.scientificamerican.com/observations/obamas-war-on-alzheimers-will-we-be-able-to-treat-the-disease-by-2025/

[10] ARD, "Die Auslöschung," 2013. For a more detailed analysis of the cultural metaphors used for dementia, see Zeilig (2014).

of othering in order to understand and ultimately improve the dynamics of social relationships for patients with dementia.[11] Scholars like Doyle and Rubinstein identify "multiple marginalized groups: 'woman,' 'demented,' 'incontinent,' 'dependent,' 'old,' or 'aggressive'" (2014, 953) that can sometimes even be attributed to one and the same individual. It stands out that being demented and being a woman are both named as categories equally susceptible to social othering. Amelia deFalco points out that social objectification and "otherness" are issues encountered primarily by women:

> As feminism has made clear, gender is largely responsible for the formation of subjectivity, and one need only glance at any representation within popular media [...] to quickly recognize that aging is distinctly gendered. [...] Without the concealment of cosmetics, dyes, clothing, even surgeries, without appropriate adjustments in activity and behavior made to hide what the not-yet-old, the not-yet-aged, largely interpret as a process of decline and degeneration, the old female subject is rendered benign in other ways, [for example] through infantilization. (2010, x–xi)

Ageing women are more stigmatised than ageing men because being female is already a marginalising category. Being an old woman evokes more stigma, and in the depiction of old women with dementia, one should expect to find even more signs of othering. The analysis of narratives is crucial to uncover these underlying mechanisms. *Iris* and *The Iron Lady*, the two biopics considered in the following discussion, are highly apt for such an analysis as they narrate the stories of women who have become symbols of independence and individualism, and both developed dementia in their later lives.

Both Iris Murdoch and Margaret Thatcher are known in the collective cultural memory for being unconventional women and they both challenged the predominantly traditional female role model of their time. In times when a woman's place in society was mostly propagandised as being that of a homemaker and a mother, depending mostly on the income of their husbands, both Iris Murdoch and Margaret Thatcher chose a career in which they stood out through their own hard work, excellency and independence.

---

[11] See, for example, McCall (2005) or Doyle and Rubinstein (2014).

This aspect of Thatcher's personality is at the core of how her character is introduced in *The Iron Lady*. The young Margaret Roberts[12] is portrayed as the exact counterpart to the traditional role model embodied by other characters around her. At a political function, she prefers listening to the speech of her father to clearing the dirty tea cups with the other women; other girls her age are shown making fun of her because she prefers working hard to going out in fancy clothes. When she receives a letter of acceptance for the University of Oxford, her mother just comes out of the kitchen and stands by the threshold of the shop. She apologises for not congratulating her properly, "My hands are still damp," and goes back to washing up tea cups (a recurring motif in the film). From a distance, Margaret is shown from behind, looking at her mother in the kitchen. The contrast is made to appear even more drastic by the optical division of the frame: between Margaret and her mother, there are two doorframes and a dark corridor (*TIL*, 08:16-09:19). Accordingly, when the young Margaret accepts Denis' marriage proposal, she immediately makes her role and intentions clear:

> I love you so much, but... I will never be one of those women, Denis, who stay silent and pretty on the arm of her husband or remote and alone in the kitchen doing the washing up, for that matter. One's life must matter, Denis. Beyond all the cooking and the cleaning and the children. One's life must mean more than that. I cannot die washing up a teacup. I mean it, Denis. (*TIL*, 26:09-26:53)

Again, washing up tea cups occurs as a symbol of the traditional role model that young Margaret refuses to take on. In their relationship, Margaret is portrayed as the one who takes all the decisions, for example when she decides to run for party leader. Denis and their daughter Carol are outraged at her decision, which she makes without even consulting them (*TIL*, 36:35-38:20), whereas she cannot understand their anger.

In the scenes that feature Margaret (Meryl Streep) as the old AD patient, she still sees, and interacts with, her deceased husband Denis but their relationship changes over the course of the film. At first, the viewer does not know that Denis is dead as the couple are having conversations and recalling memories together, but it gradually becomes apparent that

[12] Margaret Roberts was Margaret Thatcher's maiden name.

Margaret is the only person who can see Denis. At first, Denis seems to be on her side, conspiring with her against her housekeeper and guards, and watching out for her interests. Throughout the film, Margaret becomes more and more aware that there must be something wrong about Denis' presence and the hallucinations become increasingly intrusive and aggressive. Denis' comments on her actions become harsher, he is suddenly critical about her and she becomes increasingly annoyed by seeing him. It all culminates in one scene where she switches on every electrical device in her flat just to drown out his voice in her head (*TIL*, 53:52-56:06). The fight she puts up against the hallucinations, which are part of her disease, illustrates her struggle to remain in the familiar role of her younger self, and her bewilderment at the changes she perceives in herself and Denis. The Denis in her head grows to be the dominant and almost sadistic part of the relationship now, mocking her, her incompetence and her memory problems. She endeavours to rid herself of him to prove to herself that she does not need to rely on her husband for giving her the answer to questions or telling her what to do. In a dramatic scene, she rigorously starts packing Denis' clothes into bin bags to give them to charity. The mood then suddenly changes and she carefully packs Denis' suitcase for him, helping him lovingly into his coat and bidding him farewell as he goes off through the dark corridor into a bright light (*TIL*, 1:28:14-1:32:07). It is at this point that the viewer can perceive a change in her personality. She suddenly incorporates all the "womanly" features that the young Margaret rejected or could not fulfil in her time: the caring wife, the doting mother, the housewife and the dependent part of the relationship. Margaret has apparently lost the distinctive features of her unconventional young self and has almost become selfless. The next morning, she allows her daughter to help her get ready for the day, whereas at the beginning of the film she had insisted that she found being fussed over very inappropriate. After breakfast, she proceeds to wash her teacup and wanders off to another room, leaving the viewer with a view of the empty kitchen table until the end title begins.

It is clear that one of the main issues addressed in the portrayal of Margaret Thatcher is that of her struggle with the transformation from an unusually independent and self-reliant woman into a dependent dementia sufferer. The dichotomy between her young self and her old self is highlighted in the film, not only by using different actresses, but also by emphasising their positioning in terms of their role as a woman. The relationship between Margaret and Denis serves as a metaphor to illustrate this role: Margaret is portrayed as a woman who has always had to earn men's respect and Denis is portrayed as the one man who admires her strength and who is willing to subjugate himself to her. When dementia is increasingly robbing her of her mental capacities, the alienation from herself and the world expresses itself in a changing relationship with the Denis in her head. As the later Denis in the film is merely a figment of her imagination, his mean comments may be interpreted as projections of her own subconscious fears. In the last scene, old Margaret has become the feared "other"—the dependent, old and helpless housewife who she never wanted to be, the one washing up teacups.

The Iron Lady and *Iris* share many similarities, such as the prominence and exceptionality of their protagonists and the dual narrative structure featuring a young Iris and an old one (Kate Winslet and Judi Dench). Yet, there is one main difference in the narrative strategy. As Rose Capp (2013) points out, "[in *The Iron Lady*], from the outset, events are presented consistently from Thatcher's point of view [...] The dominant point of view [in *Iris*] is ultimately that of the spouse" (2).[13] The relationship between the headstrong, outgoing Iris and her quiet and almost submissive husband John Bayley is central to the film. Young Iris is shown as an outspoken and sexually free young woman who does not think much of sexual exclusiveness in her relationships. Young John, on the other hand, is portrayed as shy and sexually inexperienced. He falls in love with Iris over her artistic use of words and the intellectually stimulating conversations they have. In contrast to her eloquence, John does not speak much and has a stammer. Of her many lovers, he is the only one who does not attempt to tame her and rather admires her free spirit. He respects her secrecy about her work and complies with her wish that he not read her unfinished novel. When she eventually asks him to read it, their relationship becomes serious, indicating that her secrecy and his acceptance of it is one of the cornerstones of their relationship. Whenever John describes her secrecy, he sees her as metaphorically wandering off into another world where no one is allowed to follow her. When she falls ill, this becomes his interpretation of what happens to her mind: she is disappearing more and more into her own world, which he cannot access, thus recalling the common metaphor of dementia as a one-way journey.

[13]The film is based on John Bayley's *Elegy for Iris: A Memoir* (1999).

When the first signs of AD become evident, a young doctor comes to Iris' and John's house to examine her. In the early stages of the disease, John refuses to see his wife as an "other" Iris and reacts to the changes in her with disavowal. Unable to answer the question about the name of the current Prime Minister, she responds evasively, to which John reacts with understanding ("Not knowing the Prime Minister's name is not a capital offence," she says and he agrees: "Absolutely."). He even admires her skillfulness at evading questions. When the doctor tries to gain more information about her state of mind from John, he refuses to speak about her as if she was not capable of having her own say in the matter. He defends Iris' "first class mind," emphasising how "she does everything. Always has. Food, shopping, tickets… I never know how she manages and does her books as well." The doctor's suggestion about putting her in a nursing home is rejected straight away. John clings to his belief in Iris' unchanged personality, even though it is undeniable that something is wrong (*Iris*, 25:25-27:15).

The further the illness progresses, the more changes become evident. The biggest change is Iris' loss of speech. John still hangs on to the belief that it is not lost but just hidden in the secret land of Iris' thoughts that he is forbidden to enter. At a later stage of her illness, he is reading to her when she suddenly utters the words "I wrote" as if she remembered her past. He answers, "Such things you wrote. Special things. Secret things… Do you know many secrets now, Iris?" The scene then blends into a neurologist's office where John is shown Iris' brain scans. He says, "You have shown me a map of Iris' brain world, empty. You tell me that all the hidden mysteries and unknown life in there has gone, has been wiped. How then can she say things with such a terrible lucidity? […] So perhaps we ought to learn her language?" (*Iris*, 45:06-47:06). John is determined not to see Iris' dementia as the loss of her personality and a decline into absolute dependency as it is seen by the neurologist. He establishes the idea for himself that her dementia is the absolute independence from worldly strings and habits and that she is moving into a completely free world of the mind that is no longer attached to the real world. Even communication between the two worlds is cut off, an idea that is represented in his thought of her "speaking another language." Although the neurologist insists that John has to accept that Iris is a different person to the one she used to be, he chooses to interpret the changes he sees in her as the expression of one of her typical particularities: the inaccessibility of her thoughts.

Several cut-backs reveal that John had always been jealous of Iris' lovers and had great difficulty accepting Iris' infidelity throughout their relationship. When she enters one of the later stages of her illness, she wanders off one day and is brought home by one of her former lovers. This opens old wounds for John, who is already overwhelmed by his attempt to care for Iris on his own. When they go to bed at night, he shouts at Iris, who does not even understand what is going on anymore:

> Who are you with now, Iris? Who is it?! [...] All your friends are finished with you! I've got you now! Nobody else has you anymore, except your fucking best friend, Dr. Fucking Alzheimer with all his fucking gifts! I've got you now and I don't want you! I've never known anything about you at all, and now I don't care! (*Iris*, 1:07:56-1:08:47)

In his rant, John personifies the illness and feels rejected by Iris' assumed decision to live in the world of Alzheimer's rather than with him. Even at this stage, he refuses to let go of his image of her, interpreting her behaviour in patterns that he knows from young Iris. It becomes clear that all he ever wanted from Iris was to know her inner secrets, to have some grasp of what goes on inside her mind and to make her confirm that their relationship is special, in order to give him a sense of security. After his outbreak, in which he claims not to care about her secrets anymore, there is a shift in his relationship to Iris. Both attend a friend's funeral together where he holds the eulogy and mentions Iris in his speech as if she was dead as well. He goes on to say that "Well, the love is over. And life will soon be over," while the camera is focused on an empty-faced Iris (*Iris*, 1:14:45-1:15:05).

On their way back, Iris panics and breaks out of the moving car. John rushes out to find her, shouting "My old mouse! My old cat-mouse, where are you?" When he finds her eventually, she utters the words that she had never said to John before: "I love you." The interpretation of whether Iris means and understands what she says or whether she just strings together words that seem appropriate is left to the viewer. John, however, answers with delight: "My little mouse! I know you do!" (*Iris*, 1:15:52-1:16:42). His choice of words shows John's sudden inclination to think of Iris as two different people. At the beginning of the scene, when he is just concerned for her well-being, more like a carer, he refers to her as "old mouse" but when she reinstates the love relationship, he lovingly refers to her as "little." His lover and beloved is young (little)

Iris, who he feels is still somehow accessible to him in lucid moments, whereas "old Iris" just seems an "other" and an empty shell. In a cathartic moment, he seems now able to differentiate between the two, finally accepting the reality of the disease.

In the next few takes, he moves her into a nursing home where she dies eventually. Sadie Wearing points out that the scene in the nursing home is not in line with the rest of the film in terms of aesthetics and the "affective register" (2013, 5) of the film. She writes:

> The care home is literally bathed in light. Iris is pictured in a white nightgown twirling around in a wide corridor with light coming in from windows on both sides. This imagery is familiar from both Christian iconographies of beatific angels in heavenly robes and spaces and, more prosaically, might be linked to the ways that people have described 'near death' experiences. (2013, 5)

The angelic interpretation of the scene underpins the positive light in which the nursing home is now presented. Formerly seen by John as the ultimate place of dependency and incapacitation, it is now presented as a heavenly place where body and space do not matter anymore and where Iris can just roam further into her peaceful secret world. John, who has accepted both the "other" and the inaccessible Iris, is finally able to let her go, and she dies shortly after.

The outside perspective on Iris' illness lets the viewer perceive John's struggle as the main plot of the film. Their love story is in the limelight of the narrative and provides the glue that keeps the increasingly conflicting personalities of Iris in accordance with each other. The viewer gets to know both Irises (the consistent young one and the increasingly demented old one) throughout the nonlinear narrative and experiences John's exertions in trying to overcome the intensifying uncanniness he feels regarding his wife. The third-person perspective on Iris and her illness in this film recalls Laura Mulvey's concept of the "male gaze" (see Mulvey 2009)—the viewer can only experience the narrative through the eyes of John who gazes actively at an increasingly passive Iris. Amelia deFalco criticises the placidity with which Iris' narrative depiction distances the viewer from the old person Iris, whose inside perspective is not told. Her character is left devoid of personality and thus open to associations and instrumentalisation:

> Though *Iris* polarizes human life into categories of old and young, it also evokes continuity, a blurring of boundaries that exposes age as uncannily fluid and nonlinear. Furthermore, the film simultaneously sympathizes with the pathos of Iris's illness, elegizing the gradual erasure of her memory and abilities, and actually contributes to such erasure, substituting one version for many: the undoubtedly abundant narratives that constitute Iris the writer, Iris the mature, accomplished woman, Iris the public intellectual, are overwritten with narratives of illness and loss. As such, the film threatens to transform Iris Murdoch into a mascot for dementia. (deFalco 2010, 70)

Both biopics emphasise this image of the young selves in contrast to other female figures and portray them as extraordinary and rebellious. Both films share the strategy of splitting the protagonist's role into a young and an old self to contrast not only the difference in age but also the difference between healthy and ill, which makes the uncanny aspect of othering even more visible. Yet, the difference between the films is primarily the narrative perspective: in *The Iron Lady,* Margaret herself has to cope with the changes, whereas in *Iris,* John is the protagonist. The first-person perspective of the illness through the eyes of Margaret Thatcher lets the viewer experience all the confusion and illogical fractures in her perception first-hand. Eventually, it is hard to make sense of what is happening around her and hard to make sense of her own actions. Through the use of this perspective, the viewer will understand that the old Margaret is an unreliable narrator and that their only points of reference to her real personality lie in the cut-back scenes. They can compare her to her former self and experience the uncanniness of her transformation but the effect of othering is constrained by letting them experience her suffering first-hand. The outside view of AD in *Iris* offers more narrative consistency but at the same time does not attribute the ill Iris any personality, transforming her selfless existence into a palimpsest for any possible interpretation. As viewers are aware that the film is narrated from John's perspective, they can only experience the uncanniness second-hand by adopting John's perception of the events. The film's eponymous protagonist remains voiceless in the end and John's angle is the only one remaining.

Both women end up in the places where they never wanted to be, the one powerless and washing up a tea cup, the other speechless in a nursing home. However, both films still aim to provide the viewer with a conciliatory and somehow cathartic ending. In the final scenes, the protagonists are shown at peace, without the often violent struggles of coping with the disease and the impact of othering. Yet, both films fail to address how Margaret and Iris themselves come to terms with having become an "other." Instead, the peaceful resolution at the end of both films suggests that they have gone beyond the point of noticing the change as they have already forgotten who they were. However, it seems bizarre to think that the completion of othering, the very process that is criticised by feminists in society's interaction with aged women, is used as a cathartic solution to a narrative about AD patients whose younger selves are distinctively portrayed as the incorporation of feminist ideals. This only comes to show the uncanniness of a disease that is as inaccessible to the outer world as it is frightening.

Works Cited

Beauvoir, Simone de. 2012. *Das Alter*, trans. Anjuta Aigner-Dünnwald and Ruth Henry. Reinbek bei Hamburg: Rowohlt Taschenbuch Verlag.

Capp, Rose. 2013. Dementia on the Silver Screen. *The Gerontologist* 53 (1): 172–173.

DeFalco, Amelia. 2010. *Uncanny Subjects: Aging in Contemporary Narrative*. Columbus: Ohio State UP.

Donnelly, Gabrielle. 2016. 'I wouldn't be young again for anything': Jane Fonda says she loves being old... and she still looks like herself. *The Daily Mail Online*, June 23.

Doyle, Patrick, and Robert Rubinstein. 2014. Person-Centered Dementia Care and the Cultural Matrix of Othering. *The Gerontologist* 54 (6): 952–963.

Eakin, Paul Ian. 2006. Narrative Identity and Narrative Imperialism: A Response to Galen Strawson and James Phelan. *Narrative* 14 (2): 180–187.

Freud, Sigmund. 1928. Fetischismus. *Almanach der Psychoanalyse* 1928: 17–25.

Gullette, Margaret M. 2004. *Aged by Culture*. Chicago: Chicago UP.

Iris. 2001. United Kingdom/United States of America: Miramax.

Lacan, Jacques. 1956–1957. *Le séminaire-livre IV, la relation d'objet*. Paris: Le Seuil.

McCall, Leslie. 2005. The Complexity of Intersectionality. *Signs: Journal of Women in Culture & Society* 30: 1771–1800.

Mulvey, Laura. 2009. Visual Pleasure and Narrative Cinema. In *Visual and Other Pleasures*, ed. Laura Mulyey, 14–30. New York: Palgrave Macmillan.

Sontag, Susan. 1978. *Illness as Metaphor*. New York: Farrar, Straus and Giroux.

The Iron Lady. 2011. United Kingdom/France: 20th Century Fox.

Wearing, Sadie. 2013. Dementia and the Biopolitics of the Biopic. *Dementia* 5: 315–325.

Zeilig, Hannah. 2014. Dementia as a Cultural Metaphor. *The Gerontologist* 54 (2): 258–267.

CHAPTER 4

"Embarking, Not Dying": Clare Boylan's *Beloved Stranger* as *Reifungsroman*

Michaela Schrage-Früh

This chapter reads Clare Boylan's *Beloved Stranger* (1999) as an example of the recently emerged genre of the *Reifungsroman*, or novel of ripening. In doing so, it argues that Boylan's novel about seventy-five-year-old Lily Butler counteracts the cultural myth of ageing as a narrative of decline without denying its validity. In fact, it is precisely her elderly husband Dick's mental and physical decline, and eventual death, that forces Lily to review her own life and embark on a difficult journey toward self-discovery, renewal and liberation. Initially, Lily is presented as a character not at all unhappy with her life. She has settled into an apparently comfortable routine with her retired husband in their Dublin home and, when her daughter Ruth questions the happiness of her parents' marriage, Lily insists: "We need each other. We're halves of the same part. It's nothing you could write a book about. We're old pals, Ruth" (Boylan 7). This quiet routine, however, is shattered when Dick is diagnosed with bipolar disorder, showing "signs of severe paranoid delusion" (Boylan 59). After the crisis culminates and Dick threatens his wife at

M. Schrage-Früh (✉)
Languages, Literatures and Cultures, National University of Ireland Galway, Galway, Ireland
e-mail: Michaela.Schrage-Frueh@nuigalway.ie

C. McGlynn et al. (eds.), *Ageing Women in Literature and Visual Culture*,
DOI 10.1007/978-3-319-63609-2_4

gun point, he is put in the care of a mental institution and later a nursing home. This situation unhinges not only his own, but also his wife's and daughter's lives. Both women are prompted to reassess their life stories and for both this process will be one of self-awareness and growth, ultimately leading to a closer mother-daughter bond and a hopeful future.

Lily's journey is inextricably entwined with the lives of her husband and daughter, whose stories impact on and serve as a foil to her own. In fact, a case could be made that *Beloved Stranger* comprises three novels in one; while Dick's story is representative of the narrative of decline, Ruth's story might be said to exemplify what Margaret Morganroth Gullette has termed the "midlife women's progress novel" (1997, 77). Through their individual developments, the two female characters also redefine the mother-daughter relationship in terms of what Kathleen Woodward calls "a model of generational continuity" (1999b, 153). Nevertheless, Lily's development remains at the heart of the novel. Thus, after briefly outlining the most important features of the *Reifungsroman*, this chapter will analyse Lily's multifaceted and intimate psychological journey inward and backward in time as an example of fictional life review. In doing so, it will show how the reader is made to share Lily's rich inner life, which is not only well worth "writing a book about," but complicates conventional notions of the protagonist's identity as wife, widow and elderly mother as well as the concept of ageing as a linear narrative of decline.

As Susan Watkins notes, "the conventional age narrative (and one that is often used by male authors) is one of decline accompanied by nostalgia for past glories" (2013, 224).[1] This traditional decline narrative is challenged by the *Reifungsroman*, a term coined by Barbara Frey Waxman to describe a new type of novel in which "an aging heroine grapples with aging's problems while also finding in old age opportunities for true *reifung*, or ripening, of intellect and spirit" (1993, 28). Accordingly, this type of novel foregrounds the ageing, often female protagonist's "quest of self-knowledge, self-development, and a role for the future" (Waxman 1990, 16). Taking her cue from May Sarton's "optimistic concept of 'ripening toward death in a fruitful way,'" Waxman argues that this *Bildungsroman* of the second half of life not only opposes "its central tenet to the usual notion of deterioration in old age" but also "rejects

[1] See, for instance, John Updike's *Toward the End of Time* (1997), Philip Roth's *The Human Stain* (2000) and *Everyman* (2006), or Martin Amis' *The Pregnant Widow* (2010).

negative cultural stereotypes of the old woman and aging, seeking to change the society that created these stereotypes" (1990, 2). Waxman's exploration of the genre in her seminal study *From the Hearth to the Open Road* (1990) focuses on works by North American and British writers, most notably Doris Lessing, Elizabeth Taylor, Barbara Pym, May Sarton and Margaret Laurence. These writers, alongside Penelope Lively and Angela Carter, also feature in later studies by Brennan (2005) and King (2013). The genre has been less popular in the Irish literary context, where older women in fiction tend to bear symbolic overtones and often feature in narratives of decline.[2] Boylan's novel, a fictionalised account of her own parents' relationship,[3] provides a noteworthy exception that adds some facets to the generic features of the *Reifungsroman*.

Reifungsromane often involve either real or internal journeys. In the latter case, the protagonists experience the past through frequent recollections, reminiscences and dreams. Through these internal travels they come to terms with the past and, crucially, "try to chart a new course either into or through old age, which they embark on at the end of the work" (Waxman 1990, 17). Often, these explorations of the characters' past take the form of life review, a geriatric concept defined by Robert Butler as a "naturally occurring, universal mental process characterized by the progressive return to consciousness of past experience, and particularly, the resurgence of unresolved conflicts; simultaneously, and normally, these revived experiences and conflicts are surveyed and reintegrated" (1963, 66). While Butler considers the life review as a process occurring naturally and automatically in elderly or terminally ill people faced with the prospect of "dissolution and death" (1963, 66), writers of *Reifungsromane* employ the concept less rigidly. Nevertheless they maintain the emphasis on life review's therapeutic potential, as the "dialogue between past and present selves [...] makes it possible for the subject to see the experience of change as constructive" (King 2013, 101). At the end of the novel, the protagonists typically "have become revitalized, newly self-knowledgeable, self-confident, and independent before they

---

[2]Recent examples include Anne Enright's *The Green Road* (2015) and Joseph O'Connor's *Ghost Light* (2010), the latter of which is analysed in Margaret O'Neill's chapter in this collection.

[3]The autobiographical background of *Beloved Stranger* is provided in Clare Boylan's obituary from 2006 in *The Telegraph*. See http://www.telegraph.co.uk/news/obituaries/1518643/Clare-Boylan.html.

move forward" (Waxman 1990, 17). Ultimately, as Waxman notes, the protagonists "develop and expand more as they grow old than they did as they grew up—or perhaps they truly grow up at last" (1990, 17). In this sense, the genre of the *Reifungsroman* contributes to a positive conception of ageing in terms of "growth and change" rather than "decline" (Woodward 1999a, xiii).

Often the protagonist's actual and inner journeys are linked. This is also the case in Boylan's novel in which Lily undertakes a number of short but crucial trips as well as more extensive internal journeys into the past. In many of the examples discussed by Waxman, these inner journeys are conveyed by means of a confessional first-person narrator or a third-person narrative point of view described as "limited omniscient, confined to the elder in a youthful world" (1990, 16). In contrast, *Beloved Stranger* offers three closely interwoven, constantly shifting third-person narrations so that Lily's perspective is complemented by that of her elderly husband and her middle-aged daughter. Memories are further evoked in the form of dialogues and shared reminiscences. Arguably, this type of narration reinforces one of the central aims of the *Reifungsroman* as defined by Waxman, namely dissolving barriers between constructed categories such as young and old or real and imagined (1990, 17). The exchange of reminiscences between Lily and younger characters also furthers what Rosario Arias Doblas identifies as the two core elements of the process of ripening, namely "forging links with the younger generation and the recapitulation of past experience" (2005, 8).

At the start of the novel the reader learns that Lily and Dick, who have lived in the same neighbourhood for almost fifty years, were "such a familiar sight that people scarcely noticed them" (Boylan 4). However, each being "in the care of the other" (Boylan 4), neither Dick nor Lily are fully aware of their social invisibility. Lily is looking after the household and Dick is assisting her with health issues, such as her ingrown toenail, or is accompanying her to the shops and to church. It soon becomes obvious that all is not well though. Early in the novel, Dick is showing the first signs of illness as manifested in his secretive and increasingly strange behaviour. For instance, Lily discovers that he keeps a gun in their bedroom with which he threatens to kill both his wife and himself. It becomes obvious that he has not been able to settle into old age and find a fulfilling new role for himself after his retirement. Dick himself articulates this insight while pointing the gun at his wife:

> No one expects their life to change. No man does. [...] I am not an old man either. Not old, merely a prisoner inside this rotting cage, having to stand by helpless while his manliness is spat upon and kicked to the ground, and his obedient wife slopes away to be replaced by a nanny who treats him like a pet dog. (Boylan 50)

This passage shows the extent to which Dick has internalised patriarchal role models, including his traditional position as head of household, breadwinner and protector, and how deeply incompatible these roles are with his current situation as elderly and increasingly frail pensioner. Accordingly, as Brooke Allan notes, *Beloved Stranger* is only superficially

> a book about madness; in reality it is a book about marriage and family, and the function of the mania is simply to underscore, intensify, the patterns that have been there all along. The illness reveals Dick's true nature without distorting it [...] and the countless unspoken problems are thrown into sudden and disconcerting relief. (2001, n.p.)

These "unspoken problems," however, point to a broader social context, highlighting the damaging consequences that rigid gender conventions, such as those enshrined in the 1937 Irish Constitution and permeating Irish society throughout the twentieth century, can entail for an individual family.

Partly due to his disease, partly due to his inability to come to terms with his ageing process and find a new role not determined by economic and sexual power, Dick fails to complete a successful life review. Thus, when he revisits Lily's and his shared past with the help of their old photo album, he fabricates a romantic tale of courtship that evades all problems of their later married and family life. Moreover, his attempts to ignore his old age lead him to re-enact scripts of romance and sexuality which he firmly associates with youth and which are therefore doomed to failure. This failure, in turn, brings to light Dick's internalisation of misogynist views. He slights his wife by stating "You can't have a good time with an old woman" (Boylan 243) or torments her with his *idée fixe* that Lily is having a sexual affair with the much younger Tim Walcott, a gay psychiatrist with whom both Ruth and Lily develop a friendship. At the climax of the crisis, he tries to set fire to both his wife and the house while resorting to derogatory stereotypes associated with older women:

> Nobody wants to come to the house of an old man who is married to a hag, a shrew. [...] I can smell you. I could smell you when we were dancing. The whole place stinks of your unwashed body. There is nothing left for me to do but to burn the whole bloody place down. (Boylan 132, 133)

These manic "episodes" (Boylan 241) are contrasted with Dick's continual decline in health as well as his poignantly described moments of fear, confusion and alienation. Shortly before his death Lily gently reminds her husband of his old age, and Dick's reaction succinctly sums up the narrative of decline exemplified by his story: "Then it's all over. The game's up. [...] You get old and then you die—that's it, isn't it?" (Boylan 243).

While Dick's story exemplifies the narrative of ageing as decline, for Lily the crisis caused by his illness provides an opportunity to undergo a liberating, if painful, process of ripening and growth. In contrast to her husband, Lily, after a lifetime of compromises and self-denial, has had less difficulty settling into old age. Early on in the novel, she muses about the passage of time and the various selves she has accumulated over the years:

> 'I'm seventy-five,' she thought. 'How did I get to seventy-five?' The people she had been were all still inside her, very neatly packaged. She used to imagine that old age must be awful, the death of everything. But it wasn't so. Nothing died. The child and the young girl and the mother and the middle-aged woman full of rage and grief and dawning wisdom were there all together, and she reigned as peacemaker over this tribe. She understood them now and knew they had done their best. (Boylan 19)

This insight at the beginning of the novel suggests that Lily is at peace with old age, envisioning this phase of her life as a time of wisdom and reconciliation. Having maintained a sense of continuity between her younger selves and her present self, she does not resent the visible signs of ageing, and only focuses on her bodily changes when they cause her discomfort; in one scene, for instance, she is amazed at the "hoofed extension" (Boylan 9) of her toes. As her daughter Ruth reflects: "Lily never thought about her appearance. [...] She had been a lovely-looking woman but hadn't minded getting old. Old age was a fine excuse to wear comfortable clothes" (Boylan 85). Accordingly, unlike other *Reifungsromane*, the novel does not contain any mirror scenes in which Lily gazes at her own reflection, feeling detached from her aged body.[4] Old age, to her, is not a "mask or disguise concealing the essentially youthful self beneath" (Featherstone and Hepworth 2001, 379), but it is part of the identity she has grown into and that still contains her former selves. During the brief spell in which Lily and Dick experience what their daughter describes as "crazy love affair" (Boylan 85), triggered by the perusal of their photo album, we learn that Lily "didn't feel self-conscious about being old, or about him being old and talking in this heartfelt way. The girl with the big breasts and modest legs was still inside her, she had always known that. And if she had been insecure then, she was insecure now. Let her have her romance at full volume. Better late than never" (Boylan 98). For a while, Lily thrives in this blissful fantasy. She experiences a second spring when she is 'dating' Dick during his hospital sojourn, remembering "with pleasure that it was a visiting day" (Boylan 94).

However, while Lily enjoys Dick's reminiscences, his romantic tale is at the same time subverted by her own spontaneous recollections, which she can't share and hardly admits to herself as they call into question her entire life story. In Lily's early years *Bildung* did not take place because she simply followed the script, living her life according to the social conventions and rules of her time. For a young woman in 1950s Dublin, this meant getting married and raising a family. In this sense, Allan's description of Lily as "product of a pre-feminist age" is accurate (2001, n.p.). Lily becomes acutely aware of her youthful lack of reflection and growth as she is leafing through the pages of her old photo album. At first she eagerly joins Dick on his "fascinating journey" into their early courtship days: "The surprise of seeing their young selves there, pristine under dust, was like finding some delicate flower in a neglected part of the garden. She could not tell if the past had been as Dick said. If not, it should have been" (Boylan 98). However, despite her eagerness to share Dick's idealised tale of their courtship, Lily ultimately remains detached from his version of the past and even her own younger self, unable to "remember the details of each date as he could, nor the feelings he

[4] For the importance of mirror scenes in the *Reifungsroman*, see Brennan (2005, 24–25) and Waxman (1990).

described. She couldn't even clearly recall the girl in the picture. It was like looking at an old cigarette ad" (Boylan 96). The fact that Lily detaches herself from her own image by likening her younger self to a girl in "an old cigarette ad" throws into relief Dick's and Lily's very different views of the past. Accordingly, even at this relatively early stage of Dick's illness and despite the second spring they briefly enjoy together, Lily's own memories continually seep in and can't be suppressed. These memories tell a different story from the one constructed by Dick, most crucially when she recalls a moment shortly before their marriage when "a thought swooped in like a pirate. *I don't want to marry him.* It was such an awful thought that she couldn't bear to consider it. Was it him, or did she just not want to marry?" (Boylan 98). As Susan Sontag rightly reminds us, "A way of certifying experience, taking photographs is also a way of refusing it—by limiting experience to a search for the photogenic, by converting experience into an image, a souvenir" (1979, 9). Lily's recollections may be elicited by the photographs, yet they focus on her undocumented emotional history that runs counter to the more photogenic "souvenirs" of the past.

Lily's disconcerting memories confirm Ruth's doubt that her mother "had ever really been happy in her early married life" (Boylan 85). This suspicion is increasingly shared by the reader as the alternative history of Lily's and Dick's marriage gradually emerges through Lily's spontaneous recollections and reminiscences. Even before their journey into the past, Lily's occasional recollections of their early married life suggest the extent to which her marriage thwarted her own potential and growth. Thus, Lily recalls how Dick forcefully prevented her from returning to her office job, even though her "office days [...] had been among the happiest of her life" (Boylan 23). Firmly insisting on Lily's exclusive role as housewife and mother, Dick simultaneously denied her "luxuries" such as central heating or a washing machine. Similarly, it becomes obvious that Lily's sexual desire has been stifled throughout her marriage. Returning from a trip to the local stores with Dick, she recalls how fifty years ago they had made love in a doorway while sheltering from the rain, and she realises: "That was the only time she had been swept away in the way she read about in novels" (Boylan 3). However, owing to Dick's "prudish side" (Boylan 3), they never discussed each other's needs and wishes so that sex became an act of unpleasurable duty on Lily's part. A number of sex scenes in the novel focus on Lily's thoughts as "his old bones clamped around her" (Boylan 29) or as "she sighed as silently as possible as she was butted on the iron mattress" (Boylan 119). While in the earlier scene Lily distracts herself by musing that she "mostly hadn't cared for sex" (Boylan 29), in the later scene she admits to herself that her husband has never "been a good lover" (Boylan 119). These remarkable scenes belie what Sandberg calls the "longstanding history that dissociates sexuality and later life" (2015, 219). In fact, sexuality is presented as a persistent yet increasingly troubling aspect of Lily's and Dick's relationship. At the same time, Lily's continuing curiosity about sexual matters—for instance, she repeatedly reflects on and even mentions to her daughter how she once walked in on a couple engaged in oral sex in a sauna—suggests that this lack of interest is caused less by Lily's old age than by her own impoverished marital intimacy.

While Lily's life has been defined by compromises and self-denial, Dick's hospital sojourn provides her with the opportunity to enjoy both romance and a life of her own. According to Ruth, she "had at last achieved the perfect existence—a life entirely free of compromise. She did not have to live with a man and yet she wasn't alone. [...] Whenever she saw Pa it was at the fever pitch of courtship. And then she went home again" (Boylan 86). Ruth also notices a visible change in her mother's personality: "She was growing sleek and almost assertive. She no longer felt the need to please or justify" (Boylan 99). The difference between what Ruth refers to as "new" versus "old Ma" (Boylan 100) is caused by Lily's sudden freedom to live her life the way she wants, at liberty to neglect her household chores, to eat simple food and read the books she is interested in. The latter include mainly feminist works ranging from Germaine Greer's *The Female Eunuch* to Doris Lessing's *The Golden Notebook*, an interest first sparked by the small library Ruth left behind two decades ago and one that Lily pursues not so much in order to change her life as "to make sense of it" (Boylan 93). This blissful state, however, is dramatically disrupted when Dick's condition takes a turn for the worse during his stay home for Christmas, and it is precisely Lily's feminist books that become a target for his fury when he tries to set fire to the books, the house and his wife. This traumatic event disrupts Lily's life and causes her to temporarily exchange her home for a squalid "ghost room, totally devoid of history or memory" (Boylan 147). Interestingly, her escape to this bedsitter in an anonymous building block not far from her own neighbourhood is likened to a teenager's first flight from home: "She had done an awful thing. She had run away. […] What would her daughter think? She felt like a teenager giving trouble to a parent" (Boylan 147). Throughout the novel seventy-five-year-old Lily is repeatedly likened to a child, for instance when Dick tells his daughter that Lily is "a child, always had every decision made for her" and that she is therefore "not able to look after herself" (Boylan 155). It is thus not surprising that the horror of her own dependent state begins to dawn on Lily in her new surroundings: "What have I done with my life? Why have I no money, no courage, no life of my own? She was like a child being sent to the shops for the messages, not quite understanding the money that had been put into her fist" (Boylan 149). Simultaneously, associating Lily's escape from home with a teenager's first independent steps serves to destabilise clear-cut notions of the life-course and suggests the prospect of growth.

Accordingly, Lily's bedsitter experiences provide her with a valuable first sense of independence. Even when she has difficulty unlocking the gate that leads to her flat and fears a passer-by has stolen her handbag, she refuses to give up her newly gained freedom by calling Ruth, who "would take over her life, destroy this little, bitter scrap of independence she had found for herself" (Boylan 151). Before the outbreak of Dick's illness, Lily had been sheltered in the close, if restrictive, embrace of their marriage, symbolised by the tight grip of his arm around her at night. Now she has to face everyday challenges on her own. She also has to grapple with the experience of isolation, loneliness and lack of money. While Lily's isolated and economically strained condition is only temporary, it evokes what Brennan calls "the spectre of the penniless older woman" (2005, 33). Lily tries in vain to make contact with her neighbours; for instance she offers to babysit the child of a young single mother, only to be rudely rejected. She also feels vulnerable, exposed to the gaze of a male stranger who occupies the converted garage opposite her apartment. Increasingly isolated and socially invisible in her bedsitter, with only the company of a mouse that she befriends, feeds and talks to, Lily drinks to take "the edge off her loneliness" (Boylan 166) and eventually attempts suicide by taking an overdose of painkillers. The liminal state in which Lily finds herself during this phase of her life forces her to face uncomfortable truths about herself, such as the following:

> 'I've lied to Ruth. All the talk about marriage! In fact, I used to envy single women. I used to think it must be lovely for a woman to have her own income and no one to tell her what to do. I always imagined single women

> hadn't any worries. […] I never imagined them short of money or growing old alone in a room like this, day after day, year upon year, with no human touch and no one to talk to.' (Boylan 184–185)

Shortly after her failed suicide attempt, the building block catches fire and Lily saves her neighbour's neglected baby from the burning house. In her reading of the novel, Carmen Zamorano Llena interprets this act as a symbol of Lily's completed *Bildung*. As she states, while the fire caused by Dick forces Lily out of her home to begin a re-examination of her own life,

> Her *Bildung* comes full circle with the fire that burns down the block of apartments. […] In a Phoenix-like image, Lily emerges from the collapsing building with a baby that she has risked her life to save in her arms, and which becomes the symbol of Lily's new life emerging out of the ashes. (2004, 193)

This interpretation is appealing in its sense of neat symbolic closure. However, while the fire and Lily's return home after a prolonged hospital sojourn are important steps in her process of recovery and ripening, there is still a long way ahead before Lily's insights about what she considers her wasted life (cf. Boylan 185) can be transformed into a positive vision for the future. It is only when Lily starts sharing her reminiscences with others, such as Tim Walcott or her daughter Ruth, that a healing process can set in and reconciliation with the past can occur. This process is anything but clear-cut and is complicated by an array of contradictory emotions. Thus, when Lily returns home from hospital, she feels frustrated by her house, where "the face of marriage became her own face, feeding off her life and energy until she was old and used up and calmed down" (Boylan 208). On the other hand, her short excursion into the world of the less privileged makes her aware of the blessings of having a family and a home: "And family life, she thought, in spite of its wars and waste, was all there was. What would she do without Ruth to take her home from hospital and turn on her electric blanket? What if there was no Dick to act as a mirror for her vanished life?" (Boylan 212).

Lily also has to grapple with Dick's death, which occurs shortly after her return home, and which leaves her full of conflicting emotions ranging from grief to anger. Her initial reaction is a sense of liberation, expressed by a significant dream in the night after his death, in which a priest tells her to "Go in peace" as her marriage "is ended." The dream seems to restore Lily's youth, promising a bright future full of opportunities: "When she went out the sun was shining. She walked away on high-heeled shoes and she realised that she was young again; she was a young girl and she was free. Her body and her spirits were buoyant and her whole life was ahead of her" (Boylan 252). Even though Lily's physical youth cannot be restored, and she soon realises that she will have to work through her grief for Dick, she still feels "light and euphoric" even after waking. Despite simultaneously feeling "a rush of pain," her dominant emotion is relief: "'I'm free,' she thought. The notion swam into her, seductive and profane. The marriage is ended" (Boylan 252). In order to successfully complete her life review and embark on a new life, however, Lily needs to reconcile herself with past choices and conflicts. She thus spends the time following Dick's death withdrawing from her daughter and friends, restlessly "navigating the underworld" (Boylan 264) in order to "find the happy memories and gather them in" (Boylan 259). However, she is increasingly filled with anger and frustration as "Her only memories were of the cruelty and chaos of his recent behaviour" (Boylan 260). Moreover, she is haunted by Dick's ghost who climbs into bed with her at night in what Ruth considers "vivid dreams" and what Lily fears are "supernatural experience[s]" (Boylan 278).

Lily's relationship to Ruth plays a key role both in her recovery and in her process of ripening. Thus, her recovery is facilitated by a weekend in Nice spent together with her daughter. During this regenerative trip "Ruth marvelled at Ma's healing powers, her childish curiosity and willingness to be pleased" (Boylan 284). While Lily is once more likened to a child, this time the comparison suggests openness to new experience rather than dependence. The short journey also contrasts with an earlier weekend trip to a seaside resort, which she had undertaken with Dick at the start of his illness and during which Lily's own sense of happiness mainly seemed to be prompted by his: "'I've never seen him look so happy,' she thought, and then with surprise, 'I'm happy too.' It had been a memorable weekend, a glowing time, an autumn blaze" (Boylan 29). However, during Lily's first trip abroad, carefully organised by her daughter, she spends a weekend she really enjoys, confiding to Ruth that her father never really understood her dreams, one of which was to travel: "Do you think if I hadn't married Pa I'd have got to see the world?" (Boylan 282). The two contrasting weekend trips, then, bring into sharp relief the inner distance that Lily has covered in the course of her journey.

Lily's willingness and ability to embark on a new course of her life is shown when she decides to use the free space in Dick's photo album for the holiday photos with Ruth. Looking at the pictures, she sees "for the first time that there were similarities between herself and her daughter. They had the same frank gaze, an ironic edge to their smile. Had that developed over the years, through common understanding?" (Boylan 289). Busying herself with the photos, she also realises "that an hour had passed, a pleasant and absorbing hour in which self-pity and anxiety played no part" (Boylan 289). Prompted by this realisation, Lily returns to the photos from her younger years:

> Like a diver coming on sunken treasure, she plunged, turning back to the early pages. [...] She traced her own features – unconsciously beautiful, selfish, hopeful. She had never lived. She had seized the first good thing that came her way, Dick Butler's unconditional worship. She had been seeking herself in Dick – an acceptable, lovable version of herself. She felt a rush of forgiveness for her young self. (Boylan 289)

Her forgiveness extends to her husband's younger self as she tries to imagine Dick's hopes and struggles. This journey back in time completes Lily's life review in that she not only comes to terms with past choices but re-evaluates her life in such a way that she discovers meaning and purpose in her marriage: "Going through the pictures she was surprised by how right they looked together, the boy and girl, Lily and Dick. [...] She felt very strongly now that they had been put together for some purpose. That notion had not struck her before. It had all seemed random and blurred" (Boylan 290). This insight into a purposeful meaning of their shared life story is a turning point for Lily, which finally allows her to come to terms with her past and to let go of her dead husband. When she falls asleep shortly afterwards, Dick visits her a final time and while his former visits had been terrifying, defined by Dick's cold touch and his unwanted sexual demands on her, this time she desires the intimacy that she had only endured before: "'Could you put your arms around me, Dick?' His hands were warm. He was still old but he had the freshness of a boy. Warmth and light enfolded her. 'Don't go yet', she appealed. The stiff, sour feeling of grief dissolved as she clung to him. She felt light as summer" (Boylan 291).

Lily's completion of her life review is assisted and accompanied by her forging of cross-generational friendships. One of these friends is Tim

Walcott, the psychiatrist who assists Ruth and Lily throughout the course of Dick's illness. It is Tim who sums up the value of their friendship: "She was anybody's fancy, really, but he liked her. Maybe mad old Dick was right to be jealous. She was nearly half a century older than him and he had never got to grips with women anyway, but it was a rare thing to find a person of any age or sex with whom you could be honest and at ease" (Boylan 199). Most important, however, is Lily's relationship with Ruth.

Ruth's story is closely interwoven with Lily's and serves as a foil to her mother's. Having suffered from her father's domestic tyranny and her mother's perceived subservience, Ruth left her family home early to become a successful architect. Now in her early forties she enjoys the pleasurable life of a well-off single woman with good friends and occasional lovers. Her process of ripening in the novel includes coming to terms with her childhood and adolescence, both of which impacted negatively on her conception of family life. In one of the mirror scenes that mark the development of Ruth throughout the novel, she muses on the fact that her decision to "let her appearance go" is in part a reaction to her mother's restricted way of life. Looking at herself in the mirror, Ruth sees "greying hair, that forbidding look women get when they think too much. She didn't lack confidence. She had a successful career, she had lovers and she knew she could get a husband if she put her mind to it, but years of looking at Ma had led her to believe that pretty women were like a rabbit in trap" (Boylan 15). As Zamorano Llena observes, the mother–daughter relationship is "marked by the generational gap, but most especially by the feminist age and the disruption of social and cultural constructs of femininity with the consequent alterations on the course and expectations of women's lives" (2004, 181). While this is true, in the course of the novel mother and daughter move closer to each other as Ruth understands that Lily has not chosen, but rather has been forced into, the role of the traditionally minded housewife. This recognition is partly brought about by shared reminiscence, for instance when Ruth learns that Lily, after reading the feminist books left behind by her daughter, "had felt angry and cheated of her life" and had walked out on her husband. Planning to start a new life in England, Lily had been "quite excited" (Boylan 210) but ultimately returned home to continue her life with Dick. As Ruth is beginning to see her mother in a different light and finds a way to reconcile herself with her dead father, she is able to move forward with her own life and open up to others, for instance Tim Walcott, with whom she decides to raise a family. Ruth's reconciliation with the past and the strengthened bond with her mother manifest themselves in her changed outward appearance, including her use of make-up and a new hairstyle: "She was quite pleased with the end result. It wasn't exactly a transformation, it was a truce. She had given up her battle. She was no longer at war with the world" (Boylan 303).

At the end of the novel, generational conflict has given way to "generational continuity" in which "three generations are linked to each other through a heritage of care for the next generation" (Woodward 1999b, 153). For the first time, Lily realises that Ruth, from whom she had been quite estranged at the start of the novel, is in many ways similar to herself and might turn into her woman friend. Conversely, Ruth, who "had always assumed that being grown-up meant being free of your family," now understands that "there was a sequel, that getting older brought a need to rediscover your source" (Boylan 292). In a similar vein, Ruth's pregnancy is presented in terms of generational continuity. Significantly, Ruth realises that she is pregnant while she and her mother are visiting Dick's grave. The symbolically fraught setting of the cemetery in winter appears to Ruth as "the perfect venue for her tidings" because "If any news were to matter to the dead, it must be that life goes on" (Boylan 309). It is Lily's reasoning, however, which provides the ironic conclusion to the novel when she abruptly informs her daughter that the unborn child will be "your father, coming back" (Boylan 309). This sense of intergenerational connectedness, ultimately replacing the narrative of decline with a cyclical model of time, is also encapsulated in Ruth's vision of a new housing project called Ocean Village, which she has developed in the spirit of intergenerational community and which is to "incorporate a row of retirement cottages into a smart new town-house scheme" informed by the insight that it is "neither safe nor natural for children to grow up with no elderly people around" (Boylan 200). Accordingly, the positive vision offered in Boylan's novel is grounded in a notion of family life and cross-generational bonding. While Lily's tentative travels, her late-life romance with Dick and her experiences in the bedsitter gesture at alternative possibilities, the plot thus ultimately returns to the more conventional mother/grandmother narrative. In this narrative, however, Dick, representative of outdated patriarchal values, is replaced by the boyish and gentle Tim, and the traditional nuclear family is radically reimagined.

Within these parameters, moreover, Boylan paints a picture of Lily as an intellectually curious, courageous and independent woman, whose potential to grow and enjoy life has just begun to come into its own at the end of the novel. As Lily realises shortly after Dick's death, "deep inside she would be sustained by the seed of her own life, reaching up for the light. There wasn't much left of her life, but it was money unspent" (Boylan 252). This potential is captured by the beautifully wrought image of a falling leaf. At the start of the novel, Lily watches the descent of a leaf in autumn and discards the more obvious association with death for the image of a teenager leaving home: "She watched a leaf come down, a frivolous descent, as if it was embarking, not dying. It did not simply drop off the tree but detached itself fastidiously and then glided into freefall, a flimsy scrap of gold against the wide, cold sky, like a teenager leaving home. Ruth" (Boylan 25). At the end of the novel it becomes clear that this image might just as well represent Lily's own "embarking, not dying," thus subverting clear-cut notions of the life-course as a linear narrative of decline. While Boylan does not refrain from exploring the hardships of old age, including physical and mental deterioration as well as the challenges of coming to terms with grief, loss and the passage of time, she leaves the reader with an optimistic vision of the future and thus provides an important example of what Waxman calls a "groundbreaking literary genre that celebrates aging" (1990, 188).

Works Cited

Allan, Brooke. 2001. Blurring the Borders. Review of Pat Barker, *Border Crossing*, Clare Boylan, *Beloved Stranger* and Michael Dibdin, *Thanksgiving*. *New Criterion*, vol. 19. https://www.newcriterion.com/articles.cfm/Blurring-the-borders-2195. Accessed April 25 2017.

Boylan, Clare. 1999. *Beloved Stranger*. London: Abacus.

Brennan, Zoe. 2005. *The Older Woman in Recent Fiction*. Jefferson, North Carolina: McFarland & Company.

Butler, Robert N. 1963. The Life Review: An Interpretation of Reminiscence in the Aged. *Psychiatry* 26 (1): 65–76.

Doblas, Rosario Arias. 2005. Moments of Ageing: The *Reifungsroman* in Contemporary Fiction. In *Women Ageing Through Literature and Experience*, ed. Brian J. Worsfold, 3–12. Lleida: DEDAL-LIT 4.

Featherstone, Mike, and Mike Hepworth. 2001. The Mask of Ageing and the Postmodern Life Course. In *The Body: Social Process and Cultural Theory*, ed. Mike Feathersone, Mike Hepworth, and Bryan S. Turner, 371–389. London: Sage.

Gullette, Margaret Morganroth. 1997. *Declining to Decline: Cultural Combat and the Politics of the Midlife*. Charlottesville: University Press of Virginia.

King, Jeanette. 2013. *Discourses of Ageing in Fiction and Feminism: The Invisible Woman*. Basingstoke: Palgrave Macmillan.

Sandberg, Linn. 2015. Sex, Sexuality and Later Life. In *The Routledge Handbook of Cultural Gerontology*, ed. Julia Twigg and Wendy Martin, 218–225. New York: Routledge.

Sontag, Susan. 1979. *On Photography*. London: Penguin Books.

Watkins, Susan. 2013. 'Summoning Your Youth at Will': Memory, Time, and Aging in the Work of Penelope Lively, Margaret Atwood, and Doris Lessing. *Frontiers: A Journal of Women's Studies* 34 (2): 222–244.

Waxman, Barbara Frey. 1990. *From the Hearth to the Open Road: A Feminist Study of Aging in Contemporary Literature*. New York: Greenwood's Press.

Waxman, Barbara Frey. 1993. Linking Women Across Generations: The Journals and Letters of Lessing and Sarton. In *Communications and Women's Friendships: Parallels and Intersections in Literature and Life*, ed. Janet Doubler Ward and Joanna Stephens Mink, 27–44. Bowling Green, OH: Bowling Green State University Popular Press.

Woodward, Kathleen. 1999a. Introduction. In *Figuring Age: Women, Bodies, Generations*, ed. Kathleen Woodward, ix–xxix. Bloomington: Indiana University Press.

Woodward, Kathleen. 1999b. Inventing Generational Models: Psychoanalysis, Feminism, Literature. In *Figuring Age: Women, Bodies, Generations*, ed. Kathleen Woodward, 149–168. Bloomington: Indiana University Press.

Zamorano Llena, Carmen. 2004. From Loneliness to Solitude in a Post-feminist Age: Redefining Love in the Second Half of Life in Clare Boylan's *Beloved Stranger*. In *The Polemics of Ageing as Reflected in Literatures in English*, ed. Maria Vidal Grau and Núria Casado Gual, 177–200. Lleida: DEDAL-LIT 3.

CHAPTER 5

The Age Performances of Peggy Shaw: Intersection, Interoception and Interruption

Bridie Moore

I first saw Peggy Shaw perform in her co-production with Clod Ensemble *MUST—The Inside Story* (2009), at the King's College Anatomy Theatre in London. I was struck by the charismatic sexiness of her performance and the unusual, abstract nature of this autobiographical show. Jill Dolan notes that "Shaw has always been a stunning presence in the lesbian performance world" (2011, 3), having her own brand of what Judith Halberstam describes as "female masculinity" (1998, 30). Shaw presents herself in what she calls "Gentleman Drag," taking on the significations of masculinity, the sharp suit and tie, short hairstyle and so on.[1] However, even though at times she has quipped about passing for a 35-year-old man (see below), she always draws attention to the female body that inhabits this dapper, gentlemanly costume. Born in 1944, Shaw is now a veteran performer, and as such her disruptive gender-play also complicates the figure of the "old woman" in performance.

[1] Shaw described her attire as "Gentleman Drag" at the post-show discussion of the performance of *Must* on 15 November, 2011.

B. Moore (✉)
University of Huddersfield, Huddersfield, England, UK
e-mail: b.moore@hud.ac.uk

C. McGlynn et al. (eds.), *Ageing Women in Literature and Visual Culture*,
DOI 10.1007/978-3-319-63609-2_5

I saw *MUST* at the beginning of my research into age and ageing on the contemporary British stage. During that autumn/winter season of 2011–2012 and then beyond it, I sought out plays in which old people were central, yet it became increasingly clear to me that, although there were a surprising number of these, the old folks often didn't make it out alive![2] The original spur to my research was an awareness that (with the exception of Alan Bennett's and Samuel Beckett's plays) old characters in many canonical and contemporary dramatic works are often either secondary—functioning as comic relief for example—or, when they *are* central, play out what Margaret Morganroth Gullette calls a "narrative of decline" (2004, 28). When vigorous old characters *are* shown on stage, they can be placed in a disturbing binary opposition to frail old characters, as is the case in Nicholas Wright's *The Last of the Duchess* (2011).[3] Here the eponymous octogenarian Duchess actually fails to appear on stage and thus the frailty, which often develops with extreme old age, is rendered "obscene"; that is, beyond representation. In contrast, the Duchess's preternaturally vital eighty-one-year-old lawyer Suzanne Blum occupies the stage during the majority of the drama, finally taking the Duchess's place as the subject of Caroline Blackwood's article. The Duchess only ever appears in a dream-like apparition as her younger, iconic self. The complexity of the lived experience of old people, particularly old women, is unrepresented. The figure of the "old woman"—disassociated with what Kathleen Woodward describes as "the feared image of death" (1991, 66)—is rarely seen centre stage in British drama and certainly not in my snapshot survey of the autumn/winter 2011–2012 British mainstream theatre offering.[4] The complexities of ageing femininity in what Peter Laslett named "the fourth age of true dependency

[2] My 2014 article "Depth, Significance and Absence: Age-Effects in New British Theatre" in *Age, Culture, Humanities*, elaborates on this snapshot survey of contemporary British drama and glosses the early twenty first Century turn towards old age as an increasing focus of dramatic representation.

[3] The play, based on the book of the same name by Caroline Blackwood, details Blackwood's failed attempts to interview the eighty-six-year-old Duchess of Windsor for a *Sunday Times* article.

[4] In this Autumn/Winter season, I counted twenty-five productions, twenty-two of which were new works, which explicitly highlighted issues of age and/or ageing in their publicity or content. There was therefore a perceived increase in roles for elders and middle-aged actors. However, my critique concluded that more roles for old people do not

and decrepitude" (1989, x), that is, age so advanced that it represents a state of "irredeemable abjection," lying "beyond the social and [...] the scope for agentic transgression" (Gilleard and Higgs 2011, 138), were not, as far as could be detected, visible in this arena.

My focus at that time was almost exclusively on narrative and dramatic representations, which were textual in form and which featured, as Hans-Thies Lehmann puts it, "dialogue, charged with suspense and pregnant with decisions; the subject whose reality can essentially be expressed in interpersonal speech; [and] action that unfolds primarily in an absolute present" (2006, 49). "Drama" (which Lehmann sees as distinct from "performance"), precisely because it is the conventional theatrical form, can struggle to counter dominant narratives or accommodate a plurality of meanings. For instance, dramatic narratives often conform to oppositional binaries, which in age terms in *The Last of the Duchess* set decline against "positive ageing."[5] However, specific experiences of longevity do not readily conform to such a dualism. For instance, we might become more playful as we age, or our health, while challenged in one area, may actually improve in others, such as with laser eye surgery or the resolution of mental health problems. Individual experience, therefore, might not conform to the cultural meanings that generally attach to age.[6] Michael Mangan has outlined the various ways in which gerontology distinguishes between different conceptions of age, these being "chronological age, social age and physiological age" (2013, 24). It follows, then, that if performance is to speak more astutely of the ageing experience, it must take into account this multiplicity of meanings by offering a multifaceted, layered, reflective and reflecting staging of age; by which I mean one that takes in a multitude of perspectives on old age, or, conversely, illuminates the specificity of an individual ageing process or elder experience. Looking to what Lehmann calls "the new theatre"

necessarily guarantee a subversion of the accepted script of ageing but may inadvertently amplify the normative construction of old age.

[5] Positive ageing according to Katz and Campbell involves "activity, independence, resourcefulness, and creativity" (2009, 106). The World Health Organisation defines "active ageing" as "the process of optimizing opportunities for health, participation and security in order to enhance quality of life as people age" (2002, 12).

[6] See Oscar H. Franco, et al. (2012) "Cross-cultural Comparison of Correlates of Quality of Life and Health Status: The Whitehall II Study (UK) and the Western New York Health Study (US)," *European Journal of Epidemiology*.

(2006, 18) (which he sets in opposition to "drama") and to the genre of "performance" (which Lehmann sees as distinct from but associated with "theatre" [2006, 134–144]) offers the promise that such complex age representations might be realised.[7] Shaw's performances, as Dolan states, "avoid the essentialisms of psychology: little 'happens' in them" (2011, 13). Instead, she espouses non-linear performance conventions, "weaves stories cut through with recorded music and refers to politics [and] world events" (Dolan 2011, 13). Her shows "move in fits and starts accumulating images and actions" (Dolan 2011, 14) and so Shaw's work embraces "performance" as a genre capable of expressing the complexity of her experience as a butch, lesbian, and now elder, performance artist.

The practice of "performance" has developed under the converging influences of performance art, and both the historical and neo-avant-gardes (Lehmann 2006, 48). It has been variously described as "post-dramatic" (Lehmann 2006, ix), "experimental" (Kershaw 1999, 69) or "postmodernist" (Auslander 1997, 7), and it challenges what Kershaw calls the "sticky heat of a middle-class and ageing theatre" (1999, 30). Kershaw asserts that "It would be my generation that flew past the old constraints to make a new kind of world and a new kind of art and unlike Billy [Liar] we would do it without lying" (1999, 30–31). This move away from what Kershaw calls "lying"—that is, pretending to be someone else through mimetic character and dialogue within a fictional world—towards the performance of a multi-layered consideration of specific themes, is the subject of Lehmann's groundbreaking *Postdramatic Theatre*, in which Lehmann locates the "new theatre" as part of "a simultaneous and multi-perspectival form of perceiving," brought about, in large part, by a reaction to the dominance of the written text (2006, 16). Among other definitions of the new theatre, Lehmann suggests the notion of the "performer as theme and protagonist" (2006, 25). So, in postdramatic theatre, or what Auslander calls postmodern performance, a focus on the idea and the materiality of the performer as both the content of the work and the locus of its politics, is arguably a central element.

[7] I acknowledge that Lehmann's definition of "the new theatre" is contested, however, here I am not primarily concerned with debates about the specific differences between dramatic and postdramatic theatre; more I wish to draw—as Lehmann does—a broad distinction between mainstream forms and those of contemporary, experimental, postmodern theatre, which are not circumscribed by the considerations of text, character and plot.

It follows then that performance has the capacity to disrupt the normative figure of ageing femininity through an idiosyncratic performance by a particular old woman, who is the theme and protagonist of the work.

Deirdre Heddon draws attention to the opportunities presented by autobiographical performance to "communicate and unsettle a particular identity position" (2008, 13), noting that most performers "who use autobiography in their work are marginalised subjects" (2008, 2). She comments that "the lived experience that pertains to a certain identity position provides the foundation of the autobiographical act, but at the same time that foundation is strategically (and politically) unsettled *through* the autobiographical act" (2008, 13). It would follow, then, that autobiographical, postdramatic performance by an old woman might at once stage *and* unsettle the complex of meanings that attach to ageing femininity.[8] Moreover, the cumulative effect on an individual spectator of attending a *range* of solo performances by old women, or one particular woman, might develop an understanding of the diversity of meanings that the ageing female subject *can* embody. Philip Auslander argues that "the body in some postmodern performance can be understood as a body that exposes the ideological discourses producing it, [insisting] on the body's status as a historical and cultural construct and assert[ing] the body's materiality" (1997, 92). It might be expected, therefore, that postdramatic/postmodern performances by an old female performer would yield insights into the discourses through which the ageing female body is produced. Such discourses may be exposed by performance, not only by revealing the old woman's perspective and experience or by exposing the discourses that influence any encounter with her, but also by witnessing her old body engaged in the act of performing per se. The materiality of the ageing female body in such performance has the potential to trouble the normative representation of the "old woman" and also to scrutinise the possibilities and limitations of a specific old female body. In addition, following Auslander's assertion that "a body that is understood to be discursively produced and ideologically encoded can also

[8]These might include positive meanings such as longevity (Bond and Coleman 1993, 343), or care giving (Jerrome 1993, 228), but will also, and I would argue more readily, incorporate negative associations such as loss, loneliness and widowhood (ibid., 252), and a decline in power that corresponds to loss of physical beauty (Featherstone and Hepworth 1993, 312) or poverty (Walker 1993, 288–289).

be seen as a site of resistance where hegemonic discourses and codings can be exposed, deconstructed, and, perhaps, rewritten" (1997, 140), solo/autobiographical performance might have the potential to disrupt the scripts of ageing femininity by offering multi-layered representations of ageing. With this in mind, this chapter will focus on three solo autobiographical performances by Peggy Shaw. The first section will discuss the way in which Shaw plays with the quality of age in its intersection with gender and class in *Menopausal Gentleman* (1998). The second will analyse how her 2009 performance, *Must—The Inside Story*, disrupts the normative surface significations of the ageing body through her metaphorical, interoceptive journey "inside."[9] Finally, the third section will explore the methods, including that of interruption, which Shaw employs in *Ruff* (2013), in order to perform resilient frailty after she suffered a serious stroke in 2011. First, a brief biography will be useful.

Ageing Centre Stage

Peggy Shaw began performing with Lois Weaver in the 1970s; they founded Split Britches and the W.O.W. Cafe theatre collective in New York in 1980 and toured through the 1980s and 1990s, performing first with Deb Margolin and later as a butch/femme duo,[10] creating what Sue-Ellen Case describes as a

> unique postmodern style that served to embed feminist and lesbian issues of the times, economic debates, national agendas, personal relationships, and sex-radical role playing in spectacular and humorous deconstructions of canonical texts, vaudeville shtick, cabaret forms, lip-synching satire, lyrical love scenes and dark, frightening explorations of class and gender violence. (1996, 1)

As they have aged beyond the middle years, Weaver and Shaw have singly and collectively explored the subject of ageing in a number of shows. Their 2009 collaboration *Lost Lounge* explored lost social, cultural,

[9]The "interoceptive field" is a phrase used by Drew Leder (1990, 39) to describe the perception of the interior of the body. He sets this in a phenomenological framework against the experience of exteroception that is the subject's perception of the exterior, the surface of the body and beyond.

[10]See Peggy Shaw's Resume (2011, splitbritches.files.wordpress.com).

concrete and abstract spaces and was billed as "a tribute to last holdouts; both the people and places people gather to face or fend off encroaching cultural extinction," "riffing on aging and losses of all kind" and speaking "of how fantasy remains even as age reminds us of our limitations" (qtd. in Hughes 2009, 135, 136). As Shaw's solo, autobiographical work developed in the 1990s and 2000s, it incorporated the particular physical and cultural realities of growing older. For example, in her solo show in *To My Chagrin* (2001) she role-modelled masculinity in the driving seat of a pickup truck and gave grave advice—born of many years as an ostracised butch woman—to her mixed-race grandson. Resilience is evident in her work as much as it is in her continued presence on the stage; in a BBC Radio 4 interview she sums up her performing career as she moves into her eighth decade: "All my shows are about all the changes I've been through, I was a lesbian then a butch lesbian, then a mother then a grandmother then a grandmother to a mixed race grandson, then I had a lesbian old age and then I had a stroke" (*Loose Ends*, 2016). Her work is inflected throughout with questions of identity, taking delight in unsettling identity constructions through playful inversions and subversions; her "old woman" identity is modulated by a multiplicity of other designations.

Intersection

Shaw's 1997 solo show *Menopausal Gentleman*, "about a menopausal body and the fires of its ageless heart" (Ferguson 1998, 375), explored the intersection of feminine ageing and butch lesbian identity in a heteronormative context. Dolan describes *Menopausal Gentleman* as telling "mournful, melancholic, piercing tales about the passage of time playing over and within a female body lived in a masculine style for which biology provides a kind of necessary historical referent," arguing that Shaw's performances "thoughtfully chart the intersection of gender, sexuality, race and class" (2011, 15). Although Dolan omits age as an intersecting factor, Shaw foregrounds age in its intersection with femininity and butch lesbian identity, by declaring herself "a 54 year old woman/who passes as a 35-year-old man" and by asserting "I keep young by passing you see. / I sacrifice being a woman for youth. It's a trade off" (2011, 76–77).

In the late 1980s, Kimberle Crenshaw drew attention to the issue of intersectionality in the fields of American law and politics. She exposed the ways in which the experience of being both Black and female were erased in legal cases concerning sex and race discrimination, and obscured in both antiracist politics and feminist theory, arguing that "Both feminist theory and antiracist politics have been organized, in part, around the equation of racism with what happens to the Black middle-class or to Black men, and the equation of sexism with what happens to white women" (1989, 152). In a similar way, feminist theory has also failed to take account of the subject positions of old women. As Barbara Macdonald notes, "so far the women's movement has resonated with its silence on the subject of old women" (2001, 36); and Calasanti, Slevin and King assert that "Although women's studies scholars and activists do not deny the reality of ageism, they have relegated it to secondary status, neglecting to theorize age relations or place old age at the center of analysis" (2006, 13). Consequently, Crenshaw's insight, with respect to the invisibility of Black women's experience in law and politics, can illuminate the erasure of old women's experience in feminist discourse. The concept of intersectionality is a useful lens through which to view Shaw's performances, which expose the intersecting discourses that construct the stroke-surviving, old, lesbian, butch, working-class, grandmother (of a mixed-race grandson).

It seems safe to say that for everyone, as we age, an increasing multiplicity of identities accrue and necessarily intersect with each other. Crenshaw problematises the "authoritative universal voice," which is in part claimed by white feminists, outlining the ways in which "feminist theories are constructed around white women's experiences" (1989, 154). It is necessary, then, not to universalise the experience of a specific identity position as if it were not also impacted by others, including the category of age. An old woman can exemplify a complex intersectionality of disadvantaged subject positions; having already occupied (among others) the position of "woman," she has subsequently grown into the designation "old woman." In addition, all other non-normative locations such as "lesbian," "Black," "service user," "disabled" and/or "widow" could accumulate to complicate her experience, only finally to be overshadowed by the overriding and disqualifying position of "old." This designation, as Calasanti et al. argue, "does not just exacerbate other inequalities but is a social location in its own right, conferring a loss of power for all those designated as 'old' regardless of their advantages in other hierarchies" (2006, 17). How much more so can the designation "old" operate to hyper-marginalise subjects, where it intersects with and erases experience of *dis*advantage? By playfully refracting and reflecting her now multifarious identity positions, Shaw's performances bring into focus the intersectionality of identities that proliferate as age advances.

Shaw's assertion that she "keep[s] young by passing" claims her sexuality and butch self-presentation as an opportunity to escape the reductive trap of ageing femininity. In spite of her constant referral to the female body that lies beneath her sharp suit, her "gentlemanly" appearance works to co-opt the cultural flexibility of 35-year-old masculinity into her project of evading the disqualifications of age and gender; thus, she side-steps ageist and sexist constructions of her body. However, in spite of Shaw's playful claim to pass as a man, Dolan observes that "both and multiple genders cohabit in Shaw's work" (2011, 19), and notes that she constructs

> her own foundational brand of female masculinity, always complicating the combination of genders across her body and her performances but [she is] never willing to forgo the one for the other. In fact, female biology is inescapable in Shaw's performances, keeping her poised within complex gendered contradictions. (2011, 18)

Shaw's stated femininity—expressed in the title "Menopausal Gentleman"—evidences the complexity of her age/gender performance and her aim to "pass" as young both exposes and disrupts the complex interplay of meanings that attach to age and to femininity.

Class, as an intersecting factor, also plays into her performance of masculinity and complicates the suite of identities Shaw inhabits. She portrays herself as a "gentleman"—literally a man who is also gentle—mixing commonly ascribed masculine, feminine and middle-class attributes in one designation. But this profession of middle-class gentlemanliness, as Dolan notes, is a class migration (2011, 19); Shaw was brought up as a working-class Irish–American, a heritage that seeps through her tailored image to generate a crotch-adjusting, wide-legged, drawling energy. Shaw also claims that she is a beast "trying to pass as a person" (2011, 71), placing her outside class and gender distinctions altogether. This "tiger" (Dolan 2011, 72)—the hot flush of menopause—that she says lurks inside her is a facet of her ageing self that complicates her surface gender assignment and gentlemanly aspirations. Exposing this intersection of age, class, sexuality and gender, she simply says, "it's hard to be a gentleman in menopause" (Dolan 2011, 76). By 2010, as she reaches her mid-sixties Shaw has relinquished any claim to gentility and has come to describe herself as "a sixty-plus year old, second-generation Irish, working-class, grand-butch-mother" (Dolan 2011, 41).

Shaw's intersectional focus is also reflected in her performance *Must—The Inside Story*. Presented in "the nonlinear, imagistic, melancholic yet hopeful, dark but funny style that Split Breeches pioneered" (Dolan 2011, 6), it charts the medical history of her body and likens her physical and psychological condition to that periodic state of high aggression in male elephants known as "must."[11] Shaw compares herself to an elephant with, as Dolan puts it, "thick and ancient skin, experience crafted on its deep and hanging folds" (2011, 33). The association of elephants, not only with rogue aggression but also with resilience, longevity and memory, privileges these qualities as a central focus of the piece.[12] In a sensational list of medical events, Shaw describes experiences that have marked her, both on and beneath the surface of her elephant hide:

> I cracked my pelvis. I broke my heels. I smashed my knuckles on my right hand. I smashed my knees in the woods. [...] I got pneumococcal meningitis when I slept with a woman for the first time. I died for three minutes. I was in a coma for two weeks. I had mononucleosis and couldn't kiss a boy for a year. [...] I had a lump removed from my breast. I have lumps on my forearms and the front of my thighs where I store my original thoughts. I smashed out my two front teeth on the ice fighting over a girl. I had a baby. (Dolan 2011, 146)

The litany of medical emergencies is complicated by the underlying fluidity of gender and sexual indicators. Shaw is sleeping with, fighting over and (not) kissing both boys and girls; and while the medical events attest to a kind of activity and aggression that is associated with masculinity, this is contradicted by the punch line: "I had a baby." Clearly, the age and experience demonstrated by Shaw's performance of her body-history is not circumscribed by the normative life narrative of a woman in her mid- to late sixties, and as such her performance exposes and resists the sort of discourse that would construct her ageing as much as it would her femininity.

---

[11] This state, also known as "musth," is associated with a spike in testosterone and is defined as "a state or condition of violent, destructive frenzy occurring with the rutting season in male elephants, accompanied by the exudation of an oily substance from glands between the eyes and mouth" (dictionary.reference.com).

[12] See the entry "Elephant" in *The Continuum Encyclopaedia of Symbols* 99–100.

Interoception: The Journey Inside

Peggy Shaw's investigation into her body history in *Must* brings into appearance, as the title suggests, her "Inside Story," a term that plays on the sense of the inside as both a physical phenomenon and one indicative of identity. Shaw's "Inside Story" is an invocation of what philosopher Drew Leder calls the "interoceptive field" (1990, 39): the perception of the interior of the body. In *The Absent Body* Leder writes, from a phenomenological perspective, of the differences between "exteroception" and "interoception," that is, what we perceive as detailed sensation on the surface of (and beyond) our bodies, compared with the more generalised impressions that we have of our physical interior. He explains that "Interoception does not share the multi-dimensionality of exteroception [...] interoception is not devoid of an expressive range [...] Yet these are experienced as modulating a single dimension of perception i.e., 'inner sensation,' rather than opening on to distinct perceptual worlds" (Leder 1990, 40). In *Must*, however, Shaw works to "sensationalise" the interior regions of the body. As Lyn Gardner comments: "This is an exquisite lesson in anatomy, a journey underneath the skin, a mapping of the human body in which the sites of love and loss are placed under the microscope and analysed" (*The Guardian*, 2009).

With advancing age, the awareness of the interiority of the body becomes increasingly acute: developing medical problems can result in heightened awareness of joints, bones, muscles and organs; levels of subcutaneous fat diminish and the veins and bones of, say, the hand, begin to be discernable through the thinning membrane of the skin; or as Leder asserts: "a medical mishap can suddenly awaken us to the significance of such bodily lacunae" (1990, 43).[13] Shaw displaces this dominant image of ageing—the sign of the interior breaking through the surface—by reversing the focus, switching from the external—the surface, where culturally constructed signs are at play—towards an imagined journey into the uncharted territory of the internal, where the production or encoding of signs has no dominion. In cultural terms, the audience are now lost in the *terra incognita* of the organs, muscles, joints and bones. Being unable to rank the social value of organs, veins or bones—of whatever age—leaves the audience without cultural reference

[13] According to the Cleveland Clinic website, "Underlying structures—veins and bones in particular—become more prominent," and "The skin becomes more transparent as we

points. This offers Shaw an opportunity to displace the surface signs that denote the ageing body. Given the lack of coordinates that would help the non-medic differentiate, for example, a younger spleen from an older one, no value system presents itself that would ascribe a greater sense of worth to one or the other. Shaw's words—which evoke her epic interior journey—and the series of fascinating Welcome Collection Archive micrographs that are projected, both onto the upstage wall, and finally onto Shaw's naked back, evince the fascinating beauty of bodily structures of whatever age.[14] Shaw's poetic journey into the interior exposes the audience to what Leder calls a new "perceptual world" (1990, 40), where age falls away and what is glimpsed is an alternative, half-remembered, half-fantastical realm in which you can find traces of the hidden subject.

> When my skin cracks open
> You will find my meat.
> My carnivore body.
> You will see the anthills and mole tunnels underground and food being carried from place to place by millions of workers. You will see a magical landscape, like New York City in the seventies [...] Evidence that someone lives in here. Really lives here and leaves traces. (Shaw 2011, 140)

Imagining her body's fantastical interior opens up a fluid territory outside the region where identity is circumscribed by discursive practices. Shaw becomes self-inscriptive through this performance; placing herself at the centre of the interoceptive action, she defines and inscribes her own identity upon her own interior, she is the one who "leaves traces." As she begins her journey, she is not without a fear that is fuelled by the discourses that construct old age: "I'm afraid of finding something I didn't know about—like a bear shitting in my woods, or a field of Irish potatoes in my uterus" (Shaw 2011, 140–41). Identifying her old body

age. This is caused by thinning of the epidermis (surface layer of the skin)." (my.clevelandclinic.org)

[14]These projections came courtesy of the Welcome Library in London and included images of: "cells of the upper respiratory tract," "the uterus," "network of collagen fibrils" and "spinal chord motor neurons" (Shaw and Willson [Clod Ensemble] 2010, n.p.).

with The Planet Earth, she elevates her physical losses by likening them to ecological losses: "Underneath my thighs is where all the oil is being stolen from, leaving empty pockets inside" (Shaw 2011, 141). In addition, by taking this interoceptive journey she also repeats a familiar plea made by old people to see behind the visible surface of the ageing body. However, she goes further than a mere plea for insight by leading us into the texture and detail of this epic "underground" space, evoking a multiplicity of images, from the geology of landscapes and the sporadic appearance of memories to mechanistic systems and the evolution of flora and fauna, revealing her emotional, interior sense of self in visceral terms. Shaw, as Lyn Gardner says, "is taking a scalpel to herself, opening up old wounds, so that the shadows of a lifetime are rendered visible" (*The Guardian*, 2009). Shaw enlists the powers of performance to disrupt the discourses that construct her aged identity by telling her "Inside Story," which is, paradoxically, a story about "coming from the darkness into the light" (2011, 143).

In this sense, Shaw's interior journey resonates with the notion of the internal that Judith Butler proposes. If we replace the notion of "gender" with that of "age," Butler's explanation of how the idea of the "internal" operates in establishing gender identity is pertinent here: "Gender is [...] a norm that can never be fully internalized; the 'internal' is a surface signification, and gender norms are finally *phantasmatic*, impossible to embody" (2006, 192, my emphasis). So Butler clears the ground of the "internal" field (whether it be "internal" in physical, emotional or psychological terms), rendering it virgin territory. By engaging in a fantastical interoception and imagining her own interiority in physical/visual terms, Shaw opens up the possibility of an alternative discourse that might re-construct her identity within an ageing body:

> There are different ways of seeing inside me:
> You could guess what's in here
> You could touch me
> You could X-Ray me
> Or you could believe what I tell you. (2011, 142)

Shaw's fantasy has the potential to destabilise the "phantasmatic" surface significations (of age in this instance) that Butler identifies, and to refuse such significations as being "impossible to embody." Shaw even attempts to refuse the markers of age that are present on her body's surface as cultural disqualifiers; she presents the lines on her face as products of an inquisitive, lifelong quest of self-discovery: "It's a journey through the shadows of a city. A map. The wrinkles on my face are where the map gets folded over and over" (Shaw 2011, 143). She also plays with global-epic notions of age-identity and imagines the ageing process extending over geological time, by proposing a perceptual world beneath her "elephant's hide" (Shaw 2011, 146), in which she identifies herself with tectonic and evolutionary forces: "I am sizematic. My back is slowly moving away from my hip-bone toward America, my vertebrae curving toward the horizon, slipping underneath the sea of love, taking a million years to crawl up out of the water" (Shaw 2011, 154). Here Shaw complicates her relationship to time, identifying her interiority not only with geological time but also with processes of evolution and even embryogenesis; her claims echo the description that Leder gives of the way embryonic development leaves traces of vestigial organs in the mature body:

> visceral sensations are often vaguely situated with indistinct borders [...] This reflects the embryological origins; sensation is referred to that level of the body the viscus occupied in the developing foetus before it descended, dragging nerves along, to its mature position [...] An almost magical transfer of experience is effected along both spatial and temporal dimensions, weaving the inner body into an ambiguous space. (1990, 41)

Shaw's performance of her inside story constructs just such an "ambiguous space," reclaiming her interior as a radically fluid location that effects a similar spatial and temporal "transfer of experience" in metaphorical terms and resists distinct locations. Through this inside journey, Shaw evokes a continuum of forms and imagines a body that in all its particularity has an ontological unity with all other bodies, and so unites the particular and the universal, the individual and the communal, the owned and the shared. In the final act, Shaw slowly disrobes from the waist up and with her back to the audience, standing against the upstage wall, her body is lit by, and overlaid with, projections of magnified cell structures and tissue formations, archive material from the Welcome Collection. Through this action, Shaw overlays the external with the indecipherably internal and brings into appearance the archived "inside stories" of many anonymous lives, associating herself, and by extension the audience, with a biological continuum that could encompass all of life and any age.

Interruption

According to director Lois Weaver, *Ruff*—Shaw's most recent performance—"visually and verbally translates Shaw's internal experience of illness and aging into an external assemblage of her multifaceted, creatively capable, aging brain" (Queen Mary University of London 2016). The show's publicity flyer says that Shaw does this by bringing to life the "host of Lounge singers, movie stars, rock and roll bands and eccentric family members living inside her," all of whom, she claims, have been with her all her performing life and are now released because of the stroke she suffered in 2011. *Ruff* focuses on the moment of the stroke, and in a conceit, which collapses five and a half decades of her life, she conflates a time-displacing incident where she saw film footage of herself *in a dress* at the age of thirteen, with the moment of the stroke, thus equating the questions in her thirteen-year-old brain with gaps in her understanding that still remain:

> But when my sixty-seven-year-old self saw my thirteen-year-old self wearing a green dress I could see a picture of my thoughts before I even thought them. Back then in the 50s, in a world that was not ready for me, I could see myself trying to fill in the blanks with information I needed, to be able to carry my brain on the top of my body. And then suddenly I was exhausted from still trying to hold my brain in my head and my head on my neck [...] fifty-four years later [...] My old brain met my young brain and that one look shattered my insides all at once. (Extract from *Ruff*, BBC Radio 4's *Loose Ends*, 2/4/2016)

Shaw implies that her uninterrupted confusion has caused her stroke and that her current cognitive "blanks" have as much to do with a long-term bewilderment over cultural notions of femininity as the physiological state of either her adolescent or her sixty-seven-year-old stroke-surviving brain.

Shaw "channels" a plethora of charismatic characters, embodying Elvis's sexual potency in the rock-star persona who sings "The Okey Pokey" in a strutting, fist-in-the-air, microphone-tilting style, and even linking the physical site of the stroke to a favourite TV character, asserting that her stroke happened in her "PONS, which rhymes, with The

Fonz" (*Loose Ends*, 2/4/2016).[15] In her BBC Radio 4 interview, she explained: "After my stroke I was able to define that I wasn't an original person, that I had a combination of a lot of people inside of me that I wanted to talk about and thank for all their help. Like Leonard Cohen, and Marlon Brando and Elizabeth Taylor, Malcolm X, Otis Redding" (*Loose Ends*, 2/4/2016). These figures supply both her gender-troubling, performative script and her supporting cast. Her allies—including an all-female backing band who are projected onto the green screen behind her and who set the pulse of the blood in her veins—support her in a performance that is openly "compromised" by the impairment of her stroke. Shaw's sexy performance style now accommodates the limitations of her post-stroke body, and, as Auslander notes of postmodern performance, clearly "asserts the body's materiality" (1997, 2). Shaw still has much of the vocal and physical presence and comic mastery of former performances but her reliance on autocue and her occasional interruptions of the show to ask her director Weaver—who sits in the audience—about the next sequence or move, make explicit the fragility which the stroke has produced and incorporate this into the performance aesthetic. Shaw comments:

> In my performances it doesn't matter whether I mess up or not because that's part of the performance. When I started performing after my stroke I would just tell the audience 'hey I just had a stroke!' They'd say, 'Wow you look great!' or 'you're lucky,' or something [...] So we had, immediately, a conversation about it. (*Loose Ends*, 2/4/2016)

In this way *Ruff* is demonstrably a performance of old age, one that accommodates the limitations of Shaw's post-stroke memory by employing the technical aid of autocue, making her cognitive losses explicit. However, she still shows an ability to push the limits of performance through the use of green screen technology; in a metaphor for the "dark holes left by her stroke" (flyer, n.p.), the green screen populates the stage with her co-opted helpmates. The upstage projections show footage and computer-generated images, for instance her backing band, who appear

[15] Originally played by Henry Winkler in the ABC TV series *Happy Days* from 1974–1984, The Fonz, a cool 1950s- style, quiffed, leather-jacketed character, reminiscent of Brando in his films of the 1950s, is one of Shaw's appropriated characters (www.imdb.com).

one by one, building the tune behind her. These sustaining personnel, springing from Shaw's post-stroke imagination, show through the points of transparency on the green screen, which, in a resilient performance of fragility, materialises the stroke damage she has suffered. The green screen both acts as a metaphor for the losses Shaw has suffered and enables the performance of Shaw's hopeful, creative response to these losses. This device and Shaw's performance disrupt the binary of positive ageing versus a narrative of decline discussed above. *Ruff* demonstrates a reassuring continuity of the Shaw persona and with its humour, its plethora of colourful characters and its openness about assistive techniques, shows Shaw's resilience as a creative force and performs her determination to overcome cognitive obstacles. As much as Shaw's female masculinity challenges gender ascriptions, her performance of resilient fragility challenges age ascriptions. This exuberant and technically sophisticated piece ultimately confounds normative expectations that an old female stroke-sufferer is a clear case for retirement from the theatre.

Conclusion

Petra Kuppers points out that "Knowledge has arrived into powerstructures (sic) when it translates itself from its living form into public discourse. And in turn, knowledge feeds back into new forms of aliveness and seeing life" (2003, 3). The project undertaken by Shaw since 1998 to translate her elder experience into public discourse springs from an identity-unsettling, autobiographical impetus. She produces performances that explicitly materialise frailty, bringing disruptive images and subversive performances of the "old woman" into appearance, and consequently exposing and troubling the figure of ageing femininity.[16] Shaw evades normative constructions of ageing femininity by adopting the gentleman drag that "strategically unsettles" her explicitly female body, concealed beneath the clothing, voice and body-style assigned to masculinity. Moving deeper into her interiority, Shaw defines her subjectivity from the perspective of interoception, where fantastical, epic imaginings of her interior replace the normative surface constructions of the

[16] The chapter evidences, in part, the bringing of such narratives and performances into public discourse; this arrival is also evidenced by numerous reviews, and by the audience attendance at the shows under discussion here.

"old woman." Her multifaceted, non-linear, postdramatic performances have the potential, especially when taken together, to offer new ways of understanding and discussing the phenomenon of ageing femininity. Her continued presence on stage challenges the normalised decline narrative, which speaks of burden and excess; instead Shaw presents an "old woman" who counters the figure popularly staged as dependent, obsolete or obscene.

Works Cited

Publications

Auslander, Philip. 1997. *From Acting to Performance: Essays in Modernism and Postmodernism*. London: Routledge.

Bond, John, and Peter Coleman. 1993. Ageing into the 21st Century. In *Ageing in Society: An Introduction to Social Gerontology*, 2nd ed, ed. John Bond, Peter Coleman, and Sheila Peace, 333–350. London: Sage.

Butler, Judith. 2006. *Gender Trouble: Feminism and the Subversion of Identity*. Abingdon: Routledge.

Calasanti, Toni M., Kathleen F. Slevin., and Neal King. 2006. Ageism and Feminism: From 'Et Cetera' to Centre. *National Women's Studies Association Journal* 18 (1): 13–30. Accessed 12 February, 2012. https://muse.jhu.edu/article/195212.

Case, Sue-Ellen (ed.). 1996. *Split Britches: Lesbian Practice/Feminist Performance*. London: Routledge.

Crenshaw, Kimberle. 1989. Demarginalising the Intersection of Race and Sex: A Black Feminist Critique of Antidiscrimination Doctrine, Feminist Theory and Anti Racist Politics. *University of Chicago Legal Forum*, 139–167. Accessed 10 Feb 2012. http://heinonline.org/HOL/LandingPage?handle=hein.journals/uchclf1989&div=10&.

Dolan, Jill. 2011. Introduction to *Menopausal Gentleman: The Solo Performances of Peggy Shaw*. Ann Arbor: University of Michigan Press.

Featherstone, Mike, and Mike Hepworth. 1993. Images of Ageing. In *Ageing in Society: An Introduction to Social Gerontology*, 2nd ed, ed. John Bond, Peter Coleman, and Sheila Peace, 304–332. London: Sage.

Ferguson, Marcia, L. 1998. Performance Review: *Menopausal Gentleman*. *Theatre Journal*, 50 (3): 374–375. Accessed 22 Jan 2017. http://www.jstor.org/stable/25068559.

Franco, Oscar H. et al. 2012. Cross-cultural Comparison of Correlates of Quality of Life and Health Status: The Whitehall II Study (UK) and the

Western New York Health Study (US). *European Journal of Epidemiology*, Apr 27 (4): 255–265. Accessed 21 Jan 2017. doi:10.1007/s10654-012-9664-z.

Gardner, Lyn. *Must—The Inside Story* Review. Accessed 30 May 2016. http://www.theguardian.com/culture/2009/aug/24/must-the-inside-story-review.

Gilleard, Chris, and Paul Higgs. 2011. Ageing Abjection and Embodiment in the Fourth Age. *Journal of Aging Studies.* 25 (2011): 135–142. Accessed 13 Aug 2013. doi:10.1016/j.jaging.2010.08.018.

Gullette, Margaret Morganroth. 2004. *Aged By Culture.* Chicago & London: University of Chicago Press.

Halberstam, Judith. 1998. *Female Masculinity.* Durham: Duke University Press.

Heddon, Deirdre. 2008. *Autobiography and Performance.* Basingstoke: Palgrave Macmillan.

Hughes, Holly. 2012. Faith Not Lost: Holly Hughes interviews Lois Weaver about Split Britches *Lost Lounge* (2009). *Women & Performance: A Journal of Feminist Theory* 22 (1): 135–140. Accessed 22 Jan 2017. doi:10.1080/0740770X.2012.68539.

Jerrome, Dorothy. 1993. Intimate Relationships. In *Ageing in Society: An Introduction to Social Gerontology*, 2nd ed, ed. John Bond, Peter Coleman, and Sheila Peace, 226–254. London: Sage.

Katz, Stephen, and Erin Campbell. 2009. Creativity Across the Life Course? Titian, Michelangelo, and older Artist Narratives. In *Cultural Aging: Life Course, Lifestyle and Senior Worlds*, ed. Stephen Katz, 101–117. Ontario: University of Toronto Press.

Kershaw, Baz. 1999. *The Radical in Performance: Between Brecht and Baudrillard.* Abingdon: Routledge.

Kuppers, Petra. 2003. *Disability and Contemporary Performance: Bodies on Edge.* Abingdon: Routledge.

Laslett, Peter. 1989. *A Fresh Map of Life.* London: Weidenfeld & Nicholson.

Leder, Drew. 1990. *The Absent Body.* Chicago: University of Chicago Press.

Lehmann, Hans-Thies. 2006. *Postdramatic Theatre.* Translated by. Karen Jürs-Munby. Abingdon: Routledge.

Macdonald, Barbara. 2001. *Look Me in the Eye.* Denver: Spinsters Ink Books.

Mangan, Michael. 2013. *Staging Ageing: Theatre, Performance and the Narrative of Decline.* Bristol: Intellect.

Moore, Bridie. 2014. Depth, Significance and Absence: Age-Effects in New British Theatre. *Age, Culture, Humanities.* Issue 1: 163–195. Accessed 22 Jan 2017. http://ageculturehumanities.org/WP/depth-significance-and-absence-age-effects-in-new-british-theatre/.

Shaw, Peggy. 2011. *Menopausal Gentleman: The Solo Performances of Peggy Shaw*, edited and introduced by Jill Dolan. Ann Arbor: University of Michigan Press.

Shaw, Peggy. Resume. 2016. Accessed 28 May. http://splitbritches.files.wordpress.com/2011/02/peggy-shaw-resumc3a9.pdf.

Shaw, Peggy, Suzy Willson, and (Clod Ensemble). 2010. *Must: The Inside Story*, 2nd ed. London: Shaw and Willson.

Walker, Alan. 1993. Poverty and Inequality in Old Age. In *Ageing in Society: An Introduction to Social Gerontology*, 2nd ed, ed. John Bond, Peter Coleman, and Sheila Peace, 280–303. London: Sage.

Woodward, Kathleen. 1991. *Aging and its Discontents: Freud and Other Fictions.* Bloomington and Indianapolis: Indiana University Press.

World Health Organisation. 2002. *Active Ageing: A Policy Framework.* Accessed 22 Feb 2015. http://whqlibdoc.who.int/hq/2002/WHO_NMH_NPH_02.8.pdf?ua=1.

Online

Ageing Skin, condition of. Accessed 6 Aug 2014. http://my.clevelandclinic.org/health/diseases_conditions/derm_overview.

Happy Days (The Fonz). Accessed 30 May 2016. http://www.imdb.com/title/tt0070992/.

Lois Weaver's Queen Mary University of London Staff Profile. Accessed 30 May 2016. http://www.sed.qmul.ac.uk/staff/weaverl.html.

Musth, definition of. Accessed 6 Aug 2014. http://dictionary.reference.com/browse/musth.

Peggy Shaw's interview with Arthur Smith on BBC Radio 4 *Loose Ends*, (radio programme, online), 18:15 2 April 2016, BBC Radio 4, 47mins. Accessed 30 May 2016. http://bobnational.net/record/_omIGI0I7XG3hBIqIxIbxxl.

Performances

Shaw, Peggy. *Menopausal Gentleman.* Video Recording Accessed 30 May 2016 http://hidvl.nyu.edu/video/000515761.html.

Shaw, Peggy. *Must: The Inside Story* at The Kings College Anatomy Theatre, London, Tuesday 15 Nov 2011. Produced with Clod Ensemble.

Split Britches. *Ruff.* Performed by Peggy Shaw and directed by Lois Weaver. Contact Theatre, Manchester, Wednesday 28 May 2014. Produced by Split Britches.

Wright, Nicholas. *The Last of the Duchess*, at The Hampstead Theatre, London, on Saturday 29 Oct 2011.

Other

Publicity flyer for the May 2014 Performance of Split Britches' *Ruff*, at Contact Theatre, Manchester.

PART II

Social Roles: Mothers, Widows, Spinsters

CHAPTER 6

Closing In: Restrictive Spaces for Ageing Mothers in Jane Austen's Novels

Amber Jones

Jane Austen's six novels abound with examples of ageing mothers, poor parenting styles and dysfunctional mother-daughter relationships. Although the representation of mothers as foolish caricatures may be amusing, it is important to consider what causes the maladapted mother-daughter relationships, which play a vital role in Austen's narratives. Austen portrays the ageing mothers as foils for their young daughters and highlights recurring themes of duty, wise choices and the role of education and understanding in long-term happiness. These relationships give rise to important questions about Austen's themes of parenting, family politics and individuality, and underlying these are questions about the origins of conflict in the mother-daughter relationships. One possible cause is that the ageing process coincides with changes in the physical, social and psychological spaces to which women are assigned. Another cause is how inadequate education, exclusion from intellectual spaces, objectification and infantilization leave these characters unprepared to adapt to their changing physical, social and psychological landscapes. The closing in of those spaces leads to conflict in the

A. Jones (✉)
Ivy Tech Community College, Richmond, IN, USA
e-mail: ajones40@ivytech.edu

C. McGlynn et al. (eds.), *Ageing Women in Literature and Visual Culture*,
DOI 10.1007/978-3-319-63609-2_6

mother-daughter dynamic. As Austen's matronly characters age, limitations inherent in the strict social and cultural norms of the late eighteenth and early nineteenth centuries manifest as physical boundaries, and mothers are left physically, socially and psychologically static. With limited power to act on their own interests and desires, these ageing female characters attempt to avoid their constraints, and their efforts result in competition with, dependence upon, or withdrawal from their daughters.

When surveying physical, social and psychological boundaries for ageing female characters in Austen's novels, it is important to take into account their experiences in both youth and middle age. Although brief, Austen provides some background about these mothers' young adult years through references to the past and through frequent comparisons to their favoured daughters. Austen describes the young Mrs. Bennet as having an "appearance of good humour" and beauty but also of a "weak understanding and illiberal mind," which make her so similar to Lydia (2001, 155). Similarly, an understanding of Mrs. Dashwood's youth is established primarily through the frequent comparisons between her and Marianne, who are more like sisters, one might even say twins, than mother and daughter. As John Wiltshire notes, "Mrs. Dashwood, though a very kind and sensitive woman, is as romantic, as impulsive, as little inclined to calculation and caution, as her daughter Marianne" (1992, 25). Lady Bertram is known to have been a beautiful young woman of some fortune whose character was marked by her lassitude and indifference (cf. Austen 1998, 5; 16). By providing these descriptions, Austen invites readers to consider these middle-aged female characters as foils for their daughters both in their present age and state of life and during their younger years and stages of life. As a plot device, the motherly role would generally be to guide their daughters, but due to the disparity between their physical ages and their adolescent behaviours in Austen's novels they more often function as a barrier to be overcome rather than as sage, experienced guides.

One point of conflict which Austen frequently highlights in the mother-daughter dynamic is that of education and intellect. In the context of educational and gendered exclusion for young women of the era, the details Austen provides of the ageing mothers' youths indicate that this parent-child conflict has its roots in the mothers' formative years. As youths, the characters and temperaments of women were influenced by the spaces they were permitted to access. The "gendering of rooms in the eighteenth and early nineteenth century was a product of patriarchal ideas about domestic and public spaces" (Posusta 2014, 76), and it created empowering spaces of male inclusion but marginalizing spaces of female exclusion. Rooms traditionally associated with education, business and politics had strong masculine connotations and included such rooms as libraries, studies and offices. Feminine exclusion from such spaces occurs in *Pride and Prejudice* as Mr. Bennet employs his library both as place of business and as refuge from his wife and daughters: "In his library he had always been sure of leisure and tranquility; and though prepared, as he told Elizabeth, to meet with folly and conceit in every other room in the house, he was used to be free from them there" (Austen 2001, 49). Unfortunately, Mr. Bennet's endeavours to exclude his wife from his space are, at times, harsh and derisive.

After Mr. Collins's failed proposal to Elizabeth, Mrs. Bennet invades the library, demanding her husband force an engagement on their second daughter. Mr. Bennet rebuffs both her intellectual and physical presence saying, "My dear, [...] I have two small favours to request. First that you allow me the free use of my understanding on the present occasion; and secondly, of my room. I shall be glad to have the library to myself as soon as may be" (Austen 2001, 75). His dismissal illustrates how Mrs. Bennet has overstepped her assigned psychological and physical spaces within the family, and his continual exclusion of her from the traditionally masculine space of the library simultaneously excludes her from any position of authority or respect within the family and within the mother-daughter dynamic. This dismissal of her limited understanding infantilizes her and effectively reduces Mrs. Bennet to a childlike role within the family; it renders her powerless and ridiculous as it reinforces the strict boundaries of her permitted existence.

While Mrs. Bennet's exclusion from this space is not a direct result of her age any more so than Mary's, Kitty's or Lydia's, the combination of ageing and her long-term exclusion results in a perpetually adolescent character whom Austen describes as "a woman of mean understanding, little information, and uncertain temper" (2001, 4). Though limited, access to public and private spaces associated with education and intellect could potentially alter Mrs. Bennet into a woman of deeper understanding, respected by her husband and daughters. Rather than avail herself of such resources, Mrs. Bennet made it "[t]he business of her life [...] to get her daughters married; its solace was visiting and news," and when meddling and gossip are insufficient to distract her from "discontent[ment], she fancied herself nervous" (Austen 2001, 4).

The implication here is that, as time passes, both her ignorance and her nervous complaints will increase, and neither age nor the stress of ill health, whether real or imagined, are conducive to intellectual growth. During Austen's era, this process of decline was a common theme in the discourse of ageing women as it was believed to be an inevitability of menopause. Post-menopausal women, such as the mothers in Austen's novels, were viewed as regressing into a "second girlhood" and were perceived as a threat to "moral and social order" due to their "failing mental powers" and "loss of concentration and memory" (King 2013, 10–11). This perception of dangerous, infantilized decline pervaded medical, social and literary thought in the eighteenth and nineteenth centuries, and it further explains why ageing women were increasingly restricted in the physical, social and psychological spaces they inhabited.

At the end of the novel, Austen draws her readers' attention to the sharp contrast between Elizabeth and Mrs. Bennet. Elizabeth has journeyed to overcome her prejudice (as well as her pride) and to learn to function as an individual, and she is rewarded by a socially and financially advantageous marriage to Mr. Darcy, who reciprocates her love and respect. Austen clarifies, however, that Mrs. Bennet remains unchanged: "I wish I could say, for the sake of her family, that the accomplishment of her earnest desire [...] produced so happy an effect as to make her a sensible, well-informed woman for the rest of her life [but] she still was occasionally nervous and invariably silly" (2001, 251). This enduring resistance to change and self-improvement prevents intellectual growth, which would improve Mrs. Bennet's psychological space (the way she feels, thinks and relates to others within the spaces she inhabits) within the home. Due to the combination of long-standing gendered exclusion, lacking self-discipline and the cognitive decline of age, Mrs. Bennet remains a static, childlike character and improves neither her mind nor her abilities as a mother.

In a more subtle fashion, Mrs. Dashwood and Lady Bertram demonstrate the same behaviour. Neither in *Mansfield Park* nor in *Sense and Sensibility* does Austen include scenes of overt intellectual-spatial exclusion for these ageing female characters; however, the distinct absence of scenes of inclusion may reasonably be interpreted as established, normalized exclusion. Mrs. Dashwood's departure from Norland Park after the death of her husband necessitates her exclusion from any library or educational resources available within the property. As for Lady Bertram, she is simply too "indolent," too unmotivated to engage in any intellectual pursuit: "She was a woman who spent her days in sitting, nicely dressed, on a sofa, doing some long piece of needlework, of little use and no beauty, thinking more of her pug than her children" (Austen 1998, 26; 16). Throughout the novels, Austen never places Mrs. Bennet, Mrs. Dashwood or Lady Bertram in an intellectually rich or stimulating environment, such as a library, for the purpose of education or self-improvement. As a result, one of their functions within Austen's narrative is as an object lesson about the relationship between age, intellect and family function, the lesson being that neither their ridiculousness nor their physical and social boundaries can be improved until their understanding and psychological age are better suited to their physical age.

Additionally, Austen increases the mother-daughter conflict by establishing psychological and social constraints for these ageing women. Eighteenth- and nineteenth-century fiction and sermons focused strongly on women's psychological development, and though feared to be morally inferior, women were expected to epitomise their culture's moral standard. As such, proper education and psychological conditioning would produce a gentlewoman who would "aspire [to] every amiable, every noble quality that is adapted to [her] state" (Fordyce 1814, 8). Mothers should have modeled those standards of modesty, courtesy, piety, devotion and diligence to her children or have been willing to personally, and perhaps solely, accept responsibility for their failings (Fordyce 1814, 9). Such romanticized perceptions of motherhood were fostered by popular publications such as the *Lady's Magazine* which published from 1770 to 1837 "with a circulation of 15,000 to 16,000 a month" (Tobin 1990, 205). These, in combination with sermons from men like James Fordyce on matters of humility, chastity and propriety, created a sense of noble, maternal sacrifice. For some, "there was even a certain pleasure in martyrdom" and they "were enthralled by saintly lives of self-abnegation, service to God and/or mankind, and sublimation of sensual gratification" (Perkin 1989, 282).

In contrast, Austen created mother characters who, rather than being "the best standard of [their] sex" (Fordyce 1814, 9), are often psychologically and socially absent when their daughters require support or guidance. Particularly in late eighteenth- and early nineteenth-century fiction, "Whether she is dead, missing, emotionally detached, or present without the daughter's realizing it, the mother is conspicuous in her absence" (Greenfield 2002, 18), and Mrs. Bennet, Mrs. Dashwood and Lady Bertram are more often psychologically and physically absent than present. Austen possibly intended for her nineteenth-century readers to see these middle-aged female characters both as foils for their daughters and as a direct contrast with the popular, romanticized mother characters of the day. At times, the function of their absence within the narrative is to motivate the heroines, their daughters, on their journeys; at other times, it is to create a vacuum of moral guidance and support which permits one of their daughters—such as Lydia Bennet, Marianne Dashwood or Mrs. Maria Rushworth née Bertram—to overcome a seemingly insurmountable social conflict for the true heroines—Elizabeth Bennet, Elinor Dashwood and Fanny Price.

Unfortunately for ageing women, both in fiction and real life, the navigation of social spaces had the potential to become constraining and treacherous, as missteps bore severe consequences. When speaking of the women of the age, Nancy Locklin explains that "An active social life could be a liability or a source of support. If a woman's relationships were perceived as dishonorable, no matter what their true nature, the impact on her and her family could be disastrous" (2007, 115), and she cites Jean-Jacques Rosseau's assertion that "there are no good morals for a woman outside of a withdrawn and domestic life" (2007, 113). In her youth, a gentlewoman's social concerns focused on how perceptions of her behaviour could help or harm her in attracting a suitable match. As she aged, a gentlewoman's focus should have shifted from her present, of which there was little hope of change, to her daughters' futures and how her behaviour impacted their chances of making a good match. As Jeannette King points out, once a mother's childbearing years are past, she ought to focus on being useful to her family and on promoting her children's future success rather than re-engaging the social sphere for her own personal gain or pleasure (2013, 12–13). As Mary Bennet points out in the wake of Lydia's elopement, "loss of virtue in a female is irretrievable [...] and [...] she cannot be too much guarded in her behaviour towards the other sex" (Austen 2001, 187–188). Mothers, in short, could not be too cautious in their public behaviour.

Because a matron's public behaviour was judged according to society's expectations of education and moral superiority, following "the proper direction of her earlier emotional life" would directly influence behaviour as an ageing mother (King 2013, 26). As a result of patriarchal gendering of domestic spaces and "through the tutelage of their fathers, brothers and guidebooks (often written by men) specifically designed to school them on how they should occupy space physically, socially and psychologically" (Posusta 2014, 76), women learned about which spaces they could occupy as well as what they could do within those spaces as they aged. All three ways of occupying space—physical, social and psychological—influence one another. Austen understood, especially when creating a cohesive narrative, that acceptance within particular social circles can both limit and be limited by the physical spaces one occupies. As such, she sets up ageing mothers like Mrs. Bennet and Mrs. Dashwood to fail in their respective attempts to occupy certain physical and social spaces because, due to their adolescent sensibilities and mindsets, they are psychologically unprepared to navigate or claim ownership within these spaces. Lady Bertram fails as a mother not because of her failure to navigate public spaces but because she has withdrawn from those spaces altogether. She has abdicated her role as social and moral guide to Aunt Norris who attends public outings with Maria and Julia; at the same time, the rest of the family reinforces and perpetuates her childlike state as they endeavour to "sav[e] her from all possible fatigue or exertion in every particular but that of directing her letters" (Austen 1998, 26).

With regards to Mrs. Bennet, this inability to navigate public space is particularly obvious at the Netherfield ball when her unchecked irritation with Darcy and her loud, inappropriate discussion of wealthy suitors violates social standards of feminine courtesy, propriety and reserve. For Mrs. Dashwood, this manifests not as an inability to navigate public social circles but as an inability to take on the role of head of household after her husband's death. Each of these women are at an age when their understanding of navigating social spaces should allow them to guide their daughters; instead, Austen uses their inability to do so to reveal "the fallacy of contemporary maternal ideals—that successful motherhood does not exist in [her] novels because it does not exist in real life" (Greenfield 2002, 18).

Austen frequently draws attention to the nonexistent ideal mother by creating middle-aged female characters, like Mrs. Dashwood, who bear the title "mother" but frequently do not function in the role of mother within the family dynamic. With the exception of *Emma*, all the heroines' mothers are alive, but "each heroine finds it increasingly important to detach herself from her parent" (Greenfield 2002, 148). To justify this separation within the narrative, Austen establishes each mother's flaws and social or psychological absence by contrasting their adolescent behaviour with their increasing age and their overall character with that of their daughters. In both *Pride and Prejudice* and *Sense and Sensibility*,

Austen does this by designing a middle-aged female who mirrors one daughter—Mrs. Bennet mirrors Lydia just as Mrs. Dashwood mirrors Marianne—even as she acts as the foil for another daughter—Elizabeth and Elinor respectively. In both cases, the mother is known to be solidly in middle age, yet she most closely resembles one of her younger daughters in personality and behaviour. Mrs. Dashwood acknowledges her age as "forty," and Marianne is "sixteen and a half" (Austen 2002, 30; 38). As Jane Bennet is "almost three-and-twenty," Mrs. Bennet is likely at or approaching mid-forty, but she identifies most strongly with fifteen-year-old Lydia (Austen 2001, 145; 31). Much like Marianne, her favourite daughter, Mrs. Dashwood is driven by sensibility, and being a woman of "affections naturally warm, but not carefully disciplined […] [she] falls a victim to the excesses of uncontrolled feelings" (More 2002, 297). Much to Elinor's dismay, Mrs. Dashwood cannot teach Marianne to balance her sensibility with sense because she herself does not know how. Instead, the conflict between her and Elinor builds as she encourages and lives vicariously through the emotional intensity of Marianne's relationship with Willoughby and criticizes her eldest daughter's caution: "I should scold [Elinor] myself, if she were capable of wishing to check the delight of your conversation with our new friend" (Austen 2002, 37). Austen sets Mrs. Dashwood up as a mirror for Marianne but as a foil for Elinor, "whose advice was so effectual, possessed a strength of understanding, and coolness of judgment, which qualified her […] to be the counsellor of her mother, and enabled her frequently to counteract […] that eagerness of mind in Mrs. Dashwood which must generally have led to imprudence" (Austen 2002, 8). The conflict arising from Mrs. Dashwood's perpetually youthful mindset strengthens Elinor's desire to marry and have as much control as possible over her own home.

Unfortunately for Elinor, Mrs. Dashwood never grows from the psychological space of a romantic youth to provide useful aid or helpful social and moral guidance for her daughters, but Austen provides her with some little praise by indicating that "Mrs. Dashwood was prudent enough to remain at the cottage, without attempting a removal to Delaford" (Austen 2002, 269). This seems to imply that she considered such a removal, which would have made her financially dependent upon Marianne, and thus would have put her in a psychological space even more distant from her age than the one she currently occupies. While Austen assures readers at the novel's conclusion that these relationships are mended, she provides no indication that Mrs. Dashwood undergoes self-evaluation or attempts to adopt a behaviour more suited to her age.

Austen also establishes in Mrs. Bennet a conflict between physical age and psychological age which undermines her relationships with her daughters. In Mrs. Bennet's (née Gardiner's) youth, Austen reveals that Mr. Bennet, "captivated by youth and beauty, and that appearance of good humour which youth and beauty generally give, had married a woman whose weak understanding and illiberal mind had very early in their marriage put an end to all real affection for her. Respect, esteem, and confidence had vanished for ever" (Austen 2001, 155). Without mutual respect and affection, the Bennet marriage was based upon a "continual breach of conjugal obligation and decorum which, in exposing his wife to the contempt of her own children, was so highly reprehensible" (Austen 2001, 155). It can reasonably be concluded that this marital conflict, which creates and fosters conflict between mother and daughters and often aggravates Mrs. Bennet's nervous complaints, contributes to her ageing process by increasing her stress. Furthermore, by decreasing her opportunities to improve her mind, this conflict reduces her to the familial role of an adolescent young woman and leaves her open to scorn, ridicule and pity from her own daughters.

To make the situation worse, Mr. Bennet's mockery assigns Mrs. Bennet to a psychological space to which she no longer belongs—the space of a young woman. In fact, Mr. Bennet continues to contribute to the problem when, early in the novel, he teases Mrs. Bennet about her beauty in comparison to her young daughters by encouraging her to take his place in calling upon Mr. Bingley: "for as you are as handsome as any of them, Mr. Bingley may like you the best of the party" (Austen 2001, 3). In a surprisingly calm fashion, Mrs. Bennet replies with: "I certainly have had my share of beauty, but I do not pretend to be anything extraordinary now. When a woman has five grown-up daughters, she ought to give over thinking of her own beauty" (Austen 2001, 4). The passage of nearly a quarter of a century in a contentious marriage along with the physical burdens of bearing five children has clearly had a visible effect on Mrs. Bennet as she has aged, and yet she still finds herself being compared to, and therefore in direct competition with, her daughters.

Austen revisits the potential for conflict between ageing mother and youthful daughter in *Mansfield Park* with Lady Bertram, who "had been a [...] prosperous beauty, all her life" (1998, 225) and who is confronted with the beauty of her daughters and of Fanny Price, an adopted niece who had been raised in the Bertram household. Like Mrs. Bennet, Lady Bertram does not occupy the psychological space of a mother within the household; however, in contrast to Mrs. Bennet, Lady Bertram's husband has never forced her to compete with her daughters to feel beautiful. For Mrs. Bennet there is "a tinge of insecurity in [Mr. Bennet's taunts,] but Lady Bertram, whose husband never teases and never criticizes, is left with her self-satisfaction intact" (Lane 2014, 25). For both women, their respective loss of beauty as they age has the potential to create or deepen conflict between them and their daughters. For Lady Bertram, this conflict is mediated because of an extraordinarily passive nature and because she is "either pleased to see her beauty replicated or, more likely, unable to perceive any alteration in herself" (Austen 1998, 26). As for Mrs. Bennet, her increasing age and decreasing beauty serve to further complicate her relationship with her daughters in general, due to comparisons of beauty, and with Elizabeth in particular, due to the added sting of Mr. Bennet's frequent praise of Lizzy's intellect.

Although the outward appearance of Lady Bertram's age causes less conflict for her than it does for Mrs. Bennet, Austen characterizes Lady Bertram's natural versus psychological ages as being even more disparate than Mrs. Bennet's and Mrs. Dashwood's. Early in the novel, Austen reveals to her readers that Lady Bertram allows her sister, Aunt Norris, to take charge of the family and has surrendered virtually all wifely (excepting conjugal) and motherly duties. In fact, Lady Bertram fundamentally ceases to exist as a wife and mother because she has receded so far into the boundaries of her life as a married woman—partly for propriety, which takes effort, and largely for laziness—and can no longer function independently. In addition to occupying a very limited physical space, mostly the sofa, she also occupies a very limited and childlike psychological space; as a result, she cannot function as a wife and mother. Her dependence on Fanny is frequently evident; for instance, Lady Bertram declares how she "cannot spare her" and, when challenged or asked to make a decision, she must consult her husband asking, "But can I do without her, Sir Thomas?" (Austen 1998, 149–150). Due to how far Lady Bertram has receded from independence, autonomy and the psychological landscape of an adult, she is naturally of no support to her husband or children when troubles occur; in fact, her husband and children actively shield her from difficulties which a mother would typically try to shield her children from or guide them through. For example, during the illness of her eldest son Tom, rather than assisting with his care, Lady Bertram largely remains unaffected as Sir Thomas and Edmund "judged it best that Lady Bertram should not be harassed by alarms which, it was to be hoped, would prove unfounded"

(Austen 1998, 291). Being denied a true understanding of the situation, the boundaries around Lady Bertram's life are complete: no mobility, no intellectual interaction or development, no emotional growth and no beneficial position or constructive function within the family.

Just as Austen reveals that these middle-aged mothers are less beautiful than they once were, she also shows how they are less physically and socially mobile than they once were, and they are considerably less mobile than their daughters are. Perhaps due to the popularity of travel narratives at the time, journeys and mobility are recurring themes in Austen's works. Thus, a gentlewoman's adaptation of the heroic journey archetype is evident in each heroine's story: departure, initiation, road of trials, innermost cave, return to and reintegration with society (cf. "Archetypes" 2015, 2). Mobility and the journey archetype are integral to Austen's characters, but compared to other primary characters, Mrs. Dashwood, Mrs. Bennet and Lady Bertram are some of the least mobile. Their immobility contrasts sharply with the mobility of their daughters because travel is synonymous with vitality, individuality and character development; as such, a lack of travel signifies physical decline, intellectual limitations and character stagnation.

In *Pride and Prejudice*, *Sense and Sensibility* and *Mansfield Park*, each heroine must undertake a journey, both as archetypal symbol and as a literal journey between homes, estates and cities, which guides her to a deeper understanding of herself, her role within society and her future spouse. As Benson points out, "The Austen heroine must, to be a heroine, have her own personal sense of morality well established—even if it is separate from that of her family—before she can grow up and become a mother" (1989, 117), and to accomplish this, she must, for a time, be separate from her family prior to marrying. She must define her own moral code and take responsibility for her moral conduct before she can, through marriage, permanently detach herself from her parents' authority and moral guidance. Elizabeth Bennet's journey to Derbyshire reveals Mr. Darcy's true character; Fanny Price's visit with her parents strengthens her conviction in rejecting Mr. Crawford's suit; Elinor and Marianne Dashwood's stay in London reveals harsh truths about the men they love. In contrast, Austen rarely sets their respective mothers outside their husbands' (or other male relatives') estates, and thereby rarely outside of their care and supervision. They no longer exist as individuals with an independent moral code but as appendages, and, in Lady Bertram's case, almost as a dependent child. Austen uses their lack of mobility to symbolize their lack of maturity, productivity and social capital, which only serves to further isolate them in limited physical, psychological and social spaces, and causes the ongoing deterioration of their relationships with their daughters, who can neither rely on them nor respect them.

Of the three mothers, *Sense and Sensibility*'s Mrs. Dashwood is unique in the Austen novels, in being the only widowed biological mother and in being forced to relinquish her home. While, at a glance, she is the most mobile of the mothers, her travel is involuntary; therefore, it cannot function as a symbol of growth or maturation. Of her two instances of travel (being two more than Mrs. Bennet and one more than Lady Bertram), both are necessitated by outside forces. At the beginning of the novel, it is clear that the recently widowed Mrs. Dashwood does not wish to leave Norland Park; in fact, she deliberately stays, hoping for some of the promised aid from her stepson (Austen 2002, 22). Her departure from Norland comes down to two reasons: her stepson's meanness and her stepdaughter-in-law's vindictive pettiness.

In addition to her transition to Barton Cottage not being voluntary and not being symbolic of choice or empowerment, it is also, at least in part, a direct result of her age. She is too young for her stepson and his wife to want to support as "people always live for ever when there is an annuity to be paid them; and she is very stout and healthy, and hardly forty" (Austen 2002, 11). Yet she is too old to re-enter the marriage market without causing a scandal as it may be seen as proof that sexual urges had "overpower[ed] her judgement or sense of propriety" (Lane 2014, 132). Due to her age and widow status, the best she can do is relocate herself and her daughters from her husband's estate to her cousin's, Sir John Middleton's, cottage. Once there, the chance that she should re-emerge into a broader and wealthier society is slim, as her age simultaneously makes marriage unlikely and increases the likelihood that her financial resources, like Miss Bates' in *Emma*, will become scarcer if she lives a long life.

The journey from Norland to Barton Cottage, despite being a decided step down in social and financial status and in the quality of her home environment, might provide an opportunity for Mrs. Dashwood to grow more autonomous and responsible. Instead, the move is primarily orchestrated by her eldest daughter Elinor, and it places her on the property and therefore under the care of her boisterous and intrusive cousin, Sir John Middleton. She moves from one house which is not her own to another which is not her own, replaces the guidance of her husband with the guidance of her eldest daughter, and trades inconsiderate landlords for intrusive ones, Sir John and his mother-in-law, Mrs. Jennings. Despite the potential for her to grow psychologically in this move, she gains no significant peace, autonomy or financial security from the exchange, and once settled in this new physical space, she seems to accept the inherent limitations and becomes even more isolated than *Pride and Prejudice*'s Mrs. Bennet and almost as isolated as *Mansfield Park*'s Lady Bertram.

Just as Mrs. Dashwood's isolated country existence symbolizes her status as an ageing widow and her decline into invisibility as an ageing woman, so does Mrs. Bennet's restrictive home life represent her ineffectiveness and weakness of character in *Pride and Prejudice*. Like the other mothers in Austen's novels, Mrs. Bennet is locationally static, and despite being a primary character, Austen rarely depicts her outside of Longbourn, Mr. Bennet's estate. Other than a party at Lucas Lodge, another at Netherfield Park, and a quick day trip to check on Jane at Netherfield, Mrs. Bennet predominately stays at home. Her one time assertion that "At our time of life, it is not so pleasant, I can tell you, to be making new acquaintances every day" (Austen 2001, 6) is all the more unconvincing because twice she expresses a desire to travel. On both occasions, Mrs. Bennet's desire to travel is directly related to where Lydia, her favourite daughter to whom she is most alike, is travelling, first to Brighton and later to Newcastle (cf. Austen 2001, 150; 214). Because she never expresses a desire to travel with Jane to London or with Elizabeth, her least favourite daughter, to Kent or to Derbyshire, it is clear that her desire to travel is strictly related to the daughter through whom she is most able to vicariously re-live the freedom and romance of her youth. She is attempting to forestall her age and to move beyond her assigned space by feeding off of Lydia's youth, and this perhaps also explains her refusal to acknowledge or to temper Lydia's behaviour—to deny Lydia is to deny herself the only escape she has.

Mrs. Bennet's desire to travel exclusively with Lydia as well as her unwillingness to discipline her wilful youngest daughter not only prove her a contentious mother, they also show her as occupying the same psychological space within the family as Lydia occupies. Unfortunately for Mrs. Bennet, adolescent mindsets and behaviours are difficult to overlook in a woman of middle age, and she is no longer permitted to navigate the same social spaces (at least not in the same manner) as her daughters. As a result, her attempts to be the centre of attention and to dominate social spaces reserved for younger, husband-seeking women backfire and result in the exposure of her ridiculousness and in humiliation for her daughters, which nearly eliminates their chances of successful, happy marriages.

While Austen shows both Mrs. Dashwood and Mrs. Bennet as attempting to engage, albeit ineffectually, with their daughters and be involved in their lives, she takes Lady Bertram to a different extreme of physical, social and psychological restriction. From the beginning of *Mansfield Park*, Austen alerts her readers not to expect much of Lady Bertram as a mother by describing her as having "very tranquil feelings, and a temper remarkably easy and indolent" (Austen 1998, 6); however, this does not fully reveal the extent to which Lady Bertram has essentially ceased to exist not only outside of her husband's home but also within it. In the early chapters of *Mansfield Park*, Austen outlines how Lady Bertram grew up in Huntingdon, moved to Northampton upon the advent of her marriage, and used to travel seasonally to London with her husband (1998, 5; 17), but by the time she and Sir Thomas decide to adopt their niece, Fanny Price, Lady Bertram no longer travels with her husband to London nor even fulfils a mother's fundamental role of attending local public functions with her young daughters: "Lady Bertram did not go out into public with her daughters. She was too indolent even to accept a mother's gratification in witnessing their success and enjoyment at the expense of any personal trouble" (Austen 1998, 26). Whereas Mrs. Bennet still desires the mobility of her youth and Mrs. Dashwood the diversity of company in more settled areas, Lady Bertram has surrendered and withdrawn from almost all social interaction as well as motherly duty.

While Mrs. Dashwood, Mrs. Bennet and Lady Bertram each behave and interact with family and society in very different ways, as ageing mothers all three share the same problems: as a result of adolescent behaviours, insufficient education and being infantilized by others, they lack the necessary ownership over their physical, social and psychological spaces to function as effective mothers according to the social values of the era. Because they are unable to function as mothers, as they age they are increasingly constrained from moving beyond the limitations of their husband's property, where their social and behavioural infractions would be viewed in a far harsher light. Trapped within their husband's (or cousin's) estates, they remain static, which only adds to their limitations as they cannot function as would be expected either within the family or beyond, and this adds to their conflict with their young adult daughters. Because of the heavy social and moral restrictions placed upon mothers, it is easier for mothers like Mrs. Bennet, Mrs. Dashwood and Lady Bertram, who are lacking in conventional "motherly" qualities, to remain safely within their assigned spaces rather than to attempt navigating society in the same ways that younger female characters do.

Works Cited

"Archetypes." Hillsborough Community College 2015. https://www.hccfl.edu/media/724354/archetypesforliteraryanalysis.pdf. Accessed 18 May 2015.

Austen, Jane. 1998. *Mansfield Park*, ed. Claudia L. Johnson. New York: W. W. Norton.

Austen, Jane. 2001. *Pride and Prejudice*, 3rd ed., ed. Donald J. Gray. New York: W. W. Norton.

Austen, Jane. 2002. *Sense and Sensibility*, ed. Claudia L. Johnson. New York: W. W. Norton.

Benson, Mary Margaret. 1989. Mothers, Substitute Mothers, and Daughters in the Novels of Jane Austen. *Persuasions* 11: 117–124. *Jane Austen Society of North America*. http://www.jasna.org/persuasions/printed/number11/benson.htm. Accessed 15 May 2015.

Fordyce, James. 1814. *Sermons to Young Women, In Two Volumes*, vol. 1, 14th ed. London: T. Cadell and W. Davies.

Greenfield, Susan C. 2002. *Mothering Daughters: Novels and the Politics of Family Romance: Frances Burney to Jane Austen*. Detroit: Wayne State University Press.

King, Jeannette. 2013. *Discourses of Ageing in Fiction and Feminism: The Invisible Woman*. New York: Palgrave Macmillan.

Lane, Maggie. 2014. *Growing Older with Jane Austen*. London: Robert Hale.

Locklin, Nancy. 2007. *Women's Work and Identity in Eighteenth-Century Brittany*. Abingdon: Ashgate.

More, Hannah. 2002. From Strictures on the Modern System of Female Education. In *Sense and Sensibility by Jane Austen*, ed. Claudia L. Johnson, 269–299. New York: W. W. Norton.

Perkin, Joan. 1989. *Women and Marriage in Nineteenth-Century England*. 1988. London: Routledge.

Posusta, Rebecca. 2014. Architecture of the Mind and Place in Jane Austen's Persuasion. *Critical Survey* 26 (1): 76–91. doi: 10.3167/cs.2014.260106.

Tobin, Beth Fowkes. 1990. 'The Tender Mother': The Social Construction of Motherhood and the *Lady's Magazine*. *Women's Studies* 18 (2/3): 205–221.

Wiltshire, John. 1992. *Jane Austen and the Body: 'The Picture of Health.'* New York: Cambridge University Press.

CHAPTER 7

"No One Noticed Her": Ageing Spinsters and Youth Culture in Sylvia Townsend Warner's Short Stories

Cathy McGlynn

Sylvia Townsend Warner's first novel, *Lolly Willowes* (1926), documents its ageing spinster protagonist's attempts to defy the limitations placed upon her by an ageist, patriarchal social order. In her wish to "have a life of one's own" (Warner 2012, 196), Laura (Lolly) abandons the conventional urban middle-class respectability she experiences living with her brother and his family, in favour of an independent existence in the country where, at the novel's climax, she makes a pact with Satan and begins practising witchcraft. Her description to Satan of the state of ageing women raises significant issues in relation to the experience of the ageing spinster, and the social construction and invisibility of the ageing woman in a deeply patriarchal culture:

> When I think of witches, I seem to see all over England, all over Europe, women living and growing old, as common as blackberries, and as unregarded. I see them as wives and sisters of respectable men [...] Well, there

C. McGlynn (✉)
Independent Researcher, Limerick, Ireland
e-mail: cathymcglynn@gmail.com

C. McGlynn et al. (eds.), *Ageing Women in Literature and Visual Culture*,
DOI 10.1007/978-3-319-63609-2_7

> they were, there they are, child-rearing, housekeeping [...] And they think how they were young once, and they see new young women, just like what they were. (Warner 2012, 193-194)

The practice of witchcraft is Lolly's response to a culture that renders "unregarded" older women invisible and silent. Women's social function is limited to their roles as wives or sisters, dependent on male relatives, situated firmly within a domestic space, confined to gendered activities such as "child-rearing" and "housekeeping." And as they grow older they become less culturally visible—Lolly adds that "If they could be passive and unnoticed, it wouldn't matter. But they must be active, and still not noticed" (Warner 2012, 194). Their activities must be appropriate to their gender, and yet they must accept that they are "not noticed" and invisible. If the ageing woman's lot in the interwar era is a dismal one, as indicated here, the fate of the ageing spinster is worse. Lolly describes a local spinster, Miss Carloe, as a "typical witch, people would say. Really she's the typical genteel spinster who's spent her life being useful to people who didn't want her. If you'd got her younger she'd never be like that" (Warner 2012, 196). Lolly's definition of a spinster alludes to the dominant contemporary view that the spinster was a useless burden on society. Unmarried at the age of 47, Lolly has experienced this sense of being unwanted and the subsequent need to feel "useful to people." Instead, she decides to be useful to no one but herself, and her embrace of witchcraft is her assertion of autonomy and rejection of convention. As Barbara Brothers observes, "Lolly, in seeing herself as another in the long line of witches about which she has read, casts herself as one of those women who have chosen to exercise their own powers and are therefore society's outcasts" (1991, 208). In exercising her own powers, Lolly rejects the ideological value system that positions the ageing spinster as deviant and threatening.

The alignment of spinsterhood with ageing in *Lolly Willowes* is a motif that is repeated throughout Warner's work, and in particular her short stories. Warner's subversiveness in relation to gender has been well documented in critical responses to this novel and yet her 14 collections of short stories, many of which were published in *The New Yorker* over a period of five decades, have received comparatively less critical attention than her novels. Furthermore, with the exception of Brothers' article on spinsterhood in *Lolly Willowes*, research on Warner to date has overlooked the dominance of ageing characters in her work, in spite of Dean

Baldwin's brief recognition of her "sympathy with the aged" (1986, 79). This chapter will focus on the representation of the ageing spinster in a selection of Warner's stories from both the interwar period and the 1960s, and will examine Warner's foregrounding of the anti-ageing discourse of invisibility that was produced by the respective cultures, and indeed cults of youth, that defined both eras. Ultimately, Warner's representation of the ageing spinster in both her early and later stories demonstrates continuity rather than change in the cultural discourses that construct the ageing spinster as invisible, abnormal and surplus to society's requirements. Her later stories, however, more overtly foreground the chasm between the inner life of the ageing woman and society's view of her, and can therefore be viewed as more subversive. Warner uses several tactics to facilitate a critique of dominant age ideology: the representation of a generational clash that is characteristic of cultures in which the idealization of youth dominates; a "dual-voiced narrative" (Doan 1991, 151) where the portrayal of the ageing woman's subjective inner life serves to undercut other characters' objective view of her; the foregrounding of what Jeannette King refers to as the "relationship between identity and the body" which is "deeply problematic and one wrestled with in most fictions of ageing" (2013, 124); and the use of domestic objects and surroundings to metaphorically comment on the experience of the ageing spinster.

The stories under discussion here date from the interwar period (the 1920s and 1930s) and the 1960s. *Lolly Willowes* was published in 1926, and the stories "The Property of a Lady" and "The Nosegay" were published in the collection *More Joy in Heaven* in 1935. The later stories, "An Aging Head" and "The Listening Woman," were written in 1963 and 1967, respectively. The 1920s was a decade in which youth was elevated into a cult status, and this idealization of youth persisted into the 1930s. Cynthia Port discusses the "increased valorization of youth in the 1920s and 1930s" and links this to "the widespread distrust of the older generation, which had sent hundreds of thousands of young men to their deaths." This generational clash resulted in an "emerging hostility toward age" which, in Port's view, "had significantly gendered connotations" (2006, 141, 142). Significantly, this "growing interest in the 'problem' of old age led to the establishment in the 1920s and '30s of gerontology as a discipline" (Port 2006, 147). Ageing women in particular were denigrated and associated with what Margaret Morganroth Gullette refers to as "decline." She writes that in the 1920s, "aging seen as an unmitigated decline had never started so early in the life course or [had been] made so central to identity and mental accomplishment" (1993, 44). In this context, Port argues that "the consequences of aging" in fiction in the interwar period, "are often experienced as particularly dire for women, whose sense of self-worth and of evaluation by others is so frequently tied to youthful beauty and fertility" (2006, 144), and she cites examples of female characters from the fiction of James Joyce, Virginia Woolf and Jean Rhys. Similar characters proliferate in Warner's stories at the time, and, significantly, still appear in her work thirty years later. This can be attributed to the fact that, as Elizabeth Wilson observes, "the sexual discourse of the sixties was obsessively about youth" (1980, 107). Ruth Adam associates the sixties with the emergence of the "teenager" as a social phenomenon, and links the youth of the decade to their predecessors in the interwar period: "The 'Teenagers' who dominated British social life for the best part of a decade were in some ways the successors of the 'Bright Young Things' of the Twenties. Like them, they had their own music and dancing, defied their elders [and] believed that they were the first generation to make the most of being young" (1975, 179). King likewise observes that in the sixties, "to be old, for women in particular, was to be invisible, since the visual codes of the fashionable in all areas of cultural life were predicated on the young, immature body" (2013, 58). As in the 1920s and 1930s, the centrality and adulation of youth in the cultural discourse of the 1960s resulted in the subsequent marginalization and denigration of the ageing woman. The cultural invisibility of the ageing woman is reflected in Warner's stories from both periods and the stories under discussion here focus specifically on the double marginalization of the ageing woman who is also a spinster.

If the ageing woman in the interwar period was ignored and sidelined from mainstream culture, then the ageing spinster was abhorred and rendered abnormal and deviant. In fact, Gullette attributes the profoundly gendered ageism of the era to the existence of spinsters: "early twentieth-century ageism may have been harder on women as they aged, if only because many women did not marry, and celibacy was condemned" (1993, 44). Of course by its very definition, the spinster is an ageing woman, and within the context of interwar youth culture, this figure was doubly marginalised—according to her age and her assumed celibacy. The double burden of spinsterhood and age is encapsulated in the derogatory term "Old Maid," a term which originated in England as far back as the seventeenth century (Israel 2003, 16). In the interwar period, this figure of the "Old Maid" was greeted with dread, and, as King observes, there are "contradictions" in this stereotype, where on the one hand "concern about non-reproductive sexuality in the older woman leads to recommendations to celibacy," and on the other "the sterility of the spinster generates its own hostility because it represents a non-productive role in society. It is therefore unsurprising that most sociological discussion of ageing femininity focuses on this figure, a figure of both ridicule and dread" (2013, 14–15). Unmarried women, according to the logic of contemporary gender ideology, should remain celibate, and yet this celibacy is precisely what rendered them Other to normative models of proper femininity, and furthermore, led to the conflation of spinsterhood with frigidity. Sheila Jeffreys notes that while spinsterhood was gradually perceived positively as the nineteenth century progressed, in the early twentieth century a backlash occurred that resulted in the equation of spinsterhood with frigidity and abnormality. She notes that "while previously the word spinster had simply meant unmarried woman, it was coming to mean specifically, women who had not done sexual intercourse with men" (1985, 175). Judy Little supports this with the view that between the late Victorian era and the 1930s, "the spinster rises from the status of being perceived as an unhappy, deprived, 'surplus' person, to being a major agent in the social reform and suffrage movements, to once again being seen as an unhappy and even suspect person by the 1930s" (1991, 20). This was due in part to the massive surplus of unmarried women in Britain in the decades following the First World War, which created a social anxiety about unmarried women, and a social obsession with marriage as a marker of stability and progress.

At the same time, the new fashionable discipline of sexology promoted sexual activity within marriage and assumed "that the 'normal' woman would enthusiastically embrace sexual intercourse" (Jeffreys 1985, 169). The acknowledgement that women could feel sexual desire was groundbreaking, but this desire could only be exercised within the heterosexual marriage bond. Sexology can therefore be viewed as part of the general "campaign to promote marriage and motherhood throughout the 1920s" (Jeffreys 1985, 168). Whereas before, the spinster's unmarried and barren state was denigrated, it was, as Sybil Oldfield notes, "her virginity rather than her barrenness or her perverted lust for power that stigmatized the spinster now. If heterosexual intercourse is the only path to human maturity and fulfilment, the spinster, by definition, must be sexually retarded and psychologically subnormal" (1991, 99). The result of this "new ideology of the spinster" was that, by the 1930s, "a very limiting new legend or code defined the spinster as unfulfilled, sexually, and in every other way" (Little 1991, 22). The damning construction of spinsterhood in the interwar period occurred along with the idealisation of marriage and youth, and, as Warner's stories show, the cultural stereotype of the ageing spinster persists decades later. As Jeffreys observes, writing in 1985, the new meaning attached to spinsterhood in the interwar period persisted throughout the twentieth century and "is much-closer to the present-day meaning of the word" (1985, 175). The difference between Warner's earlier and later stories is arguably a more complex and developed technique, which allows for a more sustained critique of discourses of ageing.

Warner's arguably most disheartening treatment of the ageing spinster occurs in "The Property of a Lady" (1935), in which the discourse of invisibility that marginalizes the ageing spinster is the main theme. Warner eschews subtlety in favour of a stark, devastating portrait of a lonely, ignored ageing spinster living alone. Miss Cruttwell adheres to society's definition of what constitutes "a lady" and devotes herself to diligent housework that will produce the visual effect of "the property of a lady" (Warner 2002b, 311). Each day she finishes her household duties, content that at least "if anyone comes, it's ready for them," and then, in weary resignation, remembers "how lonely she was, how old, and how neglected, and how, all her life long, she had kept the lady-standard flying, had been scrupulously clean, scrupulously honest, scrupulously refined, and nothing had come of it save to be old and neglected and lonely" (2002b, 311). In this story, Warner uses the domestic space inhabited by Miss Crutwell to reflect the battle between selfhood and the physical manifestation of ageing, and this is a motif that is used to a fuller extent in her later stories. Miss Crutwell's rooms have the appearance of "the property of a lady" due to her diligent housework and this masks the "empty room" (2002b, 312), devoid of visitors, just as Miss Crutwell's physical attire suggests a ladylike demeanour that hides the desperation and emptiness of the ageing self: "she dressed with her usual exact care, lacing her shoes briskly, smoothing on her gloves; for a lady is always known by her neatness of hand and foot" (2002b, 313). The "neatness" of her domestic space, "the property" of this lady, is reiterated in her attire, and both serve to mask the loneliness within. The ageing spinster in this story reflects the fact that, as King (2013, xiii) notes, "women's bodies inevitably become invisible, if not objects of disgust" as they get older. Now 65, Miss Crutwell is painfully conscious of her own invisibility. She knows that "No one noticed her, she glided through the wet streets unscanned. No one would notice if she died" (2002b, 312). Her invisibility is also linked to her spinsterhood. Her rare guests include "the wife of the clergyman" and "the widow of the gentleman whose secretary Miss Crutwell had been" (2002b, 311). She is the wife of no one and has spent most of her life in a job that was typically considered suitable for spinsters. Though, as Rebecca D'Monte observes, "the Great War afforded many middle-class women their first opportunity to work, and therefore earn their own money [...] employment mainly consisted of monotonous drudgery in shops, offices and schools" (2012, 7). This monotonous work is the spinster's lot as long as she is unmarried. It is worth noting that the "wives" who visit Miss Crutwell are not named—she alludes to them only in relation to their husbands and this evokes the central position marriage occupied in the interwar social scene and in the imagination of the lonely unwed spinster.

Determined to be noticed, to be visible, Miss Crutwell first considers, then rejects suicide and makes the radical decision to be a "shop-lifter," because this, she decides, will at least make her visible. Heading to a local department store, she walks around, stealing "two cakes of soap, a swansdown powder-puff, a scent-spray and a bottle of golden perfume [...] and then [...] she stole a brooch on a velvet pad, an enamelled cigarette case, and a bracelet of weighty false pearls." The expectation of finally being noticed brings a sense of "rapture" and she remembers "the need to be discovered and arrested and taken to the police and put into the papers" (2002b, 314). Proud of her subversiveness, she leaves the store, expecting to be followed and apprehended. However, she remains painfully invisible and the story's conclusion reiterates her earlier feeling of invisibility: "She waited. She waited. People went in and out, but no one noticed her [...] She waited. But no one came, no one noticed her" (2002b, 315).

This last paragraph encapsulates the invisibility suffered by ageing women at a time when there was "a widespread obsession with women's ages" (Port 2006, 139). It is telling that the obsession with youth in the interwar era was linked to an emerging culture of consumerism that, as Port explains, "positioned women in an increasingly complicated dual role as both ideal consumers and consumed objects" where in an attempt to regain or retain a youthful body, women "were expected to purchase and apply cosmetics or any of a growing range of other goods and services." At the same time, the new physical ideal of womanhood was embodied in the adolescent, infantilized girl (Port 2006, 149).

The older woman, therefore, was an outcast in a society that valorized the youthful body. It is significant that Miss Crutwell's attempt to make herself visible occurs in a department store full of objects to be consumed by the ideal female consumer. The stolen "swansdown powder-puff, a scent-spray and a bottle of golden perfume" are not, both literally and figuratively, the property of this lady. The trappings of youth do not belong to this ageing spinster. If "the growth of a consumer-based economy served to further elevate the value of the young and the new" (Port 2006, 149), then Miss Crutwell's social value as an ageing consumer is, to use Gullette's term, in "decline."

The "decline" associated with the figure of the ageing spinster is explored again in "The Nosegay" (1935). Here, generational clash is foregrounded to emphasise the older spinster's incongruity with youth culture, and Warner adopts the technique of "dual perspective," the function of which, according to Laura L. Doan,[1] is to subvert "the dominant ideology" so that "two voices, articulating differing positions, resonate from the literary text" (1991, 149). This reflects the "chasm [that] existed between appearance and reality, between how society viewed spinsters and how they really were" (Doan 1991, 146). Much of the story is narrated from the perspective of Mary Matlask, an ageing unmarried woman. At the beginning of the story, she is described from the perspective of a third-person omniscient narrator as "an old woman, so bleached and brittle that it seemed as though the rays of the sun, beating down on her, might snap her in two" (Warner 2002a, 283). The setting is Mary Matlask's garden, and, as in "The Property of a Lady" where the domestic space in which the protagonist lives serves as a symbolic reflection of her ageing body, here, the garden so lovingly tended to by Mary Matlask, can be read as a metaphorical commentary on her decline. In the opening she is standing on her kitchen chair in the garden, "snipping off the withered blooms" (2002a, 283). Ageing conventionally conceived of as "fading bloom" is of course connoted by this, and the metaphor is reiterated several times throughout the story. She cuts, with delight, "a pink rosebud" from the tree and muses "It was the last bud the tree would put forth that summer. It had only opened that morning, it was still faultlessly virginal and brilliant" (2002a, 284). The description

[1] Doan's identification of this technique specifically relates to the representation of the spinster in the fiction of Barbara Pym, but is applicable to Warner's stories.

of the new, young rosebud as "virginal" takes on significance in relation to the story's title, the implication of which only becomes fully evident at the end of the story.

We learn that "All her life, Mary Matlask had made nosegays [...] she gave them to children, to brides, to the bed-ridden, to the dead."[2] For the first time, she has been commissioned to make a nosegay for an old employer's daughter who "wants one for a dance." She is instructed to "put a rose in the middle" and this rose is the very one that she describes as "virginal" (2002a, 284). The association of flowers with female sexuality and development is further cemented in Mary's insistence that "a nosegay for a young lady should contain a good deal of white, to be suitable. But she had the essential, the rose, the year's last and loveliest. There was a song about that, thought Mary Matlask. '*All its lovely companions are faded and gone*'" (2002a, 285). This passage provides an important interpretive framework for the story. The colour white, traditionally associated with virginity, is "suitable" for a "young lady"; but she chooses instead a pink rose, which has also already been explicitly associated with virginity. The rose, however, has contradictory connotations as indicated in the song lyric quoted by Mary, which conflates its virginal youthful associations with friends who are "faded and gone." The rose therefore symbolises virginity, but its connotations relating to the withered blooms that surround it evoke the chastity of the ageing spinster. The "flowering" of young girls is therefore linked to sexuality and this is opposed to the "brittle" ageing chaste body of Mary Matlask.

The opposition between youth and old age is further cemented in the generation clash that is foregrounded in the story. Before the arrival of the young Miss Ursula and her friend, Mary expresses her old-fashioned views of the lifestyle of the privileged youth. She envisions "a car driving up to the door, two young ladies, both in the height of fashion, stepping out, the chauffeur attending on them" and wonders if "this very night, some fine young gentleman might not beg one of Mary Matlask's clove carnations from Miss Ursula's nosegay" (2002a, 285). She makes assumptions such as "Ladies drank China tea, she knew" and her discourse recalls Miss Crutwell's adherence to society's definition of what a "lady" should look and behave like, in "The Property of a Lady." Proud

[2] A nosegay is an old term for a small posy of flowers, which can be worn as a decorative adornment for the purposes of a special occasion.

of her commission, and aware of being watched, Mary makes sure to tell her interfering neighbour that "Two young ladies […] will come in a car" (2002a, 286). The phrase "young ladies" is repeated throughout the story, and this has the effect of drawing attention to the opposition between their youth, and Mary's old age. Their arrival, however, confounds Mary's expectations, as "There was no chauffeur to spring out and hold open the door. It was a tiny car, open, little larger than the coffin of a motor-bicycle." Furthermore "the young ladies […] were so queerly dressed, Miss Ursula's friend even in trousers" and the stark contrast between the "young ladies" and old spinster is highlighted in Miss Ursula's patronising exclamation, "Darling old Mat! […] Of course we should love an egg to our tea. How sweet of you to think of it!" (2002a, 286). Miss Ursula's view of Mary as "old" and "sweet" is reiterated in the infantilizing "isn't she an old pet?" that she murmurs to her friend later on (2002a, 288). The "young ladies" upend tradition, by, in spite of their obvious genteel backgrounds, driving independently of a chauffeur, and by wearing trousers. They are, then, part of what Gullette describes as "the cult of youth, the youth rebellion that resulted in the creation of a generation gap" (1993, 25–26).

The story's conclusion emphasises this generation gap with the use of dual perspective, which reflects contemporary age ideology. Warner uses the technique only at the very end. From the outset of the young ladies' visit, Mary is aware of being watched and overheard by her neighbour. Deciding to make a second nosegay for Miss Ursula's friend, she disappears into the garden, and the reader is privy to the conversation that takes place between the two young friends, which crucially, is overheard by Mrs Colley:

> 'Isn't she an old pet?'said Miss Ursula […]
>
> 'Enchanting,' answered the friend, 'and makes the sweetest lettuce sandwiches. But my dear, what will you do with that vegetation? You don't propose to wear it, do you, all chewed up with greenfly, and crawling with earwigs?'
>
> 'My God, no! But I wanted a specimen of the genuine Victorian article, for Wallers to copy in proper flowers.' (2002a, 288)

The metaphors associated with flowering, age and sexuality are reiterated in the final cruel perspective of the young women. In an instant, Mary's work is demolished. The earlier association of the rose with ageing and chastity is recalled in Miss Ursula's description of the nosegay as the "genuine Victorian article," to be discarded for a more modern version. The use of the term "Victorian" emphasises the generation clash in the story, and renders Mary Matlask as irrelevant and out-of-touch. This generation clash is articulated through the clashing perspectives of Mary, who adheres to "Victorian" notions of how a young lady behaves and looks, and the young women, who subscribe to the "postwar disgust with the older generation and its 'Victorian' values" (Port 2006, 153).

The celebration of youth and denigration of the old in the interwar era lost its relevance during the trauma of the Second World War, and the surplus women problem caused by the deaths of so many young men in the First World War was not an issue after 1945. Adam explains that 'the difference between the peace of 1945 and the peace of 1918 was that this time so many more of the men came home," with the result that in the immediate post-war climate, "a phenomenal number of young husbands and wives settled down to live with each other for the first time" (1975, 159). Marriage was, for different reasons than in the 1920s and 1930s, elevated as the normative state towards which men and women should aspire, and in the 1950s, the "home and motherhood school of thought" and the "back-to-the-kitchen movement" (Adam 1975, 164) were promoted in multiple cultural discourses, including women's magazines, which focused almost exclusively on "child-centred mothering as well as on the importance of domestic skills" (Wilson 1980, 39). In this decade, Betty Israel notes that "single life more than ever stood out as a social aberration" (2003, 184). No longer a "surplus woman," the spinster remained stigmatized, and the ageing spinster doubly so. In 1949, Simone de Beauvoir's groundbreaking book *The Second Sex* (translated into English in 1953) was published, and is one of the few accounts of the experience of female ageing in the postwar period. There is nothing positive in her descriptions; she claims that "woman is haunted by the horror of growing old," and "useless, unjustified, she looks forward to the long, unpromising years she has yet to live, and she mutters: 'No one needs me'" (1997, 587). The ageing woman's increasing invisibility and sense of uselessness is highlighted and recalls Miss Crutwell's experience in "The Property of a Lady." The ageing spinster then was still firmly positioned as Other in the decades following the interwar period.

Of course the advent of a second "youth culture" in the 1960s made ageing women even less relevant and visible. Like their predecessors in the 1920s and 1930s, the "teenagers" of the 1960s also "believed they were the first generation to make the most of being young" (Adam 1975, 179) and became sexually active before marriage. As a result, the fiction of the period, which for the most part was "part of the general obsession with youth," accordingly focused on themes such as "the loss of virginity, the experience of motherhood, the portrayal of young women from the inside" (Wilson 1980, 155). The ageing spinster was simply not relevant. Warner, however, retained and even increased her attention to ageing women in her later fiction. Two of her stories from the period feature ageing spinsters, and while the stigmas expressed in her interwar stories still exist, age ideology is, I would argue, more effectively critiqued.

Warner's 1963 story, "An Aging Head," features Georgina, another older single woman, living alone, who is convalescing after an illness and is being looked after by her niece Antonia. From the outset, Georgie is subjected to what King refers to as "the second childhood view of ageing" which "assumes the old person's physical dependency on 'adults' from whom the 'elderly' are routinely differentiated in medical contexts" (2013, 123). At the story's outset, Antonia must leave "Aunt Georgie" and fusses over her, calling her "reckless" and wishing she "could keep an eye on her" (2001a, 42). Here again, and to a greater extent than before, Warner uses a dual perspective to contrast Georgina's experience as an ageing woman with Antonia's view of her. Georgina yearns for release from this physical dependency on Antonia, and when the latter leaves, it is with a "sigh of relief" that "Georgina turned back to her solitude" (2001a, 42). Here is the first hint that Warner's depiction of the ageing spinster might be more subversive than before: Georgina is utterly content to be alone. Her first task is to tend to the garden, and, as in "The Nosegay," Warner uses the space inhabited by her protagonist to comment on her ageing process. Georgina observes that "nature, in a last fling of fertility, had been doing a great deal" and that consequently it looked like "someone else's garden" (2001a, 42). The reference to fertility, or impending lack of it, is evocative of Georgina's ageing body, and this is ominously linked to the idea that soon this may well be "someone else's garden." She is determined, however, to resist the necessary dependence that comes with physical frailty and busies herself in the garden. However, when she finishes, "the weight of the basket with the snowdrop bulbs in it made her stagger" and "she was cold with fatigue" (2001a, 43). This is indicative of the split between the "I" (self) who has not aged, and the ageing physical body that signals decline.

This split between body and identity is cemented when Georgina looks at her reflection in the mirror. Confronted "with her image in the looking glass" she "saw that the object confronting her was on the brink of tears. She turned away with a toss of her head" and her response is to seek out "male society" in the form of "George," who "was faithful and admiring and in the past had often asked her to marry him" (2001a, 44–45). Georgina's sense of self is in conflict with the physical experience of ageing, to the extent that the body she sees in the mirror is "an object," with which she has has no identification, and this is the body that Antonia and others see. This corresponds to what de Beauvoir calls "a sense of doubling; when one feels oneself a conscious, active, free being, the passive object on which the fatality is operating seems necessarily as if it were another [...] this cannot be I, this old woman reflected in the mirror!" (1997, 592). Georgina's response is to immediately transform herself into an object of desire, by meeting George, who has always been attracted to her. This is evident in the fact that he has proposed to her several times and it is important to note that Georgina has *chosen* spinsterhood by rejecting his proposals, and in doing so, recalls the subversive Lolly Willowes, who chooses to resist what society expects of her. Nevertheless, she cannot halt the ageing process, which makes her dependent on others. She goes out for dinner with George, who has also been ill with bronchitis. Warner's choice of names in this story is not accidental—"George," a bachelor (not by choice), is "Georgina's" male counterpart. Both are ageing, both are alone, and both have been ill. Crucially, however, one is male and the other female and this allows Warner to critique the profoundly gendered aspect of ageing.

After an enjoyable dinner, Georgina is shocked "to be told that she was looking tired and should be taken home" (2001a, 48). This alternative perspective is the first indication that George no longer sees her as an object of desire. On arrival at Georgina's house, they are greeted with a frantic Antonia who has been worrying about her sick Aunt. While Georgina busies herself in the kitchen, she overhears the conversation between her niece and George in the next room. Antonia offers "soothing, diagnosing words" to George, "who liberally as to a midwife was declaring the state of his bronchial tubes" (2001a, 51). The story concludes with Georgina's knowing prediction that the two will soon be "hyphenated into George-and-Antonia—one of those late marriages that at first seem so surprising and soon after seem so natural [...] And she would go on pretty much as usual—an aunt to Antonia, to George an old acquaintance" (2001a, 52). Due to her illness and ageing body, Georgina is no longer an object of desire, and is symbolically replaced by her younger niece in George's affections. Her younger niece, however—and here the generation clash of youth and old age is painfully evident—views George as an object of desire, in spite of the fact that he is ageing and frail like Georgina. This suggests that the experience of ageing is gendered in favour of men. Meanwhile, if Georgina is subversive in her younger self's refusal of marriage and desire to be alone, she cannot halt the ageing process that transforms her into the state she loathes most—dependent. The story does at least allow the ageing spinster a certain amount of agency, and her refusal to marry, together with her labelling of George and Antonia as "A Boy Scout, a Girl Guide," suggests that the traditional institution of marriage that relies on old gender stereotypes is not for her.

Perhaps Warner's most striking attack on anti-ageing discourse occurs in "The Listening Woman" (1967). The story is one of five stories set in Abbey Antique Galleries, run by Mr. Edom, and the narrative is constructed according to two perspectives; the first is that of Miss Mainwaring, a visitor to the gallery, and a woman in advanced old age, and the second is Mr. Collins, the assistant to Mr. Edom, who functions to articulate the objectifying discourses of ageing that dominate the contemporary culture of youth. The two opposing viewpoints allow Warner to undercut the stereotypical view of ageing articulated by Mr. Collins with the inner experience of Miss Mainwaring, which is mostly articulated through free indirect discourse, allowing direct access to her thoughts. As in her earlier stories, Warner connects external objects/space to the ageing woman, to comment on her experience, and this technique is fully realized in this story, where in the first line Miss Mainwaring reflects on the "possessions of one's childhood" which "vanish…all scattered, all gone, broken or left behind." Clearly, these possessions represent her youth, which has vanished, and, with an acute self-awareness, she muses "then suddenly, when you are an old woman—though not in your case a rare and valued antique—they flock back […] [and] you discover that you remember everything about them" (2001b, 136). This sentence captures several thematic threads which the story will develop. Miss Mainwaring, though "antique" herself, knows full well that she is not "rare and valued" and this suggests, as in "The Property of a Lady," the declining value that is considered, in contemporary discourses of ageing, synonymous with old age. Furthermore, though ostensibly her youth is lost, it has not wholly vanished—in fact, it flocks back.

This suggests the interpenetration of past and present experienced by the inner ageing self, which is hidden by what King describes as the "mask of age" that "conceals identity that is unchanging" (2013, 125). Memory functions to combine the young and old selves in a complex identity that is at odds with the visible manifestation of ageing.

Mr. Collins's perspective interrupts her flow of thought and it is clear that he sees a woman in decline, and makes an immediate association between ageing and invisibility, which is reiterated many times throughout the story. In his objectifying view, "her presence was so contained and her examination so unobtrusive [...] that to all intents and purposes he might have been alone [...] she was one of the old lot" (2001b, 136). Miss Mainwaring's age renders her almost absent. The reader is then jolted back to Miss Mainwaring's narrative. She sees a painting that belonged to her family in her youth and Mr. Collins hears her murmur "So here you are" (2001b, 137). As the narrative progresses, it is clear that Miss Mainwaring wholly identifies with the woman in the painting, who "was no darker than she had always been" and with relief, she thinks, "There she was. No restorer, no flaying turpentine hand, had come between them. Unchanged, she was still watching from her window" (2001b, 138). The woman in the painting represents Miss Mainwaring's youthful self and remains "unchanged." As the painting transports her to youthful reminiscence, we learn that her name is "Lucy," that this was "Lucy's picture" and that, in spite of various potential suitors in her life, "Lucy remained a spinster" and during this time, her picture was "lost." Now, "here it was" (2001b, 138–139). The picture fuses memories of her past self with her present self and cements her complex identity in the here and now ("There she was," "here it was"). This subjective self fuses memory with the present and therefore the painting represents the complex inner life of the ageing self, which is firmly at odds with the social constructions of ageing articulated by Mr. Collins. When Lucy tells him the painting (by the artist Schlacken) used to belong to her, he disbelieves her, infantilizes her, and assumes that she is insane: "Poor old thing, she must be a little mad. He must deal with her gently" (2001b, 139). He worries that "she was going to work herself up, *idée fixe*, persecution mania and all that. How on earth was he to deal gently with an elderly maniac, convinced that the Schlacken was her picture and had been stolen from her?" (2001b, 140). The picture has already been equated with Lucy's young self and Mr. Collins, who embodies anti-ageing discourse, wishes to deny the validity of her youthful identity, to retain the property that has indeed "been stolen from her."

The invisibility of Lucy's ageing body is again suggested when a younger couple in the shop shows interest in the painting and as "they stood on her heels [...] being polite, she moved aside" (2001b, 141). They decide they will buy her painting, though they want it for the frame and not the picture, deciding that the picture is disposable and that the frame could be used "for something else" (2001b, 142). This suggests that the ageing body of Miss Mainwaring, whose visibility they ignore, is disposable. The price, however, is too high, and they leave, and this equates both the ageing body and the antique painting with declining value. Mr. Edom returns to the shop, and, unlike Mr. Collins, he treats Miss Mainwaring with respect and dignity. He immediately believes her when she tells him about the painting's history, with the result that "Mr. Collins felt an oncome of second thoughts" and decides that "nothing could be less like madness" than Miss Mainwaring's behaviour. Lucy discovers that the painting has been hanging in the snug of a pub for decades. If the snug traditionally allowed drinkers privacy in a pub, and in particular female drinkers, then this again evokes invisibility and marginality. Mr. Edom bought the painting for a mere "eighty-five pounds" and this makes Lucy "extremely angry" (2001b, 144), and reiterates the theme of declining value in the ageing body. She buys the painting and regains what she has lost, metaphorically uniting her youthful self with her ageing self. Lucy's final re-reading of the painting's meaning forges a connection between youth, old age, and death. Studying the painting, she says, "I've made a discovery. I thought I knew everything about her, but I've made a discovery. She's not watching. She's listening," to which Mr. Edom replies, "Listening for a step she is waiting for, I should say" (2001b, 145). This suggests approaching death, and Lucy's final thoughts cement this association: "She was listening for a step in the darkness, the step of someone nearing the end of a journey [...] or for a last heartbeat" (2001b, 146). Lucy knows she is approaching the end of her life and if the painting represents the "journey" and progression of her life from youth to old age, then at the story's conclusion the painting makes the journey complete; in regaining her property (though it has declined in value), she fuses her memories with the present, her past younger self with her present self, and articulates a complex subjectivity that challenges the social codes that render ageing spinsters invisible and mad.

In "The Listening Woman," Warner allows her protagonist's inner thoughts to frame the story—it both begins and ends with an insight into her inner self. This ageing spinster, unlike her counterparts in "The

Property of a Lady" and "The Nosegay," is wholly self-aware, and the reader's immediate access to her thought process allows her to regain visibility and a voice in a culture that tries to deny her both. Though the dominance of youth culture in the interwar era and the 1960s produced anti-ageing discourses, particularly in relation to the ageing spinster, Warner's treatment and subversion of these discourses is more fully developed in her later stories. The generational clash depicted in "A Nosegay" (1935) highlights its protagonist spinster's lack of self-awareness, whereas in "An Aging Head" (1963) it is used as an effective means of foregrounding the discourses of ageing of which Georgina is only too aware, and which she actively tries to resist. The dual perspective, used tentatively by Warner in both these stories, and completely absent in "The Property of a Lady," is more fully realized in "The Listening Woman," and the use of free indirect discourse allows the ageing woman's voice and experience to dominate the story, and order the narrative, symbolically allowing its protagonist to dictate the terms of how she is perceived. If Warner's earlier stories paint a devastating portrait of both the cultural perception and experience of ageing spinsters, her later stories, through a more subversive and extensive use of the dual-voiced narrative, portray these "old maids" as assertive, complex women, with rich inner lives, who, in spite of physical frailty, resist dependence in all its forms.

Works Cited

Adam, Ruth. 1975. *A Woman's Place, 1910–1975*. London: Chatto & Windus Ltd.

Baldwin, Dean. 1986. The Stories of Sylvia Townsend Warner. *Crazy Horse* 31: 71–80.

Beauvoir, Simone de. 1997. *The Second Sex*. London: Vintage.

Brothers, Barbara. 1991. Flying the Nets at Forty: Lolly Willowes as Female Bildungsroman. In *Old Maids to Radical Spinsters: Unmarried Women in the Twentieth-Century Novel*, ed. Laura L. Doan, 195–212. Urbana and Chicago: University of Illinois Press.

D'Monte, Rebecca. 2012. Passion, Penury, and Psychosis: Representations of the Spinster by Interwar Dramatists. In *Aging Femininities: Troubling Representations*, eds. Josephine Dolan, and Estella Tincknell, 3–16. Cambridge: Cambridge Scholars Press.

Doan, Laura L. 1991. Pym's Singular Interest: The Self as Spinster. In *Old Maids to Radical Spinsters: Unmarried Women in the Twentieth-Century Novel*, ed. Laura L. Doan, 139–154. Urbana and Chicago: University of Illinois Press.

Gullette, Margaret Morganroth. 1993. Creativity, Aging, Gender: A Study of Their Intersections, 1910–1935. In *Aging and Gender in Literature: Studies in Creativity*, eds. M. Anne, Wyatt-Brown and Janice Rosen, 19–48. University of Virginia Press.

Israel, Betty. 2003. *Bachelor Girl: The Secret History of Single Women in the 20th Century*. London: Aurum Press.

Jeffreys, Sheila. 1985. *The Spinster and Her Enemies: Feminism and Sexuality 1880-1930*. London: Pandora Press.

King, Jeannette. 2013. *Discourses of Ageing in Fiction and Feminism: The Invisible Woman*. Palgrave Macmillan.

Little, Judy. 1991. "Endless Different Ways": Muriel Spark's Re-Visions of the Spinster. In *Old Maids to Radical Spinsters: Unmarried Women in the 20th Century Novel*, ed. Laura L. Doan, 19–36. Urbana and Chicago: University of Illinois Press.

Oldfield, Sybil. 1991. From Rachel's Aunts to Miss La Trobe: Spinsters in the Fiction of Virginia Woolf. In *Old Maids to Radical Spinsters: Unmarried Women in the Twentieth-Century Novel*, ed. Laura L. Doan, 85–104. Urbana and Chicago: University of Illinois Press.

Port, Cynthia. 2006. Ages Are the Stuff: The Traffic in Ages in Interwar Britain. *The National Women's Studies Association Journal* 18 (1) (Spring): 138–160.

Warner, Sylvia Townsend. 2001a. An Aging Head. In *The Music at Long Verney: Twenty Stories*, ed. Michael Steinman, 41–52. Washington: Counterpoint.

Warner, Sylvia Townsend. 2001b. The Listening Woman. In *The Music at Long Verney: Twenty Stories*, ed. Michael Steinman, 135–146. Washington: Counterpoint.

Warner, Sylvia Townsend. 2002a. The Nosegay. In *Selected Stories*, ed. Susannah Pinney, 283–288. London: Virago Press.

Warner, Sylvia Townsend. 2002b. The Property of a Lady. In *Selected Stories*, ed. Susannah Pinney, 311–315. London: Virago Press.

Warner, Sylvia Townsend. 2012. *Lolly Willowes or The Loving Huntsman*. London: Virago Press.

Wilson, Elizabeth. 1980. *Only Halfway to Paradise: Women in Postwar Britain 1945-1968*. London and New York: Tavistock Publications.

CHAPTER 8

Stories of Motherhood and Ageing in ABC's Television Programme *Once Upon a Time*

Katherine Whitehurst

Bringing together scholarship on gender, feminism, ageing, adaptation, television and fairy tales, this chapter explores how complex stories about female ageing and motherhood are told in the first two seasons of ABC's television programme *Once Upon a Time* (2011–present). "Snow White" is the ideal tale for this work as Snow White and the queen's story in preceding versions centres on their changing bodies and social roles as developing and ageing females, and their relationship as (step)mother and daughter. The tension between these characters stems from a social system that sees the newly developed youthful woman usurp and erase her older counterpart, with the resulting generational tensions leading to the respective depiction of Snow White and the queen as the angel and devil woman, the virgin and the crone. Through an exploration of *Once Upon a Time*'s representation of character conflicts and relationships, this chapter draws upon age studies to consider how the adaptation reflects, refracts and reimagines dominant stigmas and perceptions around female ageing.

K. Whitehurst (✉)
University of Liverpool, Liverpool, UK
e-mail: katherine.whitehurst@stir.ac.uk

C. McGlynn et al. (eds.), *Ageing Women in Literature and Visual Culture*,
DOI 10.1007/978-3-319-63609-2_8

This chapter, in addition to examining the portrayal of an "older" generation of women, builds on ageing studies by demonstrating how characters transition, grow, age or remain in flux at different moments in their lives. It analyses the relationship between characters' changing identities as mothers and the roles they assume within *Once Upon a Time*'s central storyline. Accounting for the interplay between television, "Snow White" and stories of motherhood, this chapter examines the dominant discourses and ideologies that frame the characters' changing identities and relationships as they align with or seek to separate themselves from different age-cohorts.

Fairy tales provide the ideal space to conduct this research because their ability to project utopic realities or mirror society's beliefs and attitudes means these tales are just as likely to communicate reductive narratives about females as transformative ones. Additionally, as fairy tales are not subject to chronometric time, they can resist and challenge chronological processes of growth and ageing. As Donald Haase asserts:

> The formulaic 'once upon a time' stereotypically associated with the fairy tale would seem to suggest that the genre is largely about time—about temporal displacement from the present to the mythical past or to an imaginative time not governed by the laws of everyday life. [...] If the fairy tale is in fact 'timeless,' that timelessness derives largely from its *structural disinterest* in time. (2000, 362)

Fairy tales' loose temporal engagement means that the characters' temporal experiences of ageing are ungoverned by the laws of everyday life. When female ageing occurs, it serves specific ideological functions within the tales rather than reflecting a chronometric temporal reality. Fairy tales consequently offer a potentially productive space to examine the sociocultural and ideological function female ageing serves in Western contemporary popular culture.

In turn, an analysis of female growth and ageing in *Once Upon a Time* contributes to fairy-tale scholarship's growing interest in the increasingly complex depiction of human experiences, societal constructs and characters' psychology in contemporary fairy tales. Historically, fairy tales depicted one-dimensional, psychologically undeveloped characters. Consequently, early feminist fairy-tale scholars largely focused on female characters' generic narrative function and/or figurative roles. However, the expansion and reimagining of fairy tales in contemporary television has enabled the emergence of psychologically and socially complex female characters. As this chapter illustrates, the process of adaptation becomes central to character complexity as the tale's content is defamiliarised, with television enabling different avenues to enunciate and explore fairy tales. In considering the televisual adaptation of "Snow White," I detail how the issues of time and temporality, and growth and ageing that play out in *Once Upon a Time* simultaneously muddle age categories while reinforcing narratives about ideal female development that cast the older woman into invisibility, and stereotypically reduce her social value.

Focusing on the programme's overarching storyline, this chapter argues that despite the characters' youthful appearances, they are connected to different generations of women based on their differing ideological associations. As I illustrate, the characters' connection to specific generations of women signifies their value as mothers within the programme. Specifically, I detail how the queen's association with older mothers generates a storyline where emotionally maturing female characters must abandon "older" values (and by extension the older woman) to gain social acceptance within the world of the programme. Centrally, this chapter analyses how the text's representation of time and temporality, and growth and ageing, facilitates a narrative of self-improvement (specifically in relation to motherhood) that entrenches dominant stigmas surrounding ageing/aged women.

Adapting "Snow White"

Adaptations are not simple acts of replication. They are palimpsestuous works that function on the level of discourse—both haunted by and moving from preceding versions (Hutcheon 2006). In this process of adaptation, the interplay between a tale and its medium provides different spaces to engage with and/or reimagine "Snow White," its female characters and the tale's representation of female growth and ageing. When considering television, Hutcheon asserts that television differs from other media, such as film, as it is less compressed. Television's expansive nature accommodates different avenues for "Snow White" and its characters to take shape through multiple episodes and/or series. Additionally, television's complex structures and interweaving of storylines of varying length create further opportunities for adaptation.

As scholars have explained when considering television's structural elements,[1] series and serial programming have been traditionally divided. Series take shape as "never-ending" episodes that can be broadcast in any order—mimicking "an anthology of short stories" (Kozloff 1992, 91). In contrast, serials "follow [...] an unfolding and episodic narrative structure that moves progressively towards a conclusion" over a number of episodes or across a season (Creeber 2004, 8).[2] Despite this distinction, scholars are in agreement that since the 1990s it has become difficult to differentiate between series and serial due to the hybridisation of the structures.[3] This hybridisation is "characterised by both the serial format for the long story arc with open storylines and their combination with [...] shorter more contained plotlines that come to an end within one episode" (Hammond 2005, 76). Although the breakdown of the series/serial divide is now commonplace and familiar to audiences, this hybridisation makes it difficult to use series and serial terminology when analysing structurally dynamic dramas. As such, to clarify this narrative complexity, scholars such as Jason Mittell (2006), Susan Berridge (2010) and Trisha Dunleavy (2009) have associated series' self-contained episode structure with the term "episodic," and overarching storylines with the term "serial." Like many scholars,[4] I view these two structures as interrelated.

The interweaving of episodic and serial storylines facilitates the emergence of complex stories of character development and informs how time and temporality are used and represented within the programme. Specifically, the show's use of flashbacks within an episodic framework enables the programme to engage in temporal jumps that, while only shared with the viewer, link the past with the present and break down chronological time. It is the characters' histories which inform critical events, happenings and relationships in each season. This temporal overlap significantly influences a reading of the characters' growth and development,

[1] Berridge (2010), Creeber (2004), Corner (1999), Holland (1997) and Kozloff (1992).

[2] Dunleavy (2009) has since asserted, and I would agree, that the serial's overarching story has "no prescribed length and can be either 'open' (potentially never-ending) or 'closed' (resolving within a limited number of episodes)" (51), or as I would contend, at the end of a season.

[3] Jowett and Abbott (2013), Berridge (2010), Dunleavy (2009), Mittell (2006), Hammond and Mazdon (2005) and Creeber (2004).

[4] Jowett and Abbott (2013), Dunleavy (2009), Mittell (2006), Hammond and Mazdon (2005) and Creeber (2004).

particularly as the linking of past and present bridges the gap between childhood and adulthood, and draws attention to the complex layering of identity that occurs as character development is explored through non-linear understandings of time, temporality, growth and ageing.

Programme Overview

Once Upon a Time draws on fantasy, romance, adventure and detective genres. Rated 12 and 15 (season one, UK) and 15 (season two, UK), the programme follows the lives of various fairy-tale characters,[5] after Snow White's (Ginnifer Goodwin) evil stepmother, Regina (Lana Parrilla), cast a curse that banished them to a small town in New England, USA called Storybrooke. Under this curse, the characters are separated from their loved ones and have lost their memories (save Regina and Rumpelstiltskin). Although the programme incorporates and adapts just about every fairy-tale character and story, Snow White, the queen and their conflict remain at the heart of the show's first two seasons.

First aired 23 October 2011 (IMDb 2016), the series completed its fifth season in May 2016. This chapter looks at the first two seasons (44 hour-long episodes) as the third, fourth and fifth seasons focus on other stories, such as *The Wizard of Oz, Frozen*, "Sleeping Beauty" and the Arthurian legend. While Snow White and the queen remain as main characters in the third, fourth and fifth seasons, the "Snow White" storyline is no longer the programme's central focus and the women's conflict is largely resolved.

The serial storyline primarily takes place in Storybrooke, with the characters' histories and their fairy-tale stories shown in flashbacks of the fairy world. These flashbacks provide episodic stories that run concurrently with the primary plotline in Storybrooke. The two storylines are played off each other, giving further insight into the characters' identities and relationships. Primarily, the stories reflect a heterosexual, Caucasian, middle-class perspective, with the episodes focusing on the female characters' emotional development as youths, lovers, mothers, wives and women.

[5] Such as Rumpelstiltskin (Robert Carlyle), Cinderella (Jessy Schram) and Belle (Emilie de Ravin) to name a few.

The first season begins when Henry finds and brings his biological mother, Emma, to Storybrooke. Henry, believing that his adoptive mother, Regina, has cursed the town, wants Emma to save the community by breaking the curse. Though Emma doesn't believe Henry, she remains in Storybrooke out of concern for him. The remainder of the season explores the townspeople's relationships; Emma's relationship to Henry; Emma's friendship with Mary Margaret (Snow White); Regina's conflict with Emma and Mary Margaret; and Mary Margaret and David's (Prince Charming) affair. The season progresses with Emma finding clues that suggest Henry's story is true, until she ultimately breaks the curse. The second season, using an open narrative structure, primarily focuses on the community's social upheaval following their release from the curse. It explores Snow White's and the queen's (in)ability to move beyond their history and to emotionally develop as selfless and caring mothers. Unlike the first season, the second season's overarching story is driven by a variety of smaller conflicts, with characters motivated by different goals.

Following a serial structure, *Once Upon a Time*'s overarching story "unfolds in a sequential, usually linear, fashion, with each episode contributing [to] new developments" (Dunleavy 2009, 51). The linear build-up of the overarching story, like a serial programme, slows down time by displaying the mundane elements of daily life (Dunleavy 2009; Creeber 2004). In slowing down time, one might expect the representation of daily life in Storybrooke to naturalise growth and ageing by confining it to a linear progression. The first episode fulfils this expectation by beginning with clear markers of time, such as Emma's 28th birthday, the arrival of her 10-year-old son (who she gave up for adoption) and the starting of chronological time in Storybrooke, which had previously been frozen for 28 years. However, though the first episode is contextualised with chronometric measures, as the Storybrooke community develops, the measures of age become less marked: many characters' ages are unknown, and there is non-linear (magical) movement through age brackets (for example, a man may be transformed back into a boy). Storybrooke moves between measured and magical experiences of time as characters partially participate in chronological progressions of daily life, while continuing their magical engagement with growth/ageing.

The ambiguity of characters' ages and their temporal experiences is emphasised by muddled generational divisions. For example, although Regina is Emma's stepgrandmother, and Mary Margaret is her mother,

Regina, Mary Margaret and Emma are played respectively by actresses aged 34, 33 and 32.[6] While the lack of division is explained by the curse, their relative ages flatten generations, as explored below, working at odds with the serial storyline's focus on daily life and development by unsettling the experiences of character growth associated with specific age categories or groups.

Only Henry (the sole main character born on earth) verbalises the passing of chronometric time by stating his age at 10 in the first season and 11 in the second. Although Henry's growth reinforces the linear movement of the serial storyline, as Henry is neither from the fairy world nor subject to the queen's curse, he does not reflect the Storybrooke community's temporal experience. For example, while Henry questions why none of the adults are aware of how long they have been in Storybrooke, the adults never compare or contextualise Henry's age with their own, or with the children he would assumedly outgrow. Therefore, despite the linear development of the serial storyline and Henry's growth, Henry's embodiment and understanding of chronometric time and temporality simply reveals the Storybrooke community's disconnect from chronometric experiences of time, temporality, growth and ageing.

As the remainder of this article illustrates, because the characters' growth (physical and emotional) is not driven by chronometric measures, the serial's overarching structure and its plotline's attention to characters' daily lives becomes a means to explore the emotional and sociocultural hurdles that characters must continuously overcome as adults. For Mary Margaret and Regina, their social and emotional growth is shaped by their roles as mothers and their ideological alignment with different generations of women.

A Continued Maturation: Motherhood, Ageing and the Serial Storyline

In her consideration of age as an identity category, Kathleen Karlyn notes, "Like gender and race, age is a culturally created identity category that defines us [and] applies to the entire lifespan. [However], just as ideology applies the concept of race only to the nonwhite, age belongs mainly to the old" (2011, 243).

[6] The actresses' ages when the programme first aired.

Whereas age and ageing are applied to the old, growth is associated with the young (see James 2000). Consequently, the adult becomes a fluid figure as its symbolic shape and identity shifts in relation and difference to the categorisation of the young and old. This fluidity allows the adult female figure to obtain a dominant position—her youth offering the promise of reproduction, and her maturity offering motherhood and stability. However, the inevitable biological process of ageing prevents real people from maintaining this position as they transition into middle/old age. This biological reality directly affects the dominant discourses concerning female ageing. As such, the "Images of the young mother [are] at the boundaries of what is acceptable not least because motherhood and sexuality, while inevitably linked, are symbolically incompatible" but because post-motherhood is linked to menopause (Whelehan 2013, 81).

For women, who are seen to decrease in sexual value as they age,[7] the ideal state of adulthood is placed under threat as the ageing body struggles or fails to perform youth. The dominant discourses of adulthood thus present this stage of life as a temporary period of independence, knowledge, maturity and a stabilisation of identity that eventually leads to decline and decay (namely, (post-)menopause/old age) (Whelehan 2013; Karlyn 2011; Driscoll 2002). However, in *Once Upon a Time* the characters' muddled chronometric engagement allows them to sustain their position on this boundary by shifting in relation to and difference from the categorisation of the young and old. As I will illustrate, the adaptation expands "Snow White," and reimagines and reaffirms character roles by refuting the stabilisation of identity associated with adulthood—casting it as a period of continual growth. In so doing, the characters' experiences, trials, relationships and renegotiation of self enable them to evade discourses of decline through their continued association with progression.

Motherhood is one way that characters' continued progression is explored. Whereas previous adaptations represented motherhood through Snow White's relationship with the queen, in *Once Upon a Time* motherhood is primarily explored through Henry's relationship with all three female leads—each character assuming a motherly role as Henry's biological mother (Emma), adoptive mother/stepgreat-grandmother

[7] Jermyn (2014), King (2013), Segal (2013), Whelehan (2013) and Jennings (2012).

(Regina) and biological grandmother/teacher (Mary Margaret)—and secondly through the reunion of daughter and mother (Emma and Mary Margaret). Significantly less time is spent in the serial storyline considering Regina and Mary Margaret's familial ties, with the two actresses presented as peers. In moving away from an exploration of a mother/ daughter rivalry, connecting all three women around the needs of a loved child and framing mothering as fundamental to their development, the programme "participat[es] in the representational trend that posits motherhood as salvation" (Negra 2009, 29).

The framing of motherhood as transformative takes shape through the programme's contrasting representations of "good" and "bad" mothering, and the characters' struggles to become "good" mothers. In the first two seasons, good mothers are depicted as emotionally giving and supportive, while bad mothers are framed as self-serving and self-interested. Unsurprisingly, Regina, as the evil queen, is initially represented as an inadequate mother. Mirroring Tania Modleski's (1997) description of the villainous mother in soaps, Regina puts her needs above Henry's, uses him to manipulate other characters, and even temporarily kills him when attempting to poison Emma ("An Apple Red as Blood," 1.21). Her failure as a mother, aligning her with the queen's aggressive and violent nature in preceding versions of "Snow White," is further marked by Henry's need for therapy and Mary Margaret's insinuation that Regina is not catering to Henry's emotional needs ("Pilot," 1.01).

Though marked as deficient, Regina rationalises her shortcomings with her single mother status, stating:

> You have to understand, ever since I became mayor, balancing things has been tricky. You have a job I assume? [...] Imagine having another one on top of it, that's being a single mom, so I push for order. Am I strict? I suppose, but I do it for his own good. I want Henry to excel in life. I don't think that makes me evil, do you? ("Pilot," 1.01)

Regina's remarks, paired with Henry's unhappiness, aligns her with the single-mother figure who, Amy Benfer (2000) suggests, is seen to "struggle socially; sexually or financially" (paraphrased in Feasey 2012, 73). Though not connected to the financially struggling working mom—as evidenced by her large house, Burberry clothing (Saxton 2013) and high-level position as mayor—Regina's remarks connect her to the socially struggling mother Rebecca Feasey (2012), Kathleen Rowe

Karlyn (2011) and Ritch Calvin (2008) identify in popular culture, as she attempts to negotiate a public and private life. Regina's struggle to exist within both spheres as well as her authoritative and aggressive identity frame her as deficient, but, as I will explain, deficient in so far as she stereotypically embodies a postfeminist depiction of second-wave feminist "values" and "goals," which are presented as "misguided" and "dated."

As Karlyn (2011), Radner and Stringer (2011) and Modleski (1999) note, postfeminism often depicts second-wave feminists as hostile towards or distant from the maternal, while, as Dow (1996) explains, postfeminists romanticise the return to the home and see the immersion of women into the public sphere as ideally accomplished through maternal roles. Regina's role as mayor (specifically, her non-maternal position in the public sphere), and her desire for control, power and authority over Henry and the community disconnects her from the maternal. Further, while Regina is visually aligned with Emma and Mary Margaret in terms of age, she differs from their new-momist approach. As a central justifying ideology in postfeminism (Negra 2009; Douglas and Michaels 2004), new-momism consists of a set of ideals, norms and practices, which—demanding an unachievable standard of perfection from mothers—idealises women's return to the home and the self-sacrificing mother (Karlyn 2011; Douglas and Michaels 2004). Centrally, new-momism "purports to celebrate motherhood, but by making mothers subservient to their children rather than their husbands" (Karlyn 2011, 3). While Mary Margaret and Emma largely conform to new-momism (and by extension postfeminism) by seeking to put their child's needs and desires over their own, Regina does not attempt to put Henry's needs first and alternatively expects Henry to conform to her wants and wishes. As a consequence, Regina's distance from the sacrificing mother and the framing of her character as hostile, positions her as the antithesis to the postfeminist new-momist and contextualises her in relation to a stereotypical postfeminist depiction of second-wave feminists.

Although Regina's parenting might simply be read as an example of "bad" parenting and/or "misplaced" values, as the programme draws parallels between Regina and her mother Cora (Barbara Hershey), *Once Upon a Time* roots Regina's parenting style and ideological associations in her connection to a preceding generation. Regina's parenting, framed as stifling, mirrors her mother Cora's parenting in the fairy world. The connection between the women takes shape through the paralleling of episodic and serial storylines in "We Are Both" (2.02). In a flashback, a young Regina is shown running away from her mother and upcoming union to Snow White's father. Cora stops Regina with bewitched tree branches and denies her the freedom she longs for. Similarly, when Henry tries to run away from Regina, she mimics Cora's behaviour by stopping Henry with bewitched tree branches and imprisoning him in their family home. The paralleling of the two storylines and both scenes' imagery aligns Regina and Cora in terms of parenting style and amoral behaviour. This overlap rationalises Regina's conduct by implying that Regina's "bad" parenting was learned from Cora and shaped by her own abuse in youth—simultaneously depicting Regina as victim and abuser. With Regina's parenting echoing Cora's, the "inadequacies" of her and Cora's parenting are contrasted with Mary Margaret's and Emma's new-momist approach. In so doing, the programme reaffirms the perception that, as motherhood is reimagined and past practices are abandoned, the mothering of previous generations is framed as dated, harmful and insufficient (Feasey 2012; Karlyn 2011; Kaplan 1992).

Interestingly, though Regina is framed as a misguided and parentally dated mother, one might argue that her youthful appearance allows her to evade the visual connection made between the aged/ageing woman and devil woman in preceding and subsequent versions of "Snow White." It would consequently appear that it is a woman's ability to "correctly" parent and reflect contemporary parenting practices and not her wrinkle free skin that determines her "goodness." However, as I will demonstrate, Regina's connection to Cora allows for the continued critique of aged women, perpetuating ideas of the devil woman as crone.

Regina's association with the aged devil woman is made explicit through the visual overlap between Regina and her villainous, post-menopausal mother Cora (played by then 64-year-old Hershey). Throughout the programme, the characters are similarly costumed. Regina's villainous actions and use of magic also mirror Cora's, with both characters ripping their victims' still beating hearts from their chests. Consequently, Regina's excessive control over Henry, the stylisation of her character and her abuse of magic directly connect her to the selfish, violent and manipulative characteristics that Cora displays as a villain, mother and an aged woman. In this way, Regina's youth does not disconnect the evil woman from the figure of the crone; alternatively, the narrative of devil woman as crone persists through Regina's connection and overlap with Cora. Further, *Once Upon a Time* adds depth to the depiction of devil woman as crone by connecting both to the reductive postfeminist depictions of second-wave feminists as hostile, power-hungry and non-maternal. With this in mind, as Regina continues to "develop" as a mother across the first two seasons, questions remain about how her emotional and social "growth," and Emma's and Mary Margaret's contrasting positions, speak to contemporary perceptions of female ageing and the generational tensions often found in postfeminist rhetoric.

Regina's faulty parenting is contrasted with Emma, who seeks to foster a relationship with Henry by indulging his beliefs and spending time with him. When Emma resists Henry's belief in fairy tales, treats him as a possession or lies to protect her own interest, she faces Henry's reproof and is told that she is behaving like Regina ("Manhattan," 2.14). In presenting Emma's failures as a less extreme version of Regina's, the programme distinguishes Regina's parenting as a model for Emma and other "good" mother figures to avoid. Further, when Emma is reproofed for failing to consistently act selflessly, the policing of Emma's conduct denies the legitimacy, acceptability and even inevitability of being a fallible woman and mother—demanding a level of "perfectionism" from the characters that is promulgated in postfeminist celebrations of motherhood (Negra 2009; Douglas and Michaels 2004). Ultimately, Emma's desire to become a giving and supportive mother, and to distance herself from Regina, depicts mothers who unselfishly and wholly dedicate themselves to their child as ideal.

Though Regina's and Emma's parenting styles are easily contrasted because they are both Henry's mothers, Emma's single parenting is not the antithesis to Regina's model. Despite being the youngest mother in terms of generations, Emma struggles to become the unselfish and emotionally available contemporary mother that Henry desires. Alternatively, Mary Margaret embodies the new-momist role. Like Regina, Mary Margaret's mothering mirrors her mother's (Eva; Rena Sofer) parenting style. However, where Cora provides Regina with a "harmful" and "insufficient" example of parenting, Eva embodies a new-momist approach—functioning as the ultimate selfless mother by dying to protect her child's innocence and well-being. Further, Eva's relative youth (marked by Sofer's status as a 44-year-old woman at the time of production) visually disconnects her from the image and stigmatisation of the post-menopausal woman, with her death preventing her from entering old age and seeing her crystallised as the forever-youthful mother. In this way, her relative youth in death and association with new-momist mothering practices aligns her with a contemporary, postfeminist generation.

Following Eva's new-momist example, and with Emma fully grown, Mary Margaret becomes Emma's friend and emotional confidant. Although in popular culture mothers who befriend their daughters are often depicted as incompetent or immature,[8] Mary Margaret's parenting and girlfriend-like bond differs in three ways: first, Mary Margaret and Emma are friends and roommates for 22 episodes before she realises that Emma is her daughter; second, Emma is an adult; and third, Mary Margaret is married to Emma's father when she realises that Emma is her daughter—thus separating her from single motherhood. These differences allow Mary Margaret to emotionally support Emma—resembling contemporary depictions of the nurturing girlfriend-mother figure—without succumbing to the social stigmas connected to single mothers or to the emotional immaturity of other "best friend" mothers on television (for example, Lorelai and Rory Gilmore from *Gilmore Girls* 2000–2007; and Susan and Julie Mayer from *Desperate Housewives* 2004–2012).[9]

Further, in flattening the generational divides, Mary Margaret continues to parent Emma into adulthood—framing mothering as a lifetime commitment and means for character growth—without being visually, and as such ideologically, associated with older mothers. While, inevitably, Mary Margaret's parenting struggles differ from the problems that Regina and Emma face when trying to raise a 10/11 year-old-boy, her parenting, which focuses on her daughter's emotional needs, mirrors Judith Warner's (2006) definition of the contemporary "good" (young) mother of the new millennium. She states, "The new definition of good motherhood was, in the popular imagination, the state of being 'almost always on-duty.' [...] Your love for your child was judged not just by the amount of time you spent with him or her but by the amount of time you spent *doing for* him or her" (116). Similarly, Mary Margaret's life is consumed by what she can do for Emma and how she can develop a supportive relationship with her daughter. As a result, she develops a caring and mature relationship with Emma, reinforcing the value of child/parent bonding, postfeminism and the contemporary "good" mother (new-momist) role.

Mary Margaret's parenting serves to exaggerate the "dysfunctional" nature of Regina's approach. Yet, despite the overt divisions between

---

[8] Feasey (2012), Karlyn (2011), Diffrient and Lavery (2010) and Calvin (2008).

[9] Feasey (2012), Karlyn (2011), Diffrient and Lavery (2010) and Calvin (2008).

the women's parenting and single or married status, the open and long-running structure of the serial storyline provides the space for all three women to develop as mothers, with their attempts at self-improvement signalling and representing their continued emotional growth in adulthood. Though each characters' "success" varies, Regina particularly struggles to change her parenting style. Consequently, in the second season Regina is faced with losing Henry if she does not change ("Broken," 2.01). She struggles to become a "better" mother across nine episodes and in so doing becomes the self-surveilling and self-improving subject commonly found in postfeminism (Fairclough-Isaacs 2014; McRobbie 2009; Gill 2007). For example, in "Lady of the Lake" (2.03) she respects Henry's wishes by keeping her distance, and she steps down from her position as Mayor; in "The Doctor" (2.05) she begins therapy; in "Child of the Moon" (2.07) she cares for Henry after he is burned (taking on a nurturer role); in "Into the Deep" (2.08) she selflessly works with Henry and David to save Mary Margaret and Emma; in "The Cricket Game" (2.10) she joins in community celebrations, demonstrating her domestic skills by bringing a lasagna; and in "And Straight on 'til Morning" (2.22) she becomes the ultimate self-sacrificing figure as she decides to give up her life and power for the needs of Henry and the community.

While the programme's focus on Regina's self-improvement refutes the stabilisation of identity associated with adulthood by casting it as a period of continual growth, it nonetheless links her "development" to her movement away from Cora's "outdated" and "inappropriate" parenting practices towards a (youthful) new-momist approach. Her character change is rewarded across these episodes as she develops a relationship with Henry, reinforcing the division between good (contemporary, emotionally compassionate and giving mothers) and bad (dated, authoritative and selfish mothers) parenting. Her transformation highlights the way postfeminism makes use of generational tensions when reaffirming the notion that "young women [...] can gain social and sexual recognition only by distancing themselves from feminism" (Karlyn 2011, 27). With feminism caricatured and often wilfully misunderstood as "rigid, serious, anti-sex and romance, difficult and extremist" (Negra 2009, 2), postfeminism positions feminism and by extension the older woman (a figure who commonly embodies these caricaturised traits in postfeminist popular culture) as harmful and in need of effacement. In this way, although Regina's character transformation enables the adaptation to branch away from versions that condemn the ageing queen to death, Regina's "emotional growth," confined to a postfeminist rhetoric, serves to devalue an "older" generation of women and "their" ideological values.

In conclusion, the serial storyline critiques past generations of women and "their" social and ideological perspectives. However, the characters' ability to move beyond the "shortcomings" of aged women/"older" ideologies suggests that female characters' "failings" are not a product of physically ageing but occur when characters mistakenly assume "faulty" (read, "dated") values. Although, in a small way, the serial storyline provides the space for female development to be explored in terms of "gains" rather than losses—with the characters undergoing continued character growth in adulthood—ultimately, the programme erases the aged woman by reductively representing her value and contributions. Further, in suggesting that ideal character development can only take place when adult women align themselves with their younger counterparts, the first two seasons reinforce already dominant postfeminist discourses that stigmatise and erase the older woman by encouraging her symbolic and literal death. Thus, while *Once Upon a Time*'s casting flattens generational divides, the women's relative ages simply mask a narrative of devil woman as crone, with the text further entrenching dominant stigmas surrounding ageing/aged women through narratives of motherhood.

Works Cited

Berridge, Susan. 2010. Serialised Sexual Violence in Teen Television Drama Series. PhD dissertation, University of Glasgow.

Calvin, Ritch. 2008. *Gilmore Girls and the Politics of Identity: Essays on Family and Feminism in the Television Series.* North Carolina: McFarland.

Corner, John. 1999. *Critical Ideas in Television Studies.* Oxford: Clarendon Press.

Creeber, Glen. 2004. *Serial Television: Big Drama on the Small Screen.* London, UK: BFI.

Diffrient, David Scott, and David Lavery. 2010. *Screwball Television: Critical Perspectives on Gilmore Girls.* Syracuse: Syracuse University Press.

Douglas, Susan, and Meredith Michaels. 2004. *The Mommy Myth: The Idealization of Motherhood and How it Has Undermined All Women.* New York: Simon and Schuster.

Dow, Bonnie. 1996. *Prime-Time Feminism: Television, Media Culture and the Women's Movement Since 1970.* Philadelphia: University of Pennsylvania Press.

Driscoll, Catherine. 2002. *Girls: Feminine Adolescence in Popular Culture and Cultural Theory.* New York: Columbia University Press.

Dunleavy, Trisha. 2009. *Television Drama: Form, Agency, Innovation*. London: Palgrave Macmillan.

Fairclough-Isaacs, Kirsty. 2014. Mature Meryl and Hot Helen: Hollywood, Gossip and the 'Appropriately' Ageing Actress. In *Ageing, Popular Culture and Contemporary Feminism: Harleys and Hormones*, eds. Imelda Whelehan and Joel Gwynne, 140–155. London: Palgrave Macmillan.

Feasey, Rebecca. 2012. *From Happy Homemaker to Desperate Housewives: Motherhood and Popular Television*. London: Anthem Press.

Gill, Rosalind. 2007. Postfeminist Media Culture: Elements of a Sensibility. *Cultural Studies* 10 (2): 147–166.

Haase, Donald. 2000. Children, War, and the Imaginative Space of Fairy Tales. *The Lion and the Unicorn* 24 (3): 360–377.

Hammond, Michael. 2005. Introduction: The Series/Serial Form. In *The Contemporary Television Series*, ed. Michael Hammond and Lucy Mazdon, 75–82. Edinburgh: Edinburgh University Press.

Hammond, Michael, and Lucy Mazdon (eds.). 2005. *The Contemporary Television Series*. Edinburgh: Edinburgh University Press.

Holland, Patricia. 1997. *The Television Handbook*. London: Routledge.

Hutcheon, Linda. 2006. *A Theory of Adaptation*. New York: Routledge.

IMDb. 2016. Once Upon a Time. http://www.imdb.com/title/tt1843230/?ref_=ttep_ep_tt.

James, Allison. 2000. Embodied Being(s): Understanding the Self and the Body in Childhood. In *The Body, Childhood and Society*, ed. Alan Prout, 19–37. Houndmills: Macmillan.

Jennings, Ros. 2012. It's all Just a Little Bit of History Repeating: Pop Stars, Audiences, Performance and Ageing—Exploring the Performance Strategies of Shirley Bassey and Petula Clark. In *'Rock on': Women, Ageing and Popular Music*, eds. Ros Jennings and Abigail Gardner, 35–52. Surrey: Ashgate.

Jermyn, Deborah. 2014. *Female Celebrity and Ageing: Back in the Spotlight*. London: Routledge.

Jowett, Lorna, and Stacey Abbott. 2013. *TV Horror: Investigating the Dark Side of the Small Screen*. London: I.B. Tauris.

Kaplan, Ann. 1992. *Motherhood and Representation: The Mother in Popular Culture and Melodrama*. London: Routledge.

Karlyn, Kathleen Rowe. 2011. *Unruly Girls, Unrepentant Mothers: Redefining Feminism on Screen*. Austin: University of Texas.

King, Jeannette. 2013. *Discourses of Ageing in Fiction and Feminism: The Invisible Woman*. London: Palgrave.

Kozloff, Sarah. 1992. Narrative Theory and Television. In *Channels of Discourse, Reassembled: Television and Contemporary Criticism*, ed. Robert Allen, 67–100. Chaple Hill: The University of North Carolina Press.

McRobbie, Angela. 2009. *The Aftermath of Feminism: Gender, Culture and Social Change*. Los Angeles: SAGE.

Mittell, Jason. 2006. Narrative Complexity in Contemporary American Television. *The Velvet Light Trap* 58 (1): 29–40.

Modleski, Tania. 1997. The Search for Tomorrow in Today's Soap Operas. In *Feminist Television Criticism: A Reader*, eds. Charlotte Brunsdon, Julia D'Acci and Lynn Spigel, 36–47. Oxford: Clarendon.

Modleski, Tania. 1999. *Old Wives' Tales: Feminist Re-Visions of Film and Other Fictions*. London: I.B. Tauris.

Negra, Diane. 2009. *What a Girl Wants?: Fantasizing the Reclamation of Self in Postfeminism*. London: Routledge.

Once Upon a Time. Produced by Brian Wankum, Kathy Gilroy, Samantha Thomas, Christina Boylan and Robert Hull. Created by Adam Horowitz and Edward Kitsis. 2011–present. United States: ABC. DVD.

Radner, Hilary, and Rebecca Stringer. 2011. *Feminism at the Movies: Understanding Gender in Contemporary Popular Cinema*. London: Routledge.

Saxton, Daphne. 2013. Once Upon a Time—The Style of Storytelling—Best Buy Exclusive. Last Modified Aug 13. https://www.youtube.com/watch?v=4w6Png7SqAM.

Segal, Lynne. 2013. *Out of Time: The Pleasures and the Perils of Ageing*. London: Verso Books.

Warner, Judith. 2006. *Perfect Madness: Motherhood in the Age of Anxiety*. London: Random House.

Whelehan, Imelda. 2013. Ageing Appropriately: Postfeminist Discourses of Ageing in Contemporary Hollywood. In *Postfeminism and Contemporary Hollywood Cinema*, eds. Joel Gwynne and Nadine Muller, 78–95. London: Palgrave Macmillan.

CHAPTER 9

"She Says She's Thirty-Five but She's Really Fifty-One": Rebranding the Middle-Aged Postfeminist Protagonist in Helen Fielding's *Bridget Jones: Mad about The Boy*

Lucinda Rasmussen

Initially, news that British author Helen Fielding would be publishing a sequel to *Bridget Jones's Diary* (1996) and *Bridget Jones: The Edge of Reason* (1999) was greeted with considerable enthusiasm by the author's fanbase.[1] However, many of these same readers were disappointed once they discovered that *Bridget Jones: Mad about The Boy* would not be about the chick-lit protagonist's engagement, new marriage or

[1] Christian Lenz comments that the "eagerly awaited third novel about the famous Singleton was not what readers expected" (2016, 9). Lenz explains that while the sequel's preliminary sales were substantial, "neither fans nor critics seem to like the novel" (2016, 10).

L. Rasmussen (✉)
University of Alberta, Edmonton, Canada
e-mail: lmr4@ualberta.ca

C. McGlynn et al. (eds.), *Ageing Women in Literature and Visual Culture*,
DOI 10.1007/978-3-319-63609-2_9

pregnancies but, rather, about her life as a fifty-one-year-old widowed mother.[2] Indeed, such readers were shocked to discover that Fielding bypasses more than a decade of Bridget's life with Mark Darcy to instead focus on Bridget's decision to begin a romantic relationship with "toy boy" Roxter, a man twenty-one years her junior. Although Bridget and Roxter care deeply for each other, Bridget is ultimately troubled by society's pejorative labelling of her as a "cougar." As a consequence, she succumbs to social pressure to end this relationship and then to begin a romantic partnership with alpha male Mr. Wallaker, the man whom we are to read as an age-appropriate partner for her. Perhaps what is most troubling about this development is that the ageism taking place within the novel also happens in the real world outside the text, where critics direct violent ageist rhetoric at Bridget and, occasionally, at Fielding herself. Consequently, I read Bridget's failed attempts to articulate a forceful feminism that might have been her defence against the ageism she experiences within the text, as an index to what midlife women as postfeminist subjects within western society can experience in the so-called real world as they attempt to exercise their agency.

As this chapter's titular quote[3] spoken by Bridget's five-year-old daughter Mabel suggests, *Mad about The Boy* is about Bridget's anxious experience of growing older in a postfeminist society where mainstream institutions generate rhetoric targeting women's ages in attempts to regulate female conduct. It has been pointed out that ageing women can experience postfeminism as an "intensification" of social pressures to perform femininity in a narrow range of ways (Wearing 2012, 147). Some of the most important work currently being done by theorists who study ways that media and celebrity culture perpetuate ageism focuses on postfeminism and its impacts (see Dolan and Tincknell 2012; Jermyn and Holmes 2015; Whelehan and Gwynne 2014; Whelehan 2013). While postfeminism is a term that has been defined variably in critical conversations, in this chapter its use corresponds to work by cultural critics who

[2]See Dan Evon (2013) for a compilation of reader responses to Fielding's novel titled "Bridget Jones Spoiler: Twitter Furious About Mark Darcy News." The respondents, including one who states that there is no reason to "live in a world where Mark Darcy and Bridget Jones aren't living happily ever after" (purpleclaire, cited in Devon) are distraught by news of Mark Darcy's death. See also Derschowitz (2013).

[3]The original quote in the novel reads: "She says she'th thirty-five but she'th really fifty-one" (Fielding 2013, 4).

regard it as an ideology disseminated through popular media to interfere with forms of feminist expression seeking to bring about gender equality (see McRobbie 2011, 2012; Gill 2007, 2016; Gill and Scharff 2013; Negra 2009; Tasker and Negra 2007). Perhaps no critic has stated this point as forcefully as Angela McRobbie who regards postfeminism as capitalism's "ferocious attack on feminism" (2012). While Rosalind Gill does not "require a static notion of one single authentic feminism" to explore the term (2007, 148), the characteristics she identifies as taking place within a postfeminist media culture are certainly antithetical to feminism as an activist-oriented social movement. For instance, Gill points out how postfeminist media encourages women to subject themselves to rigid forms of self surveillance, always by constructing discourses that remind women of bodily imperfections, and that suggest they are at "risk of 'failing'" (2007, 149). By defining a model of ideal femininity that is impossible to achieve, through physical beauty and dress in particular, the postfeminist media encourages women to conform to what are ultimately conservative gender politics that privilege a heteronormative masculine perspective. As part of this process, women are aggressively hailed as consumers. Postfeminism's deception, however, is to carry out this hailing through a clever subversion of feminism: in postfeminist rhetoric there is a conflation or "entanglement of feminist and antifeminist themes" in which women's compliance with heteropatriarchal rules comes to be understood as them making their own choices freely (Gill 2007, 149). For Tasker and Negra also, feminism is commodified "via the figure of woman as empowered consumer" (2007, 2). The naturalization of an understanding of feminism as a consumer-oriented activity means that women are not encouraged to pursue roles as activists who seek gender equality and social conditions under which all people can thrive.

Discussions about postfeminism have of course been taking place for some time, to situate postfeminism within a particular timeframe while also noting the pressures this ideology places on girls and those who are young. McRobbie's work on postfeminism, for instance, has focussed on the time between 1997 and 2007 when "a sharp disidentification with feminism on the part of young women" can be identified (2012). Her argument is predicated on the assumption that hegemonic forces will be able to encourage young women to associate militant feminism with "old and unglamorous women" (2011, 180). McRobbie does not explicitly discuss ageism in her critique; yet, her concern for young women and claims that postfeminism will polarize women on the basis of age is a recurrent theme in her analysis. This suggests that as young women from the postfeminist decade grow older, their bodies will become particularly fraught sites of ideological struggle. For this reason, Gill contends that future studies of postfeminism focussing on "*intersectional terms*" such as age are particularly needed (2016, 620). The figure of Bridget and the reception of *Mad about The Boy* can, in fact, alert us to the validity of this assertion. One way to explore postfeminism in the contemporary moment is to ask how those subjects who flourished during the postfeminist decade identified by McRobbie are now experiencing that ideology years later. This question—of how years of exposure to postfeminist discourses can impact women in midlife—is central to discussions about ways that postfeminism is continuing to impede feminism.

Chick lit, a genre of romantic fiction associated with postfeminism, provides an opportunity to contemplate the long-term effects and resilience of postfeminist ideology. Indeed, *Bridget Jones's Diary* and *Bridget Jones: The Edge of Reason* are considered two of the genre's foundational texts.[4] As romantic novels about a white, educated, middle-class heterosexual woman, the Bridget novels all include the characteristics of what Margaret O'Neill describes as "dominant" chick lit (2015, 59). In such novels, privileged women work through problems such as overeating and, most importantly, finding the right man. Of course, some chick-lit novels do also probe matters related to race and class, and, as a result, debates have taken place over whether or not chick lit has the capacity to work as social commentary, with some arguing that chick-lit authors are well positioned to adapt the genre's conventions—or to morph it into new sub-genres—to create protagonists who speak from positions of marginality to challenge various forms of oppression.[5] This speculation suggests that Fielding should be able to transition the once youthful Bridget into a mature, self-determining protagonist whom her former fanbase will readily accept. As I will discuss in due course, although Fielding allows Bridget to grow older and gives the protagonist some latitude to speak from a position of marginality as an ageing woman, she does not transform the genre to challenge the status quo because,

[4] See Ferriss and Young (2006, 1–13) for a comprehensive introduction to chick lit, its relationship to postfeminism and the critical debates surrounding the genre.

[5] See O'Neill (2015), Butler and Desai (2008) as well as Ferris and Young (2006), who discuss the emergence of Black chick lit and Latinalit (2006, 8).

in *Mad about The Boy*, Bridget is affirmed for making an enormous sacrifice based on how she believes mainstream society expects a middle-aged woman to behave. Although Bridget seems, by the end of the novel, to have made the choice to reject postfeminist media culture's more superficial aspects such as the importance of hiding wrinkles through botox, she does so by retreating with her new romantic partner Mr. Wallaker to a "big old messy house near Hampstead Heath" (Fielding 2013, 386).

I would argue that *Mad about The Boy* provides an opportunity to consider ways in which the now more mature protagonist of postfeminist fiction continues to be influenced, and often silenced, by postfeminist ideology. In *Declining to Decline*, Margaret Morganroth Gullette credits feminism with the emergence of several progressive midlife heroines in fiction, as she expresses optimism over the emergence of the "female midlife progress novel" (1997, 78). While Gullette could not, at the time, have fully appreciated postfeminism's interference in the literary marketplace and, by extension, the dissemination of feminist texts, she did anticipate resistance when cautioning feminist writers that "the temptation for mainstream representation will be to portray midlife women (and men) as emotionally weak, intellectually mediocre, morally inadequate, repeatedly failing in the workforce, unlucky in love—declining" (1997, 92). As the protagonist of mainstream chick lit, the middle-aged Bridget ends up embodying most of these unfortunate qualities. While Bridget is frustrated by the way ageing women are treated, her frustration does not challenge the objectification of mature women. Since Fielding's novel does not become the bold articulation of midlife that Gullette craves—one where the heroine "editorializes more explicitly about midlife ageism" to produce social change (1997, 96)—it is thus important to consider systemic reasons for and conditions under which Bridget's attempts to fight against ageism fail to gain any real momentum.

Reviews of *Mad about The Boy*, while not unanimously negative, nonetheless provide several striking examples of how ageist rhetoric has been naturalized within contemporary postfeminist media culture. In her analysis of *Bridget Jones's Diary*, Anthea Taylor analyses the novel's paratexts to locate discriminatory attitudes directed at young single women (2012, 96–98). Certainly Bridget has always had detractors; however, in *Mad about The Boy*, she enters a discursive terrain far more hostile than any she has experienced before. For example, Maureen Corrigan (2013) begins her review of *Mad about The Boy* with the observation that "dizzy dames don't age well." Corrigan, a former fan, believes that Bridget used to be "an attractive young thing doing prat falls." Somewhat crassly, she now regards the fifty-one-year-old Bridget as "spell[ing] hip replacement" (2013). Commentaries with titles such as "Bridget in Middle Age: We're Not So 'Mad About' This Girl" (Wolitzer 2013), "Bridget Jones: Wanton Cougar, Calorie Counter, Widowed Mother of Two" (Newman 2013) and even "Helen Fielding On Bridget Jones: Still Looking Good at 51" (Martin 2013) all signal that Bridget's age is a problem, and do so in condescending or hostile ways.

As noted, some of the frustration that is directed at *Mad about The Boy* relates to Fielding's decision to kill off Mark Darcy. Readers were disappointed by this development, as were moviegoers who, over the course of two film adaptations, grew to love actor Colin Firth in the role. Despite Fielding's reasons for choosing to write Darcy out of her third novel, she perhaps failed to anticipate her fans' investment in the leading male character.[6] However, the upset over Mark's death does not fully account for *Mad about The Boy*'s mixed reception. Sarah Richards' remark that "The real disappointment isn't that Darcy is dead [...] but that Bridget Jones hasn't grown up" is typical of many reviewers who repeat the charge that the middle-aged Bridget ought to behave differently than she did when she was young (2013).[7] Elsewhere, the frustration that Heddus Blackwell articulates over the classism in *Mad about The Boy* materializes as an ageist slur when she writes: "The thirty something Bridget was imperfect, insecure and loveable; the 51 year old Bridget is just a silly mare" (2013). Even Wolitzer, who does commend Fielding for representing Bridget in middle age, still claims that this older Bridget is less appealing than the "classic Bridget" who is originally depicted in her thirties (2013). Readers seeking weightier representations of ageing women are certainly not wrong to point out their frustrations with this character. Nonetheless, criticisms of Bridget at fifty-one are uttered in such ways as to starkly confirm postfeminist culture's tendency to resort to ageist discourse as a means to discipline women.

---

[6] Fielding wanted to write Bridget as a middle-aged, single mother and thus chose to have Mark Darcy die, as she felt that it would be out of character for him to leave Bridget (qtd. in Carter 2013).

[7] For additional examples, see Lanzito (2013) and Crompton (2013).

To summarize, Bridget's loss of popularity is interpreted as an outcome of a postfeminist hegemony that has worked, and continues to work, to separate women from feminism. Regarded by many critics as a quintessential representation of a postfeminist woman, the first two Bridget novels have functioned as touchstones in many critical conversations about how postfeminism manifests itself in culture and women's lives (cf. Taylor 2012; McRobbie 2011, 2012; Gill and Scharff 2013; Negra 2009). Diane Negra observes that postfeminism perpetuates "time panic" and that once a young woman reaches middle age, the media only really affords her a narrow range of sanctioned identities (2009, 47). The comments about *Mad about The Boy* previously cited confirm the validity of her claim. In addition, it is interesting that the motion picture industry did not, as was the case with the earlier Bridget novels, move quickly to adapt *Mad about The Boy* as a film. Rather, an attempt appears to have been made to sate the postfeminist culture's desire for Bridget's courtship and pregnancy story with the film *Bridget Jones's Baby* (2016), a complicated move on the part of filmmakers, as Renée Zellweger, the actress who plays Bridget in the films, and Colin Firth, who plays Mark Darcy, are respectively near or older than fifty themselves. It may, of course, be the case that *Mad about The Boy* will still become a film. While a full discussion of *Bridget Jones's Baby* and the many complex dynamics it raises in discussions of ageing and postfeminism is beyond the scope of this chapter, it must be noted that the film, which begins by showing its audience that Bridget is single and alone at forty-three, is much preoccupied with biological clocks and with telling a story that ultimately is about women who are younger than fifty.[8]

To Fielding's credit, her decision to depict Bridget as a fifty-one-year-old widow was a defiance of genre norms. Imelda Whelehan has commented on the scarcity of mum-lit narratives featuring women over fifty, asking whether Bridget's failure to grow up in *Mad about The Boy* "prove[s] cause for reflection on whether romance narratives can express mature

[8]The film *Bridget Jones's Baby* (2016) is not to be confused with Fielding's novel *Bridget Jones's Baby: The Diaries*, also published in 2016. While both texts are about a younger Bridget's pregnancy, and both involve a love triangle, the novel includes the character of Daniel Cleaver. Daniel Cleaver (Hugh Grant) does not appear in the movie adaptation. The confusing chronology of these texts has caused one commentator to remark on the "monetisation" of the Bridget Jones brand (Williams 2016). Further exploration of Bridget Jones as a franchise would be productive.

themes?" (2014, 42). Through her observations of the literary market's complex politics of inclusion and exclusion, Whelehan prompts critics to notice how the postfeminist media culture influences the public to recognize which women are and are not worthy of attention. As genre scholar John Frow explains:

> Genre [...] is a shared convention with a social force. The imputations or guesses that we make about the appropriate and relevant conventions to apply in a particular case will structure our reading, guiding the course it will take, our expectations of what it will encounter. But they are grounded in institutions in which genre has its social being. (2015, 112)

Frow's statement helps to show why disappointment in Bridget is rooted in ideological expectations regarding who she is allowed to be as an ageing chick-lit protagonist. Crucially, prior to *Mad about The Boy,* Bridget already exists in the public's imagination as a chick-lit heroine, with chick lit understood as a postfeminist commodity (cf. Gill and Herdieckerhoff 2006, 489). The argument is that the backlash against Bridget when she re-enters the literary marketplace as an older chick happens because she, as a prior and extraordinarily successful representation of young postfeminist womanhood, functions as a brand. According to feminist journalist and social commentator Andi Zeisler, who argues that feminism itself is currently being marketed as a brand, "Branding [is] the series of stories, images, and vocabularies associated with a company and its products" (2016, 71). While Fielding could be read as transitioning her chick-lit heroine into hen or mommy lit—derivatives of chick lit which some commenters believe answer a demand for more mature themes (cf. Reid 2002; Cooke 2002)—the challenge that Fielding faces in having her readership accept an older Bridget prove considerable. Frow has argued that framing plays a key role in how genre is understood and that paratexts, for instance, form the "anticipatory structure [...] based on the cues we receive when we first encounter a text" (2015, 113). As a postfeminist commodity, Bridget has been extensively framed as a youthful subject; take, for instance, the semiotics associated with media coverage of *Mad about The Boy,* which frequently included images of a young Renée Zellweger. In short, as "a constructed point of identification" within postfeminist media culture (Gill and Herdieckerhoff 2006, 489), Bridget is a youthful brand, and a specific site of ideological struggle when she crosses the threshold to middle age. Indeed, Zellweger has been the subject of hostile commentary on changes to her appearance as she has aged. For example, the IMDb movie database message board contains at least one post by a viewer who suggests that *Bridget Jones's Baby* will be problematic because, given her age and too much plastic surgery, "Renée Zellweger no longer looks like Renée Zellweger" (ScienceGuy 2015).

What the mixed reception to *Mad about The Boy* suggests is that an older Bridget is no longer considered a suitable chick-lit protagonist. On the surface, this observation seems extraordinary: while it is true that in this novel Bridget lacks self-discipline, that she consequently still subjects herself to rigid policing of the self, and that she is still obsessive when it comes to her relationships, it is also the case that Bridget is simply behaving as she has always done. Given that Fielding is routinely credited as having established chick lit as a genre, one would suppose that she would have the freedom to reshape its conventions to accommodate an older protagonist. Yet when Bridget is contextualised in criticisms of postfeminism, her difficulties are predictable. The "new sexual contract" which McRobbie describes as granting young postfeminist women some limited freedom without inviting their "active *political* participation" comes with an expiration date (2011, 182). While midlife Bridget articulates desire and has satisfying sex with Roxter and later with Mr. Wallaker, she also discovers that as a fifty-one-year old, the postfeminist sexual contract's benefits are much more difficult to claim. In effect, both inside and outside the novel, Bridget is shamed for her attempts to claim the empowerment that the sexual contract promised her as a young woman, and these same forces encourage her to recede at a point in life when experience and economic security would allow her to be most powerful.

This refusal to take Bridget seriously happens inside and outside the novel, and is interpreted here as an outcome of postfeminist ideology's interference in feminism. Of key significance is the manner in which Bridget's internalization of a postfeminist sensibility manifests as her misunderstanding of what feminism can do as a productive social movement. Several anecdotes in *Mad about The Boy* reveal Bridget's participation in what McRobbie describes as the subtle but relentless repudiation of feminism (2011, 2012). For instance, when Bridget's former lover Daniel Cleaver compliments her appearance and asks if a "fuck would be out of the question," Bridget is "outraged as a feminist [...] but uplifted as a female" (Fielding 2013, 77). Elsewhere, she regards her friend Shazzer with a mixture of admiration and disdain for her tendency to "rant feministically" (Fielding 2013, 13), and regards feminist icon Germaine Greer's "'Invisible Woman'" as irrelevant to her situation as a contemporary woman (Fielding 2013, 152, sic).

Bridget's inability to conceive of feminism as a way to achieve gender equality can also be contextualized in more recent conversations about feminism in the marketplace. Zeisler (2016) explains that the backlash narrative has, in recent years, shifted to accommodate the rise of the individual woman who embodies a watered-down feminism as a personal brand. Fashion and lifestyle conglomerates have continued to co-opt feminism with campaigns suggesting that feminism has a "branding problem" (Zeisler 2016, 72; Thornham 2013, 33; Gill 2016, 618), but one that can be solved through carefully managed, and strategic forms of consumption. Zeisler explains how, for instance, a company markets a particular style of woman's underpants with the word feminist stitched across the bottom (2016, 59). How this sort of scenario can play out for the ageing woman is demonstrated in *Mad about The Boy* where Bridget's friend Talitha—an attractive and avid participant in beauty culture and a sixty-year-old television personality—educates Bridget on how to "rebrand," by altering the "signposts" of ageing through the consumption of beauty products like botox and hair extensions (Fielding 2013, 33).

Bridget's understanding of feminism as a brand also impacts her professional life, and it is here that Fielding seems to point to the difficulties faced by a woman who attempts to do feminist work in the public sphere. Bridget's work to write a screenplay based on *Hedda Gabler* constitutes her attempt to articulate "feminist, pre- and anti-feminist themes" (Fielding 2013, 17). Yet, her efforts to write something which has feminist aspects to it is interrupted by hegemonic marketplace forces: in *Mad about The Boy,* Bridget's production team prefers she write a rom-com as opposed to a more dramatic storyline (cf. Fielding 2013, 211), and when Bridget attempts to convince them that her screenplay is meant to be read as a serious feminist text, her laptop—sabotaged by her five-year-old daughter—opens to "the pink and lilac home page of Princess Bride Dress Up" (Fielding 2013, 221).

The fact that Bridget grows frustrated when her feminism is hijacked suggests that Fielding might be critiquing the capitalist media. According to Frow, a text's author can "strengthen the cues by which it signals its strategic intentions, and it may do so by an internal 'modeling' of its own generic structure and of the ways in which it intends that structure to apply" (2015, 133). He adds that an author can guide readers to interpret a work in a particular way by embedding within it a second genre as a form of metacommunication on the meaning of the host text (cf. 2015, 124). The most explicit example of this sort is Fielding's incorporation of a newspaper editorial titled "The Tragic Fate of the Toy Boy," a disparaging piece which demoralizes Bridget by admonishing the cougar who preys on "young, defenseless boys" (2013, 258). Ironically, the fictitious article does not differ from real-world reviews of *Mad about The Boy*. Perhaps the strongest hint that Fielding is critiquing ageism in the media is her decision to name the novel's fictitious journalist Ellen Boschup, a name that bears a striking resemblance to that of Alison Boshoff, a real-life commentator who wrote an insensitive article about Fielding: in it Boshoff comments on Fielding's pregnancy while "pushing 50" and further describes the author as "prickly" when asked during an interview to disclose whether her child was conceived using fertility therapy (2006). Given Fielding's own experiences with the intrusive ageist media, it is reasonable to suppose that she might retaliate through her protagonist: in Bridget's words: "Don't these [media commentators] realize what harm they cause with their glib social generalizations?" (Fielding 2013, 260). Fielding has certainly stated that she wanted to show that a woman in midlife should not suddenly find herself subjected to an "outdated notion of a 'woman of a certain age'" (qtd. in Martin 2013).

However, although Fielding does call attention to the media's objectification of midlife women, it is also the case that Bridget's feminist critique is always muted. For instance, Bridget's work on a screenplay that is at least partially feminist is compromised when she misspells Gabler as Gabbler and when she also attributes her source material incorrectly to Chekhov as opposed to Ibsen (Fielding 2013, 284). While Bridget tries to pass these lapses off as "anti-intellectualist irony," such blunders cause her to lose credibility with her production crew (Fielding 2013, 284), while also confirming that she has not done the work required of her to understand feminism as a social movement with emancipatory powers. However, if this problem is understood from a systemic standpoint, we might consider how Bridget, who seeks an identity through popular culture and who by the third novel is a well-established subject of postfeminism, has become part of a cultural moment remarkably void of images of actual feminist activism as it is taking place (cf. Gill 2016, 616). Importantly, it has been pointed out that women who belong to

Bridget's generation "come to feminism, not, like earlier generations, through personal experience or involvement in social activism" but via popular culture (Thornham 2013, 45). Consequently, as a postfeminist subject, Bridget's feminism is of the sort Gill considers "feminism-weightless" (2016, 618).

What does a weightless feminism cost Bridget? Depending on how one interprets *Mad about The Boy*, it can be argued that Bridget loses a meaningful relationship due to ageist discourse that polices what women do. When Bridget's young lover Roxter tells Bridget that he wants a permanent relationship, and offers to become a stepfather to Bridget's children, Bridget declines. Curiously, her decision is based partially on what she sees happening in popular culture with "Judi Dench [and] Daniel Craig at the end of *Skyfall*" (Fielding 2013, 333). Bridget wishes that the moviemakers, instead of killing Dench's character, would have "done a beautifully lit sex scene" featuring the older actress and the younger Craig—"Now there," muses Bridget, "would be a rebranding feminist" (Fielding 2013, 334). Still, what Bridget ultimately accepts is that even powerful older women have limited representational possibilities open to them. The protagonist's insight is her realization that postfeminism's promises of empowerment are false. Although Bridget notes some positive representations of ageing celebrity women in the media, she is also aware of postfeminist media's contradictory messages, as apparent when she imagines herself unflatteringly as a "hung-over Joan Crawford figure" (Fielding 2013, 84), or when she refers to herself as a "failed cougar" (Fielding 2013, 299). Bridget's tendency to measure herself against ageist stereotypes originates from her awareness that midlife progress narratives, at least those in popular culture, are countered just as often by what critic Sadie Wearing refers to as the ageing "female grotesque" (2012, 149–150).

Mad about The Boy begins the Bridget-Roxter break-up as a critique of postfeminist media culture for its cruel treatment of ageing women, but when Bridget concludes that the relationship must end so that she does not "ruin Roxter's life" (Fielding 2013, 333), the moment's critical force is lost. Had *Mad about The Boy* ended with Roxter and Bridget as a couple who attempt to build a serious relationship, it would have legitimized a romantic union that, while still heteronormative, would have opened up a new space of legibility for the midlife woman—perhaps by showing that the so-called cougar's interest in a younger partner could come from a place of genuine caring and reciprocity as opposed to exploitation.

But as Cecily Devereux has shown, drawing on the work of Lee Edelman, the chick-lit protagonist's central role is to shore up "reproductive futurism" (2013, 222): this outcome is precisely what Bridget does by setting aside her own desires so that Roxter can become a *biological* father who can pass his name to his children (Fielding 2013, 333). Here Bridget secures reproductive certainty for Roxter by freeing him for a younger partner, and she does so despite the fact that she and Roxter care deeply for one another and are on many levels compatible. Had Bridget ended the relationship because she clearly no longer wished to participate in the self-perfecting rituals which postfeminist culture imposes on the "cougar" as part of its social arrangement with women who are involved with younger partners (Gwynne 2014, 48; Hinchliff 2014, 68), we might also have had a feminist critique. Instead, Bridget is shown to have internalized an undeniably postfeminist understanding of what it means to grow older, and even to have perpetuated such ageist beliefs with her own use of language that diminishes old age.

With Roxter's departure, Bridget finds romance with Mr. Wallaker. In addition to being an age-appropriate match for Bridget, the ultra-masculine Wallaker is a former agent with the "Special Air Service" who reminds Bridget of James Bond (Fielding 2013, 345) and whom Bridget refers to as "masterful" (Fielding 2013, 379) and "looking like he was on an assault course" (Fielding 2013, 139). Significantly, Wallaker's hyper-masculine persona affords him a degree of superiority as evidenced when he often regards Bridget with a "slight twitch of amusement" (Fielding 2013, 156) and when he gives her unsolicited advice on how to raise her children (cf. Fielding 2013, 5). He is confrontational with another father on the playground (cf. Fielding 2013, 362–368), and he is the physical aggressor when he attempts to force a kiss on Bridget during a school picnic (cf. Fielding 2013, 344). Wallaker's behaviour is unsettling for the way it returns Bridget to what Gill and Herdieckerhoff refer to, as they draw on criticism by Ann Snitow, as the "'hard' romances such as [...] Mills and Boon" (2006, 490). In such narratives, male heroes are rewarded for what is ultimately their "mocking, cynical, contemptuous" behaviours toward the women they desire (Gill and Herdieckerhoff 2006, 490). This observation matters in the context of critical discussions about postfeminism and chick lit where it was hoped that the genre would transform such restrictive paradigms. What makes this plot development particularly troublesome is that Bridget's deference to such a man becomes her way of escaping the often contradictory demands that postfeminist media culture places on women. It has been noted that in *Bridget Jones's Diary* Mark Darcy rescues Bridget, thereby emphasizing a "superior white masculinity" (Gill and Herdieckerhoff 2006, 495). Of course, in *Mad about The Boy* Mr. Wallaker is also Bridget's rescuer: he is the one who tells Bridget that she is attractive without botox, and he also reassures her that she can still accept help from him without relinquishing her status as "a top professional feminist" (Fielding 2013, 366).

To close, I would argue that Bridget's return to a hard romance marks her disavowal of the conditions under which she has been called to exist as an ageing subject of postfeminism. As a woman who comes of age during the postfeminist decade and who is its loyal subject, Bridget has learned how to rebrand so as not to be regarded as "non-viable, post-menopausal sitcom fodder" (Fielding 2013, 152). However, within the world of the novel, she has been reminded—and as critics we have also been reminded through an exploration of the social commentary surrounding the novel's reception—that the power Bridget possessed as a young woman was tenuous and, as McRobbie predicted, an illusion (2011, 2012). Under postfeminism, "patriarchal power" is said to be strategically given over to the fashion and beauty industries which devise means of encouraging women to present themselves as particular kinds of subjects (McRobbie 2011, 183). Ironically, Bridget's union with Wallaker upholds the patriarchy through its implicit endorsement of conservative gender politics. Bridget's choice to unite with Wallaker, while seeming to be a way for her to reject consumer-driven anti-ageing gimmicks perpetuated through fashion, beauty and celebrity industries, is nonetheless her fulfilment of postfeminism's terms.

Clearly, as Bridget Jones ages, she finds it increasingly difficult to navigate a postfeminist landscape. While feminism might have been her defence against the ageism she experiences, as a woman of postfeminism Bridget is unable to articulate a feminist position with substance. Many commentators outside the text also mirror this confusion. Critical feminist interventions undertaken by literary and cultural critics may in fact be the only way to address what Gullette regards as the inevitable "mental difficulty" that consumers of narratives about midlife women seem destined to experience (2000, xviii). Her point is that readers are socialized to be uncomfortable over ageing: in postfeminist culture especially, ageist rhetoric has been naturalized, as social commentary about Bridget Jones demonstrates. As women grow older, their calendar age is used to discredit them, and those who are long-term postfeminist subjects have little experience with an activist-oriented feminism to address this problem. It will be interesting to observe, should there be any subsequent novels about Bridget Jones after the age of fifty, how the heroine may further develop her feminist outlook. In the meantime, feminist scholars must continue to study the complex network of ageist rhetoric that pervades postfeminist genres and media forms.

Works Cited

Blackwell, Heddus. 2013. Review of *Bridget Jones: Mad about The Boy*, by Helen Fielding. *Goodreads*, Dec 4, Mad about The Boy (Bridget Jones #3). Accessed 15 June 2016. http://www.goodreads.com/book/show/17262155-mad-about-the-boy.html.

Boshoff, Alison. 2006. Is Helen Fielding About to Bump Off Bridget Jones? *MailOnline*, June 1. Accessed 20 June 2016. http://www.dailymail.co.uk/femail/article-388553/Is-Helen-Fielding-bump-Bridget-Jones.html.

Bridget Jones's Baby. 2016. Directed by Sharon Maguire. Mirimax. Released Sept 16.

Butler, Pamela, and Jigna Desai. 2008. Manolos, Marriage, and Mantras: Chick-Lit Criticism and Transnational Feminism. *Meridians: Feminism, Race, Transnationalism* 8 (2): 1–31.

Carter, Claire. 2013. Helen Fielding: Mark Darcy Had to Die so Bridget Could Be a Single Mother. *The Telegraph*, Oct 10, Accessed 15 June 2016. http://www.telegraph.co.uk/culture/books/10369815/Helen-Fielding-Mark-Darcy-had-to-die-so-Bridget-could-be-single-mother.html.

Cooke, Rachel. 2002. Now For…Hen Lit. (Book). *New Statesman* 131 (4574): 52.

Corrigan, Maureen. 2013. If You're Looking to Read 'Lady Things,' Choose Jezebel Over Jones. Review of *Bridget Jones: Mad about The Boy*, by Helen Fielding. *npr books*, Oct 21, Book Reviews. Accessed 10 June 2016. http://www.npr.org/2013/10/21/235414762/if-youre-looking-toread-lady-things-choose-jezebel-over-jones.

Crompton, Sarah. 2013. Bridget Jones: Mad about The Boy Review: 'A Clunking Disappointment.' Review of *Bridget Jones: Mad About The Boy*, by Helen Fielding. *The Telegraph*, Oct 7, Book Reviews. Accessed 10 June 2016. http://www.telegraph.co.uk/culture/books/bookreviews/10358920/Bridget-Jones-Mad-About-the-Boy-review-A-Clunking-disappointment.html.

Derschowitz, Jessica. 2013. 'Bridget Jones' Sequel Shocks Fans with Darcy's Fate. *CBS News*, Oct 3. Accessed 5 June 2016. http://www.cbsnews.com/news/bridget-jones-sequel-shocks-fans-with-darcys-fate/.html.

Devereux, Cecily. 2013. 'Chosen Representatives in the Field of Shagging': Bridget Jones, Britishness, and Reproductive Futurism. *Genre* 46 (3): 213–237.

Dolan, Josephine, and Estella Tincknell. 2012. Introduction. In *Aging Femininities: Troubling Representations*, ed. Josephine Dolan and Estella Tincknell, vii–xxi. Newcastle: Cambridge.

Evon, Dan. 2013. Bridget Jones Spoiler: Twitter Furious About Mark Darcy News. *SocialNewsDaily,* Sept 30. Accessed 17 Jan 2017. http://socialnews-daily.com/17345/bridget-jones-spoiler-twitter-furious-mark-darcy-news/.

Ferriss, Suzanne, and Mallory Young. 2006. Introduction. In *Chick Lit: The New Woman's Fiction*, ed. Suzanne Ferriss and Mallory Young, 1–13. New York: Routledge.

Fielding, Helen. 1996. *Bridget Jones's Diary*. London: Picador.

Fielding, Helen. 1999. *Bridget Jones: The Edge of Reason*. New York: Penguin.

Fielding, Helen. 2013. *Bridget Jones: Mad About The Boy*. Toronto: Knopf Canada.

Fielding, Helen. 2016. *Bridget Jones's Baby: The Diaries*. Toronto: Knopf Canada.

Frow, John. 2015. *Genre: The New Critical Idiom*. New York: Routledge.

Gill, Rosalind, and Elena Herdieckerhoff. 2006. Rewriting the Romance: New Femininities in Chick Lit? *Feminist Media Studies* 6(4): 487–504. doi:10.1080/14680770600989947.

Gill, Rosalind. 2007. Postfeminist Media Culture: Elements of a Sensibility. *European Journal of Cultural Studies* 10 (2): 147–166. doi:10.1177/1367549407075898.

Gill, Rosalind. 2016. Post-postfeminism?: New Feminist Visibilities in Postfeminist Times. *Feminist Media Studies* 16 (4): 610–630. doi:10.1080/14680777.2016.1193293.

Gill, Rosalind, and Christina Scharff. 2013. Introduction. In *New Femininities: Postfeminism, Neoliberalism, and Subjectivity*, eds. Rosalind Gill and Christina Scharff, 1–17. New York: Palgrave Macmillan.

Gullette, Margaret Morganroth. 1997. *Declining to Decline: Cultural Combat and the Politics of the Midlife*. Charlottesville: University Press of Virginia.

Gullette, Margaret Morganroth. 2000. *Safe at Last in the Middle Years: The Invention of the Midlife Progress Novel*. Lincoln: iUniverse.com.

Gwynne, Joel. 2014. 'Mrs. Robinson Seeks Benjamin': Cougars, Popular Memoirs and the Quest for Fulfillment in Midlife and Beyond. In *Ageing, Popular Culture and Contemporary Feminism: Harleys and Hormones,* eds. Imelda Whelehan and Joel Gwynne, 47–62. New York: Palgrave Macmillan.

Hinchliff, Sharron. 2014. Sexing Up the Midlife Woman: Cultural Representations of Ageing, Femininity and the Sexy Body. In *Ageing, Popular Culture and Contemporary Feminism: Harleys and Hormones*, 63–77. New York: Palgrave Macmillan.

Jermyn, Deborah, and Su Holmes. 2015. Introduction: A Timely Intervention - Unravelling the Gender/Age/Celebrity Matrix. In *Women, Celebrity and Cultures of Ageing: Freeze Frame,* ed. Deborah Jermyn and Su Holmes, 1–10. New York: Palgrave Macmillan.

Lanzito, Christina. 2013. Bridget Jones is 51: Older, But Any Wiser? Review of *Bridget Jones: Mad about The Boy,* by Helen Fielding. *AARP,* Oct 14, Entertainment. Accessed 10 June 2016. http://blog.aarp.org/2013/10/14/bridget-jones-is-51-older-but-any-wiser/.

Lenz, Christian. 2016. *Geographies of Love: The Cultural Space of Romance in Chick- and Ladlit.* Bielefeld: Transcript.

Martin, Rachel. 2013. Helen Fielding on Bridget Jones: Still Looking Good at 51. Interview with Helen Fielding. *npr books,* Oct 20, Weekend Edition Sunday. Accessed 12 June 2016. http://www.npr.org/2013/10/20/237075402/helen-fielding-on-bridget-jones-still-looking-good-at-51.

McRobbie, Angela. 2011. Beyond Post-Feminism. *Public Policy Research* 18 (3): 179–184.

McRobbie, Angela. 2012. Angela McRobbie: Post-Feminism + Beyond. *YouTube,* June 24. Accessed 29 June 2016. https://www.youtube.com/watch?v=Wk-QIXlx2wk.

Negra, Diane. 2009. *What a Girl Wants? Fantasizing the Reclamation of Self in Postfeminism.* New York: Routledge.

Newman, Brucella. 2013. Bridget Jones: Wanton Cougar, Calorie Counter, Widowed Mother of Two. Review of *Bridget Jones: Mad about The Boy,* by Helen Fielding. *The Guardian,* Sept 30. Accessed 20 June 2016. http://guardianlv.com/2013/09/bridget-jones-wanton-cougar-calorie-counter-widowed-mother-of-two/.

O'Neill, Margaret. 2015. You Can Still Have It All, But Just in Moderation: Neoliberal Gender and the Post-Celtic Tiger 'Recession Lit.' *Assuming Gender* 5 (1): 59–83.

Reid, Carmen. 2002. Here's One for my Baby. *The Sunday Times,* Sept 6.

Richards, Sarah Elizabeth. 2013. Middle-Aged Women Feel Cheated by Bridget Jones. Review of *Bridget Jones: Mad about The Boy,* by Helen Fielding. *Time.* Oct 17, Books. Accessed 1 June 2016. http://ideas.time.com/2013/10/17/women-feel-cheated-by-bridget-jones/.

ScienceGuy. 2015. Problem: Renée Zellweger No Longer Looks Like Renée Zellweger. *IMDb Message Board,* Sept 10. Accessed 16 June 2016. http://www.imdb.com/title/tt1473832/board/nest/248178896?ref_=tt_bd_1.

Tasker, Yvonne, and Diane Negra, eds. 2007. *Interrogating Postfeminism: Gender and the Politics of Popular Culture.* Texas: Duke University.

Taylor, Anthea. 2012. *Single Women in Popular Culture: The Limits of Postfeminism.* New York: Palgrave Macmillan.

Thornham, Sue. 2013. Rebranding Feminism: Post-Feminism, Popular Culture, and the Academy. In *Renewing Feminisms: Radical Narratives, Fantasies, and Futures in Media Studies,* ed. Helen Thornham and Elke Weissmann, 32–46. London: I.B. Taurus.

Wearing, Sadie. 2012. Exemplary or Exceptional Embodiment? Discourses of Aging in the Case of Helen Mirren and *Calendar Girls*. In *Aging Femininities: Troubling Representations*, eds. Josephine Dolan and Estella Tincknell, 145–160. Newcastle: Cambridge.

Whelehan, Imelda. 2013. Ageing Appropriately: Postfeminist Discourses of Ageing in Contemporary Hollywood. In *Postfeminism and Contemporary Hollywood Cinema*, eds. Nadine Müller and Joel Gwynne, 78–95. New York: Palgrave Macmillan.

Whelehan, Imelda. 2014. Fiction or Polemic? Transcending the Ageing Body in Popular Women's Fiction. In *Ageing, Popular Culture and Contemporary Feminism: Harleys and Hormones*, eds. Imelda Whelehan and Joel Gwynne, 29–46. New York: Palgrave Macmillan.

Whelehan, Imelda and Joel Gwynne. 2014. Introduction: Popular Culture's 'Silver Tsunami.' In *Ageing, Popular Culture and Contemporary Feminism: Harleys and Hormones*, eds. Imelda Whelehan and Joel Gwynne, 1–13. New York: Palgrave Macmillan.

Williams, Zoe. 2016. Bridget Jones's Baby: The Diaries--Review. Review of *Bridget Jones's Baby: The Diaries* by Helen Fielding. *The Guardian*, Oct 12. Accessed 19 Jan 2017. https://www.theguardian.com/books/2016/oct/12/bridget-jones-baby-the-diaries-helen-fielding-review.

Wolitzer, Meg. 2013. Bridget in Middle Age: We're Not So 'Mad About' This Girl. Review of *Bridget Jones: Mad about The Boy*, by Helen Fielding. *WBUR News*, Oct 16. Accessed 15 June 2016. http://www.wbur.org/npr/230153761/bridget-in-middle-age-were-not-so-mad-%09about-this-girl.html.

Zeisler, Andi. 2016. *We Were Feminists Once: From Riot Grrrl. To Covergirl©, the Buying and Selling of a Political Movement*. New York: BBS Public Affairs.

PART III

The Body and Embodiment

CHAPTER 10

Older Women and Sexuality On-Screen: Euphemism and Evasion?

Susan Liddy

Sexually active older female characters have traditionally been absent from cinema, but over the last two decades a handful of films have tentatively explored what Fine has called "the missing discourse of desire" (1988, 42) and challenged hegemonic definitions of older women as asexual (Tally 2008; Weitz 2010; Moseley 2010; Liddy 2014, 2015). Prompted by factors such as public debates about "successful ageing," the perceived power of the "grey pound" and its impact on cinemagoers, and the continuing popularity of a range of ageing female stars, the extent to which this ideological shift has continued to gain ground over the last number of years is explored here. Representation is, of course, an interpretative process; film does not re-present a pre-existing reality but offers an ideological view of aspects of the social world. Yet it remains an important research focus because it can "illuminate the cultural ideas that media producers either hold themselves or believe are most palatable to mainstream audiences" (Weitz 2010, 18). A close reading of three high-profile films, released between 2012 and 2015, will explore the parameters, both visual and narrative, of recent

S. Liddy (✉)
Mary Immaculate College, Limerick, Ireland
e-mail: Susan.Liddy@mic.ul.ie

C. McGlynn et al. (eds.), *Ageing Women in Literature and Visual Culture*,
DOI 10.1007/978-3-319-63609-2_10

representations of ageing women and sexuality: *Hope Springs* (2012), *Le Week-End* (2013) and *45 Years* (2015). After briefly reviewing the small body of literature on sexuality and ageing femininity, this chapter will assess the extent to which these films disrupt stereotypes and challenge the still widespread assumptions about ageing female sexuality.

A review of ageing female characters on-screen suggests that throughout the 1930s and 1940s, representations of mature women in American film were dominated by portrayals of motherhood; a visual reminder that "biological reproduction best fulfilled women's role in the social order" (Stoddard 1983, 27). Indeed, female actors over sixty-five years of age have primarily played minor characters such as wives and mothers or "lonely spinsters" in films spanning 1929–1995, with the majority of older women projecting "images of decline" (Markson and Taylor 2000, 156). Neither can such limiting roles be entirely consigned to Hollywood or, indeed, to the past. For instance, Josephine Dolan suggests that characterising older female characters "as marginal or abject" is part and parcel of global cinema practice and female stars are often cast in roles where "their sexuality is repressed in some way" (2013, 344). Certainly, this is evident in a range of films in which impediments to the articulation of ageing female sexuality include motherhood in *Agnes Brown* (1999), illness and discord in *The Last Station* (2009), age-inappropriate sexual couplings in *Being Julia* (2004) and addiction in *Come on Eileen* (2010). While the vast majority of mainstream films continue to exclude or marginalise older female characters, a number of films are being produced that challenge a discourse of decline associated with post-menopausal women and suggest a more ambivalent landscape: "seemingly hopeful and newly affirming one moment and destructive and retrograde the next" (Jermyn 2016, 12).

A diminishing on-screen presence in central roles is a reality for ageing male as well as female actors. However, stars such as Clint Eastwood and Jack Nicholson continue to express a masculinity that is "exaggerated and compensatory" well into their later years (Chivers 2011, 99). Older male stars more often play the romantic hero to a younger female character (cf. Jermyn 2016, 4) or have female stars bolstering their "aging virility" (Dolan 2013, 344). The portrayal of older men promises the audience a "dynamic" old age (Markson and Taylor 2000, 155) unhampered by the passage of time. In contrast, the sexuality of female characters is generally taboo; indeed, Whelehan and Gwynne describe the place of post-menopausal women in popular culture as being "on the 'scrap heap' once their hormone levels start to shift" (2014, 5). In the past, this has translated into a veritable banishment of older women from key screen roles, particularly as agentic, sexual subjects. However, there are signs that change is making its way onto the screen in the form of narratives and characters that validate the sexual desire and sexual expression of older women, albeit within carefully defined parameters.

Research on US (Weitz 2010), British and Irish narrative films (Mosely 2010; Wearing 2012; Liddy 2014, 2015) suggests that representations of mature female sexuality occur very infrequently.[1] Notwithstanding the small number of such films that are produced each year, films like *Saving Grace* (2000), *Calendar Girls* (2003) and *Ladies in Lavender* (2004) are important culturally. They affirm sexuality for older women and validate their "sexual pleasure and sexual agency" (Weitz 2010, 27), thus challenging hegemonic definitions of older women as asexual. An annexing of motherhood and sexuality is also observable in a number of US, British and Irish film co-productions such as *Keeping Mum* (2005), *A Tiger's Tail* (2006) and *Mamma Mia!* (2008) (cf. Liddy 2014). Yet the familiar desiring gaze, characteristic of much contemporary cinema, is absent, or extremely muted, even in films in which the sexuality of older female characters is in focus. Interestingly, in only two films, *Calendar Girls* (2003) and *The Mother* (2003), are female breasts even partially on display.

Within the same film, the sexuality of younger and older female characters can be portrayed quite differently. Concealing strategies are often in evidence when older women are physically intimate on-screen, yet younger female characters routinely appear in various stages of undress. For instance, in *Undertaking Betty,* downtrodden Betty, played by Brenda Blethyn, plans to leave her loveless marriage and embark on a new life with childhood sweetheart, Boris (Alfred Molina). Despite her assertion that "it's never too late for anything, ever," a single kiss in the last moments of the film is the extent of Betty's represented sexuality.

[1] US films representing mature female sexuality on screen, from 2000–2007, was half of one percent; in UK films between 1998–2011 it was just under one percent and in Irish film for the same period it was three percent. The expression of mature female sexuality was defined as any sexual activity from a passionate kiss to a sexual touch to simulated sexual intercourse.

In contrast, Meredith (Naomi Watts, aged thirty-four) romps in bed with Hugh, Betty's husband (Robert Pugh), clad in sexy lingerie, stockings and suspenders. Even when sexuality is deemed a necessary and important part of life for older women and when cultural norms that exclusively pair youth and sex are challenged, the expression of female sexuality is muted and the sexual double standard is often in operation (cf. Liddy 2014, 20; Bildtgard 2000, 180). A passionate kiss is often the only sexual expression and although scenes may *imply* that sexual activity has taken place, or is about to take place, the camera inevitably evades the sight of the older female body. Although, on one level, these films do indeed challenge discourses of an asexual old age, the sexual expression of older women is cautiously validated. The portrayals of sexual relationships tend to be romanticised and occur almost exclusively within the confines of marriage or committed relationships, implicitly ringfenced as the appropriate forum for a mature character to express her sexuality. Interestingly, comedy tends to be the genre in which older female characters are represented as sexually active and in leading roles, suggesting that mature female sexuality can be rendered more palatable when couched in comedic terms (cf. Liddy 2014, 25).

Drawing on the work of Margaret Woodward, Williams et al. observe that representations of later-life sexuality are "essentially taboo for mainstream culture—possessing an intrinsic unwatchability" (2007, 2). However, as Vares points out, there is a "gendered dimension" to the unwatchability of portrayals of later life sexuality. It is specifically the female body that remains hidden and taboo, reflecting a gendered double standard of ageing (cf. Vares 2009, 504). The severing of all traces of sexual life from depictions of older women makes a powerful statement, naturalising the invisibility of older female sexuality and rendering it abject. At a symbolic level, as Lauzen and Dozier (2009, 438) argue, the "worth" of characters can be communicated by their absence or presence on screen and, of course, by the manner in which they are represented. The exclusion of sexually desiring or sexually active older women has been widely accepted as inevitable and is customarily explained away by the perceived resistance of mainstream audiences. That said, while filmic representations of sexually active older female characters remain small, there is a shift occurring that is important to explore, despite the caveats outlined above. A close reading of three recent films tentatively points to the emergence of competing discourses relating to women, ageing and sexuality.

Hope Springs, *Le Week-End* and *45 Years* have all been released since 2012 and have been heralded in the press as evidence of the power of the older audience: "Oldies are where the gold is" (Bunbury 2014); "Lights, camera, action attract an older audience to the silver screen" (Jennings 2014). As already discussed, research suggests that on the rare occasions when older female sexuality is represented on film it is often shrouded in humour, arguably rendering it more palatable to a mainstream audience. While two of these films have moments of light comedy (*Hope Springs* and *Le Week-End*), comedy is not used as a device to diffuse or undermine explorations of age and/or ageing sexuality; indeed, such an exploration is central rather than peripheral to these narratives. All three films are concerned with the sexual lives of Baby Boomers, a cohort considered to be the twentieth century's "first teenagers" (Biggs et al. 2007, 32). Liberal, individualist and anti-establishment, this "vanguard generation" entered adulthood during a period characterised by rapid social change and lived through the so-called sexual revolution, leading to expectations that they would reimagine the ageing process and its perceived impact on later-life sexuality (cf. Huber and Skidmore 2003, 34–35).

In *Hope Springs*, Kay (Meryl Streep) and her husband of thirty-one years, Arnie (Tommy Lee Jones), sleep in separate bedrooms and live emotionally and physically detached lives. Stereotypes are doubly disrupted in this film, firstly by challenging the asexuality of older women and secondly by positioning Kay, rather than Arnie, as the sexual agent. From the opening scene, it is clear that Kay longs for sexual intimacy. Dressed in her nightdress, she regards herself in the mirror, fluffs her hair and nervously slips into her husband's bedroom. Arnie is taken aback to hear her admit tentatively "I just want it," but he claims to be feeling unwell and she accepts his excuses without challenge. Kay is a traditional suburban housewife "oriented toward private sphere, home, marriage, motherhood, care and nurture, passivity, emotionality, tenderness, reproduction, dependency" (Zeman and Geiger Zeman 2016, 451). Dutifully, she serves her husband his breakfast and dinner every day and remains pleasant in the face of his brusqueness and taciturnity; his retreat into the newspaper and golf DVDs.

Her work in the drapery store is implicitly more for "pin money" than a considered career choice. Indeed, Arnie reminds her a number of times that he is the breadwinner. His world view is an impoverished one in which indulgence and joie de vivre have long since been buried. Kay is initially a soft-spoken and compliant character but her despair at the disappearance of the sexual side of her marriage energises her and subsequently takes her on a journey of self-discovery and renewal. It is she who exhibits sexual agency and delivers an ultimatum to Arnold: she has drawn down her savings to pay for "intensive couples counselling" and is flying to Maine to see a therapist, with or without him. "I want a real marriage again Arnold," she tells him, "when was the last time you touched me that wasn't just for a picture?" Perhaps prompted by warnings delivered by his divorced work colleague, to humour Kay or "he'll end up in a condo," Arnie reluctantly joins her on the flight.

During the course of the therapy, graphic descriptions of sexual history, sexual positions and fantasy life are disclosed to the therapist, Bernie (Steve Carrell), and it is Arnie who exhibits discomfort and resistance. Despite her embarrassment and naiveté, Kay is proactive with the prescribed sexual "exercises," galvanised by the conviction that this may be her only opportunity to create a sexual life with her husband. Kay's character is constructed as sexually inexperienced and this provides much of the film's mild humour as she "practises" techniques designed to improve her ability to give oral sex, one of Arnie's declared fantasies. Hence, she experiments using bananas as props while studying a book on sex tips and tries to perform fellatio on him in a darkened cinema in order to demonstrate her desire to please him. Interestingly, the narrative constructs Kay as struggling to discover any aspect of her sexuality that does not include or reference Arnie. Neither does it posit a scenario in which Arnie tries to discover what pleases Kay sexually, reproducing a gendered hierarchy of sexual needs that privileges the male. While the inclusion of sexually active older female characters is to be welcomed, there is a danger of replicating "traditional heteronormative and gender conventional standards" (Katz and Marshall 2012, 228).

As a mature woman, Kay's unrequited sexual desire is the driving force in her life. In contrast, as a younger woman, her emotional needs were paramount, needs which Arnold could not satisfy, resulting in a withdrawal of her physical availability. Feminists have commented on the "disproportionately gendered responsibility women tend to take for emotional caretaking of the family and other home duties" which acts as a "major inhibitor of feminine sexual interest" (Rowntree 2014, 156). During therapy, after a series of awkward moments and false starts, Kay and Arnie eventually consummate their relationship. In *Hope Springs*, the menopausal ageing female body, so often a site of discourses of decline and disgust, is the site of pleasure and desire. Bildtgard has argued that films rarely show an elderly couple having sex and when they do, it is only "hinted at" (2000, 176). Hence, the myth of the asexual older person and the incongruity of later life and sexual relations is reinforced (cf. Bildtgard 2000, 180). However, while both Kay and Arnie's bodies remain concealed throughout, simulated sex scenes are enacted rather than alluded to. While it is true that more explicit representations are sidestepped, a scenario which would be very unlikely if a younger couple was driving the narrative, *Hope Springs* does not shy away from its treatment of mid-life sex and sexuality.

Sex is both present and absent in *Le Week-End* when Meg (Lindsay Duncan) and Nick (Jim Broadbent) return to Paris for their thirtieth wedding anniversary; a city they have not visited since the heady days of their youth. Their relationship is conveyed in shorthand as the Eurostar hurtles towards France: Meg is restless and impulsive while Nick is earnest and cautious. Yet, it is he who instigates the weekend and persuades her to go with him by booking them into a hotel that has some significance for their younger selves. That is his first mistake: time has taken its toll on the hotel as well as on the protagonists and it is hardly recognisable to Meg. "It's beige," she proclaims in the tiny bedroom, a metaphor for a life that is being lived by rote. Within minutes she is dispensing euros to a cab driver who drops them at an exclusive hotel, despite Nick's remonstrations that they cannot afford it. Meg's reappraisal of her life is articulated through conspicuous consumption as she spends lavishly on goods and services for the duration of her stay. The action of the film, always walking a fine line between humour and pathos, is constructed around their reflections, debates and exploits over the course of the weekend: ducking out of restaurants without paying and zigzagging through the hotel foyer.

Meg's problem, in a narrative sense, can be encapsulated in what Chivers has called "the banality" of middle age (2011, xvi). Meg and Nick are cut adrift from each other emotionally and physically as they face retirement and growing old together. The sexual dynamic is immediately established; in a reworking of an old trope, Nick desires his wife but his feelings are not reciprocated. As she lies on the bed rolling up her black stockings, before they go out for the evening, Nick asks: "Can I touch you?" to which Meg replies "What for?" She would rather see the Eiffel Tower, she tells him, "than your partially erect sausage." Many stereotypes are confounded in Meg's character construction. In an industry that seeks to create "likeable" and "relatable" female characters for fear of alienating mainstream audiences, Meg is breaking the mould.

Like Kay, she is an "empty nester" but neither woman exhibits any regret that this part of their lives is over. Meg has finally succeeded in getting their son to leave the family home and is holding firm that he will not return, despite his pleading phone calls to Nick while they are in Paris. She is characterised as a woman who yearns for passion; in a moment of defiance she flashes her breasts for Nick; toys with the phallic toothbrush; dresses in lingerie, black stockings and stilettoes and toys with him sexually. She tells him of the young man who tried to pick her up in Waterstones; briefly considers a tryst with a Frenchman she meets at a party and tells Nick that she wants to leave him during their anniversary dinner. But ultimately these encounters seem to be mere rehearsals for something she longs for but cannot fully manifest. For now, somewhat like Kay in *Hope Springs*, she is at a point in her life when she feels "boredom, dissatisfaction, fury and the clock ticking by."

When Nick unexpectedly encounters his one-time protégé, Morgan, the angst that has been building between him and Kay, and within themselves, erupts at a formal dinner party. Here Meg and Nick both come to some understanding of what is troubling them; Nick has never lived up to his youthful potential; he has been forced into early retirement and his wife has little respect for him. But hearing Morgan's glowing description of the young Nick reminds Meg of the man he was and might be again. She recounts to the dinner guests how a friend heard her chatting to Nick on the phone and assumed she was talking to a lover. They leave the party hand in hand. But there is no earth-shattering reunion or Hollywood-style choreographed sex here. The dilemma for Meg is that she no longer desires her husband though she is fond of him, perhaps still loves him. This begs the question raised throughout the film: is it possible to continue to feel sexual passion for someone with whom you have shared a long marriage? Or is it inevitable that, for some at least, lust and passion will eventually burn out? Love will, perhaps, survive; desire, maybe not. It is unclear what the future, long- or short-term, holds for Meg and Nick; they have exceeded their credit card limit, spent all their euros, and been presented with a huge hotel bill which they have no way of paying. But as we leave Paris, they joyfully enact the dance from Jean Luc Godard's *Bande a Part* in a small bar, suggesting that new horizons may yet lie ahead though it is unlikely to deliver the sexual passion Meg longs for; at least not with her husband.

45 Years recounts a tumultuous week in the lives of retired teacher, Kate (Charlotte Rampling), and her husband Geoff (Tom Courtney), living a companionable but somewhat isolated life in the bleak Norfolk countryside. Out of the blue, a letter brings the startling news that a beloved girlfriend from Geoff's youth, Katya, who had plunged to her death in an Alpine crevice fifty years earlier, has been found preserved in the ice. The fallout from the discovery exhumes secrets and emotions that play out in the lead-up to a party belatedly celebrating their 45th wedding anniversary. Katya's "return"–"my Katya" as Geoff refers to her—throws a spotlight on the choices made within their (childless) marriage, who it was that made those choices and why. Initially, Kate tolerates Geoff's brooding; he is nearly eighty years old, nearly a decade older than her and this event provokes thoughts of mortality and melancholy—"she looks like she did in 1962 and I look like this." But as Kate witnesses Geoff's growing obsession with the dead girl; the distraction; the emotional withdrawal from her; the endless stories of their time together; the visits to the attic during the night to pour over old photos and memorabilia of a life that might have been, her distress and rage escalate. The gradual unveiling of the details of their youthful relationship and the circumstances surrounding their last journey into the Alps suggest that they were much closer than Geoff had ever indicated. In fact, he was her next of kin and they would certainly have married had fate not delivered such a cruel blow. It is implied that Kate, like Kay in *Hope Springs*, was somewhat more sheltered and sexually inexperienced than Geoff and was captivated by his confidence and his "passion."

As a couple, they still like to "cuddle," which may be indicative of sexual intimacy and "a crucial aspect of women's sexual desire and arousal" (Rowntree 2014, 15) in the real world, but on film it can suggest companionship rather than passion. However, like *Hope Springs*, *45 Years* breaks with convention and includes a simulated sex scene between the seventy-one-year-old Rampling and the eighty-year-old Courtney. After an impromptu dance in their living room, which references their early years together, the camera follows them upstairs. Geoff tells Kate that he hopes he will remember what to do, suggesting that intercourse is no longer a regular practice, arguably because he suffers from ill health. However, just as Kay was the proactive partner in *Hope Springs*, Kate also takes the sexual initiative. Hers is the voice of reassurance and confidence as she runs a teasing finger down his chest telling him: "Don't worry, I'll remind you." Geoff prepares for bed dressed only in his underpants but Kate's body remains covered in a nightshirt, supporting Sally Chivers's observation that "North American society dictates that aged bodies should be covered up to allow for a comfortable distancing; they should be prevented from telling 'stories of getting old"' (2003, xxvii). However, it is specifically the spectacle of the ageing female body from which the audience is shielded, despite the acknowledgement in the narrative that age is not a barrier to sexual desire.

Unusually, the camera follows the couple into the bedroom where they begin to have sex until Geoff loses his erection. Thereafter, his concern is directed solely to his lack of performance—"bugger it." Neither one of them suggest that he might help Kate to sexual satisfaction; the narrative sidelines the sexual desire of the older woman, even as it affirms it. As Sandberg has observed, "sexuality as lifelong and as part of positive ageing is a markedly masculinist and heterosexual discourse in which most of the focus is placed on restoring men's potential for penile-vaginal penetration" (2013, 14). Again, the gendered hierarchy of sexual needs is established and, as in *Hope Springs,* Kate clearly exhibits sexual agency and sexual desire. However, the sexual double standard emerges in the implicit primacy of male sexuality and the male sexual imperative. In shoring up Geoff's ego after the loss of his erection, Kate's actions are a reminder that ageing female and male bodies "reflect gender ideologies and cultural constructions of femininity and/or masculinity, which include gender relations, stereotypes and, unavoidably, particular power relations" (Zeman and Geiger Zeman 2016, 449).

The lives of Kate and Geoff seem strangely undocumented; the few photographs on the walls are not of children or family members, but of beloved pets—"there's Tess when she was a puppy"—something that Kate had started to question even before the answer is revealed. Unable to contain her curiosity, she climbs into the attic and scans the slides to see for herself what has beguiled Geoff over a lifetime. A young, pretty, dark-haired woman, Katya, comes into focus. She is wearing a wooden "wedding ring," a ploy to permit them to share a bedroom in less liberated times, her hand resting on what appears to be a pregnant belly. Kate's world implodes, suggestive of the realisation that major life decisions, such as remaining childless, devoting themselves to each other, were driven by Geoff and predicated on a lie. Everything she believed she knew is now on shifting sand. At the celebration party, Geoff makes a public declaration of his love for her but it rings hollow to her ears even as she plays the part of the happy wife. Forty-five years of marriage collapses under the burden of lies and buried emotions. Kate takes to the floor with Geoff for their celebratory dance to the song, *Smoke Gets in Your Eyes*, with a smile pasted on her face. As it ends Geoff raises his arm in jubilation but Kate untangles herself and her face is riddled with unspoken, and perhaps unspeakable, emotion.

Cinema is an important site for struggle "over meanings we give to aging and old age" (Katz 2005, 14). A focus on sexuality is only one lens through which we can interrogate the representation of ageing women in contemporary culture; a culture in which older women are "discounted socially" as sexual beings (Rowntree 2014, 157), particularly if they are mothers (cf. Tally 2008; Leamish and Muhlbauer 2012). Yet, such narratives are important because they challenge the cultural myth that sexual desire and sexual passion belong solely to the young. Meryl Streep, Charlotte Rampling and Lindsay Duncan were sixty-three, sixty-four and sixty-nine years of age, respectively, at the time the film in which they starred was released. This is about a decade older than most of the protagonists identified in current literature on the portrayal of ageing women in film—suggestive, perhaps, of a growing acceptance of the portrayal of ageing female sexuality. The films explore a range of issues around age and ageing and present some new ways of viewing older women, "who have generally been perceived as disinterested in sex or as undesirable and unattractive sexual partners" (Montemurro and Siefken 2014, 35). All three films partially challenge the manner in which a youth-obsessed culture steers older women towards specific and quite limiting performances of age: such as the cultural norms which exclusively pair youth and sex and which "make middle-aged and older people ashamed of their sexual desires" (Carpenter et al. 2006, 95).

Kay, Meg and Kate, as protagonists, are central to the narratives and are positioned as sexual beings in all three films; desiring of and, in the case of *Hope Springs* and *45 Years*, engaging in simulated sexual intercourse on-screen, a new departure for ageing female stars. However, echoing existing research on ageing women in film (Weitz 2010, 30; Liddy 2014, 39) the characters are all white, middle-class, slim women, and sexual relations are still expressed within committed, romanticised and heterosexual relationships. The display of the ageing female body remains taboo; "the antithesis of beauty and desirability" (Rowntree 2014, 156), which, for Margaret Cruikshank, perpetuates the "shame" of ageing (2003, 149). Despite the thrust of the narrative, which positions these characters as sexual subjects, their ageing bodies remain hidden from view, even during scenes of sexual intimacy, ensuring no breach in what Wearing calls "chronological decorum" (2007) and arguably allaying cultural anxiety about the flimsy veneer of "successful ageing." Nonetheless,

Hope Springs, *Le Week-End* and *45 Years* do offer alternative identities for older female characters as dynamic, sexual subjects and thus offer different ways of performing age and sexuality by disrupting naturalised assumptions about the asexual nature of post-menopausal women.

Works Cited

Biggs, Simon, Chris Phillipson, Rebecca Leach, and Ann-Marie Money. 2007. The Mature Imagination and Consumption Strategies: Age and Generation in the Development of a United Kingdom Baby Boomer Identity. *International Journal of Ageing and Later Life* 2 (2): 31–59.

Biltgard, Torbjorn. 2000. The Sexuality of Elderly People on Film-Visual Limitations. *Journal of Aging and Identity* 5 (3): 169–183.

Bunbury, Stephanie. 2014. Le Week-End: Oldies Are Where the Gold Is. *Sydney Morning Herald*, Feb 20.

Carpenter, L.M., C.A. Nathanson, and J.K. Young. 2006. Sex after 40? Gender, Ageism and Sexual Partnering in Midlife. *Journal of Aging Studies* 20: 93–106.

Chivers, Sally. 2003. *From Old Woman to Older Women: Contemporary Culture and Women's Narratives*. Ohio: The Ohio State University Press.

Chivers, Sally. 2011. *The Silvering Screen: Old Age and Disability in Cinema*. Toronto, Buffalo and London: University of Toronto Press.

Cruikshank, Margaret. 2003. *Learning to Be Old: Gender, Culture and Aging*. Maryland: Rowan and Littlefield Publishers Inc.

Dolan, Josephine. 2013. Smoothing the Wrinkles: Hollywood, Successful Aging and the New Visibility of Older Female Stars. In *The Routledge Companion to Media and Gender*, ed. Cindy Carter, Linda Steiner, and Lisa McLaughlin, 324–351. London and New York: Routledge.

Fine, Michelle. 1988. Sexuality, Schooling and Adolescent Females: The Missing Discourse of Desire. *Harvard Educational Review* 58 (1): 29–54.

Huber, J., and P. Skidmore. 2003. *The New Old*. London: Demos.

Jennings, Margaret. 2014. Lights, Camera, Action Attract an Older Audience to the Silver Screen. *The Irish Examiner*, April 20.

Jermyn, Deborah. 2016. Get a Life, Ladies: Your Old One is Not Coming Back. In *Female Celebrity and Ageing: Back in the Spotlight*, ed. Deborah Jermyn, 1–14. London and New York: Routledge.

Katz, Stephen. 2005. *Cultural Aging: Life Course, Lifestyle and Senior Worlds*. Toronto: University of Toronto Press.

Lauzen, M., and D. Dozier. 2009. Recognition and Respect Revisited: Portrayals of Age and Gender in Prime-Time Television. *Mass Communication and Society* 8 (3): 241–256.

Lemish, Dafna, and Varda Muhlbauer. 2012. 'Can't Have It All': Representations of Older Women in Popular Culture. *Women and Therapy* 35 (3-4): 165–180.

Liddy, Susan. 2014. The Representation of Mature Female Sexuality in British and Irish Film, 1998–2013. *Postgraduate Journal of Women, Ageing and Media* 1 (1): 38–66.
Liddy, Susan. 2015. Stories We Tell Ourselves: Writing the Mature Female Protagonist. *Sexuality and Culture* 19 (4): 599–616.
Markson, Elizabeth W., and Carol A. Taylor. 2000. The Mirror Has Two Faces. *Aging and Society* 20: 137–160.
Marshall, Barbara L., and Stephen Katz. 2012. The Embodied Life Course: Post-Ageism or the Renaturalzation of Gender. *Societies* 2: 222–234. Accessed 10 Feb 2017. doi:10.3390/soc2040222.
Montemurro, Beth, and Jenn Marie Siefken. 2014. Cougars on the Prowl? New Perceptions of Older Women's Sexuality. *Journal of Aging Studies* 28: 35–43.
Moseley, Rachel. 2010. A Landscape of Desire: Cornwall as Romantic Setting in Love Story and Ladies in Lavender. In *British Women's Cinema*, ed. Melanie Bell and Melanie Williams, 77–93. London and New York: Routledge.
Rowntree, Margaret R. 2014. 'Comfortable in My Own Skin': A New Form of Sexual Freedom for Ageing Baby Boomers. *Journal of Aging Studies* 31: 150–158.
Sandberg, Linn. 2013. Affirmative Old Age: The Ageing Body and Feminist Theories on Difference. *International Journal of Ageing and Later Life* 8 (1): 11–40.
Stoddard, Karen. 1983. *Saints and Shrews: Women and Aging in American Popular Film*. Westport, Connecticut: Greenwood Press.
Tally, Margaret. 2008. Something's Gotta Give: Hollywood, Female Sexuality and the 'Older Bird' Chick Flick. In *Chick Flicks: Contemporary Women at the Movies*, ed. Suzanne Ferriss and Mallory Young, 119–131. London and New York: Routledge.
Vares, Tiina. 2009. Reading the 'Sexy Oldie': Gender, Age(ing) and Embodiment. *Sexualities* 12 (4): 503–524.
Wearing, S. 2007. 'Subjects of Rejuvenation': Aging in Postfeminist Culture. In *Interrogating Postfeminism: Gender and the Politics of Popular Culture*, ed. Yvonne Tasker and Diane Negra, 277–310. Durham, NC and London: Duke University Press.
Wearing, Sadie. 2012. Exemplary or Exceptional Embodiment? Discourses of Aging in the Case of Helen Mirren and 'Calendar Girls.' In *Ageing Femininities: Troubling Representations*, ed. Josephine Dolan and Estella Tincknell, 145–160. Cambridge, UK: Cambridge Scholars Press.
Weitz, Rose. 2010. Changing the Scripts: Midlife Women's Sexuality in Contemporary U.S. Film. *Sexuality and Culture* 14: 17–32.
Whelehan, Imelda, and Joel Gwynne (eds.). 2014. *Ageing, Popular Culture and Contemporary Feminism: Harleys and Hormones*. Basingstoke: Palgrave Macmillan.

Williams, Angie, Virpi Ylanne, and Paul Mark Wadleigh. 2007. 'Selling the Elixir of Life': Images of Elderly in an Olivio Advertising Campaign. *Journal of Aging Studies* 21 (1): 1–21.

Zeman, Zdenko, and Marija Geiger Zeman. 2016. 'Such is Life that People Get Old and Change': Gendered Experiences of Ageing Bodies from Older Persons' View. *Slovak Ethnology* 4 (64): 447–462.

Films

Agnes Brown, Dir. Anjelica Huston. Written by Brendan O Carroll and John Goldsmith. USA: Polygram, 1999. Film.

A Tiger's Tail, Dir. John Boorman. Written by John Boorman. Buena Vista International (Ireland), 2006. Film.

Being Julia (2004/2005) [DVD]. Directed by Istvan Szabo. Written by Ronald Harwood and W. Somerset Maugham (book). USA: Sony Pictures Home Entertainment.

Calendar Girls. Dir. Nigel Cole. Written by Juliette Towhidi and Tim Firth. USA: Touchstone Home Entertainment, 2003. Film.

Come on Eileen (2010/2011) [DVD]. Directed by Finola Geraghty. Written by Finola Geraghty. UK: High Fliers.

Hope Springs. Dir. David Frankel. Written by Vanessa Taylor. Columbia Pictures/ Metro-Goldwyn Mayer, 2012. Film.

Keeping Mum. Dir. Niall Johnson. Written by Richard Russo and Niall Johnson. Summit Entertainment, Isle of Man Film, Azure Films. 2005. Film.

Ladies in Lavender. Dir. Charles Dance. Written by William J. Locke and Charles Dance. Lakeshore International, 2004. Film.

The Last Station. (2009/2010) [DVD]. Dir. by Michael Hoffman. Written by Michael Hoffman. UK: Optimum Home Entertainment.

Le Week-End. Dir. Roger Michell. Written by Hanif Kureishi. Curzon Film World, 2013. Film.

The Mother (2003/2004) [DVD]. Directed by Roger Michell. Written by Hanif Kureishi. UK: Momentum.

Undertaking Betty (2002/2006) [DVD]. Directed by Nick Hurran. Written by Fred Ponzlov. USA: Miramax.

45 Years. 2015. Dir. Andrew Haigh. Written by Andrew Haigh and David Constantine. Curzon Artificial Eye, 2015. Film.

CHAPTER 11

A Certain Truth in Fiction: Perceptions of the Ageing Process in Irish Women's Fiction

Theresa Wray

World Cultures have long histories of storytelling practices that guide, educate and entertain. As readers, our immersion into worlds of fiction and the myriad of invented personalities within should never be underestimated in light of what we may learn about ourselves and the world around us. For instance, in the twenty-first century there exists an ever-expanding market in print and online literatures. These short stories, blogs, mini sagas, flash fictions or novels often provide particular insight into the broad spectrum of human activity. It is often the very familiarity of the narrative that draws us to it in that we recognise, even if we do not always experience, common grounds of knowledge and understanding within. In "Being a Product of Your Dwelling Place," Nadine Gordimer acknowledges this, simply stating that "For me, writing has been and is an exploration of life" (2003, 60). Alice Munro suggests a similar focus in recognising the value of intersecting personal narratives with fictive ones, admitting: "I'm not an autobiographical writer, but [...] I think we

T. Wray (✉)
Independent Researcher, Wales, UK
e-mail: theresawray.tw@gmail.com

C. McGlynn et al. (eds.), *Ageing Women in Literature and Visual Culture*,
DOI 10.1007/978-3-319-63609-2_11

all tell stories of our lives to ourselves, as well as to other people. Well, women do, anyway. Women do this a lot. [...] What interests me is how these stories are made [...] how you use the stories to see yourself, or sometimes just to make life bearable for yourself" (Feinberg 2012).

It is worth noting that Munro's sentiment of synthesising the imagined with the locus of real experience is one that Irish writers Mary Lavin, Bridget O'Connor, Mary Costello and Claire Kilroy appear also to be attuned to; not in the prosaic sense of only relaying personal experience directly into their fictions, but in recognising that the voices captured in their work have some genuineness to us as readers. This is why their writing has been chosen here, among other women's voices, to provide a small but significant exemplar base from which to extrapolate various insights into how women might experience the ageing process and its negative cultural repercussions. While the focus is primarily on Irish women's short fiction, in one instance looking at a section from a novel, discussion will also include examples from online interviews and advertising campaigns. These forms of popular and visual culture will offer currency in an ever-changing forum of discussion about aspects of ageing pertinent to women.

In *Truth and Fiction*, broadcast in 1956, Elizabeth Bowen raises the question of readers' investment in literature, foregrounding veracity and authenticity, "a most extraordinary and imperative reality," in those characters that she draws: "Would you or I as readers be drawn into a novel implicated with what may be its other issues at all if our interest was not pegged to the personalities and the outlook and the actions of the people who we encounter inside the story? They are the attractive element in the book" (Bowen 1956). Bowen's own compelling and complex creation of Mme Fisher, a woman of advanced age in *The House in Paris* (1935), for instance, is testimony to her conservation of the "human interest" factor. As the success of any text relies on our resolve to complete the reading process, connection, not necessarily positive, with protagonists, is vital. In making those fictional entities "real," by awakening our curiosity in them, perhaps linking them to concerns, experiences or locations within our own lives, fictive communities such as Bowen's breathe life into real-time discussions on critical management of topics such as the ageing process. As part of the dialogue then between writer and reader, these individuals become potential vocal ambassadors for any subject matter.

What drives ageing women's experiences is well summarised by Lynne Segal in *Out of Time: The Perils and the Pleasures of Ageing*:

> Ageing affects us all, and affects us all differently, but it is women who have often reported a very specific horror of ageing. It is associated, of course, with the place of the body, and fertility, in women's lives; above all, with what is seen as beauty, attractiveness, good looks, in defining the quintessentially "feminine", however fleeting, however unattainable, this will prove. (2014, 13)

Segal's disquieting honesty regarding the disappointments we face as we get older is welcome, but thankfully alleviated somewhat later in *Out of Time* by her focus on the "enduring ways of remaining open and attached to the world," so providing some encouragement at a time when I find myself somewhat more pessimistic about my own future, and frankly that of other older women (2014, 4). This is no panacea—she is fully aware of tensions between "the possibilities for and impediments to staying alive to life itself, whatever our age" (2014, 4). Her use of the noun "horror" heightens the affect impact that women have to negotiate, a point made some forty-one years previously by Susan Sontag: "Being physically attractive counts much more in a woman's life than in a man's, but beauty, identified as it is for women, with youthfulness, does not stand up well to age" (1972, 31). Seemingly invisible to employers, till assistants, hairdressers, other pedestrians, acutely aware of the double standard that Sontag highlights, I consider myself at a crossroads, questioning what exactly has altered since her essay.

Divorcée Antonia, from Kilroy's *All Names Have Been Changed* (2010), is such a victim to interrogation of her own viability. Thirty-nine when she joins a writing group at Trinity College Dublin, at least fourteen years older than Declan—a firm believer that "Age was a delicate matter amongst women who were past it"—her confidence is so shattered after the break-up of her marriage, that after a night out she ends up bringing Declan home in a calculated, if drunken, move to have sex with him (Kilroy 2010, 204). Declan is fighting his own demons following the breakdown of his relationship with a much younger woman from the group, Guinevere. What follows is an unsettling night of bravado sex on both sides and the language of the encounter, "bitch," "fucked," "fuck," "shag" intentionally corrupts its desperation (Kilroy 2010, 210–212). Declan sees Antonia in the role of victim, prepared to be roughed up, hurt in the process; well, he thinks, "Two could play at that game" (Kilroy 2010, 210). Yet he is the one who loses control over the course of the night, admitting to thoughts of murder and regret: "I didn't really understand the grace of youth until Antonia drained it out of me, tainting it with knowledge of what it was to have lost youth, or to have never possessed it in the first place" (Kilroy 2010, 210). Ironically, Declan is articulating the revulsion surrounding the ageing process that Segal highlights, while experiencing a form of critical insight into the double standard of ageing that Sontag draws attention to regarding women.

As the narrative plays with the vampire myth, unsettling in its exploitation of a distraught woman, Antonia is the one who attempts mock-humour in order to cajole Declan's wounded pride as she teases him with, "I burgled your bank of youth" (Kilroy 2010, 211). The night is played out through Declan's point of view, so the complex depth of Antonia's unhappiness is lost in translation. When later in the night she tells Declan that he is, in fact, the only other man she has slept with besides her ex-husband, this makes him angry. He does not understand how rejected she has felt, neither does he want to invest by staying to find out. Antonia has passed into what Sontag identifies for women as "a humiliating process of gradual disqualification [...] old as soon as they are no longer very young" (1972, 32). The motif of a disparate group drawn together by misplaced admiration for their tutor, each searching for some form of personal validation within the discrete drama of their lives, allows for *All Names Have Been Changed* to be profitably read as a series of connected short tales and vignettes. Laying bare human frailty, this particular chapter, "Castle Rackrent," filters a wholly negative and brutal response to a woman, through the perspective of a male protagonist. Declan's actions make clear Sontag's concerns regarding the labels of youth and age. Antonia is the parasite, the predator, with Declan the injured party, as he sees it.

Today, the bombardment of health advice, the destructive idealisation of beauty and age discrimination at all life stages (can you ever be the right age?), has given rise to a genuine need for multiple forums in which to explore the complexities of ageing, especially in women's lives. One of the questions posed in Bernadette Whelan's research, for example, "American Influences on Irish Advertising and Consumerism 1900–1960: Fashioning Irishwomen," recognises the difficulties that Irish women and Irish society faced in the early twentieth century simply to navigate quite complicated yet "contradictory" messages in advertising (2014, 159–182).[1] The American film industry proved a lucrative vehicle for advertisers in Ireland, with "product placement, endorsement and merchandising," steering a model of glamour and sexuality across the water, essentially providing a new cultural database from which Irish women could draw (Whelan 2014, 10). I would argue that speculative images of successful women have now become endemically positioned worldwide below 30, 35 if I am being generous, destabilising women's ease with positive self-esteem. No area of life is immune. In an interview, actress Juliet Stevenson talks of the paucity of good female roles: "The few roles on screen for women between 45 and 65 are rarely leads. They tend to be secondary—somebody's wife, somebody's mother, somebody's boss. They rarely reflect the rich, challenging, multi-layered complexity of being a woman in her middle years, a woman who's lived" (Grice and Stevenson 2013). As Betty Friedan argues, "there is a crucial difference between society's image of old people [for instance] and 'us' as we know and feel ourselves to be […] To break through that image, we must first understand why, how, and by whom it is perpetuated" (1993, 31). Segal's *Out of Time* also raises the spectre of an increasingly aged population in Britain and North America, a "greying of society [that] has not only been largely either disregarded or deplored, it has also amplified rather than diminished social antipathy towards the elderly" (2013, 2). Women can create a palimpsest to inscribe alternatives to the stigma of "greying." For example, Laura Dodsworth celebrates women's diversity in her photography (2016) and Jenny Joseph rails against prescriptive notions of age-appropriate behaviour in "Warning" (1985, 174). Yet it seems as if the discussion has barely begun. A bombardment of discordant messages still exists—redundancy, decline and marginalisation—alongside destabilising, culturally constructed perceptions of what can make us still viable and attractive to others. The various narratives discussed here are set within that context of a twenty-first century crisis surrounding an ageing demographic.

We do not even have to look to old age (a curiously difficult number to settle on) to see the extent to which women showing visible signs of ageing are marginalised. Susie Orbach starkly reminds us that "We are judged physically and our social and economic position has depended on how our bodies are seen and where we are then placed socially and

[1] My thanks to Professor Whelan for generously forwarding this paper to me.

economically" (2010, 134). Agony aunt and presenter Mariella Forstrup admits "Hitting 50 is traumatic" (2015). Erica Jong is predictably more forthright about turning 50, hitting out at media manipulation that extols the virtues of middle age while astutely pointing out that women find it difficult to come to terms with getting older in a culture "in love with youth and out of love with women as human beings" (1994, 5). In tune with Segal's "horror of ageing," Jong states "We are terrified at fifty because we do not know what on earth we can become when we are no longer young and cute" (1994, 5). Well, some of us have never been cute! This incremental level of hysteria exposes a narrative that must be addressed more fully.[2]

Where might successful expressions of concern surrounding the ageing process for women be found in Irish fiction? The Irish short story even now, a viable space alongside the novel and other media, offers such a space. Despite an evident increase in popularity as a genre for a woman writer, and renewed interest in the form by readers, there is, unfortunately, still a sense of "risk" apparent in publishing collections (cf. D'hoker 2016, 215). Heather Ingman argues that it is "relegated to the margins of critical discourse" and, as such, that does allow the form a certain freedom, positioning the short story as an innovative forum within which to examine pressing social concerns (2009, 1). Bridget O'Connor's first collection of short stories, *Here Comes John* (1995), is full of unsettling, achingly brittle pictures of life: Fiona, reclaiming intimacy with an old lover running from the shadow of death in "Time in Lieu," squalid unsatisfying sex in "After a Dance," the disappointed manipulator in "Here Comes John." However, it is O'Connor's "Kissing Time" that is the most shocking. A twenty-five-year-old woman leaves a particularly confrontational dentist's appointment shocked by the realisation that her decayed teeth will have to be removed. She tries to regain some control over her sexual destiny by sleeping with the first available man she sees, a road-worker, nearby. She craves contact with someone, anyone, while rationalising what the loss of her teeth will bring.

[2] See blogs such as "Beauty Redefined Blog/ Invisible Women Over 40: Anti-Aging and Symbolic Annihilation," [accessed 10/4/16] < http://www.beautyredefined.net/anti-aging-and-symbolic-annihilation/> and articles such as Keo Nozari's "Madonna, Annie Lennox and 'Acting Your Age,'" *The Huffington Post*, 2 October 2015, [accessed 3/4/15].

Her femininity is challenged. The possibility of future sexual encounters is dismissed by her, rejected even before she undergoes any surgery. Kissing, that generous gift of first encounters, the gateway to repeated intimacies with lovers, will be denied her:

> Twenty-five years old: down to the bone
>
> No one would kiss her.
>
> In the park, in the no-breeze, it hit her: no one would kiss her. No one would kiss her. She saw lovers in swim-suits. She saw kissers everywhere, kissing. She saw her face turned up and her lids going down like blinds. The air thickening. She felt emotions load in her chest and launched herself home.
>
> No one would kiss her with false teeth. (O'Connor 1995, 4)

Her real sensitivity to what it means to be attractive to someone is bound up entirely in physical terms. The poignancy of this story is that the woman is never named, yet her past lovers are as she recalls them. She is an everywoman, old before her time, redundant.

This short story allies itself to negative associations with growing older, yet unlike this everywoman whose smoking and poor dental hygiene destroyed her teeth at an early age, it does appear that we can *choose* how we grow older—simply eat well, exercise and keep the mind active. Yet we are assailed by conflicting messages about our value as we undergo this journey. Ashton Applewhite points out that "we live in a culture that drowns out all but the negative about growing old, or even just again past youth [since] social and economic forces frame aging as a problem, so they can sell us remedies to 'fix' or 'stop' or 'cure' it" (2016). The redundant, patronising soundbite of L'Oreal's anti-ageing cosmetic campaign, "*age is just a number and maths was never my thing!*" reflects what Sara Mills addresses as "the semantic derogation of women" through gender-specific derogatory terms (1995, 110–116). The flippant blonde-syndrome disclaimer about mathematical ability did not last long in this campaign; we are now exhorted to "*live another year **bolder***" (Richardson 2015). A series of actresses who have fronted the L'Oreal campaigns—Jane Fonda, Rachel Weisz, Julianne Moore, Helen Mirren—it might be argued, have not, in Susan Bordo's terms, "made the aging female body sexually more acceptable. They have established a new norm" (1995, 26). Audiences/readers identify with this. Yet ironically, they are also the subject of intense scrutiny, where L'Oreal has been forced to defend their photographic techniques to establish that Helen Mirren is not the victim of airbrushing.[3] Bordo's words in *Unbearable Weight: Feminism, Western Culture, and the Body*, connect with Segal's and Orbach's and resonate here:

> What, after all, is more personal than the life of the body? And for women, associated with the body and largely confined to a life centred on the body (both the beautification of one's own body and the reproduction, care, and maintenance of the bodies of others), culture's grip on the body is a constant, intimate fact of everyday life. (1995, 17)

Bordo recognises that culture "not only has taught women to be insecure bodies, constantly monitoring themselves for signs of imperfection, constantly engaged in physical 'improvement'; it also is constantly teaching women (and, let us not forget, men as well) how to *see* bodies" (1995, 57).

In other words, new socially constructed representations of best practice or successful body image, and I include the ageing body here, distort existing perceptions, rendering them redundant and requiring a new appraisal of whatever health/beauty/age model is ideal. Bordo also reminds us that as images constructed within a culture homogenise and normalise the framing of women, so deciphering meaning can be complicated—yet: "People *know* the routes to success in this culture—they are advertised widely enough—and they are not 'dopes' to pursue them. Often, given the racism, sexism, and narcissism of the culture, their personal happiness and economic security may depend on it" (1995, 30). Orbach reiterates similar sentiments in *Bodies*. Bordo's earlier caution in *Unbearable Weight* against a simplistic essentialist discourse of women as without agency over their lives is interesting some twenty-three years after Sontag's essay (1995, 23). It suggests a more nuanced resonance of discussion in certain circles. However, I would argue that within Irish women's fiction, the conversation is not yet fully realised.

The American born Irish writer Mary Lavin weaves the subject of ageing throughout her fiction long before Sontag's essay, though her focus does alter as she herself matures, perhaps reflecting her own adjustment to the ageing process. The older spinster features in "The Long Ago" (1944) and "A Single Lady" (1951)—where single women can be at

[3]BBC Entertainment and Arts, "L'Oreal's Helen Mirren ads cleared of airbrushing." Accessed May 16 2016. http://www.bbc.co.uk/news/entertainment-arts-33440127.

once obsessed and repulsed by sexual activity in old age. "The Becker Wives" (1946) lays bare the earthy reality of a couple's active love-life. "The Will" (1944) illustrates the toll that poverty has on a woman, to the extent that her siblings hardly recognise her when she returns for her mother's funeral. Forty-nine years before O'Connor's young woman in "Kissing Time" is terrified by the loss of her teeth, here Lally is taken to task by her siblings for how badly her teeth have decayed. "Happiness" (1969) and "Senility" (1977) monitor the older woman living in a frenzy of activity or losing control as memory loss and incontinence take a hold on her life. Some twenty-eight years before Sontag's essay, Lavin's short story "The Nun's Mother" from *The Long Ago* (1944), bravely articulates an appreciation of an active and pleasurable sex life for married women, at a time when Irish writers faced the prospect of their books being banned, without recourse to appeal, under the Censorship of Publications Act (1929). The Appeal Board was not introduced until 1946. As Julia Carlson points out, "Writers whose books were banned immediately became stigmatized" (1990, 11). Somehow, Lavin's body of work passes below that particular radar despite its challenges on many fronts to Church and State discourse. The story examines the impact upon two parents of a decision by their daughter to enter into a religious order and the narrative is driven through the lens of a mother's, Mrs. Latimer's, contemplation on the ride home from her daughter's final mass. "The Nun's Mother" offers a bold and explicit rendition of female sexuality in the 1940s, through its close reference to the pleasurable intimacies of married life.

Although there is minimal communication between husband and wife on the journey, it is through Maud Latimer that her husband's fears and insecurities are also channelled. Yet, despite the fact that their daughter Angela's choice affected both of them, and would have taken its toll in equal measure, Mrs. Latimer is concerned with the deterioration in her own appearance as "it had taken more effect on herself all the same [where] only this morning she had seen a fleck or two of grey reflected in the mirror" (Lavin 1944, 195–196). Maud Latimer recognises the implications of her daughter's decision upon herself, and the ensuing loss of sexual identity in her new role.

Maud is confidently, albeit internally articulate about how she views the sexual connection between men and women, and about her own sexual desires and successes. She believes, "None of all the women she knew had lived with love as long and as intimately as she had done.

No one knew what love was as well as she" (Lavin 1944, 204). Yet sadly, above all this she believes that relinquishing her daughter to the Church is going to stop the intimate exchanges between herself and her husband; she must now "act and think like a nun's mother" (Lavin 1944, 203). Lavin's frequent reminders in interviews that she was a Catholic suggest that there is more than mere railing against the system here. Lavin implies that women rationalise various routes in order to negotiate religious, social and personal obstacles, much as Bordo suggests in *Unbearable Weight*. Lavin does not deny a woman's right to experience pleasure. In fact, in an interview with the *Boston Sunday Globe* in 1974, thirty years after "The Nun's Mother," and two years after Sontag's "The Double Standard of Ageing," she says: "I don't think Irish women are as oppressed as many think them to be. Irish women enjoy sex. Many enjoy it before they are married and it's not a test of whether or not they are fertile. They have happy lives" (McManus and Lavin 1974).

Lavin's understanding of Irish women's control over their own fulfilment sits well alongside Whelan's assertion, in "American Influences," of a more open and liberal Irish society than has been previously appreciated. Yet in the short story, Maud's ease with the pleasures of the body still falters when her own public status alters. Her journey demonstrates some real progress in claiming command over one's own body earlier in the narrative, but the conclusion plays to the cultural restraints that Bordo, Friedan, Orbach, Segal and Sontag later identify.

Interestingly, Mary Costello's "Things I See," from the collection *The China Factory* (2012), suggests that women are becoming more, not less, reticent about articulating their concerns to partners, families, friends, echoing Jong's suggestion that, "As women, we still need practice in making alliances with other women. We still tend to see other women as competitors to be eliminated (1994, 303). The female protagonist in "Things I See" is one of what Anne Enright marks as Costello's "lonely [characters] especially when they are in a relationship" (Enright 2012). Early on we discover that Ann feels distanced from her husband as she considers: "I have become concerned for our future. It is not the fact of growing old but of growing different [...] [of] how I will never know him but always imagine him" (Costello 2012, 35, 43). Her denial of ageing, yet her focus on time passing, strains the narrative as she fails to recognise the enormous toll that childbirth can have on the body. She also questions her previous perception of her husband: this could be postpartum depression, or wariness in light of new responsibilities. She obsesses about her husband's closeness to her sister Lucy. However, as tableaus are painted showing Don and Lucy in both relaxed and intimate situations it becomes clear that Ann may have been betrayed by her sister and her husband just after her daughter was born. A brief incident as her husband, daughter and sister enter the household one day prompts a memory of that obvious sexual attraction between Don and Lucy. The cinematic quality of her dissociative observation of their secret liaison in the weeks after Robin was born is rendered distinctly—almost too raw for the reader (2012, 41). In her fragile condition, Ann lacks the emotional resources to confront either her husband or her sister—she is trapped, cornered, as she reveals, by her love for him (2012, 43). "Things I See" reminds the reader that it is not always a simple decision to stand up for oneself, to have the confidence in one's own sense of worth, a theme that Costello returns to in "The Sewing Room" from the same collection. Sometimes we are undone.

This chapter asks, has much altered since Sontag's essay in 1972? Both the critical and fictional discourses considered show willingness to work through an enormous range of issues surrounding the ageing process for women. In some cases it would appear that women are becoming less, not more confident as time progresses; elsewhere new voices question the inevitability of passively accepting a sell by date for women. Despite the positive affirmations of alternative life choices for older women posited by Applewhite, Dodsworth, Friedan and Segal, Irish women writers such as Lavin, O'Connor, Costello and Kilroy still tap into the uncertainties we readers actually experience. This suggests that much is still needed to manage the ageing process with dignity, without discrimination, and with some sense of personal value as women in Irish writing. In Sontag's words, "Women should tell the truth." If they cannot, who else will?

Works Cited

Applewhite, Ashton. 2016. Why I Dislike the Term 'Successful Aging.' Accessed 16 May 2016. http://www.huffingtonpost.com/ashtonapplewhite/ageism-age-discrimination_b_9543050.html.

BBC Entertainment and Arts, L'Oreal's Helen Mirren Ads Cleared of Airbrushing. Accessed 16 May 2016. http://www.bbc.co.uk/news/entertainment-arts-33440127.

Beauty Redefined Blog/ Invisible Women Over 40: Anti-Aging and Symbolic Annihilation. Accessed 10 April 2016. http://www.beautyredefined.net/anti-aging-and-symbolic-annihilation/.

Bordo, Susan. 1995. *Unbearable Weight: Feminism, Western Culture, and the Body*. Berkeley, Los Angeles and London: University of California Press.
Bowen, Elizabeth. 1935. *The House in Paris*. Middlesex and New York: Penguin Books.
Bowen, Elizabeth. 1956. *Truth and Fiction*. http://www.bbc.co.uk/archive/writers/12246.shtml.
Carlson, Julia. 1990. *Banned in Ireland: Censorship & the Irish Writer*. London: Routledge.
Costello, Mary. 2012. Things I See. *The China Factory*. Dublin: The Stinging Fly Press.
D'hoker, Elke. 2016. *Irish Women Writers and the Modern Short Story*. London: Palgrave Macmillan.
Dodsworth, Laura. 2016. Why I Am Embracing, Not Erasing, Experience. *The Huffington Post*, March 1. Accessed 16 May 2016. http://www.huffingtonpost.co.uk/laura-dodsworth/women-embracing-experience_b_9354926.html.
Enright, Anne. 2012. *The Guardian*, June 7. Accessed 9 May 2015. http://www.theguardian.com/books/2012/jun/07/china-factory-mary-costello-review.
Feinberg, Cara. 2012. Bringing Life to Life: A Conversation with Alice Munro. Accessed 8 May 2011. http://theatlantic.com/magazine/archive/2001/12/bringing-life-to-life/3056/.
Forstrup, Mariella. 2015. Life after 50. *The Guardian*, Feb 22. Accessed 16 May 2016. http://www.theguardian.com/lifeandstyle/2015/feb/22/mariella-frostrup-life-after-50?CMP=share_btn_link.
Friedan, Betty. 1993. *The Fountain of Age*. New York and London: Simon and Schuster.
Gordimer, Nadine. 2003. Being a Product of Your Dwelling Place. In *The Writing Life: Writers on How They Think and Work*, ed. Marie Arana. New York: Public Affairs.
Grice, Elizabeth. 2013. Interview with Juliet Stevenson. *The Telegraph*, Nov 18. Accessed 12 May 2015. http://www.telegraph.co.uk/culture/theatre/10457417/Juliet-Stevenson-interview-I-can-imagine-a-time-when-Im-free-of-it-all.-Id-love-it.html.
Ingman, Heather. 2009. *A History of the Irish Short Story*. Cambridge: Cambridge University Press.
Jong, Erica. 1994. *Fear of Fifty: A Midlife Memoir*. London: Chatto and Windus.
Joseph, Jenny. 1985. "Warning," *The Bloodaxe Book of Contemporary Women Poets*, ed. Jeni Couzyn. Newcastle upon Tyne: Bloodaxe Books.
Kilroy, Claire. 2010. *All Names Have Been Changed*. London: Faber and Faber.
Lavin, Mary. 1944. The Nun's Mother. In *The Long Ago and Other Stories*. London: Michael Joseph Ltd.

McManus, Otile. 1974. Mary Lavin: A Jolly Irish Story Teller. *Boston Sunday Globe*, May 5.

Mills, Sara. 1995. *Feminist Stylistics*. London and New York: Routledge.

Nozari, Keo. 2015. Madonna, Annie Lennox and 'Acting Your Age.' *The Huffington Post*, Oct 2. Accessed 3 April 2015. http://www.huffingtonpost.com/keo-nozari/madonna-annie-lennox-acti_b_6652674.html?utm_hp_ref=gay-voices.

O'Connor, Bridget. 1995. Kissing Time. In *Here Comes John*. London: Picador.

Orbach, Susie. 2010. *Bodies*. London: Profile Books.

Richardson, Hannah. 2015. BBC News, Feb 27. Accessed 16 May 2016. http://www.bbc.co.uk/news/education-31658852.

Segal, Lynne. 2014. *Out of Time: The Pleasures and the Perils of Ageing*. London and New York: Verso.

Sontag, Susan. 1972. The Double Standard of Aging. *The Saturday Review*. September 23, 29–38.

Whelan, Bernadette. 2014. American Influences on Irish Advertising and Consumerism 1900–1960: Fashioning Irishwomen. *Journal of Historical Research in Marketing* 6 (1): 159–182.

CHAPTER 12

Future and Present Imaginaries: The Politics of the Ageing Female Body in Lena Dunham's *Girls* (HBO, 2012–Present)

Ros Jennings and Hannah Grist

Lena Dunham's *Girls* (HB0, 2012–present) is a deliberately provocative television text. Betty Kaklamanidou and Margaret Talley suggest that its impact renders it amongst the "elite" of the 2000s (2014, 1). It has been simultaneously lauded as "a bold defence and a searing critique of the so-called millennial generation by a person still in her twenties" (Nussbaum 2014), and decried as an "uninspiring experience to hold up as an example to young women" (Persky 2013). The following analysis explores this tension in relation to the ways that the ageing female body is imagined within the series and within conflicting discourses of empowerment and decline that are prevalent in dominant western cultural understandings of age and within contemporary feminist approaches to ageing.

R. Jennings (✉) · H. Grist
University of Gloucestershire, Cheltenham, UK
e-mail: rjennings@glos.ac.uk

H. Grist
e-mail: hgrist@glos.ac.uk

C. McGlynn et al. (eds.), *Ageing Women in Literature and Visual Culture*,
DOI 10.1007/978-3-319-63609-2_12

As a "coming-of-age" comedy drama that focuses on the (mis)adventures of four twenty-something-year-old women in New York and centres on the experiences of protagonist Hannah Horvath (Dunham), *Girls* acts as a powerful social and cultural commentary on the imaginings of female ageing, igniting debates about feminism, gender, privilege, 'race' and sexuality (cf. Daalmans 2013; Nygaard 2013; Hamilton 2014; Saisi 2014; Kaklamanidou and Tally 2014; Nash and Grant 2015; Woods 2015). In so doing, *Girls* has deepened debates about the "body politic" (Ford 2016).

Media attention has focussed on the body of *Girls* creator, writer and actress Lena Dunham, which although young, does not correspond to the size and type of idealised heterosexual femininity. In its centrality to the drama, her body has been subject to both celebration and shame. Inextricably linked to Dunham's own avowed feminist credentials, *Girls* performs a "female sexual subjecthood [that] is emotionally intimate, reflexive, and ironic" (Ford 2016, 2). We argue that this subjecthood, famously configured around the realistic and digitally unaltered youthful body, is also constructed against the imaginary of an older, and to Dunham, fear-provoking female form.

Given that *Girls* contemplates the experiences of growing older, both emotionally and physiologically, it is curious that previous academic and popular discussion of age in the text centres solely on the representation of the millennial generation. This chapter examines the ways that *Girls* represents the older female body and envisages its ageing. The following analysis takes the concept that "we are aged by culture" (Gullette 2004) as a way to explore the intergenerational imaginings and representations of becoming/being an older woman that are manifest in *Girls*. Using the work of Margaret Morganroth Gullette in connection to a television series that displays what has been recognised as Dunham's awkward auteurship (cf. Nelson 2014) is particularly apposite, as Gullette's age-critical perspective emphasises the power of autobiography and storytelling to unravel how dominant cultural narratives shape our understanding of ageing. This connection is also underpinned by the ways that ageing and millennial experiences are played out in contemporary USA. *Girls'* articulation of generational identities against contemporary economics and attitudes is intertwined with the American dream's cultural narrative of ageing. The American dream, according to Gullette, is a basic progress narrative; "an example of a life-course story told by ordinary people, over time, about work and its consequences: first to themselves prospectively, then in medias res, and finally, retrospectively" (2003, 103).

When television is conceptualised as a form of heritage (Garde-Hansen and Grist 2015), it offers an important legacy as a resource for present and future identity formation. As a television text, *Girls* forensically explores identities, unpicking their complexities and contradictions. As Maricel Oró-Piqueras and Anita Wohlman (2016) explain, television texts constructed in serial form are able, over time, to develop strategies of identity and characterisation in enviable depth compared to other media forms. During five seasons, the complex portrayals of identities and generations in *Girls* work also to serialise age. Dunham's serialisation of identities and ageing is a highly personal project and one in which the understanding and representation of the female body is central. More especially, in *Girls*, Dunham visually foregrounds her own body as a feminist challenge to the limited range of possibilities that are acceptable as heterosexual femininity in western society. *Girls*, however, fails to conceptualise the holistic experience of ageing as a woman. Instead, as we will demonstrate, ageing is configured around millennial generational fear of growing older. We also argue that this is neither surprising nor something that the series, or indeed Dunham, should be blamed for. The limited and derivative textual and paratextual constructions of ageing and older women in *Girls* are the upshot of dominant and limiting understandings of female older age and the failure of various waves of feminisms to politically imagine a powerful older age for women. Where *Girls* does address the experience of ageing and later life, it rehearses culturally engrained tropes about older women in western societies. Ultimately, for a text that sets itself up to be simultaneously open to contradictions and to be contradictory, this weakens its impact. When read alongside Dunham's assertion that "There is nothing gutsier to me than a person announcing that their story is one that deserves to be told, especially if that person is a woman" (2015, xx), the series unfortunately, for the most part, struggles to imagine female ageing beyond rigid generational and culturally ageist constructions.

Ageing and Feminism

In 1978 Susan Sontag wrote: "Growing older is mainly an ordeal of the imagination—a moral disease, a social pathology—intrinsic to which is the fact that it afflicts women much more than men" (1978, 285). This social pathology is one that endures to this day. Older women are held up to a double standard of ageing in the workplace and in social and cultural life, and this is mirrored in their representation on screen.

Unfortunately, second-wave feminism did not engage with ageing and old age as an intersection of importance. Although there is a current upsurge in feminist approaches to ageing, this work must now contend with what Hannah Hammad refers to as "toxic intergenerationality" (2015, 170), where the life-views and cultural politics of second-wave feminism and millennial postfeminism are in conflict with each other. With regard to ageing and feminism, there is a residual vacuum that results from the failure of second-wave feminist politics to offer a legacy that permitted the second-wave feminists themselves, or women and girls younger than them, to age powerfully and to challenge the manifold ways that they are aged by patriarchal culture.

In line with a growing ageing population in western societies, there has been a proliferation of images of older women on television in recent years. As Sherryl Wilson indicates, however, "rather than presenting us with new ways of thinking about age and ageing, representations cohere to a series of somewhat retrogressive images" (2014, 189). Accompanying these images has been a surge of critical academic attention to these representations from scholars based within ageing studies, cultural gerontology and feminist media studies. With a few notable exceptions (see Krainitzki 2014; Jennings and Oró-Piqueras 2016; Jennings and Krainitzki 2015), what is in evidence is the "persistent tendency of postfeminist culture to pit women against each other, especially across generational lines" (Hammad 2015, 70). We argue that an important aspect that plays out in the serial narrative of *Girls* is the juxtaposition of millennial postfeminism with the inheritances of second-wave feminists, as women associated with second-wave feminism themselves contemplate their own transitions into older age.

In terms of representation across the media from television and film to news media, older postmenopausal women can generally be grouped as either in decline or successfully ageing (cf. Dolan and Tincknell 2012). Positioned as polar extremes on the spectrum of women's possible ageing experiences, both offer problematic constructions and imaginings of older female identities. On the one hand, older women are negatively portrayed as in decline and consequently as demented, vulnerable, asexual, dependent on others; grouped, as Kim Sawchuk and Barbara Crow (2012) have observed, within the "grey zone" where no differentiation is made between 60 and 90 year olds. On the other hand, women are considered to have aged successfully if their body shows limited signs of age: no decrepitude or disease, minimal wrinkling, sagging or greying and a dedication to an "active" lifestyle to stave off the signs of physiological old age (cf. Twigg 2004; Montemurro and Siefken 2014; Katz and Marshall 2008). In this context they are positioned as exceptions, as individuals who continue to do the upkeep work required by neoliberal understandings of femininity and invest time and material resources to deflect the physical signs of ageing by conforming to the glamourous celebrity standard of attractive and youthful femininity (cf. Montemurro and Siefken 2014, 39).

Media representations, as Ulla Kriebernegg and Roberta Maierhofer contend, "determine how we understand age and aging and influence the way we perceive others and define ourselves over the life course" (2014, 2). *Girls* is widely understood both in the media and in academia as "a generational document" (Woods 2015, 38) that explores the lives, experiences and dreams of young women. This document evidences that for the millennial female protagonists and Hannah in particular, older women's bodies provoke fear of growing up and growing older. As the next section will explore, one of the limitations of conceptualising age and ageing in relation to distinct and compartmentalised notions of generation is that it reinforces mutually ageist divisions between young and old and exacerbates the traumatic (cf. Kaplan 2005) and socially pathological imaginings of the female body in older age.

Intergenerational and Paratextual Ageism

The concept of generation is problematic. Grouped by chronological parameters and linked to certain attitudes and characteristics, generations function to naturalise the master narratives of cultural ageing. They are, at one and the same, as slippery and imprecise as they are individually meaningful and meaningless. Despite this, they contribute to the "pre-theorized, prehistoricized formulas that get automatically stocked in our mental rolodex through having been aged in our particular culture" (Gullette 2003, 107) and thus provide the core device for discussing identities and ageing in the series.

Distinctions and divergences between generations are central to the narrative of *Girls* as well as to its paratextual commentary. As Erika M. Nelson explains, the digital interface between Dunham and her anonymous fans performs a kind of "hyperculturality" (2014, 93) that channels a collective cultural understanding of generational identities and experiences textually in the series and paratextually in the context of its influence and reception. Threaded through these generational explorations are explicit and implicit investigations of ageing. The terrain of this investigation plays out via an oppositional binary between what is commonly configured as the millennial generation and the baby boomer generation. The relationship between Hannah and her parents is a key vehicle for this examination and is conducted via a knowing postmodern lens that juxtaposes millennial entitlement and boomer mid-life crises.

The term "millennial" refers to the generation born between 1984 and 1992, a generation marked by their exposure to technology, their flexibility to globalised neo-liberal economies and by their skills in constructing their presence in the world online and digitally (cf. Colloseus 2015). Crucially for the exploration here, they are understood as inhabiting a liminal time/space between childhood and adulthood; experiencing their life courses (cf. Katz 2005) in a less linear way than previous generations of baby boomers (boomers), generation Ys or Xers (cf. Colloseus 2015). Cecilia Colloseus maintains that "We live in the anticipation of the story we will tell later" (2015, 140) and, for Dunham's loosely autobiographically charged *Girls*, this suggests that what is being rehearsed in the present and the past is an anticipatory future. For millennials, their "kidult" status preserves a psychological separation between them and those who represent grown-up values and identities. In *Girls*, parents and grandparents occupy these roles and span the pre-baby boomer generation (born before 1946) and boomers (born between 1946 and 1964) (cf. Weiss 2003). The term "boomer" reflects a post-World War II surge (boom) in birth rates in the western world and, as this cohort of people have moved or are moving into old age, the sheer size as an ageing demographic has branded them as a potential economic threat to neoliberal western economies.

In terms of thinking about ageing, particularly from feminist perspectives, the maintenance of generational conflict reinforces a disempowering ageist divide, when what is required, and what we argue here, is an empathetic intergenerational solution.[1] Providing powerful visions and narratives for women will assist women to prepare each other for, and to imagine, being old women rather than live in fear and denial of what, if we are lucky enough to live that long, we must all face.

---

[1]The Centre for Women, Ageing and Media's WAM Manifesto (2012) presents one way in which scholars working in an interdisciplinary and intergenerational manner are proposing an empathetic intergenerational alternative to the maintenance of generational conflict.

In the context of writing this article, the process has been one of intergenerational feminist exchange and reflection as the authors (one fitting millennial chronology and the other boomer) have worked together to read *Girls* in its paratextual context. What follows is an exploration of the ways in which female bodies (both young and old) are constructed and represented in *Girls* and a critical discussion of the implications of these representations given the feminist credentials of the writer and the age-based premise of the series.

The Female Grotesque: Dunham's Body and Parallels in Ageist Discourse

As Jessica Ford suggests, it is the "tension between the simultaneous celebration and critique of Hannah's body [that] is the driving force behind the series' body politics" (2016, 9). Dunham's mode of display of her own naked body on *Girls* continues a tradition of feminist body performance art started in the mid-1960s and 1970s. In her autobiography, Dunham recounts seeing the nude photographs her mother took of her own body during this period—"the eye is drawn to her nakedness. Legs spread defiantly […] [There is an] appealing seriousness to her fascination with herself" (2015, 100). An auteur renowned for writing what she knows, Dunham's self-revelation representationally emphasises the series' paratextual feminist, and more specifically second-wave feminist, roots.

Dunham's display of her body (and her body itself) transgresses normative images of western heterosexual femininity: although young, Dunham is short, tattooed and larger than heteronormative hegemonic media ideals. The way in which *Girls* uses Dunham's body (clothed and unclothed) therefore unsettles and challenges common televisual representations of the female form and of women's sexuality.

Dunham's body has been held up as a celebratory alternative image of western femininity, which, in its unruliness, is unsettling (Russo 1995). Similar in some ways to the counter-hegemonic unruliness offered by Roseanne Barr in her 1990s television sit-com series *Roseanne* (Paramount, 1988–1997), Dunham's Hannah has generated "a powerful means of self-definition and a weapon for feminist appropriation" (Rowe 1995, 3). Like Barr, Dunham uses her own body in comedic and parodic ways to unsettle dominant discourses about the ideal female form and cultural norms. That is not to say that Dunham positions her body in

Girls as a prop to be laughed at, rather the contrary. Dunham's body is used in the series as one imbued with verisimilitude—she is naked in the bath and getting dressed, and she is naked (or nearly naked) having sex. The fact that Dunham's nudity continues to form a central theme in critical attention is significant in terms of the limited acceptable representational possibilities open to all women. For instance, radio personality and *American Idol* judge Howard Stern publically shamed Dunham as "that little fat chick" who hogs the camera, and likened her nude scenes to rape (Hayner 2013).

In western culture, bodies which challenge the masculine gaze and heteronormative representations of idealised femininity are often signified by codes of the Bakhtinian carnivalesque grotesque: the Medusa, the Crone, the Bearded Woman, the Fat Lady and the Tattooed Woman (cf. Russo 1995, 14). These invocations of the grotesque are regularly mapped against Dunham's body as "Fat," "Tattooed" and "Unruly" in acts of body-shaming that form part of the paratextual discourses that surround *Girls*. As Mary Russo suggests, the "grotesque body is the open, protruding, extended, secreting body, the body of becoming, process and change" (1995, 62–63). Mapped on to these configurations, Dunham's body is rendered grotesque and in the coming-of-age story narrative of *Girls*, there is a focus on the processes of becoming and change, where the body is integral (while not the sole focus of this process of transformation) to the transition from girlhood into "kidulthood."

In her seminal study, Russo notes that grotesque female bodies are "the pregnant body, the aging body, the irregular body" (1995, 55). Adult women's bodies are thus produced as abject and older women's bodies, when constructed through lenses of prevalent cultural ageism, are considered particularly grotesque. The limited and derivative representations of older bodies on screen inform audiences, as Sally Chivers suggests, "of what each individual's body could become. [...] Viewers accordingly come literally face to face with their preconceived notions of the grotesque aesthetic of age" (2003, xxvi).

In *Girls*, Hannah is troubled by her physiological body—not so much its non-conformist shape or size, as Hannah states in an early episode "I decided I would have some other concerns for my life"; or even how that body might *look* as it ages—but by the human body's propensity to breakdown and ail. Physical decline as a common trope about older age is taken for granted and rehearsed in *Girls*. In season two in particular, in the midst of an obsessive compulsive disorder (OCD) breakdown, Hannah googles "At what age does your body start melting down?"

The episodes that focus on Hannah's struggle with OCD (see Lehman 2014) are influenced by real-life narratives of ageing as decline and the body as a metaphor for decay and leakiness (cf. Shildrick 1997). Hannah's struggle is also informed by Dunham's own history of OCD and by personal fears about her own body. A self-identified "germophobe," Dunham wrote that she wished she "could be one of those young people who seems totally unaware of the fact that her gleaming nubile body is, in fact, fallible" (2014, online). Growing up in the late 1980s and 1990s, Dunham's childhood and adolescence were also marked with a hyperawareness of AIDS and a fear of HIV that is mirrored by her character Hannah in *Girls*. Dunham wrote:

> Is what's manifesting as a fear [of illness, disease and death] actually some instinct to resist being young? Youth, with its accompanying risks, humiliations and uncertainties, the pressure to do it all before it's too late. Is the sense of imminent death bound up in the desire to leave some kind of a legacy? (2014, online)

Thus Hannah's relationship with her body, and her own youth, is complexly informed by Dunham's own fear of illness and disease and by popular cultural representations of older life as degeneration and decay (cf. Dolan and Tincknell 2012; Katz 1996). It appears that neither Hannah nor Dunham have the tools to imagine a life without illness and decline in older age. The following section explores the most acute manifestation of this imagining of older age in *Girls* through the representation of Hannah's Grandma Flo and the older disabled artist Beadie.

The Ageing Body and Narratives of Decline: 'Grandma Flo' and the Artist 'Beadie'

As discussed above, in their representation in film and on television, older women are found grouped as either in decline or as successfully ageing. Whether frail or robust, both cultural constructions of older age rely on the body. Bodies thus work representationally to signify individuals' ageing processes and it is in the representation of its oldest characters that *Girls* continues this tradition by mapping the ageing experience along the continuum of physiological success or decline. Building on Dunham's penchant for narratives that focus on the medical, the roles and representations of Grandma Flo and Beadie in *Girls* offer the image of frail, ailing and disabled elders: old age as a metaphor for decline.

In season three, Hannah is drawn away from her vibrant youthful life in Brooklyn into the suburbs to visit her Grandmother 'Flo' in the hospital. Flo (June Squibb), who is in her mid- to late seventies, has been hospitalised with a broken femur. This choice of physical injury to incapacitate Flo is one that is most commonly experienced by older people, due to the lessening of bone density as we age (cf. Novak 2014, 40). While in hospital, Flo contracts pneumonia (another illness most common in people over the age of 65) and passes away from a heart attack. While Flo's pathology is undoubtedly (and unfortunately) representative of the experience of many adults in their late seventies, in the construction of this character *Girls* misses an opportunity to move away from well-rehearsed tropes about old age as decline on television.

The mother of a boomer, Flo does not quite fit the recognised chronology of oldest-old or a "Fourth Ager" (Gilleard and Higgs 2010), yet she is represented as sick, frail and close to death. Chris Gilleard and Paul Higgs posit "that the fourth age functions as a social imaginary because it represents a collectively imagined terminal destination in life—a location stripped of the social and cultural capital of later life which allows for the articulation of choice, autonomy, self-expression and pleasure" (2010, 14). Thus, through Flo, *Girls* constructs a terminal imaginary for its oldest character, one that rehearses old tropes, and in its narrative limits the possibilities of later life for its audience. Moreover, *Girls'* problematic conflation of third and fourth ages through its focus on the ailing aged body furthers the cultural representation of old people as a homogenous mass, existing within "grey zone" (Sawchuck and Crow 2012).

Margrit Shildrick holds that the body is "curiously absent to us during health, and it is only in sickness that it makes itself fully felt, and then as that which unsettles the sense of self" (1997, 10). In *Girls,* Flo is absent to us during her health, and it is only when she begins to succumb to the ailments of old age that she is revealed in the series. Although it is Flo who is dying, and because the audience accepts her prognosis as a fact of her age, a sense of "unsettling of the self" is experienced through Hannah, her mother and aunts. Hannah's mother and aunts spend much of the episode dividing up Flo's estate: her large reserve of prescription tranquilisers, sedatives and painkillers (medication itself a signifier of older age and evidence of cultural constructions of its association with pain and disease) and arguing over which of her belongings each will take when Flo dies. As such Flo herself does not feature in many scenes in the episode, but her belongings feature as a tangible legacy which must be argued over and divided. *Girls*, therefore, presents Flo as a character who Kathleen Woodward would describe as "invisible and without voice" (1999, xxvi).

The outro that covers the credits to the episode "Flo" is 'Don't Let Us Get Sick' written by Warren Zevon and performed by Jill Sebule. With the first verse and the chorus sharing the lyrics: "Don't let us get sick/Don't let us get old/Don't let us get stupid, alright?" the audience is reminded once again that old age and sickness (and here with the invocation of the term "stupid" perhaps also dementia) go hand in hand. As Margaret Cruikshank reminds us, old age and its related cultural construction as decrepitude and decline means that elderliness is "disconnected from youth and midlife rather than seen as an outgrowth of them" (2009, 5). The soundtrack reinforces notions of old age as decline, and in Hannah's return to the city she is spatially disconnected from Flo, her ageing and her death, and through her youth she is also separated from the spectre of her own future.

Later in season three, *Girls* offers an older female character with slightly more depth than Grandma Flo, though this is a narrative once again found attached to the metaphor of old age as decline. Jessa meets an artist named Beadie (Louise Lasser) in the gallery where Marnie works as an assistant, and later becomes her aide. Beadie is an older woman, whose chronological age might classify her as a "Third Ager" (Gilleard and Higgs 2010). Beadie is wheelchair bound, suffers from a nameless condition, and ultimately recruits Jessa to assist in her suicide. Beadie is first presented to the audience sitting in a wheelchair in the gallery, her face framed by white hair tied back into a ponytail and secured with a scrunchie. Beadie asks Marnie to wheel her closer to her photographs on the wall despite the fact that the wheelchair has handrails for self-movement. From the first moment, then, Beadie is presented as dependent, which does little to augment the cultural construction of elders as reliant and incapacitated (cf. Katz 1996). *Girls* conflates the experiences of third and fourth agers in constructing a terminal imaginary of later life in which dependency, decline and death drive the narrative. Ostensibly a similar narrative to that seen in Flo, the construction of Beadie furthers the sense that in the diegesis of *Girls* the multiplicity of experience of older life involves decline and decrepitude.

On the surface, as a successful artist with the associated socioeconomic and cultural capital, Beadie might be read as a character who embodies the third age disposition, as one who has the capacity to make decisions, to engage in social and cultural life with vigour. Beadie is given the agency to take control over her ailing body and its transition into the fourth age in making a decision to end her own life (cf. Gilleard and Higgs 2010). When Beadie is read by one "thinking with age" (Jennings and Gardner 2012) however, it appears that the character is a flimsy (and somewhat clumsy) attempt to bring attention to hotly politicised topics such as older age and euthanasia. As Chivers notes, "the silver tsunami discourse is tightly tied to the euthanasia debate" (2003, 75). Similarly, Beadie's dialogue is problematic as it suggests a surface-level engagement with political themes about the representation of older women on screen, yet the representation of this older character (who had the potential to be subversive) manages to perpetuate well-rehearsed tropes. Beadie states, for example: "Now I'm old, and no one looks at me anyway. [...] It is true. Getting old? It's the pits. Like, I hate watching television because all the old women are shells, and it... it just hurts to be a shell." The research carried out by members of the *Centre for Women, Ageing and Media* (*WAM*) has found this sentiment echoed in the stories of many older women, and the lack of diversity in the representation of older women on screen indeed provided one of the main reasons for the formation of the Centre in the first place. Despite her lamentation, how far is Beadie's character "just a shell"? Beadie's story is ostensibly one about care giving and euthanasia, a narrative intrinsically related to notions of ageing as decline, and one which arguably perpetuates stereotypes of disabled elders reliant on (younger) others for help to end their lives.

In one episode, Beadie tells Jessa, "Do you know that I wake up every day, disappointed that I didn't die in the night?" and when Jessa still refuses to help her end her life, Beadie insists: "Listen to me. I'm tired. My body is gone. I'm in so much pain, Jessa." As an audience, we never learn the cause of Beadie's pain although we are inclined to believe that she has a terminal illness. Without any real knowledge of Beadie's history and without any real connection to her character (she appears in only three episodes), the audience is therefore likely to simply accept her pain and her failing health as a natural by-product of her age (as with Flo's broken hip and pneumonia). Beadie's unnamed condition continues the trend set up in Grandma Flo—both older characters and their stories are reduced to physiological symptoms and the care they receive from other characters, symptoms and actions that are decoded by audiences as signifiers of old age.

After much deliberation Jessa finally agrees to help Beadie end her life by giving her an overdose of painkillers. When Beadie decides in the final moment not to end her life, however, the action is not in fact a revival of agency, rather it is a delay of dependency. At the beginning of season four, Beadie's daughter, who has learnt of the suicide attempt, arrives in New York to collect her mother and bring her to live with her in Connecticut. When the responsibility for Beadie's continuing care is transferred to her daughter, *Girls* perpetuates current media discourses that construct older age as dependency, the gendered nature of care work (cf. Twigg 2006), and old age as a net drain on resource. This is a continuation of what Gullette suggests is "the frightening side of the media's relentless longevity discourses about the demographic catastrophe of ageing" (2014, in Chivers 2003, 75).

The inclusion of older characters in mainstream television series is, of course, to be encouraged but the depictions of Grandma Flo and Beadie do little to challenge dominant narratives that represent ageing purely as decline. In the following section, we explore the ways that *Girls* also works to stress the only current culturally acceptable vision of female ageing—ageing successfully.

Neoliberal Post-feminism: Evie Michaels and "Ageing Successfully"

Maricel Oro-Piqueras argues that media discourses about older women are "ungenerous by neither constructing nor spreading a positive image of the aging process in women" (2014, 20). This lack of generosity works to exclude more in-depth explorations of older characters' experiences and fails to explore understandings of what might actually constitute a good old age for women and also for men. For instance, maintenance of good social relations and cognitive abilities, and freedom from pain (though not necessarily disease) feature in the reflections of nonagenarians interviewed by Nosraty et al. (2015) in their ethnographic study; however, such understandings do not generally contribute to televisual representations of women in mainstream series. Such lived experiences contribute to our understandings of a worthwhile older age and a meaningful imaginary or counter-narrative for ageing as decline (cf. Nelson 2001; Laceulle and Baars 2014). If, as the above suggests, we are moulded by media and cultural pressure to fear old age, then the other side of this is that we are increasingly invited by neoliberal modes of governance and the media to fight it.

What *Girls* does exceptionally well, especially within the narrative worlds of its millennial characters, is to offer in-depth explorations of the "post-traditional order" of late modernity (Laceulle and Baars 2014) and engage with the precarity of everyday existence within neoliberal America. Older women characters in *Girls*, despite generally being more financially stable, are not immune to the pressures of late modernity (cf. Laceulle and Baars 2014) but for them, their precarity lies in the lack of meaningful explorations and representations of the older female body. Central to the project of neoliberalism are discourses of individualism, individual choice and individual responsibility, and this produces older women's bodies as "consumer bodies, badly in need of special products, such as anti-ageing skincare or figure-correcting lingerie, which promise to halt the physical declining process" (Swinnen 2012, 176). In *Girls*, Evie Michaels (Marnie's mother), offers audiences neoliberal and post-feminist visions of older age informed by popular cultural narratives about ageing "successfully"—Evie's is evidence of the consumer body in action. As a self-fashioned cougar (cf. Wohlman and Reichenpfader 2016), she has attended to the self-policing of the body (including losing weight) and searches out sexual adventure. Evie Michaels encapsulates the spirit of the boomer generation as an "aging youth culture" (Higgs and McGowan 2013, 22) and while on the one hand she pursues the ideals of female sexual liberation espoused by second-wave feminism, her representation is enmeshed in the commodified search for what Barbara Marshall calls "heterohapiness". In a paper, currently in press, but first developed for the *Women, Ageing and Media International Summer School* in 2015, Marshall argues that the success of successful ageing is equated with acceptable performances of normative, gendered heterosexuality. As a result, women are now urged to maintain appropriate levels of heterosexual attractiveness throughout their lifecourse.

In contrast to the more fluid and detailed explorations of gay male sexuality at different stages of the lifecourse that are undertaken in relation to Hannah's former boyfriend, Elijah, and also her father, Tad Horvath, any attempt to represent diverse non-heterosexual possibilities for women are low on the series' horizon. Female queer potential in *Girls* is youthful and uninspiring. Apart from Adam's coterie of twenty-something lesbian friends, a soft lesbian romp between Marnie and Jessa for the heterosexual gaze/pleasure of Jessa's short-lived husband Thomas John, and a rather half-hearted and unsatisfactory encounter between Hannah and her yoga instructor at the female empowerment retreat in season 5, older women are constrained within acceptable forms of female ageing; these are primarily constituted either as successful heterosexual agers or postmenopausal mothers and asexual.

The representations of "successfully aged" older heterosexual women, such as Evie Michaels, within *Girls* contributes to the construction of the majority of other older women's bodies as being aged unsuccessfully. The limited range of possibilities explored in *Girls,* of course, only reflects the limited repertoires currently disseminated in western culture and as such provides a restricted imaginary or narrative "content on which to model our own stories" (Laceulle and Baars 2014, 36) as older women. To Dunham's credit, however, her immersion in feminist histories allows another possible narrative to emerge; a radical and controversial postmaternal identity. In the next section, we offer an analysis of the only recurring female character over the age of 50, in *Girls*, Hannah's mother Loreen. Using ideas of postmaternity, we discuss the construction of a more "everyday" alternative to successful ageing.

Ageing as Verisimilitude: Loreen Horvath and "Everyday Ageing"

When we first encounter Loreen Horvath in the first episode of *Girls*, she is introduced as an older woman who is both straight talking and strong-willed (certainly in comparison to her husband Tad). Her first intervention is to burst the bubble of her daughter's sense of entitlement, by insisting that she and Tad will no longer financially support her. She introduces both a reality check into Hannah's life, and a reality check to notions of ageing as decline and successful ageing represented in *Girls* by Grandma Flo, Beadie and Evie Michaels. Indeed, in the fifteen appearances she makes across the five series, Loreen represents ageing as verisimilitude, functioning as a generational counterpoint to Hannah's life journey through the intersections of postfeminism and late modernity. In so doing, she also produces a more ordinary or "everyday" representation of female ageing. The deliberate manipulation of a generational (boomer/millennial) and feminist/postfeminist conflict running through *Girls*, initially at least, renders Tad as a more sympathetic and approachable character and positions Loreen in what Gullette (1995) identifies as a troublesome and frightening cultural position for ageing women in patriarchal culture—the postmenopausal body.

As an "everyday" challenge to the postmenopausal body's disempowering contemporary cultural script, Loreen makes a claim for postmaternity (cf. Gullette 2002). Postmaternity attempts a feminist intervention to negotiate some of the divisions that are constructed across generational lines. It aims to give worth to both the adult child and the postmaternal mother of the adult child through a transition in identity and status for both parties. Postmaternity is a largely unrecognised position because it threatens hegemonic notions of maternal roles and generations in western societies; particularly around cultural anxieties associated with disempowered female identities and the concept of the "empty" nest, once adult children have established separate lives. In *Girls*, this places millennial and boomer identities (Loreen turns 60 during season 5) in tension and constitutes one of the most significant explorations of the older female body and older female identity in the series. Indeed, much of the narrative is driven by the ways that Hannah responds to Loreen's attempts to claim the status of postmaternity and push Hannah to become adult.

Although not completely successful in achieving postmaternity, her pursuit of it presages a distinctive space for the ageing woman in the televisual cultural imaginary. Evie Michaels, whose older female identity is still controlled by traditional expectations of heterosexual femininity, is ultimately constructed as deviant rather than powerful because her postmenopausal sexual desires are judged in relation to notions of the maternal. She is presented as being unable to provide life wisdom for her adult daughter Marnie (cf. Gorton 2016) and is branded a bad mother. Similarly, it is also in the context of the maternal that Grandma Flo and Beadie are rendered powerless. In Flo's case, this is via the legacy suggested by the onscreen squabbling and negativity of her daughters; in Beadie's case, it is by the implicated infantalisation of her by her daughter when she takes on her full-time care.

Loreen is a robust and forward thinking older woman, especially in the way she is prepared to be the unpopular parent. She has, of course, many material and educational advantages to draw on as a resource. In many ways, she is the epitome of the white middle-class second-wave feminist; a college professor who has achieved tenure; has aspirations to have time for her own interests and even a "lake house" for her leisure time. This confidence comes from a set of material stabilities that are enviable to the millennial female protagonists in the series, but as the unravelling of her thirty-year marriage to Tad reveals, her life is still, in similar ways to her daughter Hannah's, "enmeshed by the contradictory demands and mixed messages of heterosexual romance and feminist emancipation" (Genz 2010, 101).

Loreen's ageing is messy and not a linear progress narrative to either successful ageing or decline. Her ageing is in the everyday. As an older woman, of the feminist and *Cosmopolitan*-reading generation, she has expectations of a sexually fulfilled life and her relationship with Tad is testament to sexual fluidity and negotiations of desire. She does not have to have a successfully aged body to enjoy sex; her mature body is on display with the same verisimilitude as her daughter Hannah's and it is one that desires and is desired. She is ageing in the present and, as yet, not paralysed by fear of ageing in the future. As the car journey with Hannah to celebrate turning 60 in a "queening ceremony" at a female empowerment retreat reveals, she wants to figure out who she can be as an older woman. As her subsequent actions in the series indicate, part of figuring this out is navigating a transition to postmodernity. The unspoken potential of this is to provide an empowered imaginary for later life for herself and also her age-fearing daughter.

To conclude, Kathleen Woodward suggests: "Aging—for ourselves individually and for all of us, no matter our age—is a feminist issue" (2006, 181) and this sentiment explicitly underpins Lena Dunham's *Girls* in complex ways. As a widely recognised millennial generational document, it reveals contemporary anxieties about ageing populations and older female identities and thus mostly rehearses well-known tropes about older women: the dying grandmother, the powerless disabled older woman, the successfully aged, but sexually deviant postmenopausal cougar. Amid these anxieties, Dunham sneaks in, possibly unconsciously, an embryonic attempt to start to rethink the feminist politics of ageing for women that pivots around a changing understanding of ageing and motherhood. This is generated through the construction of Loreen Horvath's desire for postmaternity as a valid way for women to empower themselves and also provide cultural narratives of potential for their adult offspring. Her negotiation of the messy intersections of sexuality, motherhood and age through her desire for postmaternity thus provides an example of ageing which differs from dominant notions represented as either successful ageing or decline.

Work Cited

Centre for Women, Ageing and Media. 2012. The WAM Manifesto. Accessed 24 Oct 2016. http://wamuog.co.uk/the-wam-manifesto.

Chivers, Sally. 2003. *From Old Woman to Older Women: Contemporary Culture and Women's Narratives*. Columbus: Ohio State University Press.

Colloseus, Cecilia. 2015. Wait For It…! Temporality, Maturing and the Depiction of Life Concepts in *How I met your Mother*. In *Serializing Age: Ageing and Old Age in TV Series*, eds. Maricel Oró-Piqueras and Anita Wohlmann, 137–157. Bielefeld: Transcript Verlag.

Cruikshank, Margaret. 2009. *Learning to Be Old: Gender, Culture, and Aging*. New York: Rowman and Littlefield.

Daalmans, Serena. 2013. 'I'm Busy Trying to Become Who I Am': Self-entitlement and the City in HBO's *Girls*. *Feminist Media Studies* 13 (2): 359–362.

Dolan, Josephine, and Estella Tincknell (eds.). 2012. *Aging Femininities: Troubling Representations*. Newcastle upon Tyne: Cambridge Scholars Publishing.

Dunham, Lena. 2014. I Just Want to Work the Death Thing Out. Accessed 24 Oct 2016. https://www.theguardian.com/culture/2014/sep/20/lena-dunham-work-out-death-thing-extract.

Dunham, Lena. 2015. *Not That Kind of Girl: A Young Woman Tells You What She's Learned*. London: Fourth Estate.

Ford, Jessica. 2016. The 'Smart' Body Politics of Lena Dunham's *Girls*. *Feminist Media Studies* 16: 1029–1042.

Garde-Hansen, Joanne, and Hannah Grist. 2015. *Remembering Dennis Potter through Fans, Extras and Archives*. Basingstoke: Palgrave Pivot.

Genz, Stephanie. 2010. Singled Out: Postfeminism's 'New Woman' and the Dilemma of Having It All. *Journal of Popular Culture* 43 (1): 97–119.

Gilleard, Chris, and Paul Higgs. 2010. Aging without Agency: Theorising the Fourth Age. *Aging and Mental Health* 14 (2): 121–128.

Gorton, Kristyn. 2016. 'I'm Too Old to Pretend Anymore': Desire, Ageing and Last Tango in Halifax. In *Serializing Age: Ageing and Old Age in TV Series*, ed. Maricel Oró-Piqueras and Anita Wohlmann, 233–250. Bielefeld: Transcript.

Gullette, Margaret M. 1995. Inventing the Postmaternal Woman, 1898–1927. *Feminist Studies* 21 (3): 221–253.

Gullette, Margaret Morganroth. 2002. Postmaternity as a Revolutionary Feminist Concept. *Feminist Studies* 28 (3): 553–572.

Gullette, Margaret Morganroth. 2003. From Life Storytelling to Age Autobiography. *Journal of Aging Studies* 17: 101–111.

Gullette, Margaret Morganroth. 2004. *Aged by Culture*. Chicago: The University of Chicago Press.

Hamilton, Nikita T. 2014. So They Say You Have a Race Problem? You're in Your Twenties, You Have Way More Problems than That. In *HBO's Girls:*

Questions of Gender, Politics, and Millennial Angst, eds. Betty Kaklamanidou, and Margaret Tally, 43–58. Newcastle-upon-Tyne: Cambridge Scholars Publishing.

Hammad, Hannah. 2015. 'I'm Not Past My Sell By Date Yet!' Sarah Jane's Adventuress in Postfeminist Rejuvenation and the Later-Life Celebrity of Elisabeth Sladandn. In *Freeze Frame: Women, Celebrity and Cultures of Ageing*, eds. Susan Holmes and Deborah Jermyn, 162–177. London: Palgrave Macmillan.

Hayner, Chris. 2013. Howard Stern Sorry for Lena Dunham Remarks. Accessed 24 Oct 2016. http://screenertv.com/news-features/howard-stern-sorry-for-lena-dunham-remarks/.

Higgs, Paul, and Fiona McGowan. 2013. Ageing, Embodiments and the Negotiation of the Third and Fourth Ages. In *Aging Men, Masculinities and Modern Medicine*, eds. Antje Kampf, Barbara L. Marshall, and Alan Petersen, 21–34. New York: Routledge.

Jennings, Ros, and Abigail Gardner. 2012. *Rock On!: Women, Ageing and Popular Music*. Farnham: Ashgate.

Jennings, Ros and Eva Krainitzki. 2015. 'Call the Celebrity': Voicing the Experience of Women and Ageing through the Distinctive Vocal Presence of Vanessa Redgrave. In *Freeze Frame: Women, Celebrity and Cultures of Ageing*, eds. Deborah Jermyn and Susan Holmes, 178–196. London: Palgrave Macmillan.

Jennings, Ros, and Maricel Oró-Piqueras. 2016. Heroine And/Or Caricature? The Older Woman in Desperate Housewives. In *Serializing Age: Ageing and Old Age in TV Series*, eds. Maricel Oró-Piqueras and Anita Wohlmann, 1–17. Bielefeld: Transcript.

Kaklamanidou, Betty, and Margaret Tally (eds.). 2014. *HBO's Girls: Questions of Gender, Politics, and Millennial Angst*. Newcastle-upon-Tyne: Cambridge Scholars Publishing.

Kaplan, E. Anne. 2005. *Trauma Culture: The Politics of Terror and Loss in Media and Literature*. New Brunswick: Rutgers University Press.

Katz, Stephen. 1996. *Disciplining Old Age: The Formation of Gerontological Knowledge*. Charlottesville: University Press of Virginia.

Katz, Stephen. 2005. *Aging: Life Course, Lifestyle, and Senior Worlds*. Peterborough: Broadview Press.

Katz, Stephen, and Barbara Marshall. 2008. New Sex for Old: Lifestyle, Consumerism and the Ethics of Ageing Well. In *Ageing*, ed. S. McDaniel. London: Sage.

Krainitzki, Eva. 2014. Judi Dench's Age-inappropriateness and the Role of M: Challenging Normative Temporality. *Journal of Aging Studies* 29: 32–40.

Kriebernegg, Ulla, Roberta Maierhofer, and Barbara Raztenböck (eds.). 2014. *Alive and Kicking at All Ages: Cultural Constructions of Health and Lifecourse Identity*. Bielefeld: Transcript.

Lehman, Katherine. 2014. 'All Adventurous Women Do': HBO's Girls and the 1960–70s Single Woman. In *HBO's Girls: Questions of Gender, Politics, and Millennial Angst*, eds. Betty Kaklamanidou and Margaret Tally, 10–27. Newcastle-upon-Tyne: Cambridge Scholars Publishing.

Laceulle, Hanne, and Jan Baars. 2014. Self-realization and Cultural Narratives about Later Life. *Journal of Aging Studies* 31: 34–44.

Montemurro, Beth, and Jenna M. Siefken. 2014. Cougars on the Prowl? New Perceptions of Older Women's Sexuality. *Journal of Aging Studies* 28: 35–43.

Nash, M., and R. Grant. 2015. Twenty-Something *Girls* v. Thirty-Something *Sex and the City* Women: Paving the way for 'Post? Feminism'. *Feminist Media Studies* 15 (6): 976–991.

Nelson, E.M. 2014. Embracing the Awkwardness of AUTEURship in *Girls*. In *HBO's Girls: Questions of Gender, Politics, and Millennial Angst*, eds. Betty Kaklamanidou and Margaret Tally, 91–107. Newcastle-upon-Tyne: Cambridge Scholars Publishing.

Nelson, Hilde Lindemann. 2001. *Damaged Identities, Narrative Repair*. Ithaca: Cornell University Press.

Nosraty, L., M. Jylhä, T. Raittila, and K. Lumme-Sandt. 2015. Perceptions of the Oldest Old of Successful Ageing: Vitality 90+Study. *Journal of Aging Studies* 32: 50–58.

Novak, Mark. 2014. *Issues in Ageing*. Oxon: Routledge.

Nussbaum, Emily. 2014. It's Different for Girls. *New York Magazine*. Accessed 12 Sept 2016. http://nymag.com/arts/tv/features/girls-lena-dunham-2012-4/.

Nygaard, Taylor. 2013. Girls Just Want to be 'Quality': HBO, Lena Dunham, and Girls' Conflicting Brand Identity. *Feminist Media Studies* 13 (2): 370–374.

Oró-Piqueras, Maricel, and Anita Wohlmann (eds.). 2016. *Serializing Age: Ageing and Old Age in TV Series*. Bielefeld: Transcript.

Oró-Piqueras, Maricel. 2014. Challenging Stereotypes? The Older Woman in the TV Series Brothers & Sisters. *Journal of Aging Studies* 31: 20–25.

Persky, Bill. 2013. Viewpoint: the Problem with Lena Dunham's *Girls*. Accessed 24 Oct 2016. http://ideas.time.com/2013/02/08/viewpoint-the-problem-with-lena-dunhams-girls/.

Rowe, Kathleen. 1995. *The Unruly Woman: Gender and the Genres of Laughter*. Austin: University of Texas Press.

Russo, Mary. 1995. *The Female Grotesque: Risk, Excess and Modernity*. Oxon: Routledge.

Saisi, Boké. 2014. "(Just White) Girls?: Underrepresentation and Active Audiences in HBO's *Girls*". In *HBO's Girls: Questions of Gender, Politics, and Millennial Angst*, eds. Betty Kaklamanidou and Margaret Tally, 59–72. Newcastle-upon-Tyne: Cambridge Scholars Publishing.

Sawchuck, Kim, and Barbara Crow. 2012. 'I'm G-Mom on the Phone': Remote Grandmothering, Cell Phones and Inter-Generational Dis/Connections. *Feminist Media Studies* 12 (4): 496–505.

Shildrick, Margrit. 1997. *Leaky Bodies and Boundaries: Feminism, Postmodernism, and (Bio)Ethics*. Oxon: Routledge.

Sontag, Susan. 1978. *Illness as a Metaphor*. London: Penguin.

Swinnen, Aagje. 2012. To Pin Up or Pin Down Women of Age?: The Representation of Ageing Women's Bodies in the Photographs of Erwin Olaf. In *Aging, Performance, and Stardom: Doing Age on the Stage of Consumerist Culture*, eds. Aagje Swinnen and John A. Stotesbury, 177–196. Berlin: LIT Verlag.

Twigg, Julia. 2004. The Body, Gender, and Age: Feminist Insights in Social Gerontology. *Journal of Aging Studies* 18: 59–73.

Twigg, Julia. 2006. *The Body in Health and Social Care*. Basingstoke: Palgrave Macmillan.

Weiss, Michael. 2003. Great Expectations: Baby Boomer Wealth Forecasts Wilt. *American Demographics* 25 (4): 26–35.

Wilson, Sherryl. 2014. She's Been Away: Ageing, Madness and Memory. In *Alive and Kicking at All Ages: Cultural Constructions of Health and Lifecourse Identity*, eds. Ulla Kriebernegg, Roberta Maierhofer, and Barbara Raztenböck, 187–202. Bielefeld Germany: Transcript.

Wohlman, Anita, and Julia Reichenpfader. 2016. Serial Cougars: Representations of Non-Normative Lifestyles in a Sitcom, an Episodic Serial, and a Soap Opera. In *Serializing Age: Ageing and Old Age in TV Series*, eds. Maricel Oró-Piqueras and Anita Wohlmann, 159–186. Bielefeld: Transcript.

Woods, Faye. 2015. Girls Talk: Authorship and Authenticity in the Reception of Lena Dunham's *Girls*. *Critical Studies in Television* 10 (2): 37–54.

Woodward, Kathleen (ed.). 1999. *Figuring Age: Women, Bodies, Generations*. Bloomington: Indiana University Press.

Woodward, Kathleen. 2006. Performing Age, Performing Gender. *NWSA Journal* 18 (1): 162–189.

CHAPTER 13

The New Model Subject: "Coolness" and the Turn to Older Women Models in Lifestyle and Fashion Advertising

Deborah Jermyn and Anne Jerslev

Even the most casual observer of fashion marketing and aspirational advertising will have noted that a core value these arenas have long held dear is the desirability of *youth*. With the exception of noted style mavericks like Anna Wintour or Carine Roitfeld, as they age, older "ordinary" women are positioned as moving progressively to the margins of the world of fashion, and are expected to more or less relinquish the pleasure they might once have taken in it. For that matter too, older subjects are typically excluded broadly from the fashionable world of major lifestyle brands; the ageing body does not sit comfortably with notions of wishful longing.

Thus it is that the fashion and related industries have long entrenched a marketplace in which young, even adolescent, models are co-opted to

D. Jermyn (✉)
University of Roehampton, London, UK
e-mail: D.Jermyn@roehampton.ac.uk

A. Jerslev
University of Copenhagen, Copenhagen, Denmark
e-mail: jerslev@hum.ku.dk

C. McGlynn et al. (eds.), *Ageing Women in Literature and Visual Culture*,
DOI 10.1007/978-3-319-63609-2_13

sell clothes, accessories, all manner of beauty products and more, to adult women. As Julia Twigg notes, labels and designers commonly hold anxieties about being seen to speak to or "for" older women, fearing negative repercussions for their brand value (2013, 126–127). Yet we live now in an era of a rapidly ageing population, one in which the "grey consumer"[1] is becoming ever more prevalent; still, they are somehow both commercially desirable (in terms of the share of the market they make up) and undesirable (in terms of the longstanding cultural distaste for ageing they obviously embody). In a marketplace marked by such tensions, it is intriguing to note that of late we find ourselves in a cultural moment where this landscape appears, in some instances at least, to be shifting. Brands ranging from Marks & Spencer, to TK Maxx, to Lanvin have all in recent years adopted women models markedly older than the "norm" in their advertising campaigns, albeit styled in different ways. What are the implications of this shift, then, for understanding the cultural value that older women can, or cannot, hold at this time in the fashion sphere? In what follows, we look at how the rearticulation of the older woman as model and/or brand ambassador has taken place in two high-profile instances—the 2015 Céline campaign featuring Joan Didion, and the 2017 Pirelli calendar—arguing that the notion of *cool* is reinscribed across the brand meaning of each by way of the older woman subject.

As a preamble to this, one might note that fashion editorials and ads are about creating a certain fashionable *look*. In her study of the fashion world backstage, Ashley Mears (2011) distinguishes between a *commercial* look associated with traditional notions of a beautiful model and mainstream magazines and commercials, and an *edgy*, "strange" look in fashion editorials and ads in more niche magazines, in which "imperfect beauty" (Cotton 2000) and non-conformity (Evans 2003) are favoured. In her outlining of the difference between these two kinds of looks in fashion media, Mears furthermore opposes a *thin* and a *skinny* look; the commercial look is "young" and "thin," in contrast to the edgy look which is "teenage" and "skinny" (2011, 39). However, the many older women in fashion ads today show that the intertwining of youth and

[1] Broadly, this refers to an older demographic than those most popularly targeted by advertisers and marketing—'older' remaining a subjective and contested term here, which is, however, widely taken to indicate the 60+ market.

skinniness in fashion has loosened to some degree. The non-conformist, skinny look may be created not only through the body of the teenage waif, but also by means of the older woman's body. Accordingly, there is a contemporary tendency in a fashion context to combine the ageing face with extreme bodily thinness, creating an updated, striking version of a sought-after fashionable *edgy look*.

The older woman in fashion ads does not resemble the typical older body; her skinny-ness does not equate with the more commonly found characteristics of the ageing female body, such as a thickening of the waistline. The skinny older female body, by contrast, constitutes the perfect "hanger-body" (Mears 2011, 181), which is sought after by the "trendiest" luxury brands (cf., for example, minimalist luxury brand *The Row*, which cast 65-year-old former model, fashion editor and stylist Linda Rodin for their pre-fall 2014 collection). In addition to favouring an appearance which accords with the undisputed fashion credo that clothes look best on a thin body, the old age of the model signals that the brand may appeal to a broader age group, and it confers upon the clothes the air of (celebrity) history attached to the model. Finally, such ads adhere to fashion logic, which is always seeking the new, and, furthermore, a newness which is audacious without being scandalous.

Joan Didion for Céline

Céline is a much-hyped influential French luxury fashion brand, and acclaimed designer Phoebe Philo has been its creative director since 2008. Labelled "impeachably cool" (Hoby 2015), Céline's campaigns have been easily recognisable for several years: plain yet subtle; elegant, yet trendy, just like the clothes. Often the model is shot on the background of a bright monochrome screen or otherwise simple background; often she poses erect, unglamorous. The ads are usually shot by Jürgen Teller, and Céline often uses the same, mostly up-and-coming fashion models. Despite the ads' apparently simple, unglamorous look, they are trendsetting in fashion photography and often discretely allude to popular cultural history on the edge of the mainstream; hence, Céline has cultivated a reputation for making clothes for an intellectual audience.

The Spring/Summer (s/s) 2015 campaign confirms this brand image. By choosing writer Joan Didion (b. 1934) as the *face* of the campaign, it constructs a kind of cerebral aura around the brand. Essential to what was enthusiastically proclaimed the campaign's audaciousness by a host of online media commentators when the campaign was released, is the very realist inscription of the ageing female body and face within the field of fashion. Here, centre stage is taken not by the middle-aged, gorgeous even when "sombre" Julia Roberts (for Givenchy s/s 2015), not by the glamorous but obviously manipulated close-ups of Helen Mirren (for L'Oreal), not by the delicate and beautiful near-70 Maye Musk (for James Perse Fall/Winter (f/w) 2016). Rather, it is the over-80-year-old and old-looking American writer who is cast by Céline to confirm the brand's image of cool minimalism—of being edgy without being avant-garde.

Joan Didion is not the first older woman to appear in a Céline ad, nor is she the first older woman in a Céline ad shot by Jürgen Teller. Already for the f/w campaign 2010/11[2] the brand featured former model Gitte Lee (b. 1935), after Lee had been featured on Ari Seth Cohen's *Advanced Style* blog in July 2010. However, contrary to the 2010 Céline ad, where the shot of Gitte Lee is medium long, the portrait of Didion is a (medium) close-up in which Teller's recognisable hard and frontal, realist and almost ruthless lighting of his model is pushed to the limit.

The photograph portrays the "literary celebrity" (Ohlsson et al. 2014; Marsh 2015) Joan Didion slightly angled from above.[3] Teller's frontal lighting of her face casts a black shadow on the upper part of the wall to the left of her face; thus a balance is created with the black surface of the tight dress she is wearing, the upper part of which resembles a black turtleneck Didion wore in an ad for Gap's 1989 campaign *Individuals of Style*, in which she was photographed tête-à-tête with her adopted daughter Quintana Roe. Didion is sitting on a kind of sofa in her private home (cf. Jacobs 2015); erect but also a bit sunken, her right arm stretched to the side, the other resting on her lap and her red lips closed. She is wearing large black Céline sunglasses that, together with the black dress and a large golden pendant necklace, provide a fashionable and luxurious version of the attitude of detachment for which she is known (cf. Daum 2015). Black sunglasses have been the writer's signature accessory since she was photographed for the cover of her first

[2]Gitte Lee was also modelling in 2013 for & Other Stories' launch catalogue and later the same year for an Italian *Vogue* editorial. Gitte Lee is on the cover of Cohen's *Advanced Style* (2012).

[3]For an analysis of the Didion ad with a focus on the face, beauty and time, see Jerslev (2017).

collection of essays, *Slouching Towards Bethlehem,* in 1968. Didion's features are sharp and her figure skinny, appearing fragile. Moreover, the harsh frontal light and the over-sized dark glasses make the ageing face look pale and emphasise her wrinkled skin above the turtleneck as well as the thinness of both her facial features and the carefully combed grey page-style hair.

The dark glasses prevent us from seeing whether she looks directly at the photographer or has adopted a more withdrawn look. However, both the harsh lighting—which creates a sense of paparazzi photography—and the dark glasses worn indoors, emphasise Didion's celebrity status, and give the impression of capturing a random moment, which confers a sense of exclusivity and immediacy to the photograph. Didion is seemingly not posing, captured almost as if caught unawares, and yet the closed lips make her seem a little tense, too, as if she was not completely at ease in her home. The brand name Céline is written in large white capital letters on the background of Didion's black dress and anchors as fashionable not only clothes and accessories but also the look of the photograph as such.

Besides photographing Joan Didion for a fashion ad and simultaneously borrowing and lending her fashionability, Teller's style gives the impression of offering a realist portrait of the elderly writer: Joan Didion just like she looks now. It provides likeness as well as a "manifestation of [her] 'essence' or 'air'" (Freeland 2010, 74). The fashion photograph constructs an unsentimental, edgy clash between a temporality of time passed inscribed in the ageing face and body, and a temporality of cool presence.

Not least by virtue of the detached look accentuated by the dark glasses, the image inscribes itself within a tradition of photographing and understanding the renowned writer Joan Didion as cool (see, for example, Daum 2015). A *look of coolness* is inscribed not only across the writer's ageing appearance but across the whole ad through its invisible web of references to Didion's history and iconic portraits of her from past decades (cf. Jerslev 2017). Moreover, Joan Didion's elderly appearance boosts the *coolness* which has been attached to the brand for many years, and vice versa, as being connected with this trendy brand attaches renewed coolness to Joan Didion, the ageing yet still topical writer. This synergistic cross-fertilisation begs the question: what is cool and what is cool in a fashion context? What goes on at the intersection of cool fashion photography and the ageing Joan Didion?

Cool

Vanessa Brown (2015) suggests that sunglasses are *signs of cool* with "an incredible staying power" (2015, 2; cf. also Pountain and Robins 2000), even though Brown (like Mears 2011) also claims that what is considered cool is shifting: "cool is well known to be a slippery thing—subjective, elusive and ever changing" (2015, 2). Sunglasses are thus a means for constructing the contradictory attitude of involvement and detachment, of presence and absence, of fashionability and individuality, which epitomises cool.

As evident in the Didion ad, sunglasses and black clothes have come to signal and accentuate the cool attitude. The dress emphasises a certain individual composure and restrained affect (cf. Geiger et al. 2010). Cool is an attitude towards the world, a strategy for making sense of everyday life, a coping mechanism, a body technique and an aesthetic sensibility performed by people or in media representations. What has most often been connected with cool, though, is a sense of individual rebellion, understood as a non-conformist attitude, a tribute to a position outside of the mainstream and common. Cool is an attitude of detachment and aloofness that expresses a thought-out, individualist position on the edge meant to reject "the aesthetic values of those 'others' with whom you do not wish to be associated" (Brown 2014, 4); thus the cool sensibility is as much defined by what it is not as by what it is. As such, cool is elitist and uncompromising; its emphasis is on individual style and visibility as superior to everyone else's.

Some of the writing on cool analyses the term as a (masculine) way of communicating strength and coping with oppressive social circumstances (cf. Majors and Billson 1993; Geiger et al. 2010; Brown 2015). By contrast, cultural theorists and writers Dick Pountain and David Robins claim that the cool pose is an aesthetic kind of rebellion and therefore merely significant as a powerful mark of distinction: "The essence of Cool has always been, first of all, to look Cool" (2000, 114), hence the importance of clothes as signals of cool (cf. also Mentges 2000). Moreover, Pountain and Robins claim that "Cool does not gaze at others but appears to others; it does not gaze but wishes to be gazed at" (2000, 117); thus the importance of sunglasses, which may, however, also conceal that even though the cool attitude is detached, it is simultaneously seismographically occupied with breaking away from the mainstream.

Today, cool functions not least as a powerful and valuable signifier of distinction in consumer culture, a position of being culturally "in the know" (Nancarrow et al. 2002, 313). A cool person—or brand—inhabits a certain cultural capital and a sense of the new *edgy* in consumer culture. Cool therefore occupies an ambiguous position in relation to fashion; in opposition to fashion as a system and yet sharing with fashion the logic of constant renewal, the necessity of being at the forefront and the connection with commodification. Because cool is not an avant-garde sensibility, mainstream fashion brands may well work to confer a cool factor on their clothes—exemplified by high-street retailer Gap's autumn 1993 black-and-white ads for khakis featuring, among others, icons of coolness James Dean, Jack Kerouac, Andy Warhol and Steve McQueen. Yet, at any rate, cool both presupposes and acknowledges the system of fashion in order for edginess to function as a superior marker of distinction.

In these ways, besides undoubtedly paying homage to an old woman who is a celebrated writer and cultural icon, the Céline ad could be described as a signature of cool, fashionable yet edgy, exuding a certain intellectual detachment and also a strong sense of being *in the know*. One might ask what qualifies Joan Didion in particular for the ad, besides the fact that she is old and the ad thereby knowingly anticipated causing a stir by resisting the founding logic of fashion, the field's marriage to the young body (cf. Twigg 2013). One answer relates to bodily appearance, as previously mentioned. Joan Didion's body, though old, still fits in well with a fashion culture in which extreme thinness is one of the preconditions for the staging of an edgy look. Secondly, an aura of the fashionable and cool has been attached to Joan Didion over the years. Several writers have noted how clothes play an important part in her writing (her packing list in "The White Album" printed in the 1979 essay collection *The White Album* is renowned), not to mention that she started her career working and writing for *Vogue* in the late 1950s and early 1960s. She appeared in the above-mentioned Gap ad in 1989, but well before that, in 1968, photographer Julian Wasser's pictures of her for *Time* magazine portrayed her as cool. In one of Wasser's photos she is casually leaning on her white shining Corvette in her driveway, a cigarette in her hand and a detached look. In another she puts an arm casually out of the car's rolled-down window, a cigarette in the other hand. As stated in an article about the Céline ad in *The Atlantic*: "It's possible that no one will ever look as cool as Joan Didion does behind a dark pair of sunglasses or half-leaning out the window of a 1969 Corvette Stingray. With Didion, it's not as much the outfit you remember as the attitude" (Lafrance 2015).

Critical work in this arena has observed in passing that the cool attitude is primarily connected to masculinity (cf. Majors and Billson 1993; Nancarrow et al. 2002; Brown 2015; Quartz and Asp 2015). Though Pountain and Robins note that there is a tradition in film for "cool female role models" (2000, 23), the majority of their examples are men. Wasser's photographs of Didion are thus rather exceptional images of a cool woman, detachedly relaxed and with an air of laid-back, self-confident elitism next to her cool car.[4] In the Céline ad, Joan Didion is constituted as cool by showing off some of her signature traits—one being those large black sunglasses. One could say that old age comes into fashion in the Céline ad, not as a tribute to ageing in itself, but as a tribute to the history of an iconic woman; moreover as a means of constructing an aesthetic, edgy attitude in fashion ads, and finally as a mark of distinction which confirms Céline's reputation as fashionably cool.

"An Arty Soft-Core Ode to Pinups": Contextualising the Pirelli Calendar

By way of another example which has similarly attached the "coolness" of the ageing/older woman model to an established high-end brand in recent times, we turn now to Pirelli. At first glance, Pirelli may seem to hold little common ground with Céline, and thus this selection warrants some brief contextualisation here. Rather than an exclusive fashion brand, the company is "Europe's third-largest tire maker" (Sylvers 2011), founded in Milan in 1872, and today perhaps most particularly heralded as supplier to the exclusive, expensive—and dangerous—sport of Formula One (F1). As such, the Pirelli brand name connotes desirable "mileage" of a different sort, one which can be expanded and exploited in other arenas to help secure the kudos of a revered "lifestyle brand." Hence in 2011 Pirelli opened its first clothing and accessories store in Milan, having sold the "PZero" brand in department and clothing stores

[4]The cool factor attached to the Julian Wasser photos is furthermore alluded to in a 2015 Céline campaign, in which model Daria Werbowy, shot by photographer and filmmaker Tyrone Lebon, mimics the photo of the young Didion in her Corvette.

around the world since 2002; as Eric Sylvers observes, in this sense Pirelli and "other such brands are not much different from fashion designers themselves, who, over the past decade, have moved into accessories, beauty products and perfume, watches and even furniture and luxury hotels" (2011).

Nowhere is the Pirelli brand's particular cachet more evident, however, than in the history of the Pirelli trade calendar, known for its use of highly esteemed photographers and the top models of the day, and trademarked simply as "The Cal." The calendar was introduced by the company in 1964 according to their official history (following an unsuccessful launch in 1963), when "Pirelli's British subsidiary was looking for a marketing strategy to help Pirelli stand out from domestic competition and appointed the art director Derek Forsyth and British photographer Robert Freeman, famous for his portraits of the Beatles, to produce what was an entirely innovative project for its day" (www.pirelli.com). The "corporate freebie" went on to become a highly anticipated annual cultural artefact of sorts; as Alice White Walker observed in her Huffington Post Style blog, "This isn't your typical oil-smeared garage calendar—there are only 20,000 copies printed each year, reserved for celebrities and the company's key clientele" (2016). Received as a kind of aesthetic marker of its time, then, "The Cal" is an object which at one level has already long been invested with certain notions of "cool," albeit frequently of a risqué kind. Year on year, photographers including Bert Stern, Herb Ritts. Richard Avedon, Bruce Weber and Karl Lagerfeld have captured women subjects in a series of often nude, highly sexualised, fetishised and provocative images that have prompted debate over the boundaries between art, taste and sensationalism. Unlike Céline's Didion campaign, it might be said, these most scrutinised Pirelli pictures have featured women very much in a series of states of *un*dress, rather than dress. However, in keeping with the modalities of designer fashion, the fact that the calendar is only available in a limited edition format lends it an air of exclusivity. Its annual release date and "the reveal" surrounding each edition's choice of photographer and models, just like the seasonal new trends of fashion showcased on global catwalks and fashion magazine pages, is a media event which is widely discussed and anticipated. The Pirelli website declares the company "vision" to be that, "We constantly challenge the boundaries of technology, style and sustainability, *setting trends across the world*" (www.pirelli.com, our emphasis); and this drive to "set trends," quite outside the technology of tyre manufacturing, has clearly been encapsulated by the ambitions it evidences in "The Cal."

Pirelli's New Cool—Unveiling "The Cal" in 2017

Increasingly in recent years, however, the artefact has arguably carried notions of the passé, as its once provocative styling became predictable, at the very least in terms of content if not entirely in the detail of form. Importantly, a reimagining of The Cal was evident already in 2016, when Annie Leibovitz photographed the calendar for the second time. As with the Didion Céline campaign, it largely adopted non-models, women who were instead accomplished, respected public figures of one kind or another drawn from other fields, here encompassing a variety of races and ages. These included comedian and actor Amy Schumer—who along with tennis legend Serena Williams and model Natalia Vodianova was the only of the sitters not to be photographed fully clothed—captured in sheer knickers astride a stool, with un-airbrushed rolls of flesh on her stomach left in full view, prompting much debate about "real" women's bodies among commentators; as well as 77-year-old Agnes Gund, philanthropist and president emerita of the Museum of Modern Art; and the "godmother of punk," singer-songwriter Patti Smith.

The 2016 calendar thus became the subject of renewed critical and media interest for breaking with conceived notions about what The Cal stood for—namely "arty soft-core" (Friedman 2015) images of young, nude, perfectly proportioned women. As Vanessa Friedman observed in *The New York Times*, "Though the calendar has, on rare occasions, featured women in clothes [...] this is the first time there is no provocation in the posing, and the first time the attraction of the subjects is in their resumes, not their measurements" (2015). The Cal's role as a kind of social barometer of some sort—that is, "to a certain extent, a historical record" (Friedman 2015)—in this new guise was thus cautiously taken to perhaps herald a cultural shift; one in which brands like Pirelli might begin to win more respect for showcasing women of substance—including, importantly, older women—rather than scantily clad young models. Alternatively, some commentators asked whether Leibovitz's reimagining of the calendar constituted mere "lip service," a superficial exercise in which "this 'feminist makeover' is more about the market than some sudden enlightenment" (Moore 2015). It seemed only time might tell in this respect as one of the 2016 models, Iranian artist Shirin Neshat, presciently observed, noting that, "It would be a huge disappointment," if in 2017 Pirelli were to "abandon the idea of women who define modern life, and go back to sexy girls who are too young to have accomplished anything" (qtd. in Friedman 2015). If the calendar's original "swinging London" vision could be said to have boldly spoken to (perceptions of) women's new-found freedom and empowerment in the sexual revolution of the 1960s, does this new turn to older women in the 2010s stand for another landmark, transitional moment, then; one in which finally it appears, "the disenfranchisement and invisibility endured by older women in the fashion, beauty and celebrity industries—which are central to upholding wider social hierarchies about which women matter—have been dented" (Jermyn 2016, 576–77)?

Thus it was in 2017 that the latest Pirelli calendar, entitled "Emotional" and devoted almost entirely to women actors, found itself once more the subject of extensive contemplation in the media as, true to Leibovitz's vision, it again featured a number of celebrated older women subjects. Given The Cal's historical reputation, the very act of adopting older women as models was thus configured as "risqué" and audacious, quite in keeping with its pedigree, even while it broke with that pedigree by eschewing an entirely youthful cast. The 14 actors photographed (along with Russian professor Anastasia Ignatova), ranging in age from 28 to 71, included Helen Mirren (71), Julianne Moore (55), Robin Wright (50), Charlotte Rampling (70) and Uma Thurman (46), as well as younger stars such as Lupita Nyong'o (33), Alicia Vikander (28) and Zhang Ziyi (37). Shot by Peter Lindbergh on his third commission for The Cal, the photographer commented at the Paris launch that his calendar was "'a cry for beauty today against *the terror of perfection and youth*,' aiming to show 'real women' as they are naturally without heavy makeup or retouching" (Willsher 2016, our emphasis), again echoing a similar outlook to that adopted by Jürgen Teller's Didion image in the Céline campaign. It was this refusal of airbrushing, most particularly by older women stars, that journalists continually returned to as central to the calendar's perceived edginess, widely reproducing examples of these "candid" images of the older women for scrutiny rather than those of the younger subjects. At Vogue.com, for example, it was this feature of The Cal that prompted the headline of an article entitled, "The 2017 Pirelli Calendar Featuring Nicole Kidman, Ziyi Zhang, Kate Winslet, and Moore Was Not Retouched at All," with Kidman's portrait reproduced beneath (Yotka 2016).

Indeed, it is photos of these older stars which are also most conspicuously adopted by Pirelli on their own website to promote the 2017 calendar, where shots of Thurman, Wright, Kidman and Moore feature on the slideshow at the top of the "2017 Pirelli Calendar Unveiled" page (www.Pirelli.com) (though one might observe it is interesting they do not use the *oldest* stars, namely Mirren or Rampling). Moore is featured in a black body suit with spaghetti straps, sitting on a stool, one leg raised up to her chest, her loose hair moving freely as if a wind machine is wafting over her, in a pose which still might readily be considered "sexy," though strikingly her facial expression is dour and she appears make-up free; a tight close-up on Thurman's face reveals the "crow's feet" one might realistically expect of a woman in her mid-40s; Wright sits atop a table in loose shorts and vest, face turned from the camera, again like Moore revealing a body that is still athletic (and thus different to, though covetable in another manner from, Didion's much older " hanger-body" type), but the looser flesh around the face and neck common to women of her age is palpable. Finally, Kidman's botox usage has been the subject of endless media speculation and surveillance, earning her the grotesque and belittling moniker "Granny Freeze" from "celebrity blogger" Perez Hilton (cf. Fairclough 2012). But in her Pirelli portrait, the fine lines running atop her forehead are plain to see. If Pirelli aspires to be understood as a brand which somehow leads, rather than only reflects, on how shifts in the representation of women matter to the cultural agenda of any given moment, its attention to older women can be considered key to how it wishes to construct its "trend-setting" public image at this time. Thus if, as noted above, cool signifies a position of being "in the know" (Nancarrow et al. 2002, 313), the 2017 Pirelli calendar seems to declare to the fashionable types who admire it that right now, "old" is where it's at.

Ways of Seeing: Older Women and Visibility

However, for some commentators, Pirelli have come late to the party in adopting older women as their new model subjects in 2017. Writing at *The Atlantic*, Sophie Gilbert observed that the brand was "jumping on a bandwagon rather than taking a brave stand" (2016). Not only was The Cal's (seemingly) novel switch to older women a marketing-savvy shift adopted for the commercial benefits the subsequent publicity would bring, it was merely emulating a growing cultural resistance to unattainable youthful perfection that has been gaining momentum for some time. In Gilbert's words, this was "fashion catching up," with Pirelli "hoping a movement that's long been felt on social media and among women themselves can turn into good branding, even for a company that's historically benefitted from the promotion of impossible beauty ideals" (2016).

Many scholars have discussed the female body's ageing characteristics, how the thin, toned, shapely body denotes youthfulness in contrast to the typically ageing female body, which as noted has very often gained weight around the waist and on the stomach, for example (cf. Twigg 2013; Clarke 2011, 21–23). To that extent the ordinary "elderly" body more readily witnessed and still disdained in the everyday, despite evidence of a burgeoning opposition to such discourses, is not fashionable. Moreover, Twigg has outlined in detail how contemporary culture persistently advocates certain dress norms appropriate for the ageing female and how many older women accord with this idea: the avoidance of dramatic styles or colours and the use of "quieter, more sober and self-effacing forms" (2013, 27). Nevertheless, Twigg also emphasises that the clothes made to fit the typical elderly body are as much an expression of a certain idea of what an older woman should look like as an adjustment to a certain bodily shape. A norm of *appropriateness* (cf. Russo 1999; Wearing 2007; Railton and Watson 2012; Twigg 2013), that is, a culturally pervasive norm of acting and looking one's age as an older person, is deeply embedded in the cultural construction of the identity of the older woman: dressing appropriately as an older woman is understood as dressing to not be seen; the style of an older woman is a non-style. However, given the trend in using older women as models, the question is, as also claimed by Wearing (2007): if invisibility has given way to visibility when it comes to representations of older women, in some recent cultural sites at least, what kind of visibility is afforded?

One potentially "daring" form of visibility, as discussed above, in taking the 2017 Pirelli calendar and the 2015 Céline ad as examples, is to construct the older woman as cool—self-confidently inhabiting an edgy pose and exuding an attitude of detachment. Images of ageing celebrities and former models inevitably invoke layers of references to their younger selves. However, the fashion and celebrity context—modelling a cool attitude and displaying the older female body as *hanger-body*—may function to release the older woman's ageing appearance from the sentimentality and air of time-gone-by that can be associated with staged photographs of older women (cf. Richards et al. 2012). A contemporary version of an edgy sensibility, we suggest that cool constitutes an aesthetic space for the representation of the older woman, in which ageing is neither concealed nor accentuated, in which the older female body may even be photographed in different states of undress and, even more importantly, in which questions of age appropriateness, youthfulness, agelessness and dressing one's age do not make sense.

A fashionable, edgy attitude, cool is about appearance and appearing. Because a cool style is best described by what it is not—cool is essentially anti-mainstream—it may allow the older woman a range of expressions and styles devoid of age normativity but aspiring for her to be seen as what she is—an older woman, stylish and cool. As such the photos on Ari Seth Cohen's *Advanced Style* blog, which show older stylish women as more flamboyantly dressed (cf. Jermyn 2016) than the black "uniform" displayed by Didion's essentially cool edginess, exemplify another kind of cool attitude. Cohen started the blog in 2008 with the intention to capture older women (and some men) who "live full creative lives" and "show that you can be stylish at any age."[5] The women are posing self-confidently, the majority in the manner of "street-style" fashion. The blog context provides the photographs with cool fashionability, but the women are not exuding the air of detachment most often found in fashionable cool, often, in fact, smiling warmly at the photographer. However, they do display a stylish sense of individualism and anti-mainstream (hence, "Advanced") and radiate a vivid self-reliance of standing out to be looked at in their old age. Cohen's women often style themselves in complete neglect of "appropriateness," and yet they are held up as both elegant and stylish; moreover, the photographs' cool appearance is sustained by the women seemingly displaying their bodies and outfits with pleasure and pride and thus claiming, through the photographs, their place as ageing women in the world of fashion and style.

What can be garnered finally, then, from our discussion here about the cultural shift regarding the visibility of the older woman, and the increasingly prevalent tendency to cast older women in fashion ads and photography? On the one hand, the older female model ideal in fashion is overwhelmingly white and slim, just like in fashion photography in

---

[5] Cohen on http://www.advanced.style/about. For a more comprehensive discussion of Cohen's blog and documentary, as well as of Sue Bourne's *Fabulous Fashionistas* (2013), see Jermyn (2014).

general; accordingly, Jermyn (2016) has noted that it is hard to ignore even in Cohen's delightful work a certain race and class bias. Moreover as with the fashion context in general, images of older women favour a certain bodily shape—the thin body. Finally it is important to note here too, as a counter-position to "celebratory" readings of this new visibility, that some feminist critics throughout the years (most famously Germaine Greer 1991) have argued that the invisibility of old age constitutes a delicious kind of *freedom* for women from the gendered pressure of continuously being forced to think about one's looks. To that extent, one could posit that the cool unsentimental stylishness attached to older women fits in well with a postfeminist sensibility, focusing on the controlled body, on individualism, choice and thus, never endingly, on "surveillance, monitoring and discipline" (Gill 2007, 149; cf. also Jermyn 2016).

At the same time, we have suggested here that a cool appearance could be regarded as providing an aesthetic space for older women in which norms about appearance as an older woman are dissolved; in which the ageing body is constituted as a fact which should not be hidden from sight but can be adorned in a plurality of different styles; and in which a new kind of ageing edginess may be performed and developed. The many ambiguities connected with the new visibility of older women in the media and the concomitant upturn of images of fashionable older women underlines the neglect within media studies, including feminist media studies, of critical approaches to representations of older women; work which becomes ever more urgent as the fact of the ageing population makes the older woman subject, in this sense at least, more present than ever before.

Works Cited

Brown, Vanessa. 2014. Is It Cool to Be Fashionable? The Instabilities of Fashion and Cool. Conference Paper. Accessed 9 Jan 2017. http://www.inter-disciplinary.net/critical-issues/wp-content/uploads/2013/09/vBrown_wpaper-fash5.pd.

Brown, Vanessa. 2015. *Cool Shades: The History and Meaning of Sunglasses.* London and New York: Bloomsbury Academic.

Clarke, Laura Hurde. 2011. *Facing Age: Women Growing Older in Anti-Aging Culture.* Lanham, Boulder, NY, Toronto and Plymouth: Rowman & Littlefield Publishers.

Cotton, Charlotte. 2000. *Imperfect Beauty: The Making of Contemporary Fashion*. London: V&A Publications.

Daum, Meghan. 2015. The Elitist Allure of Joan Didion. *The Atlantic*, Sept. Accessed 9 Jan 2017. http://www.theatlantic.com/magazine/archive/2015/09/the-elitist-allure-of-joan-didion/399320/.

Dunbar, Polly. 2016. The High Street Has Embraced the Gold Rush and so Should YOU this Season. *Mail Online/Femail*, 21 Dec 2016. Accessed 9 Jan 2017. http://www.dailymail.co.uk/femail/article-4056386/Be-golden-girl-age-High-Street-embraced-gold-rush-season.html.

Evans, Caroline. 2003. *Fashion at the Edge: Spectacle, Modernity and Deathliness*. New Haven and London: Yale University Press.

Fairclough, Kirsty. 2012. Nothing Less Than Perfect: Female Celebrity, Ageing and Hyper-Scrutiny in the Gossip Industry. *Celebrity Studies* 3 (1): 90–103.

Freeland, Cynthia. 2010. *Portraits and Persons*. Oxford and New York: Oxford University Press.

Friedman, Vanessa. 2015. The 2016 Pirelli Calendar May Signal a Cultural Shift. *The New York Times*, Nov 30. Accessed 9 Jan 2017. http://www.nytimes.com/2015/12/03/fashion/the-2016-pirelli-calendar-may-signal-a-cultural-shift.html?_r=0.

Geiger, Annette, Gerald Schröder, and Änne Söll. 2010. Coolness—eine Kulturtechnik und ihr Forschungsfeld. Eine Einleitung. In *Coolness: Zur Ästhetik einer kulturellen Strategie und Attitüde*, ed. Annette Geiger, Gerald Schröder and Änne Söll, 7–16. Bielefeld: Transcript Verlag.

Gilbert, Sophie. 2016. The Pirelli Calendar Shows Fashion Trying to Catch Up. *The Atlantic*, Dec 2. Accessed 9 Jan 2017. https://www.theatlantic.com/entertainment/archive/2016/12/the-2017-pirelli-calendar-shows-fashion-trying-to-catch-up/509312.

Gill, Rosalind. 2007. Postfeminist Media Culture: Elements of a Sensibility. *European Journal of Cultural Studies* 10 (2): 147–166.

Greer, Germaine. 1991. *The Change: Women, Ageing and the Menopause*. Harmondsworth: Penguin.

Hoby, Hermione. 2015. From Literary Heavyweight to Lifestyle Brand: Exploring the Cult of Joan Didion. *The Guardian*, 17 Aug. Accessed 11 Jan 2017. https://www.theguardian.com/lifeandstyle/2015/aug/17/joan-didion-literary-heavyweight-lifestyle-brand-celine.

Jacobs, Alexandra. 2015. Joan Didion on the Céline Ad. *The New York Times*, Jan 7. Accessed 9 Jan 2017. http://www.nytimes.com/2015/01/07/fashion/joan-didion-on-the-celine-ad.html.

Jermyn, Deborah. 2014. 'Don't Wear Beige—It Might Kill You': The Politics of Ageing and Visibility in Fabulous Fashionistas. In *Women, Celebrity and Cultures of Ageing: Freeze Frame*, ed. Deborah Jermyn and Su Holmes, 127–145. Basingstoke: Palgrave Macmillan.

Jermyn, Deborah. 2016. Pretty Past It? Interrogating the Post-feminist Makeover of Ageing, Style and Fashion. *Feminist Media Studies* 16 (4): 573–589.

Jerslev, Anne. 2017. The Elderly Female Face in Beauty and Fashion Ads: Joan Didion for Céline. *European Journal of Cultural Studies* 20.

Lafrance, Adrienne. 2015. Slouching Towards Bendel's. *The Atlantic*, Jan 16.

Majors, Richard, and Janet Mancini Billson. 1993. *Cool Pose. The Dilemmas of Black Manhood in America*. New York: Touchstone.

Marsh, Laurie. 2015. How Joan Didion Became the Ultimate Literary Celebrity. *New Republic*, July 21. Accessed 9 Jan 2017. https://newrepublic.com/article/122337/joan-didion-celebrity.

Mears, Ashley. 2011. *Pricing Beauty: The Making of a Fashion Model*. Berkeley, Los Angeles and London: University of California Press.

Mentges, Gabriele. 2000. Cold, Coldness, Coolness: Remarks on the Relationship of Dress, Body and Technology. *Fashion Theory* 4 (1): 27–47.

Moore, Suzanne. 2015. The Pirelli Calendar's Feminist Makeover is Nothing but Lip Service. *The Guardian*, Dec 2. Accessed 9 Jan 2017. https://www.theguardian.com/commentisfree/2015/dec/02/the-pirelli-calendars-feminist-makeover-is-nothing-but-lip-service.

Nancarrow, Clive, Pamela Nancarrow, and Julie Page. 2002. An Analysis of the Concept of Cool and Its Marketing Implications. *Journal of Consumer Behaviour* 1 (4): 311–322.

Ohlsson, Anders, Torbjorn Forslid, and Ann Steiner. 2014. Literary Celebrity Reconsidered. *Celebrity Studies* 5 (1–2): 32–44.

Pountain, Dick, and David Robins. 2000. *Cool Rules: Anatomy of an Attitude*. London: Reaktion Books.

Quartz, Steven, and Anette Asp. 2015. *Cool: How the Brain's Hidden Quest for Cool Drives Our Economy and Shapes Our World*. New York: Farrar, Straus and Giroux.

Railton, Diane, and Paul Watson. 2012. 'She's so Vein': Madonna and the Drag of Aging. In *Aging Femininities: Troubling Representations*, ed. Josephine Dolan and Estella Ticknell, 183–195. Newcastle upon Tyne: Cambridge Scholar Publishing.

Richards, Naomi, Lorna Warren, and Merryn Gott. 2012. The Challenge of Creating 'Alternative' Images of Ageing: Lessons from a Project with Older Women. *Journal of Aging Studies* 26: 65–78.

Russo, Mary. 1999. Aging and the Scandal of Anachronism. In *Figuring Age: Women, Bodies, Generations*, ed. Kathleen Woodward, 20–34. Bloomington and Indianapolis: Indiana University Press.

Sylvers, Eric. 2011. Opening Up the Brand Umbrella. *The New York Times*, Sept 21. Accessed 9 Jan 2017. http://mobile.nytimes.com/2011/09/22/fashion/22iht-rproduct22.html.

Twigg, Julia. 2013. *Fashion and Age: Dress, the Body and Later Life*. London and New York: Bloomsbury.

Wearing, Sadie. 2007. Subjects of Rejuvenation: Aging in Postfeminist Culture. In *Interrogating Postfeminism: Gender and the Politics of Popular Culture*, ed. Yvonne Tasker and Diane Negra, 277–311. Durham and London: Duke University Press.

White Walker, Alice. 2016. Two Fingers to Perfection: Three Takeaways from the Pirelli 2017 Calendar. *The huffingtonpost.co.uk*, Dec 9. Accessed 9 Jan 2017. http://www.huffingtonpost.co.uk/alice-white-walker/how-to-be-naked-10-takeaw_b_13323164.html.

Willsher, Kim. 2016. Fully Clothed: The 2017 Pirelli Calendar. *The Guardian*, Nov 29. Accessed 9 Jan 2017. https://www.theguardian.com/fashion/2016/nov/29/fully-clothed-the-2017-pirelli-calendar.

Yotka, Steff. 2016. The 2017 Pirelli Calendar Featuring Nicole Kidman, Ziyi Zhang, Kate Winslet, and More Was Not Retouched at All. www.vogue.com, Nov 29. Accessed 9 Jan 2017. http://www.vogue.com/slideshow/13507093/pirelli-calendar-nicole-kidman-2017-no-retouching-peter-lindbergh.

CHAPTER 14

Performances of Situated Knowledge in the Ageing Female Body

EL Putnam

Ageing is inevitable, yet it is a contested topic in visual culture. Kathleen Woodward describes how the ageing female body is both hyper-visible and invisible: mass media representations tend to regulate expectations for how women are to behave as they age while rendering them obsolete and erasing them from view through the fetishisation of youth (cf. Woodward 2006, 163). Shifting focus from the mainstream media, where misrepresentations of ageing women flourish, artists working on the experimental edges of creative production, such as performance artists, offer alternative ways for presenting and understanding age and gender. In this chapter, I examine different strategies that performance artists use in engaging with the ageing female body. The artists under consideration—Rocio Boliver, Pauline Cummins and Frances Mezzetti, and Marilyn Arsem—have presented performances in recent years that reveal the relationship between gender and age in a non-traditional manner. In addition, these artists come from different parts of the world (Mexico, Ireland and Massachusetts, United States respectively) opening an intersectional analysis of diverse cultural contexts. Rocio Boliver

EL Putnam (✉)
Dublin Institute of Technology, Dublin, Ireland
e-mail: el@mobius.org

C. McGlynn et al. (eds.), *Ageing Women in Literature and Visual Culture*,
DOI 10.1007/978-3-319-63609-2_14

engages with the theatrics of spectacle in her repertoire of works, *Between Menopause and Old Age*, where she explores the futility of buying into the commodification of youth and beauty. In their performance series *Walking in the Way*, Pauline Cummins and Frances Mezzetti take on the dress, mannerisms, and gestures of men in public contexts, offering a nuanced approach to considering the gendered, ageing body. They create a gestural palimpsest that draws attention to how older women can occupy public space through the performance of its gendered inversion. In other words, through their performances of passing as men, Cummins and Mezzetti draw attention to gendered dissimilarities in ageing, emphasising how societies treat ageing men and women differently within the context of mundane public interactions. At first glance, Marilyn Arsem's work may not appear to consider the ageing, female body. However, in her most recent series, *100 Ways to Consider Time* (2015–2016), Arsem takes time itself as her medium, engaging in durational actions with minimal materials that ask us to reconsider our relationship to time. Emerging from her ongoing considerations of mortality, she draws attention to the female ageing body as the corporeal inscription of time. Despite the differences between these artists in how they approach ageing, their practices are united in that experiences of ageing are treated as performative through the creation of live works that emerge from embodied experiences. In doing so, they introduce new forms of knowledge that undermine gendered expectations and bring the hidden aspects of ageing into focus.

Performance art, as practiced by the artists investigated in this study, emerged as an accepted visual arts medium during the twentieth century. Performance is influenced by other live practices, including experimental theatre, dance, music and rhetoric, as well as the performance turn in academic disciplines such as linguistics (Austin 1975), anthropology (Schechner 1985), sociology (Goffman 1959) and business management (McKenzie 2001). Performance as an artistic medium is difficult to succinctly define because of its variances. Performance studies scholar Diana Taylor attempts to capture the slippery essence of the term, especially in cross-cultural contexts, noting how the word connotes simultaneously "a process, a praxis, an epitome, a mode of transmission, an accomplishment, and a means of intervening in the world" (2003, 15). With such diverse applications of "performance," it becomes difficult to solidify what unifies performance art as a creative medium. The artists discussed in this study share some characteristics, such as the embodied presence of the artist in the work, the interplay of the body and gesture with material, and the use of time and space in the creation of scenarios. In addition, even though the artists perform preconceived tasks, their actions are not scripted in the traditional sense, as in theatre. Rather, artists set a task that they aim to accomplish in real time. For example, in *100 Ways to Consider Time*, each day Arsem decided on an action to perform over the course of the day, such as building a clock, reading a text, or watching ice melt. Her interactions with audience members would vary depending on how these spectators engaged with her as she performed. Her actions also varied depending on her body's response to the material, space, and the passing of time. Boliver, Cummins and Mezzetti undertake similar methods in their performances. As such, these performances cannot be reduced to mimetic repetition or even representation, as the artists are *being* within the contexts of their *doing*.

In this chapter, attention is paid to performance art as these artists are not only creating works about bodies, but use their bodies in the process of artistic creation. Performance allows the body to behave as the means of sharing knowledge, functioning as "vital acts of transfer, transmitting social knowledge, memory, and a sense of identity through reiterated actions" (Taylor 2016, loc. 357). This knowledge is situated knowledge. Drawing from feminist thinkers of science, technology and intersectional cultural studies, Lynette Hunter offers a conglomerate definition of situated knowledge that treats knowledge as reliant on contexts of knowing that are not universal, but vary depending on the experiences of sentient beings and emerge from engaged practice (Hunter 2009, 151). For instance, Boliver's series of performances are a response to her experiences of menopause, engaging with social attitudes concerning ageing women. She performs about her ageing body with her ageing body. Hunter argues that artists play a key role in the communication and dissemination of situated knowledge, with art not merely being representational or reflective, but functioning as sites of knowledge production (1999, 32). The knowledge that Boliver, Cummins, Mezzetti, and Arsem cultivate through their performances places the female ageing body as the source of this knowledge. Each artist expresses their situated experiences and the source of their knowledge is made explicit through the incorporation of the body as artistic medium. Hunter differentiates between two types of situated knowledge. The first involves studies of knowledge that emerge from the margins of society, which include intersectional feminism, overlooked figures in scientific history, and knowledge "from those outside accepted forms of social communication" (Hunter 2009, 151). In the context of this investigation, situated knowledge comes from the neglected positionalities of ageing women. The second definition of situated knowledge involves the "study of learning that takes place in the process of engaged observation and practice, such as craftwork in silver, or children's acquisition of language, or more recently, computing skills" (Hunter 2009, 151). According to this definition, knowledge is transmitted through doing. As noted previously, performance art allows the artist to *be* through their act of doing—the embodied actions that comprise the works are the means through which knowledge is transmitted. For instance, while it is possible to discuss how ageing men and women are treated differently, Cummins and Mezzetti manifest these differences through their performances, using their bodies to highlight the subtleties of social engagement that escape verbal articulation. Moreover, both definitions of situated knowledge play a part in the artists and performances discussed.

Age Gracefully? Hell No!

In her ongoing series, *Between Menopause and Old Age*, Rocio Boliver uses her body as the impetus for exploring the perceived violence that cultural ageism has on the maturing female body. With lurid gestures, she stages vicious spectacles where she exposes herself literally and figuratively to the audience. In several renditions of this performance, she puts on a "rejuvenation mask," a plastic apparatus that is tied with taut fishing line to hooks in her face (Fig. 14.1). The line stretches her skin, pulling it over the bones of her skull, giving her the appearance of someone who has undergone extreme plastic surgery. During performances, she counters violent actions such as cutting and piercing her skin with the careful application of cosmetics, giving each task the due attention of a woman performing a daily beauty routine. In some performances, she appears nude before her audience, unashamedly showing to her viewers ageing in the flesh. She blends humour with discomfort as she mixes various signifiers of age—patent leather red heels with frilly white socks—along with acts of violence and pleasure. In one performance presented at the Slovenian "City of Women" festival in 2012, Boliver poses like an amateur supermodel between lines of barbed wire that pierce her skin. As she purses her lips and winks suggestively at the audience, blood drips down her flesh as she hides any sensations of pain she may feel. Her aim

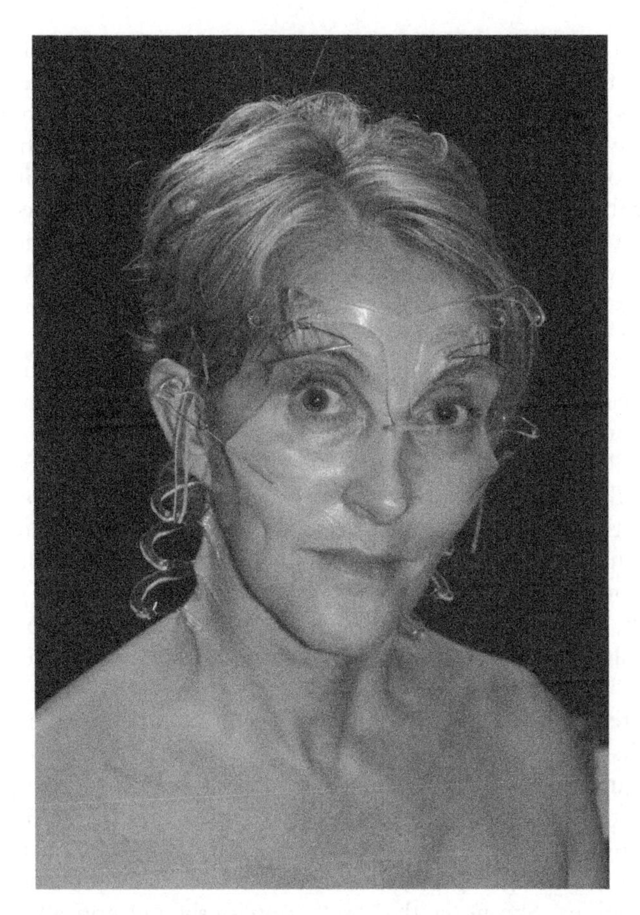

Fig. 14.1 Rocio Boliver, *Rejuvenating Mask, Between Menopause and Old Age*, 2010. Courtesy of the artist

is to "demystify the horror of old age in an ironical way, inventing [her] own deranged aesthetic and moral solutions for the 'problem of age'" (Boliver 2014, n.p.).

Kathleen Woodward describes how plastic surgery, along with other corporeal and cosmetic practices used to appear younger, such as make up, dying hair and wearing certain clothes, functions as a masquerade. In some instances, this masquerade is a denial of the inevitable ageing process; a means of keeping old age hidden (1991, 148–151). Boliver critiques this denial of ageing. Through her actions, Boliver exposes the limits of the masquerade, as if she is holding up a fun house mirror to the beauty industry that is fuelled by the commodification of the human body. As Jean Baudrillard notes in his critique of capitalist consumer culture, the body itself functions as a consumer object (1998, 131). He is particularly critical of the demands that consumer culture makes of women, whose pursuit of beauty through consumerism reaches the status of religious devotion: "being beautiful is no longer an effect of nature or a supplement to moral qualities. It is the basic, imperative quality of those who take the same care of their faces and figures as they do of their souls" (Baudrillard 1998, 132). As such, consumption takes on the form of worship to counter the visible effects of ageing on the body, fuelling individual and collective denial of the inevitability of growing old. Boliver counters this commodified masquerade of youthfulness through the creation of her own grotesque masquerade. Watching her waving and smiling self-assuredly to the audience as blood drips down her face, mingling with her lipstick so it is unclear as to what is staining her teeth, Boliver exaggerates cosmetic acts of maintenance to the point of absurdity. She is, in the words of Mary Russo, "making a spectacle out of herself" (1995, 53).

Despite the visceral strength of her performances, there are conceptual limits to Boliver's practice. Even though she explicitly draws from the masquerading body, twisting it into order to subvert it, her presentation of ageing emerges from conscious identification of the process. As Woodward points out, identifying age is not a clear-cut phenomenon. Rather, it is an ongoing process that exceeds our comprehension of its representations. She notes that "self-consciously and critically renouncing our culture's conventions of the iconography of the ageing body may enlarge the arena within which we may act, but a difference between youth and age will still exist" (Woodward 1991, 156). Through the critique that Boliver builds, she engages with the binary between youth and old age that reinforces these qualities as if they are inherently dichotomous. The dialectic between the two are what makes her performances so provocative, contributing to the shocking nature of her behaviours as she refuses to "act her age." However, her reliance on the two perpetuates the treatment of them as polar opposites. At the same time, just making a disenfranchised subject visible, which in this case is the post-menopausal woman, does not necessarily equate power. As Peggy Phelan argues in *Unmarked*, there are limitations to treating visual representation as a political goal (1993, 6). In particular, equating increased visibility with increased power carries the risk of standardising and reducing understandings of identity while overlooking the nuances affiliated with the "unmarked, unspoken, and unseen" (Phelan 1993, 7). Boliver's emphasis on making the process of ageing visible through her performances violently thrusts the ageing woman into her audience's field of vision. Not much remains unseen though, which presents the risk of perpetuating the dichotomy of youth versus age.

Generational Cross-Dressing

While Boliver creates spectacles to expose the great lengths women go to counter the visible signs of ageing, Irish artists Pauline Cummins and Frances Mezzetti engage with a more nuanced approach. Since 2010, they have been creating a series of performances, *Walking in the Way*, where they pass as men in an urban environment. The process begins by visiting a city as women, drawing connections to that particular location. They then return to these spaces performing as men, which includes dressing in male attire and adopting various masculine gestures and movements. In an early version of the performance that took place in Dublin (2009), Mezzetti and Cummins slowly pace the city centre, leaning against closed storefronts smoking or casually standing in observation of the urban milieu (see Figs. 14.2 and 14.3). When Mezzetti walks down the street in her white suit jacket and black hat, she is almost strutting—letting her arms and legs move in a relaxed flow that pays no concern to how much space she occupies. At times, their actions take on a more distinctive character. At one point, Cummins starts tracing around a pillar with a piece of chalk. While this may seem odd, people in the streets overlook their actions: "The invisibility of our presence strikes us" (Cummins and Mezzetti 2016).

In later iterations, they become bolder in their actions. In Seville, Spain (2013), they carry large, discarded pieces of church furniture around the city streets. They begin their performance outside a gilder's shop, where they clean and sand their selected piece of wood—a 10-foot-long, bow-like piece that appears to have formerly adorned the top of a wardrobe or confessional. They then pick up the wood, carrying it to various pre-determined stations. Their engagement is awkward and

Fig. 14.2 Pauline Cummins, *Walking in the Way*, first Dublin performance, 21 June 2009. Cummins and Mezzetti performed this site-specific, collaborative performance series from 2009 to 2013 in ten European cities. Photo by Michelle Brown. Image courtesy of the artists

Fig. 14.3 Frances Mezzetti, *Walking in the Way*, 21 June 2009. Photo by Pauline Cummins. Image courtesy of the artists

cumbersome, allowing them to spread their proprioceptive presence as they walk along, while people give way to their movements.

They have performed the series in Dublin, Belfast, Edinburgh, London, Derry, Istanbul, Madrid, Seville and Malaga, each time carrying out meticulous research when they arrive at the site to direct their actions in a manner that integrates with the various cities. As Michelle Browne notes: "They were not hiding and were therefore not in disguise, but instead they embodied men, donning men's clothes, applying facial hair, and exploring their own relationship to maleness" (2015, 249). Their intention is to occupy positions that as women they feel they cannot access. In particular, their gestures and actions focus on the difference between how men and women occupy space, with these performances relating to Hunter's second definition of situated knowledge (the practice of learning by doing). As such, through their actions, Cummins and Mezzetti attempt to engage with the tacit knowledge affiliated with masculine occupations of space, or what Hunter considers the implied knowledge tied to experience and expertise (1999, 21–22).

Their nuanced engagement of performing as men is more than mere mimetic representation, but encompasses performative actions that transform their bodies and interactions as they move through their environment.

The aim of the artists may have emerged from their interest in gender, but what is notable about the work is how they can engage with gender difference in the ageing body. Not only do Cummins and Mezzetti appear as men, but as older men. There is no way to avoid the appearance of age; it is recognised through visual and corporeal indicators, such as the wrinkling and sagging of flesh, the greying of hair, a slowing pace, and stooping posture. Age is also communicated through clothing and gestures, indicating the passing of fashions and the timing of trends. Returning to Woodward's analysis of ageing and masquerade, Cummins and Mezzetti do not attempt to mask their age through their adoption of male personas, but their gender play taps into how the appearance of age is connected to visible signs, physical postures, and proprioceptive actions. Even though indicators of age are visually presented, the identification of age is not as clear-cut as gender, and therefore it can be difficult to pin down age (Woodward 1991, 156). One reason for this is that age is relational. As Mary Russo points out, "despite the dominant fiction of chronological ageing, one that plots our lives in continually increasing numbers, it is clear that we experience age in relation to others (although this is not, of course, the only way we experience age)" (1999, 25). The initial motivations behind Cummins and Mezzetti's performances emerge from identification with their fathers (González 2013). As such, the inspiration for masculinity is cross-generational and genealogically connected—the impressions of masculinity presented by the fathers on their daughters are relative and inevitably older. Woodward describes how masquerade functions as cover up through which age speaks (1991, 148). As Cummins and Mezzetti draw inspiration from their fathers, the version of masculinity being presented conveys qualities of age difference, even if this communication emerges unconsciously. For instance, the style of dress, especially in Mezzetti's choice of clothing—her light jacket and grey pants offset with a blue tie and red handkerchief in the breast pocket along with a black trilby hat—convey a sense of style that also comes across as anachronistic (Fig. 14.3). The formality of her attire is made more striking when contrasted with the context of the urban environment and her relaxed actions as she appears overdressed for puttering around the streets of Dublin. The results of this juxtaposition are that Mezzetti appears aged through historical misplacement.

The way that ageing emerges in *Walking in the Way* correlates and connects with the presentation of gender, resulting in a study of human relations to public places that exceeds the artists' expectations. Ageing is a lived experience both from the perception of the subject and others—a quality that is made explicit through the medium of performance art where not only the artists' bodies provide materials for creative exploration, but time, space and audience presence are key parameters to the unfolding of the work. Cummins's and Mezzetti's unpronounced gestures allow them to integrate into the urban environments they occupy, which include the physical topography and its social relations. The significance of their performance is not just evident in how they behave, but is also determined by how others respond to them, especially those who are unaware that they are performing. Moreover, ageing is co-constitutive through intersubjective relations that include the experiences of the performers and those of observers. In her analysis of Simone de Beauvoir's *The Coming of Age*, Sara Heinämaa argues that age is experienced through the perceptions of others:

> We do not experience our age 'in the for-itself mode' but encounter it in our being for others. [...] we learn to differentiate between youth and old age in the faces and bodies of others, and only later come to realise that this distinction applies to our objectified selves. We do not immediately connect the quality of age to ourselves but by mediation, via our perception of others and the other's [sic] perceptions of us. (Heinämaa 2014, 174)

Cummins and Mezzetti collapse the perception of age of their fathers onto their embodied selves, while playing with how others perceive age through the public presentation of the performance.

Drawing attention to age complicates interpretations of the performance: were Cummins and Mezzetti able to proceed as they did due to their performances as men, as they observe, or did the presentation of age create their spaces for exploration? By performing as older men, how do they draw attention to social treatments of differences in age between genders? Simone de Beauvoir describes (controversially) that ageing affects men more so than women due to the male's reliance on contributing to the community through paid labour as a means of validation. When a man ages and retires, he becomes a "mere object" as "the old man no longer does anything. He is defined by an *exis*, not by a *praxis*: a being, not a doing" (1973, 133; 322). Both Cummins and Mezzetti emphasise how their fathers engaged in skilled, manual labour, which inspires the nature of their performance actions, such as Cummins's drawing with chalk in Dublin and the transformation of the discarded piece of church furniture in Seville. However, when they perform these tasks, they do not come across as typical labourers. In part, this is due to the transformation of action through performance. For example, at one point in the Seville performance, Cummins and Mezzetti walk along a cobblestoned road at the same pace, their shoes tapping and shuffling along in rhythm, alluding to a classic tap dance move in a self-conscious harmonisation. In addition, their garments counter any presumption that they are common workers. In the Edinburgh version, they perform their tasks (stringing black ribbons along a yellow cord) in the traditional formal attire of the tartan kilt. The appearance of age helps make the seeming absurdity of their actions plausible. What may seem odd or out-of-place becomes acceptable due to the presumed ages and genders of the performers. Moreover, the responses cultivated by Cummins and Mezzetti in *Walking in the Way* do not just emerge from their play with gender, but are interconnected with their presentation of age. Their ability to integrate with social environments cannot be attributed to gender alone, but is influenced by perceptions of age. As ageing women, Cummins and Mezzetti occupy public spaces in particular ways through their performances as older men, confirming that societies treat ageing men and women differently. Subsequently, just as Boliver's practice risks reaffirming the duality of youth versus age, the performances of Cummins and Mezzetti potentially enforce the perceived binary difference of ageing between men and women.

Ageing as Corporeal Traces of Time

Boliver, Cummins and Mezzetti all engage with masquerade in their performances, highlighting the intersection of gender in relation to the ageing body. Emphasis is placed on how the ageing body appears to the audience. Marilyn Arsem takes a different approach in her practice, asking viewers to contemplate the passing of time through her corporeal, gendered presence. Through her durational performances, including her *100 Ways to Consider Time* exhibition at the Museum of Fine Arts in Boston, MA, Arsem explicitly engages with the passing of time. For 100 consecutive days, Arsem performed for six hours a day, with each day centred on a different task to mark the passage of time while considering its nature. Her actions and gestures are subtle—measuring the body with blue tape, blowing paper across the room, emulating rocks, attempting to crochet a mile, turning a sand timer, drawing a spiral with oil pastels, watching flowers bloom—and the decor of the gallery is minimal, focusing attention on Arsem's presence. With little happening in Arsem's performances, her works demand concentration, highlighting minute details and subtle transformations (Fig. 14.4).

Arsem describes how performance allows her to "perceive the nature of time. One becomes acutely aware of the immediate loss of the moment that has just passed, of the disappearance of the work, of the fading of the memory of the work, and of the eventual vanishing of one's self" (2015, 9). As such, her performances resonate with *vanitas*—works of art that symbolically convey the brevity of human life. In art history, this theme of painting incorporates various symbols, including skulls, rotting fruit, bubbles, smoke, flowers, hourglasses, to convey the brevity and ephemeral nature of human life (Van Miegroet, n.d.). The attention that Arsem draws to the subtle transformation of materials in affiliation with the passing of time welcomes her spectators to engage with similar questions as *vanitas* paintings posed, as she conveys ephemerality through the delicate disturbances that suggest the fragility of human existence.

The subdued material parameters of Arsem's performances capture the viewer's attention and slow it down through the durational quality of the task, engaging with real time as it unfolds. In her discussion of Arsem's practice, Natalie Loveless points out how very little seems to happen during the hours that the artist performs, making duration not only a test of endurance for the artist, but also the audience (2013, 131). Viewers are asked to commit to presence, giving time to engage with the artist as she performs. Traces of Arsem's actions collect in the room, providing evidence of an accumulation of the past. Adrian Heathfield posits that this type of performance constitutes durational aesthetics. Drawing from Henri Bergson's definition of duration, Heathfield describes how "for Bergson the past lives on inside the present, and is only separated from it by thought. Thoughts, language, representations operate on time by spatialising it (sectioning, containing, and cutting it); thus time is equated with incessant and irreducible movement" (2012, 29). The manipulation of time in performance art through duration, becomes a means of breaking with the regulation of time in contemporary culture.

Fig. 14.4 Marilyn Arsem, *Day 95: Black Sand, 100 Ways to Consider Time*, 100 6-hour durational performances by Marilyn Arsem at the Museum of Fine Arts, Boston, 9 November 2015–19 February 2016. Over the course of six hours Arsem swept a cone-shaped mound of black sand from the table to the floor. Photo by Bob Hall. Image courtesy of the artist

For Bergson, duration plays a key role in the formation of the subject as consciousness is informed through the accumulation of experiences "as a snowball in snow" (2009, 16). Duration is a means of transformation for the subject that always changes with the passing of time; a process that does not cease. Durational performance draws attention to this process that is present and informs all life, as both performer and spectators engage in a concentrated accumulation and exchange of time as a phenomenological aesthetic event. The accumulation of time is manifested in various ways through Arsem's performances. First of all, her repeated actions change the form of materials, which in turn impact how she engages with them. Second, the metamorphosis of the materials in real time alter the space of the performance, which also affects Arsem's actions. Finally, the engagement with visitors, which varies depending on how much time a person commits to the work and the degree of engagement that the visitor offers, also alters the outcome of the work. Through this process, attention is drawn to the present, but bodies, materials and space carry the accumulation of gestures that are transformed through the performance process. The work as a whole depends on this contingent relationship that uses time as its form and content.

Bergson's uninterrupted, subjective flow of time, according to Gail Weiss, enables an illusion that one is ageless, "remaining untouched by time" (2014, 54). Even if a consciousness carries an impression of being untouched by time, this consciousness is connected to a body that accumulates the traces of time passing. The body, as Woodward points out, is one's only constant companion throughout life (1991, 175–176). Just as Bergson describes how the present carries the past as each moment differs from the previous one through a heterogeneous flow, duration is physically demarcated on the body through the process of ageing, leaving traces of the passing of time. Lines form around the mouth due to smiling, wrinkles emerge in the forehead from being creased in worry, flesh shifts and moves because of physical use and the ongoing influence of gravity. Even if the experience of time is subjective, the body carries its visible marks. Arsem's concentrated engagement with the passing of time is in the body of the artist, where situated knowledge is conveyed through a female body ageing in real time. While the performances of Boliver, Cummins and Mezzetti evoke considerations of ageing and gender that are read as critiques, ageing in Arsem's work diverges by focusing on the ongoing relationship of time and the body through duration.

Conclusion

Bringing together these divergent artists illustrates the complex interplay between gender, age and the body in visual culture. While these artists present situated knowledge of the experience of ageing using their bodies as artistic medium, their different approaches have different outcomes. While Boliver reveals the violent effects of anti-ageing practices promoted by consumer culture through visceral and spectacular displays, Cummins and Mezzetti subtly engage with public perceptions of gender and age through transgenerational cross-dressing. A common thread between these three artists is the use of masquerade as a means of critically engaging with social perceptions of age. In contrast, shifting away from conscious modes of identity construction, Arsem pays focused attention to the passing of time, which accumulates traces of experience onto the body. As such, Arsem's work offers a different way of portraying the female ageing body in visual culture to that which is confined to dualities, such as young and old (as in Boliver) or male and female (as with Cummins and Mezzetti).

As a whole, these performances extend understandings of how ageing is presented in visual culture to emphasise unarticulated and overlooked presentations of the ageing body. The use of performance art is key in the practice of these artists. Using their bodies as artistic media allows for the artists to performatively constitute these presentations through the ageing process itself. These are not just visual representations of ageing, but instead images of ageing become malleable through the performances of the artists. The temporal, spatial, and embodied qualities of performance art engage in the intersubjective relations that constitute social presumptions concerning ageing. As such, Boliver, Cummins and Mezzetti, and Arsem provide alternative strategies for engaging with the ageing female body that undermine mass media representations in visual culture.

Works Cited

Arsem, Marilyn. 2015. The Nature of Performance Art. In *The Performance Art of Marilyn Arsem*, ed. Liz Munsell, and Edward Saywell. Boston: MFA Publications.

Austin, J.L. 1975. *How to Do Things with Words*, 2nd ed. Cambridge, MA: Harvard University Press.

Baudrillard, Jean. 1998. *The Consumer Society: Myths and Structures*. Los Angeles: Sage.

Beauvoir, Simone de. 1973. *The Coming of Age*. trans. Patrick O'Brian. New York: Warner Paperback Library.

Bergson, Henri. 2009. *Creative Evolution*. trans. Arthur Mitchell. Waiheke Island: The Floating Press.

Boliver, Rocio. 2014. Between Menopause and Old Age, Alternative Beauty. *Hemispheric Institute*. http://hemisphericinstitute.org/hemi/enc14-performances/item/2350-enc14-performances-boliver-menopause?lang=en.

Browne, Michelle. 2015. Performance Art in Ireland: The New Millennium. In *Performance Art in Ireland: A History*, ed. Áine Phillips, 244–263. London and Bristol: Live Art Development Agency and Intellect Books.

Cummins, Pauline, and Frances Mezzetti. 2016. Dublin 2009. *Walking in the Way*. 18 March. http://www.walkingintheway.net/.

Goffman, Erving. 1959. *The Presentation of Self in Everyday Life*. New York: Anchor Books.

González, Marisa. 2013. Comportamientos Masculinos: Entrevista a Pauline Cummins Y Frances Mezzetti. *M Arte Y Cultura Visual*. 2 Dec. http://www.m-arteyculturavisual.com/2013/12/02/comportamientos-masculinos/.

Hans J. Van Miegroet. n.d. Vanitas. *Grove Art Online*. Oxford: Oxford University Press.

Heathfield, Adrian. 2012. Then Again. In *Perform Repeat Record: Live Art in History*, ed. Amelia Jones, and Adrian Heathfield, 27–35. Bristol, UK and Chicago: Intellect.

Heinämaa, Sara. 2014. Transformations of Old Age. In *Simone de Beauvoir's Philosophy of Age: Gender, Ethics, and Time*, ed. Silvia Stoller. Berlin: De Gruyter.

Hunter, Lynette. 1999. *Critiques of Knowing: Situated Textualities in Science, Computing and the Arts*. New York and London: Routledge.

Hunter, Lynette. 2009. Situated Knowledge. In *Mapping Landscapes for Performance as Research*, ed. Shannon Rose Riley and Lynette Hunter, 151–153. New York: Palgrave Macmillan.

Loveless, Natalie S. 2013. The Materiality of Duration: Between Ice Time and Water Time. *Performance Research* 18 (6): 129–136.

McKenzie, Jon. 2001. *Perform or Else: From Discipline to Performance*. New York and London: Routledge.

Phelan, Peggy. 1993. *Unmarked: The Politics of Performance*. London: Routledge.

Russo, Mary. 1995. *The Female Grotesque: Risk, Excess and Modernity*. New York and London: Routledge.

Russo, Mary. 1999. Aging and the Scandal of Anachronism. In *Figuring Age: Women, Bodies, Generations*, ed. Kathleen Woodward. Bloomington and Indianapolia: Indiana University Press.

Schechner, Richard. 1985. *Between Theater and Anthropology*. Philadelphia: University of Pennsylvania Press.

Taylor, Diana. 2003. *The Archive and the Repertoire: Performing Cultural Memory in the Americas*. EBook. Durham and London: Duke University Press.

Taylor, Diana. 2016. *Performance*. Durham and London: Duke University Press.

Weiss, Gail. 2014. The Myth of Woman Meets the Myth of Old Age: An Alienating Encounter with the Aging Female Body. In *Simone de Beauvoir's Philosophy of Age: Gender, Ethics, and Time*, ed. Silvia Stoller, 47–64. Berlin: De Gruyter.

Woodward, Kathleen. 1991. *Aging and Its Discontents: Freud and Other Fictions*. Bloomington and Indianapolia: Indiana University Press.

Woodward, Kathleen. 2006. Performing Age, Performing Gender. *National Women's Studies Association Journal* 18 (1): 162–189.

PART IV

Class, 'Race' and Agency

CHAPTER 15

"I Become Shameless as a Child": Childhood, Femininity and Older Age in J.M. Coetzee's *Age of Iron*

Antoinette Pretorius

Long before J.M. Coetzee himself became older, his fiction evidenced an abiding concern with the representation of older characters as well as with what it means to age: from the Magistrate in *Waiting for the Barbarians* (1980), to Elizabeth Curren in *Age of Iron* (1990), to David Lurie in *Disgrace* (1999), to Elizabeth Costello in *Elizabeth Costello* (2003), to Paul Rayment in *Slow Man* (2005), to Señor C. in *Diary of a Bad Year* (2007). While Elizabeth Costello is perhaps the most widely discussed of Coetzee's elderly narrators, many of these (often female) characters are deeply preoccupied by the ways in which the pressures of older age seem to bifurcate body from intellect, and past from future, across different geographical spaces and moments in time. Very few studies, however, have attempted to read Coetzee's elderly characters specifically through a gerontological lens, as this chapter attempts to do in its analysis of the ways in which Coetzee deconstructs stereotypes surrounding the infantilisation of the elderly in *Age of Iron*. Even fewer studies

A. Pretorius (✉)
University of South Africa, Pretoria, South Africa
e-mail: pretoae@unisa.ac.za

C. McGlynn et al. (eds.), *Ageing Women in Literature and Visual Culture*,
DOI 10.1007/978-3-319-63609-2_15

have done so through a reading that foregrounds the ageing female body as a marker of transcendence rather than as one of inevitable decline and deterioration.

My argument will illustrate that Coetzee subverts the conventional notion of dependency associated with the concepts of childhood, femininity and older age. I will show that in doing so, he releases his elderly female protagonist from the bodily confines that doom her to the seemingly inescapable enervation conventionally associated with senescence. I will argue that he achieves this by inscribing the aged female body with images of childhood that disrupt the hegemonic flow of sequential, linear time. Instead, he posits that both childhood and older age could be read as mutable signs that resist the inscription of rigid social meanings. In the context of South Africa's transition to democracy, this suggests that the elderly female body could be seen as representative of the irony underlying the complex (and often paradoxical) tensions governing societal change and the impetus towards ideologies centred on newness and youthfulness.

Coined in 1903 by Ellie Metchnikroff, the term "gerontology" derives from "the Greek word *geront* meaning 'old man' and *logos* meaning 'study'" (Harris 1988, n.p., original emphasis). Over the last few decades gerontologists have begun to realise the need for more nuanced and interdisciplinary approaches to understanding the complex roles and identities enacted by older individuals. Sylvia Henneberg advocates the conjoining of gerontology and literary analysis as a possible space in which these inquiries can be made, suggesting that "Literature has much to offer age studies, just as the lens of age opens up new ground on which to explore literature" (2006, 126). This branch of gerontological inquiry has been termed "literary gerontology." Anne Wyatt Brown explains that "the first group of scholars to discuss literature and aging began with the problem of literary attitudes toward old age, placing particular emphasis on negative stereotyping of the elderly" (1990, 300). Soon, however, this emphasis began to shift and recent scholarship has focused on "(1) analyses of literary attitudes towards aging; (2) humanistic approaches to literature and aging; (3) psychoanalytic explorations of literary works and their authors; (4) applications of gerontological theories about autobiography, life review and midlife transitions; and (5) psychoanalytically informed studies of the creative process" (Wyatt Brown 1990, 300). These approaches allow researchers to "confront (rather than shirk) the ambiguities and complexities of age, ageing and later life" and to focus on "quizzing the cultural norms of ageing via non-scientific forms of knowing" (Zeillig 2011, 8–9). However, Hendricks and Leedham caution against the "formulation of an overarching or unified model that can be used to explain all facets of ageing in every time and place" (1987, 204). Instead, they advocate "a careful analysis of a variety of literature from other cultures" in order to "widen our horizons by sensitizing readers to the variability of aging under diverse structural, historical and cultural conditions" (1987, 204).

In *Le Deuxième Sexe,* her seminal work on gender, Simone de Beauvoir famously declared in 1949 that "One is not born, but rather becomes, a woman," demonstrating that gender functions as a mechanism which diminishes and others in order to prioritise the masculine as the prime site of experience and knowledge (1949, 267). Significantly, in 1972 she applies her lens of inquiry to older age in *The Coming of Age*, analysing "alienation, the experience of bodily disintegration, inauthenticity, recognition and reciprocity, [and] establishing competing possibilities in response to the differentials of class, race, gender, and aging" (1972, 8). As with her assertion that gender is a social construct, she argues that identity in older age is a performative state of being which is inculcated in individuals through a complex array of societal influences. Her argument, however, centres on her belief that "men suffer more because the ageing process in most men, particularly after retirement, reduces them to [...] the situation of a woman: that of being rendered an object, denied agency in the world" (Segal 2013, 77). While drawing on de Beauvoir's work on ageing throughout her research, Lynne Segal argues that while ageing "affects us all, and affects us all differently, [...] it is women who have often reported a very specific horror of ageing" (2013, 13). She associates this "with the place of the body, and fertility, in women's lives" (2013, 13). Indeed, *Age of Iron* reflects the ways in which the barrenness and infertility associated with ageing female bodies are seen as markers of decline and deterioration. Coetzee, however, counteracts this perception through re-inscribing these markers with a dangerous mutability particular to the context in which the novel is set. In contrast to de Beauvoir, Susan Sontag posits that "Growing older is mainly an ordeal of the imagination—a moral disease, a social pathology—intrinsic to which is the fact that it afflicts women much more than men" (1972, 29). Sontag's references to ageing as a "moral disease" and a "social pathology" particular to women are pertinent to the argument

I present below in my reading of the ageing female body as a complex construct that both reflects and results from societal pressures.

As de Beauvoir and Sontag note early on in the development of research on ageing, and as many contemporary cultural gerontologists such as Segal have later affirmed, older age is experienced very differently by men and by women. The gendered nature of this construction becomes most visible in the notions of dependency conventionally associated in particular with female experiences of older age. Of course, the image of the frail older woman partly results from the image of women in general being vulnerable and in need of protection, which in turn relates to women occupying a hierarchical position in relation to men, similar to that of children in relation to adults. As Burman and Stacey argue, the "infantilization of women has long been close to the feminization of childhood, as a state of dependency" (2010, 233). While the association of femininity with childhood has been thoroughly investigated, the theoretical underpinnings surrounding female experiences of older age and childhood dependency remain largely unexplored. Such a theorisation would allow age studies to benefit from the advances made by both feminist theorists and theorists working on the concept of childhood in recent years. It is with this hope in mind that I turn my attention to the connections between childhood, femininity and older age in J.M. Coetzee's *Age of Iron*.

According to Kinsella and Ferreira, South Africa's older population (as a proportion of the country's total population) is one of the largest in Africa (cf. 1997, 1). However, in a country with a population as racially diverse and economically disparate as South Africa's, defining and understanding what it means to become old poses great difficulty. While some studies have been undertaken on ageing within the South African context,[1] these studies primarily focus on the economic and social welfare of the South African elderly. As crucial as this research may be, it does not elucidate the cultural construction of ageing identity in South Africa. Very few studies have investigated the representation of this identity in South African English-language literature.[2] This chapter addresses this lacuna through its focus on Coetzee's

[1] Cf. Kimuna and Makiwane (2008); Makiwane, Ndinda and Botsis (2012); Sadie (1994) and Sagner (2000).

[2] Cf. Nashef (2009), Pretorius (2015a) and Pretorius (2015b).

Age of Iron (1990) and pays particular attention to the ways in which Coetzee conflates the categories of childhood, femininity and older age in order to grant his protagonist an, albeit fraught and problematic, measure of escape from the confines of the ageing, female body.

The novel is set in the turbulent and violent period immediately prior to South Africa's democratisation. Elizabeth Curren, an elderly white woman, is diagnosed with terminal bone cancer. The narrative is written in the form of an extended letter to her daughter who is living in self-imposed exile in North America. The process of penning this metafictive missive forces Curren into an awareness of her passive complicity with the apartheid regime, and thus compels her to re-examine before her death her position in relation to the socio-political context in which she lives. In doing so, her impending death becomes textually conflated with the death of this political structure. In this chapter I argue that this development is textually underscored through Coetzee's conflation of childhood and older age. The stereotypical view of the elderly as childlike is ubiquitous in the popular imagination, as well as in literary representations of senescence. These kinds of representations focus on older age as a period of life in which the declining elderly subject undergoes a process of regression that renders him or her enfeebled, occupying a position dependent on care. As Hepworth explains, "Our knowledge of old age, and particularly the decrements of old age is an elaboration of socially prescribed knowledge of what it is to be a child in western culture: in other words, images, both verbal and visual, of childhood" (1996, 426). Indeed, as the novel progresses and as Curren's physical state worsens, she becomes increasingly reliant on Vercueil, a vagrant she discovers sleeping in her garage and subsequently befriends. Eventually, as a child depends on her parents, Curren comes to depend entirely on Vercueil for the most intimate acts of care: he moves into her home, feeds her, washes her and sleeps next to her in bed to keep her warm at night. Commenting on this, she declares that when an "old person begins to plead for love everything turns squalid. Like a parent trying to creep into bed with a child: unnatural" (Coetzee 1990, 73). This begins to hint at the ways in which Coetzee ironically deconstructs the dependency associated with both childhood and older age.

Similarly, Curren states that her physical enervation has made her as "shameless as a child" (Coetzee 1990, 119). Nashef, commenting on Curren's enervation, explains that "Aging brings about physical deterioration and diminishing faculties. Having no control over either process is what Curren finds most disconcerting" (2009, 125). She further argues that, for Curren, "Comparing the condition of her ailing body to the state of her country makes the process a bit more acceptable, introducing a sense of resignation" (2009, 125). My argument, however, emphasises that this comparison allows Coetzee to critique and invert the traditional trope of woman as nation in order to problematise the lens of dependency through which both children and the elderly are viewed. Anne McClintock argues that the association of the female body with the body of the nation is a long-standing trope of western imperialism. Furthermore, she explains that the colonial project seeks to legitimise such hierarchical relations as natural:

> Within the family metaphor, both social hierarchy (synchronic hierarchy) and historical change (diachronic hierarchy) could be portrayed as natural and inevitable, rather than as historically constructed and therefore subject to change. Projecting the family image onto national and imperial progress enabled what was often murderously violent change to be legitimized as the progressive unfolding of natural decree. Imperial intervention could thus be figured as a linear, non-revolutionary progression that naturally contained hierarchy within unity: paternal fathers ruling benignly over immature children. The trope of the organic family became invaluable in its capacity to give state and imperial intervention the alibi of nature. (1995, 45)

While McClintock relates the above to earlier colonial projects, the "murderously violent change" to which she refers can easily be associated with the South African apartheid state's heavily militarised response to any resistance against apartheid (which forms the backdrop against which *Age of Iron* is set). However, instead of appropriating the female body as a metaphor to represent this turbulence, Coetzee subverts the naturalisation of the family unit as justification for state control. He achieves this through his conflation of body politics with the body of an ageing sickly woman. Significantly, he simultaneously undermines neoliberal investments into the promise of futurity associated with childhood.[3] The passage in which Curren's growing political awareness is presented as a pregnancy illustrates these ideas:

[3] Cf. Edelman's *No Future* (2004) for a critique of discourses that employ the image of the child in this manner.

> To have fallen pregnant with these growths, these cold, obscene swellings; to have carried and carried this brood beyond any natural term, unable to bear them, unable to sate their hunger: children inside me eating more every day, not growing but bloating, toothed, clawed, forever cold and ravenous. Dry, dry: to feel them turning at night in my dry body, not stretching and kicking as a human child does but changing their angle, finding a new place to gnaw. Like insect eggs laid in the body of a host, now grown to grubs and eating their host away. My eggs, grown within me. (Coetzee 1990, 64)

Here, Curren's growing awareness of the reality of the socio-political context in which she lives is mapped onto her cancer-ridden body in the form of a grotesque and impossible pregnancy. She describes herself as a "crone" and "motherhood" as "parodying itself," exclaiming that "For twenty years [she has] not bled" (Coetzee 1990, 64). The ethical and political awareness she feels building in her body cannot be carried to term because while "the country smoulders" she is trapped in a state of becoming (Coetzee 1990, 39). This is evidenced by the grub-cocoon-moth imagery that reflects her personal growth throughout the novel. In this passage, her cancerous cells are likened to "insect eggs" that have "grown to grubs" and that are "eating their host away." While she remains alive, the grubs cannot break free and become moths. The implication is that her death is the prerequisite that will allow her transcendence, in the same way that the death of the apartheid regime will ensure the futurity of the country.

In Coetzee's novel, the woman as land trope is presented in a complicated manner implicated with cannibalistic, grotesque images of children and childhood. This intersection of body and politics culminates in Curren's description of "[t]he dry earth soaking up the blood of its creatures" and of South Africa as a "land that drinks rivers of blood and is never sated" (Coetzee 1990, 63). The land is personified here, and may be related to Mikhail Bakhtin's description of the "earth" as an "element that swallows up" but also as an "element of birth, of renascence" (1965, 213). The body of the land itself becomes grotesque, as its hyperbolic bloodlust demands a blood tribute from its creatures. This description refers to the countless and seemingly endless deaths demanded by the apartheid system. The physical body of the earth becomes the political imperative that requires blood and death in order to perpetuate itself, implying that the placid transposition of woman onto land is in this context replaced by the dangerous and violent incorporation of the diseased land by a female body. Through the conflation of femininity, childhood and older age, Coetzee resists the colonial imperative to paint woman as nation through inscribing the nation onto the barrenness associated with the ageing female body.

The narration next turns to Curren's own child, her daughter who bleeds "every month into foreign soil" (Coetzee 1990, 64). While Curren believes that "blood is one: a pool of life dispersed among us in separate existences, but belonging by nature together," she realizes that she cannot transcend her ageing physical body through her generational continuation in her daughter, as it is foreign soil into which her daughter bleeds (Coetzee 1990, 63). Her daughter chose to exile herself to Canada because of her disgust at the apartheid system. As a result, her blood (and its possibility for Mrs Curren's transcendence) becomes something that no longer fits in the South African context. Because of Mrs Curren's conflation of her own body and the body politics of South Africa, the implication is that she cannot transcend her ageing physical body through living on in her daughter's biological reproduction (or even in her relationship with her daughter) because of the latter's decision to distance herself from South African politics. Her daughter is her "daughter life" but the "children" inside her are her "daughters death" (Coetzee 1990, 64). This comparison highlights the fact that she sees her death as the prerequisite for her own futurity, as well as the futurity of the country. She describes how a sisterhood exists between her living daughter and the daughters of death, which she cannot yet carry to term. She states that her "daughter" is her "first child" (Coetzee 1990, 82), and that she is her "life" (Coetzee 1990, 83). The word "life" in this context is not used in its colloquial sense: Curren does not mean that her daughter is the most important thing in her life. Instead, she suggests that "Once upon a time [her daughter] lived in [her] as once upon a time [she] lived in [her] mother; as [her mother] still lives in [her], as [she] grows toward her, may [she] live in [her daughter]" (Coetzee 1990, 131). This locates her daughter's genealogical corporeality as that which defines Curren herself, hinting at the disruption of hegemonic sequential time that Coetzee is working towards in his complication of childhood, femininity and older age.

Furthermore, Curren's interactions with her housekeeper Florence's son and his friend—both school children actively involved in the struggle against apartheid—compel her to interrogate her own ethical stance towards the apartheid system. This acts as the impetus that forces her into social awareness, and more importantly, demands her social re-engagement. As is suggested by its title, the novel presents the idea of childhood as a recurring and multifaceted trope. As Brittan describes, "For Hesiod, the dissolution of the emotional and ethical bonds that bind parents and children is a central symptom of the Age of Iron, which helps to explain why the unravelling of family ties is so important to Coetzee's novel of the same name" (2010, 488). Similarly, this could be read in relation to McClintock's argument surrounding patriarchal control's appropriation of the female body as metaphoric of the delineation of borders, as well as to how this informs the ways in which Coetzee resists the naturalisation of the family unit as justification for state control. Discussing the dangerous implications of a generation of children risking their lives in political activism against apartheid, Curren learns that Florence feels that "There are no more mothers and fathers" (Coetzee 1990, 63). In reaction to this, Curren argues that:

> Children cannot grow up without mothers or fathers. The burnings and killings one hears of, the shocking callousness, [...] whose fault is it in the end? Surely the blame must fall on parents who say, 'Go, do as you wish, you are your own master now, I give up authority over you.' What child in his heart truly wants to be told that? Surely he will turn away in confusion, thinking to himself, 'I have no mother now, I have no father: then let my mother be death, let my father be death.' You wash your hands of them and they turn into the children of death. (Coetzee 1990, 79)

Florence responds by stating that these children are the "monster made by the white man," while Curren insists that their hearts are "turning to stone" (Coetzee 1990, 79). Ironically, this familial fragmentation is further emphasised by Curren's daughter "who, unable to live under the regime of apartheid, has abandoned her mother and is therefore guilty of filial impiety, the distortion of the bond between mother and child. Like the township children, she and, by extension, the reader are "children of iron"—children who have rejected their parents" (Marais 1993, 21).

In contrast, while Curren initially idealises the innocence of childhood and believes that because children are exempt from moral accountability they should be excluded from any imperatives towards political action, she refers to herself as belonging to the "children of [a] bygone age" who will be held accountable for their crime of blissful ignorance:

> I remember only long sun-struck afternoons, the smell of dust under avenues of eucalyptus, the quiet rustle of water in roadside furrows, the lulling of doves. A childhood of sleep, prelude, to what was meant to be a life without trouble and a smooth passage to Nirvana. Will we at least be allowed our Nirvana, we children, of that bygone age? I doubt it. If justice reigns at all, we will find ourselves barred at the first threshold of the underworld. White as grubs in our swaddling bands, we will be dispatched to join those infant souls whose eternal whining Aeneas mistook for weeping. (Coetzee 1990, 92)

Here the conflation of childhood and older age is shown to function in a complex manner. Rust and England argue that "our culture holds the old to higher moral standards, expecting them [...] to be self-effacing and beneficent. At the same time [...] this culture views the old as impotent, so that their moral failings are dismissed as harmless and of little interest," rendering them "moral non-entities whom we exempt from moral responsibility" (2015, 84). This is a clear example of the ways in which the reification of childhood as a state of moral innocence resonates with the moral stasis associated with older age. The "children of that bygone age" are now elderly, their privileged lives literally belonging to the past as they face older age and death. Curren, however, feels that the elderly, infantilised and ironically depicted as "white grubs" in "swaddling bands," should be held accountable to the highest of ethical considerations, despite whatever moral innocence is stereotypically associated with either childhood or older age. This begins to indicate her relinquishment of her idealised vision of childhood innocence and gestures towards the developing textual alignment of childhood and old age. Unmoored from familial bonds, both the "children of death" and the "children of [a] bygone era" belong to a category of childhood wholly devoid of childishness. This implies that the socio-political context surrounding apartheid and its downfall has altered and eroded the meaning of childhood.

The representation of Curren's older age as being conflated with childhood begins to grant her a measure of agency previously denied to her. If her ageing represents to her a site of shame, the excess inherent in this physical condition allows her to transgress the borders of what would normally be deemed socially acceptable. This is most clearly seen in an episode in the novel in which Curren reluctantly harbours Bheki's friend John in her garage after Bheki is killed by the apartheid police force. The police eventually find John and invade Curren's house to arrest him but then shoot at and kill him instead. When Curren refuses to leave her house (which she had previously in disgust at her own cowardice termed her "safe house of childhood slumber" [Coetzee 1990, 109]), a policewoman is called to coax her out. The behaviour of the police ironically underscores contemporary paradoxical attitudes towards women in older age, as the police both defer to Curren and infantilise her. They feel the need to summon a female officer to persuade her to leave her home—the first mark of their misguided accommodation of her condition as an ageing, sick woman. The policewoman approaches her and begins talking to her in the brisk tone of voice she thinks will please Curren. Significantly, this is also the tone of voice one would use when speaking to a child:

> Someone else came in, a young woman in uniform with a crisp, clean air about her.
>
> 'We are going to clear the house for a little while, till this business is over. Is there anywhere you would like to go, friends or relatives?'
>
> 'I am not leaving. This is my house.'
>
> Her friendliness, her concern did not waver. 'I know,' she said, 'but it's too dangerous to stay. For just a little while we must ask you to leave.' The men at the window had stopped talking now: they were impatient for me to be gone.
>
> '*Bel die ambulans*,'[4] said one of them. '*Ag, sy kan sommer by die stasie wag*,'[5] said the woman. She turned to me. 'Come now, Mrs...' She waited for me to supply the name. I did not. 'A nice warm cup of tea,' she offered. (Coetzee 1990, 155)

Ignoring the political position that Curren assumes by refusing to leave, they believe that because of her age, a female officer will make her more receptive to being forcefully removed from her home. The police officer further undermines Curren's agency by pandering to a stereotype of old age, namely that old people can be soothed by a "nice warm cup of tea." Curren insists that she will not leave. The police respond to this by physically carrying her from her home, unintentionally parodying the

[4] "Phone the ambulance" (my translation).

[5] "She can just wait at the station" (my translation).

racialised forced removals that occurred in the apartheid era as well as mirroring the way in which parents might carry away a difficult toddler to prevent an unpleasant scene. Utterly helpless and at their mercy, she uses the only weapon left to her. She yells at them that they must "put [her] down" because she has "cancer," and describes it as a "pleasure to fling the word at them" (Coetzee 1990, 155). This quite literally concretises the interiority of her condition into something with a tangible external effect, turning against them the ways in which they have infantilised her.

Refusing to accompany the police to the station, Curren wraps herself in an old quilt and wanders down the street despite the pain and discomfort she is experiencing. As she leaves her neat, suburban area and enters the seedier area around Buitenkant Street (a name that mirrors the dislocation and disassociation she experiences, as it means "outside" or "on the other side" in Afrikaans), she notes that while within the context of her home on Schoonder Street (the root word of "Schoonder" connoting cleanliness and order) she might be seen as a spectacle, amid the "rubble and filth" of the "urban shadowland" she is not "spared […] a glance" (Coetzee 1990, 157). After witnessing an act of police brutality in her private home (signifying the impossibility of avoiding the realities of the apartheid system), she actively aligns herself with "everything indefinite, everything that gives when you press it" (Coetzee 1990, 146). This section of the novel reinforces Coetzee's distortion of the traditionally gendered and politicised nature of space, since rather than inscribing Curren as a passive receptor onto which the trope of woman as land can be written, he grants her the agency to spatially displace herself in accordance with her changing political views. Ironically, the "lassitude" and "dissolution" (Coetzee 1990, 8) of old age that she so fears at the beginning of the novel finally catch up with her, but instead of being a result of the degeneration of old age, they are the consequence of her wilful defiance against an act of police brutality.

However, the spatial dislocation that makes her defiance possible does not come without a price: she realises that she cannot survive without her pills, but that the "pills were in the house, the house in other hands" (Coetzee 1990, 157). Curren's active gesture of protest can ironically never be described as triumphal—even the police react to her leaving by declaring, "*Sy's van haar kop af.*"[6] This implies that they read her actions as delusions resulting from older age rather than as a rebellious gesture. Furthermore, because she is old and sick, this act places her in a position of extreme vulnerability, physically as well as emotionally. While in Buitenkant Street, she says that she is "beginning to feel the indifferent peace of an old animal that, sensing its time is near, creeps, cold and sluggish, into the hole in the ground where everything will contract to the slow thudding of a heart" (Coetzee 1990, 158). While this is in part a reaction to what she witnesses happening to John, Coetzee's choice of metaphor broadens the implications. The "old animal" crawls into the "hole in the ground" because it senses that "its time is near." Curren can embrace the "welcoming of dissolution" (Coetzee 1990, 8) and enact her gesture of rebellion by wilfully displacing herself spatially from Schoonder Street (representing homologous belief in the ruling ideology) to Buitenkant Street (representing, quite literally, the heterogeneous and displaced) because she too senses that her death is near. The personal nature of this act is broadened to have political ramifications when viewed in relation to her previous description of "South Africa" as a "bad-tempered old hound snoozing in the doorway, taking its time to die" (Coetzee 1990, 70). While both Curren and South Africa are compared to dying animals, a difference lies in the fact that Curren senses that her "time is near" (Coetzee 1990, 158) and that the old South Africa is "taking its time to die" (Coetzee 1990, 70). However, this private and political act of defiance neither changes the reality of her old age and impending death nor does it mitigate the extreme state of pain and discomfort she feels at being dislocated from her home. She has nothing left to do but listen "to the beat of the pain that might as well have been the beat of [her] pulse" (Coetzee 1990, 158). Here, her entire consciousness is taken up by the demands of the ill and the ageing body. Her physical dislocation has thrust her into a realm of pain in which the normal mechanics of time have been suspended and warped, allowing for the blurring of the categories of older age and childhood.

Finally, she encounters Vercueil and spends the night sleeping next to him on the street. She is again reduced to a childlike dependence on him and in an extreme state of discomfort empties her bladder on her quilt.

[6] "She has lost her mind" (my translation).

Bed-wetting is usually associated with childhood, but is also very much related to the incontinence experienced by many elderly people. Furthermore, social mores regarding decency and privacy inhibit urination in public. Following the politically motivated police invasion of the privacy of Curren's home, her urinating further expresses the extent to which she has transgressed the dictates of white apartheid South Africa that have governed her existence up until this point in her life. However, the intrinsic humiliation in not being able to govern her body's impulses reduces this to an act of ultimate shame, as it magnifies the split between her corporeality and her consciousness. She comments that "all things work together towards an easy birth" (Coetzee 1990, 158), suggesting an interweaving of the concepts of birth and death and hinting at the gendered nature of both conditions. Previously, she wonders whether one must give "birth" to one's "death" without an "anaesthetic" (Coetzee 1990, 141). In Buitenkant Street, she who has not bled "[f]or twenty years" (Coetzee 1990, 54) is giving birth to her death without any relief from the pain. She is without the ease provided by her pills and at the same time can no longer keep any ethical distance from the apartheid system as she has witnessed its atrocities in her own home. Here, Coetzee employs the ageing female body in a complex manner that inverts the woman as land trope in order to illustrate the stagnation and decay that characterises apartheid South Africa. This simultaneously allows him to question the agency afforded to older women, as it is Curren who wilfully enacts a transcription of meaning onto the land, rather than the reverse. However, despite the transcendence which could be read into this act, Coetzee is careful to emphasise that the physical discomfort and pain she experiences are difficult to avoid.

The problematic transcendence associated with this is complicated even more by what occurs subsequently: Curren is violated by a gang of homeless boys. Moreover, the diction in these passages tentatively suggests a grotesque and absurd rape scene. When she wakes up in the night, she discovers "a child kneeling beside [her], feeling inside the folds of the quilt" (Coetzee 1990, 158). She describes how his "hand crept over [her] body" (Coetzee 1990, 158). The sexual undertones of the passage become more pronounced when she describes something that is "pressed between [her] lips" and "forced between [her] gums": she "gag[s] and pull[s] away" (Coetzee 1990, 158). The fact that the "something" is unnamed heightens the horror of the situation. Her feeble attempts at repelling "the hand" only result in its pressing "all the harder" (Coetzee 1990, 158). She tries to ward off the boys but she cannot speak because her "teeth [are] loose" (Coetzee 1990, 158). Ironically, this toothlessness simultaneously confirms her old age and associates her with infanthood. Through opening herself up to heterogeneous meanings and realities (the culmination of which is John's being shot), she has placed herself in a position of vulnerability in which she is susceptible to confrontation with everything that is other. Whereas previously she is able to use her cancer as a weapon against the police officers, when she tells the children that she is "sick" and that they will "get sick from" her, they simply withdraw and are described as "waiting" like "crows" (Coetzee 1990, 158). With this likening of children to carrion birds that feed on corpses, Curren's body is further thrust towards her impending death, implying that her ageing but still living body exists in a liminal space between life and death.

The grotesque nature of this allusion to rape is made all the more incongruous by the "ravishers" being children and the victim being an elderly woman. Because these children accosting Curren are described as "ravishers," the sexual undertones of this experience could be read in relation to her previously thinking of South Africa as a land "taken by force, used, despoiled, spoiled, abandoned in its late barren years. Loved too, perhaps, by its ravishers, but loved only in the bloomtime of its youth" (Coetzee 1990, 26). The distinction between South Africa's "youth" and its "barren years," coupled with the allusion to rape, relates the childlikeness (and childlessness) of Curren's old age to the ideological context of transitional South Africa. While she had previously insisted on a valorised image of childhood, Curren here seems to suggest that she does not deserve any mercy:

> 'Don't—' I said; but my palate was sore, it was hard to form words.
>
> What did I want to say? *Don't do that!? Don't you see I have nothing?? Don't you have any mercy??* What nonsense. Why should there be mercy in the world? I thought of beetles, those big black beetles with the humped backs, dying, waving their legs feebly, and ants pouring over them, gnawing at the soft places, the joints, the eyes, tearing away the beetle flesh. (Coetzee 1990, 255)

While her inability to form words relates to the breakdown of language associated with trauma, it also suggests that she has relinquished the idealised notions she previously held surrounding children and the respect she felt they ought to display to the elderly. The politicisation of the violation can be seen in her statement that "these things happened [...] a stone's throw from Breda Street and Schoonder Street and Vrede Street, where a century ago the patricians of Cape Town gave orders that there be erected spacious homes for themselves and their descendants in perpetuity, foreseeing nothing of the day when, in their shadows, the chickens would come home to roost" (Coetzee 1990, 255). Curren's violation by the boys could be seen as the pinnacle of Coetzee's inversion of the woman as land trope: instead of the white colonial feminising of the land in order to occupy a position of the "benign patriot" residing over both female colonisers and native inhabitants, the body of an ageing female functions to illustrate the ultimate failure of the colonial project. This serves to reinforce the connections between and inversions of childhood, older age and the feminisation of land evidenced throughout the novel.

Towards the end of the novel, Curren writes that her letter "was never meant to be the story of a body, but of the soul it houses," and that because of this, she "will draw a veil soon" (Coetzee 1990, 185). However, the phrasing of her statement that her letter "was never *meant* to be the story of a body" implies that despite her intentions, her letter inevitably does centre on her body (Coetzee 1990, 185, my emphasis). The final passages of the novel evidence this: she describes the increasingly intense pain she experiences and the hallucinations brought on by her medication as well as Vercueil cooking for her, sleeping next to her on her bed for warmth and helping her hang up the underwear he has washed (Coetzee 1990, 191). This concern with embodiment is indeed also reflected throughout the novel: Coetzee continually emphasises that Curren has to speak the truth of her disapproval of the apartheid system through the pain caused by her cancer and her old age. The implication of this is that the story of her soul is inextricably entwined with that of her body, and that her embodiment shapes the ways in which her subjectivity is constructed in her old age prior to her death. The decay of her body thus becomes the impetus that propels her into attempting to stave off the decay of her soul: Curren is able to speak her soul's truth *because* of her body's pain. Furthermore, the political changes occurring in the decade before the demise of apartheid provide the necessary conditions that allow her to do so, as the transitional nature of this period reflects the transitional nature of the process of her dying.

While Coetzee represents Curren as becoming childlike in her older age (and concomitantly implies that her ageing renders her as helpless and vulnerable as a child), this childlikeness enables her to transgress the confines of her ageing physicality through the emotional and intellectual redefinition it allows. Writing on the relationship between childhood and land, Burman and Stacey comment that "This relation [...] interferes with the traditional trope of the child as iconic subject, positing the child as a figure who instead challenges the nation state's sovereign subject" (2010, 234). This rewriting of the meaning attributed to the child-figure can indeed be seen throughout *Age of Iron*. However, Coetzee complicates this even further through his blurring of images relating to childhood and older age. As Lury points out in an analysis of the role of the child in new Iranian, Turkish and Afghani cinema, the status of childhood "precisely by virtue of [its] unfinished and socially estranged character, [...] allow[s] for different configurations of the human–landscape–environment relation that might also undo prevailing nationalist (and fundamentalist) frameworks" (2010, 234). This same mutability can be seen in Coetzee's representation of Curren's elderly female body as a force that counteracts the dependency associated with both categories of childhood and older age, undermines conventional representations of women in relation to land, and to some extent liberates the figure of the ageing woman from socially prescribed meanings.

A recurring description in criticism of literature written during South Africa's interregnum makes use of Antonio Gramsci's statement that the crisis of transition lies in the fact that while "the old is dying, [...] the new cannot be born" (1971, 276). Coetzee employs older age and its reversion to childhood as a trope that reflects this crisis. The manner in which he collapses the distinctions between childhood and older age renders *both* categories ambiguous. This indicates his insistence on the intersection of the old and the new, and suggests that any reversion of power may not be as simple as the death of the old system heralding the birth of the new. As such this text highlights the necessity of viewing the construct of older age as one marked by continuity (of the past, present and future; of the personal and political; of old age and youth) rather than regarding the aged as a discrete group, marooned in a separate temporal experience. Coetzee points to the ways in which older age outgrows itself and extends itself beyond a fixed temporal significance, with Curren both breaching the confines of her present physicality and subverting the conventionally inevitable decline into moral obsolescence.

Works Cited

Bakhtin, M.M. 1965; 1984. *Rabelais and His World*, trans. Iswolsky, H. Bloomington, Ind: Indiana University Press.

Beauvoir, Simone de. 1949. *Le Deuxième Sexe*. trans. H.M. Parshley 1973. London: Vintage.

Brittan, Alice. 2010. Death and J.M. Coetzee's Disgrace. *Quarterly* 26 (3): 441–450.

Burman, Erica, and Jackie Stacey. 2010. The Child and Childhood in Feminist Theory. *Feminist Theory* 11 (3): 227–240.

Coetzee, J.M. 1980. *Waiting for the Barbarians*. London: Secker & Warburg.

Coetzee, J.M. 1990. *Age of Iron*. London: Secker & Warburg.

Coetzee, J.M. 1999. *Disgrace*. London: Secker & Warburg.

Coetzee, J.M. 2003. *Elizabeth Costello*. London: Secker & Warburg.

Coetzee, J.M. 2005. *Slow Man*. London: Secker & Warburg.

Coetzee, J.M. 2007. *Diary of a Bad Year*. London: Random House.

Douglas, Mary. 1996. *Purity and Danger*. London: Routledge & Kegan Paul.

Edelman, L. 2004. *No Future: Queer Theory and the Death Drive*. Durham: Duke University Press.

Gramsci, A. 1971. *Selections from the Prison Notebooks of Antonio Gramsci*, trans. Quentin Hoare and Geoffrey Nowell Smith. London: Lawrence & Wishart.

Harris, D. 1988. *Dictionary of Gerontology*. Westport, CN: Greenwood.

Head, Dominic. 1997. *J.M. Coetzee*. Cambridge: Cambridge University Press.

Hendricks, Jon, and Cynthia Leedham. 1987. Making Sense of Literary Aging: Relevance of Recent Gerontological Theory. *Journal of Aging Studies* 1 (2): 187–208.

Henneberg, S.B. 2006. Of Creative Crones and Poetry: Developing Age Studies through Literature. *National Women's Studies Association Journal* 18 (1): 106–125.

Hepworth, Mike. 1996. "William" and the Old Folks: Notes on Infantilisation. *Ageing & Society* 16: 423–441.

Kimuna, S.R., and M. Makiwane. 2008. Older People as Resources in South Africa. *Journal of Aging & Social Policy* 19 (1): 97–114.

Kinsella, K., and M. Ferreira. 1997. *Aging Trends: South Africa*. USA: U.S. Department of Commerce.

Lury, K. 2010. *The Child in Film: Tears, Fears and Fairy Tales*. London: I.B. Tauris.

Makiwane, M., C. Ndinda, and H. Botsis. 2012. Gender, Race and Ageing in South Africa. *Agenda* 26 (4): 15–28.

Marais, Michael. 1993. Who Clipped the Hollycocks?: J.M. Coetzee's *Age of Iron* and the Politics of Representation. *English in Africa* 20 (2): 1–24.

McClintock, Anne. 1995. *Imperial Leather: Race, Gender and Sexuality in the Colonial Contest*. New York: Routledge.

Nashef, Hania A.M. 2009. *The Politics of Humiliation in the Novels of J.M. Coetzee*. London: Routledge.

Pretorius, Antoinette. 2015a. Bodily Disintegration and Successful Ageing in *Body Bereft* by Antjie Krog. *Tydskrif vir Letterkunde* 52 (2): 21–32.

Pretorius, Antoinette. 2015b. To Eke Out the Vocabulary of Old Age: Literary Representations of Ageing in Transitional and Post-transitional South Africa. PhD thesis. University of Pretoria, South Africa.

Rust, Martha, and Suzanne England. 2015. Sweet Old Things: Moral Complexities in Old Age in Muriel Spark's *Memento Mori*. *Journal of Aging Studies* 33: 76–85.

Sadie, J.L. 1994. Economic Implications of Demographic Ageing in South Africa. *Southern African Journal of Demography* 4 (1): 40–57.

Sagner, A. 2000. Ageing and Social Policy in South Africa: Historical Perspectives with Particular Reference to the Eastern Cape. *Journal of Southern African Studies* 26 (3): 523–553.

Segal, Lynne. 2013. *Out of Time: The Pleasures and the Perils of Ageing*. London and New York: Verso.

Sontag, Susan. 1972. The Double Standard of Aging. *The Saturday Review*. September 23, 1972. 29–38.

Wyatt-Brown, Anne. 1990. The Coming of Age of Literary Gerontology. *Journal of Ageing Studies* 4 (3): 299–315.

Zeilig, Hannah. 2011. The Critical Use of Narrative and Literature in Gerontology. *International Journal of Ageing and Later Life* 6 (2): 7–37.

CHAPTER 16

African American Humour and the Construction of a Mature Female Middle-Class Identity in Clarence Major's *Such Was the Season*

Saskia Marguerita Fürst

Historically, black women have been typically portrayed in dominant discourses according to the roles of the matriarch, the Black Mammy or the Angry Black Woman, to name a few.[1] Older black women, almost invisible within mainstream print and television culture,[2] are also often featured in stereotypical roles that serve to assist the white characters

[1] For more information, see Collins (2000) and Harris-Perry (2011).

[2] See the study conducted by Judith de Luce in 2001 of 31 common US magazines, which found relatively few advertisements featuring older women and none depicting ageing black women. See also the findings of Meredith Tupper's (2015) study concerning the representation of the elderly in prime time television commercials in 1995 that featured only 0.12% of older African Americans despite their 1% population as of the 1990 US census.

S.M. Fürst (✉)
University of Salzburg, Erzabt-Klotz-Str. 1, Salzburg 5020, Austria
e-mail: Saskia.Fuerst@sbg.ac.at

C. McGlynn et al. (eds.), *Ageing Women in Literature and Visual Culture*,
DOI 10.1007/978-3-319-63609-2_16

and families, particularly in Hollywood films.[3] More recently, in television series like *Grey's Anatomy* (2005–) and *Orange is the New Black* (2013–),[4] older black women are presented as diverse characters, featuring bodily markers of ageing, such as greying and thinning hair, sagging and wrinkled skin and less able bodies. Furthermore, their social and economic needs and the specific challenges they face are made visible in this visual format. In literary fiction, African American writers have been addressing the desires and self-development of older black women since the nineteenth century. In the early twentieth century, Zora Neale Hurston's *Their Eyes Were Watching God* (1937) features an older woman who falls in love with a younger man, and both Dorothy West and Lorraine Hansberry depict the complex lives of mature black women who aspire to live among the affluent, black middle class in the novel *The Living is Easy* (1948) and the play *A Raisin in the Sun* (1959), respectively. African American painter and writer Clarence Major continues this trend in his relatively unknown novel *Such Was the Season*, published in 1987. He utilises African American speech acts and humour as key elements of the narrative to negotiate a mature identity in his 60+ protagonist, Annie Eliza.

Within the socio-historical era of the rising black middle class in the twentieth century in the US, Major's novel addresses black women's Christian moral values, homecoming and the roles of black women and men in their respective communities.[5] Annie Eliza narrates her nephew Juneboy's return to Atlanta: a description of a week-long visit which includes important references to Annie Eliza's beloved soap operas, the political aspirations of her daughter-in-law, the food scandal surrounding her son—the local preacher's—church and Juneboy's desire to reconnect with the memory of and places connected to his deceased father. While originally Major wanted to write the novel from Juneboy's perspective, he was inspired by the voices of his mother and other female

[3] See Reid (2005, 81–84).

[4] Myrna Hant (2001) makes a similar argument for an increased and more diverse representation of ageing regarding the portrayal of older white women in quality television shows in the twenty-first century. Margaret Tally analyses recent Hollywood movies that explore sexual (re)awakening in older protagonists and also notes a recent increase in mainstream films that target older female audiences (2006, 37–39).

[5] For more on issues regarding "authenticity" in the black middle class, see Smith (1998, 63–68).

relatives during a trip to Atlanta, and he decided to tell the narrative from Annie Eliza's perspective (cf. Byerman 2012, 182). According to Keith Byerman, Major creates a "credible female storyteller" (2012, 183) through Annie Eliza by retaining speech patterns found in the rural South. Elaine Richardson further comments that many black Americans utilise "language and literary practices to resist White supremacist and economically motivated stereotypes conveying subhuman or immoral images" (2003, 74). Thus, Major is part of the African American literary canon of the late twentieth century that sought to document the experiences of black women in fictional literature and to establish their lives and experiences in the US as a legitimate theme for mainstream audiences.

Already during slavery, laughter and humour served as a means to gain freedom and self-empowerment in an environment otherwise hostile toward African Americans. According to Glenda Carpio, "Black American humour began as a wrested freedom, the freedom to laugh at that which was unjust and cruel in order to create distance from that which would otherwise obliterate a sense of self and community" (2008, 4). Lisa Green (2002) further identifies specific speech events, such as signifying, playing the dozens and the fool's laugh, which only occur within African American English. For example, signifying is a speech interaction between two or more people whereby a verbal duel takes place. The winner is the person who has the better comeback (repartee), and usually there is an audience to acknowledge the more skilful participant. The content of the banter involves making exaggerated derogatory remarks about the opponent and her/his family, sexuality, physical appearance and class (cf. Green 2002, 138; Morgan 2002, 56–57). Henry Louis Gates Jr. also notes that signifying can be used to completely destroy an opponent or to make the speaker feel better about her/himself (1998, 72). A variation of signifying, playing the dozens is solely intended to verbally crush the opponent (Green 2002, 135–136). Annie Eliza displays this verbal skill throughout the novel, particularly when she plays the dozens with Renee Wright, her daughter-in-law. With the assistance of the readers, who serve as the audience to their linguistic duels, the power dynamics between the two women shift in the narration of the events during Juneboy's visit to favour Annie Eliza, despite her lower-class status.

These speech events, replicated in literature, are also a means of releasing hostile feelings towards oppression that black Americans face in the present. As Sigmund Freud notes, individuals release energy stored from repressed sexual or hostile feelings in the form of joking (cf. Smuts 2009). For example, the fool's laugh, a black woman's humorous tool, is used to signal that a person is a fool when s/he does not take the woman seriously or that the topic itself is a mockery (Green 2002, 55). The fool's laugh can also occur in situations where women are in a less powerful position, ridiculing the other person, while also acknowledging the inequality of power existing between the two persons (Morgan 2002, 55). This speech act is evident in the novel, as Annie Eliza attempts to maintain relative social power when discussing age-related health issues with a younger man. Finally, Annie Eliza occasionally embraces stereotypical roles humorously in order to criticise and deconstruct ageist perspectives in African American communities: She plays the fool. Rather than locating a source for Annie Eliza's agency within the concept of (West-African) ancestral remembering as demonstrated by contemporary authors like Toni Morrison in *Song of Solomon* (1977) and Paule Marshall in the *Praisesong for the Widow* (1983), Major provides an alternative depiction of ageing in black communities, which uses African American forms of humorous speech acts to liberate his protagonist from certain restrictive practices with regards to her ageing body and to validate her agency as a mature black woman in her chosen community.

The second major female character in the novel, Renee, is a mother and wife who is portrayed as caring predominantly about material wealth and her political career, neglecting to provide her children with love and care. Acknowledging that this is why she is "too hard" on her, Annie Eliza's pride in her class status is threatened when Renee (inappropriately) offers to give Annie Eliza one of her used mink coats. Addressing the readers, Annie Eliza says, "Child, you should have heard me carry on" (Major, 16). She continues relating the event stating, "Renee, I said, it's so thoughtful of you, honey, and you know I do'preciate the offer, but my friends would think I'd lost my mind if they saw me in an expensive coat like this. Everybody I know know I can't afford mink. Might think I stole it or something" (Major, 16). In return, Renee turns red in the face and is unable to respond. Her lack of skills at playing the dozens is thus made evident to the readers and discredits her as a competent opponent to Annie Eliza, despite her privileged upper-class status. Simultaneously, Annie Eliza's identification with the black working-class actually situates her as a more powerful agent in her communication with Renee, confirmed through this speech act of "annihilating" her opponent.

This anecdote regarding Renee highlights Annie Eliza's use of humour to resolve a class identity conflict that also intersects with her status as an older woman. Part of the working class with limited opportunities in the Jim Crow era, Annie Eliza aspires to become a member of the middle class, displayed through her adoption of strong Christian morals and values surrounding black motherhood. The widespread promotion of moral principles, attitudes and actions traditionally associated with the middle class to working-class women was largely a consequence of black women's clubs, church-based groups and charity organisation, which sought to empower black women and counter negative stereotypes surrounding black womanhood (cf. Hines 1989, 918). Aspiring to attain class mobility in her own life-time, Annie Eliza incorporates and promotes many of these values and attitudes within her own life. Economic security for herself and her sons is also important to her, which is why she is proud that her younger son, Jeremiah, becomes a preacher and marries Renee, achieving class mobility and thus a higher social status: "I just gave praise to the Lord that at least one of my boys had made it big in this world" (Major, 20). Still, with her personal goal and satisfaction in reaching a middle-class economic status in her later years, she is not interested in accommodating or adopting the (morally inferior) upper-class values which Renee displays. As a single mother and the head of her family, Annie Eliza has worked hard to provide for her children and is enjoying the luxury of retiring and not having to work. In a rural community, she would receive additional social status as an elder for her years of accumulated knowledge and her ability to support her children financially or through childcare (cf. Kivett 1993, 170). Yet, Renee's upper-class status and educational background negate Annie Eliza's involvement in her extended family as a valuable elder: Renee hires a nanny for her children, lives in a mansion down the road from Annie Eliza and is involved in local politics. Thus, in order to regain her status as a respected matriarch, Annie Eliza signifies on Renee's perceived character flaws, which she attributes to Renee's upper-class background.

After narrating the previously mentioned anecdote, Annie Eliza continues to describe Renee as "just one of them nigger gals spoiled something you wouldn't believe, and, child, so full of herself she can't smell her own stink" (Major, 19). Annie Eliza attributes Renee's laziness and spoiled character to her family's privileged status and signifies upon this. Yet despite the humorous aspect of Annie Eliza's contempt towards Renee's inferior morality and work ethic as an upper-class black woman,

Annie Eliza's criticism is harsh. Referring to Renee as a "nigger gal" is a particular slur that symbolically demotes Renee to an extremely low moral standing within African American communities. In this instance, Bernard Bell argues that Annie Eliza is a septuagenarian whose own double consciousness is revealed in her references to Renee as a "nigger." He even notes that her use of African American English is not always grammatically correct, while her "rhythm, inherent variability, and peripatetic style of the literary idiolect seem authentic enough" (1994, 91). When attending the dinner party that Renee hosts to announce her plans to run for a senate seat in the state of Georgia, Annie Eliza purposefully sits apart from everyone and remarks that Renee's guests "make [her] feel like [she's] just a pickaninny" (Major, 152). Certainly here Annie Eliza seems to have internalised white stereotypical viewpoints regarding black people, thus internalising double consciousness.

Yet why would Major portray his mature black character in such a "folksy" manner?[6] Particularly in the Harlem Renaissance, African American writers exposed the problematic of black middle-class members internalising myths of white supremacy in their desire to achieve class mobility; abandoning their African cultural roots, these characters often failed to find a place to *be* themselves in US society and suffered emotionally, despite their upper-class status. Yet on her way to the dinner party, Annie Eliza expresses her concern that Juneboy's appearance, due to his working-class upbringing, would "embarrass [her] side of the family" (Major, 18). She makes an effort with her own appearance, too, wearing her best wig to impress the upper-class black milieu at Renee's party. While at the party, she enjoys being treated by the catering staff "like [she] was somebody too" and is impressed by the variety of food Renee serves, confiding to the readers, "You wouldn't believe the food, you just wouldn't believe it" (Major, 29). Clearly, Annie Eliza is impressed by Renee's class status, yet at the same time, as an older woman who has provided the possibility for Jeremiah to marry into such a wealthy black family, she wants to be treated with a certain degree of respect, as a middle-class black woman. Annie Eliza purposefully plays the fool and internalises stereotypical roles and thought patterns in order

[6]See Bell's comment that Annie Eliza initially appears to be more "folksy than folk" (1994, 90)—a stereotypical representation of a matriarchal figure in the black community.

to destabilise the power hierarchy between herself and her wealthier (and younger) daughter-in-law. In portraying her ambiguous thoughts and actions, Major presents a fallible mature woman who is still in the process of developing her identity and is not yet able to positively identify with her daughter-in-law due to her conflicting desires surrounding black, mature, middle-class womanhood.

In her article on Ishmael Reed's *Mumbo Jumbo* (1972), Sharon Jesse points out that at times what is being signified and critically parodied in literature still refers to "something" (1996, 130). In Major's novel, that "something" is the irony of "successful" ageing for the black protagonist. Within a youth-oriented, mainstream Western culture, women's bodies are valued for their strict adherence to a particular concept of white femininity and beauty standards in order to remain marketable in a patriarchal society (Sontag 2008, 208). Female bodies which diverge from this norm, because they display ethnic features or markers of ageing, are still stigmatised as the Other. Thus, the desire to pass for a younger, more desirable female body pressures many mature women who adhere to Western gender norms to, for instance, undergo cosmetic surgery, dye their hair and consume products and adopt lifestyles that promote a younger body image.[7] Black women in the US (and internationally) can also internalise this Western discourse, striving to achieve "white-washed," idealised bodily standards as it grants them relative social power. However, as mentioned previously, there is a historical precedence of black women refuting labels and stereotypes attributed to them by the dominant society.[8] Through actively adopting black female beauty features and displaying markers of ageing, as a rejection of internalised white beauty norms, black women have contested the concept and practice of successful ageing in consumerist-focused societies.

When Annie Eliza succeeds in passing for a younger woman in the novel, Major critically signifies her actions for the readers. For example, Annie Eliza's favourite "blond but kinda red" wig, which once looked "real natural" is described by her sister Esther as making her look "like one of these here street hussies" (Major, 17). Annie Eliza retorts, "I told

[7] See, among others, Furman (1999, 10–12) and Slevin (2010, 1006).

[8] Julie Winterich notes in a small study that African American women seem less affected in their self-confidence and self-valuation by their greying hair and other markers of ageing. She attributes this to their marginalised status in US society (2007, 63).

her she never been able to tell me what to do, and she won't 'bout to start at sixty-three. I used to change her diapers, and when she tries to get smart with me I remind her. It puts her in her place. I wore my wig all over Chicago, strutting my stuff just as pretty as I pleased" (Major, 17). Annie Eliza successfully plays the dozens with Esther, nullifying her critique as well as her credibility as an opponent. She further validates her passing as younger when she "struts her stuff" all over Chicago, an empowering feeling for Annie Eliza as an older woman aware of her sexuality. Yet through inversion, Major is also able to critique her efforts. Thus readers, while acknowledging her verbal triumph, may also laugh *at* her predicament, recognizing the "infirmity" of Eliza's attempt to pass as younger. As already noted by Thomas Hobbes, "The passion of laughter is nothing else but the sudden glory arising from the sudden conception of some eminency in ourselves by comparison with the infirmity of others or with our own formerly" (qtd. in Kline 1907, 422). Thus, Major places the readers in the position to criticise the notion of and adherence to successful ageing in Western societies through their ability to exalt in their "eminency" over Annie Eliza.

Additionally, Esther serves as a foil character to highlight the lack of attention paid by mainstream gerontologists and healthcare providers to the specific needs of elderly black Americans. Already in the 1970s, Jacquelyne Johnson Jackson (1997) notes the dearth in research featuring ageing black women compared to whites. She, along with other noted African American scholars, emphasises the need to create awareness for how to reduce the health risks these women face as they age, especially for those from working-class and poor backgrounds. For example, research in the late twentieth century showed that older black women had a higher rate of coronary heart disease, stroke, breast cancer and diabetes than their black male and white counterparts and also had the poorest nutrition, in general (cf. Ralston 1997, 280–281). In the novel, Major also addresses ailments that older women are confronted with. Annie Eliza talks with Fred, the younger man present at a dinner party hosted by Renee:

> [He] ast'bout my arthritis. I didn't tell him how bad it was being lately 'cause I don't wants to bend peoples' ears with my troubles the way my sister Esther do. Child, all you want to do is get away from all that

> complaining! So I just told Fred that I was feeling tolerably well for a gal as old as I was and laughed, and he laughed with me. (Major, 25)[9]

Annie Eliza engages once again in pointed indirectness, signifying Esther's habit of complaining about her age-related health problems and thus criticising this practice in order to position herself more positively from a mainstream perspective. At the end of her conversation, Annie Eliza laughs despite the lack of humour regarding her infirmity. In this ambiguous example, Annie Eliza may be using the fool's laugh to acknowledge the power inequality between Fred and herself based on age, class and gender differences. As older people are prone to this ailment, her laughter could also signal the ridiculousness of implying that she is "feeling well." In the gendered power hierarchy with Fred, however, she is not able to discuss her illness without implying that she is not ageing "successfully."

At the end of their exchange, Annie Eliza excuses herself, as she suspects that her wig is crooked. She escapes to the upstairs bathroom and determines that her wig is properly in place. However, she realises that her girdle is too tight and is making her feel uncomfortable. She states that due to her arthritis, her body retains water, thus making the girdle even tighter. As a result, it takes her "'bout-oh-heck, a half hour [to get] it down past my hips and put that old thing in the hamper" (Major, 26). She says, "Well, girl, it was so funny, trying to get outta that God-awful thing, I had to laugh at myself right there in the bathroom" (Major, 25–26). Additionally, just as she decides to exit the restroom and go back downstairs to the party, she stumbles against the sink and her dentures fall out. They are a new set, which she is not used to wearing. She states, "After I saw they didn't break, I broke down laughing so hard at *my foolish old self* I thought I'd die from heart failure" (Major, 26; emphasis added). Here, she realises the absurdity of trying to conform to specific standards for maintaining a more youthful appearance than her body actually exhibits. Her expression of humour, her laughter, signals her exaltation in her abrupt understanding of her previous inferiority. Addressing the readers in this funny moment, Major invites us to laugh

[9] Penny Ralston notes that elderly black women are less likely to mention their health problems, as part of a coping strategy and within a "conspiracy of silence," so as not to affect the well-being of family members with their ailments (1997, 280).

with and *at* Annie Eliza, as we both suddenly gain satisfaction in realising our eminency compared to Annie Eliza's previous state. With the sudden realisation on the part of Annie Eliza, her use of the self-directed fool's laugh criticises all her previous efforts to successfully age. Through humour then, Annie Eliza acknowledges the charade of wearing a girdle, dentures and even a wig to disguise her bodily features that display signs of ageing. The girdle, for example, restricts her freedom and movement, just as engaging in passing for a younger version of herself, symbolically, restricts her freedom to *be* an older woman. Through her use of African American humour, Annie Eliza contests the concept of and loss of agency associated with successful ageing and both literally and symbolically "wrests freedom" for herself as a mature black woman in US society.

To conclude, in *Such Was the Season*, Major utilises particular forms of African American humour through the female character of Annie Eliza to give voice, agency and legitimacy to the perspective of an older black woman from a working-/middle-class, urban, Christian background in the US. While at times Annie Eliza appears to condone conservative views of ageing and black middle-class morality, her humorous approach serves as a method for critical signification: She ridicules, contests and exemplifies the absurdity of particular concepts associated with ageing and black womanhood. However, Major does not necessarily provide answers to the dilemmas Annie Eliza faces: There is no resolution to her narration whereby she has found a balance in her self-identity, nor does she resolve a major internal or community conflict that establishes her authority and position of importance within her chosen community. As Byerman notes, Major criticises the politicised, typical presentation of older matriarchal characters in contemporary novels by African American women authors through his depiction of Annie Eliza:

> In effect, Major uses a version of the idealized wise woman of black women's fiction (Baby Suggs in *Beloved* and Pilate in Morrison's *Song of Solomon* [...] and Gloria Naylor's lead character in *Mama Day*) as a means of subverting the womanist and feminist impulses of those very writers. Unlike Reed, however, he does not do this in the service of a masculinist alternative but rather as part of his lifelong resistance to using the arts for ideological purposes. (2012, 184–185)

In his female character, Major rather presents his own (a)political representation of a mature black woman in literature, purposefully highlighting Annie Eliza's ambiguity and often stereotypical viewpoints and then deconstructing them through African American forms of humour.

At the end of the novel, Annie Eliza announces her support for Renee's political ambitions, a solemn moment of solidarity among women of different generations. Still, as Annie Eliza is supposed to provide an apolitical representation of a mature black woman, Major does not provide a method for locating positive identification within the process of ageing for black women, beyond using humour to criticise mainstream views of mature black womanhood and the concept of successful ageing. Yet as Morrison points out, the goal of a literary work is to have "something in it that enlightens [...] that suggests what the conflicts are, what the problems are. But it need not solve those problems because it is not a case study, not a recipe" (1997, 2287). While at times slow-moving and seemingly monotonous, Major's novel provides another example of the disempowering aspects of passing as younger, as well as the validity and effectiveness in shifting marginalised perspectives to the centre of discussions regarding women and ageing. To this effect, he need not provide answers; rather, he provides an alternative representation of ageing as a positive, at times hilarious, part of a middle-class (black) woman's later years.

Works Cited

Bell, Bernard. 1994. Introduction: Clarence Major's Double Consciousness as a Black Postmodernist Artist. *African American Review* 28 (1): 5–9. Accessed 30 May 2016. JSTOR. http://www.jstor.org/stable/3041944.

Byerman, Keith. 2012. *The Art and Life of Clarence Major*. Athens: University of Georgia Press.

Carpio, Glenda. 2008. *Laughing Fit to Kill: Black Humor in the Fictions of Slavery*. New York: Oxford University Press.

Collins, Patricia Hill. 2000. *Black Feminist Thought: Knowledge, Consciousness, and the Politics of Empowerment*, 2nd ed. New York: Routledge.

de Luce, Judith. 2001. Silence at the Newsstands. *Generations* 3: 39–43. Accessed 26 Oct 2001. EBSCOhost. 5741268.

Furman, Frida Kerner. 1999. There Are No Old Venuses: Older Women's Responses to Their Aging Bodies. In *Mother Time: Women, Aging, and Ethics*, ed. Margaret Urban Walker, 7–22. New York: Rowman & Littlefield.

Gates Jr., Henry Louis. 1988. *The Signifying Monkey: A Theory of African American Literary Criticism*. New York: Oxford University Press.

Green, Lisa. 2002. *African American English: A Linguistic Introduction.* Cambridge: Cambridge University Press.

Hant, Myrna. 2001. Television's Mature Women: A Changing Media Archetype: From Bewitched to the Sopranos. Los Angeles: UCLA Center for the Study of Women, 2001. Accessed 2 June 2015. eScholarship. http://escholarship.org/uc/item/3357r9nz.

Harris-Perry, Melissa Victoria. 2011. *Sister Citizen: Shame, Stereotypes, and Black Women in America.* New Haven: Yale University Press.

Jackson, Jacquelyne Johnson. 1997. The Plight of Older Black Women in the US. In *The Other Within Us: Feminist Explorations of Women and Aging*, ed. Marilyn Pearsall, 37–42. Colorado: Westview Press. Originally Published in *The Black Scholar* 7 (7): 47–55 (1976).

Jesse, Sharon. 1996. Laughter and Identity in Ishmael Reed's *Mumbo Jumbo. MELUS* 21 (4): 127–139. Accessed 26 Oct 2011. doi:10.2307/467645.

Kivett, Vira. 1993. Racial Comparisons of the Grandmother Role: Implications for Strengthening the Family Support System of Older Black Women. *Family Relations* 42 (2): 165–172. Accessed 24 Jan 2013. JSTOR http://www.jstor.org/stable/585450.

Kline, L.W. 1907. The Psychology of Humor. *The American Journal of Psychology* 18 (4): 421–441. Accessed 26 Oct 2011. doi:10.2307/1412574.

Major, Clarence. 1987. *Such Was the Season.* San Francisco: Mercury House.

Morgan, Marcyliena. 2002. *Language, Discourse and Power in African American Culture.* Studies in the Social and Cultural Foundation of Language, 20. Cambridge: Cambridge University Press.

Morrison, Toni. 1997. Rootedness: The Ancestor as Foundation. In *The Norton Anthology of African American Literature*, ed. Henry Louis Gates Jr. and Nellie McKay, 2286–2290. 2nd ed. New York: W.W. Norton & Company.

Ralston, Penny A. 1997. Midlife and Older Black Women. In *Handbook on Women and Aging*, ed. Jean M. Coyle, 273–289. London: Greenwood Press.

Reid, Mark A. 2005. *Black Lenses, Black Voices: African American Film Now.* Lanham (MD): Rowman & Littlefield.

Richardson, Elaine. 2003. *African American Literacies.* New York: Routledge.

Slevin, Kathleen. 2010. "If I Had Lots of Money…I'd Have a Body Makeover": Managing the Aging Body. *Social Forces* 88 (3): 1003–1020. Accessed 24 Jan 2013. JSTOR. http://www.jstor.org/stable/40645880.

Smith, Valerie. 1998. *Not Just Race, Not Just Gender: Black Feminist Readings.* New York: Routledge.

Smuts, Aron. 2009. Humor. *Internet Encyclopedia of Philosophy.* Accessed 30 Jan 2012. http://www.iep.utm.edu/humor/.

Sontag, Susan. 2008. The Double Standard of Aging. In *Ageing*, ed. Susan McDaniel, 201–215. London: Sage Publications. Originally Published in *Sexuality Today and Tomorrow: Contemporary Issues in Human Sexuality*, ed. Sol Gordon and Roger Libby, 350–366. Belmont: Wadsworth, 1972.

Tally, Margaret. 2006. 'She Doesn't Let Age Define Her': Sexuality and Motherhood in Recent 'Middle-Aged Chick Flicks'. *Sexuality & Culture* 10 (2): 33–55. Accessed 26 Oct 2013. EBSCOhost. 21460108.

Tupper, Meredith. 2015. The Representation of Elderly People in Prime Time Television Commercials. Master's thesis, University of South Florida School of Mass Communications. Accessed 22 May 2015. http://oldpeopletvcommercials.com.

Winterich, Julie. 2007. Aging, Femininity, and the Body: What Appearance Changes Mean to Women with Age. *Gender Issues* 24: 51–69. Accessed 24 Jan 2013. EBSCOhost. 27900982.

CHAPTER 17

"This Is How Time Unfolds When You Are Old": Ageing, Subjectivity and Joseph O'Connor's *Ghost Light*

Margaret O'Neill

Ghost Light, a 2010 novel by Joseph O'Connor, tells the story of a formerly celebrated Irish actress who lives a life of loneliness and poverty in 1950s London. This chapter reads O'Connor's fictional biography of actress Molly Allgood (Máire O'Neill) (1887–1952) with reference to cultural gerontological, feminist and Neo-Freudian theories. It focuses upon Molly's experiences of time and space, whereby, through the uncanny sense of the past in the present, O'Connor's narrative underscores memory as informing meaning in later life. I read these imaginings in light of the work of Kathleen Woodward and Lynne Segal, in particular. Woodward emphasises the role of reminiscence for creating an emotional atmosphere and the role of mourning for stimulating creativity in old age (1997, 1; 1993, 89). Segal expounds the manner in which we retain traces of our previous selves as we negotiate the present, an experience that becomes more compounded the older we are (2014, 4). Through the second-person narrative perspective, "you," *Ghost Light* reveals the complexity of

M. O'Neill (✉)
University of Limerick, Limerick, Ireland
e-mail: Margaret.ONeill@ul.ie

C. McGlynn et al. (eds.), *Ageing Women in Literature and Visual Culture*,
DOI 10.1007/978-3-319-63609-2_17

the aged protagonist's inner life as she relives and recounts her memories of her younger self as an actress and her romance with playwright John Millington Synge in early twentieth-century Dublin, while simultaneously struggling to survive alone in an environment hostile to the old and the poor. The novel thus calls attention to the complexities of how the "spiraled shell" of time "unfolds when you are old" while also demonstrating the potential for art to reveal the moral failings of a wider community, eventually seen in Molly's bleak death (O'Connor, 10). This chapter further explores O'Connor's representation of the actress's life stages, focusing on her old age, against the backdrop of early twentieth-century Irish society and post-Second World War London. It illustrates that the novel draws critical attention to cultural stereotypes of Irish women and intersections of class and race, while casting a light, albeit a ghostly one, on negative expectations about ageing, to present loss and grief as forces for creativity and change.

In his depiction of Molly Allgood, O'Connor brings together historical narrative with the transformative potential of the imaginary, writing the figure of the ageing woman back into Irish cultural memory, wherein she is so often overlooked. As Leszek Drong states, "*Ghost Light* explores what history programmatically ignores: the personal, the emotional, the hypothetical, the imaginable" (2017, 40). Molly was the daughter of a Protestant father and Catholic mother, and a child of the Dublin tenements.[1] She would become a beautiful and talented actress, well known as a star of the Abbey Theatre and later of the screen. J.M. Synge was an affluent Protestant from a landowning family and a major playwright. She is believed to have been his muse; it is said that "With her in mind he wrote 'The playboy of the western world' and 'Deirdre of the sorrows'" (Lunney, n.p.). Their relationship opposed rigid social and cultural divides and was considered scandalous by family, friends and the theatre community.[2] James Pethica describes how "Their liaison, as

[1] I refer to Molly Allgood on first name basis as "Molly" because she is "Molly" in the narrative of *Ghost Light*.

[2] In addition to class, religion and age, Molly's occupation was likely also a factor in society's distaste for her and Synge's relationship. When Synge tells his mother that Molly is an actress, she exclaims that "The worst is true" and continues to describe Molly as a "whore" (55; 58). Historically and into the early twentieth century, the role of an actress had been understood to correspond with that of a prostitute, in part due to the conflation of the willingness to expose oneself on stage with the willingness to perform sexually (Pullen 2006, 9).

W.J. McCormack has observed, violated 'boundaries of class, religion and age' at the Abbey; but it also violated the sharp line of authority Gregory and Yeats had sought to draw between Directors and actors" (2004, 14). In *Ghost Light* she is perceived, bitterly, as "Johnny Synge's bit of native. The proddy's little squaw. That Kingstown playboy's huer" (O'Connor, 3). In the text, furthermore, Molly's marginalisation in relation to her class and religion when engaged to Synge is fluidly connected with the public anger that her ageing body betrays in 1950s London, when age and race further compound her lesser position. To elaborate, the older Molly's reminiscences provide an escape from her bleak reality, while at the same time reinforcing her sense of otherness. In this manner, the novel attests to the social reality of women and ageing in Ireland and Britain in a consideration that undermines categories of identity by attesting to the multiple states of being available to Molly in old age. Molly is shown to draw on her memories, emotions and experiences, enriched by the ghostly presence of a lost loved one, as she surpasses the perceived limitations of her age and status.

In this reading, I draw upon theories from Woodward and Segal, which complement one another to illuminate O'Connor's imaginary of ageing. Woodward develops a theory of reminiscence in old age, which is "concerned with a certain moment, or moments, in the past" (1997, 2). Such echoes of the past inspire a generative, comforting mood. Furthermore, reminiscence is bound up in the trust and security one feels when "at the same time one feels oneself to be in a private space, one has a sense of extending oneself in companionship—as one holds a hand" (1997, 6).[3] In *Ghost Light*, although Molly has experienced more than her share of sorrows and though she lives in isolation and neglect,[4] a sense of solace derives from recollections of moments in her career and the lingering emotions of her relationship with Synge. Such reminiscence may be read alongside Segal's recent theory that as we age we retain traces of our previous self-states, so that psychically we are, "in one

[3]Woodward draws upon the theories of psychoanalysts Helene Deutsch, Christopher Bollas and J.-B. Pontalis, as they explore emotional memory, the character of feeling, and the secure intersubjective potential of the psychoanalytic space, respectively.

[4]Synge died the year after they were engaged, she has since been widowed and divorced, and her son was killed in an air crash (cf. Lunney 2009, n.p.).

sense, all ages and no age" (2014, 4).[5] This psychic layering creates a complex identity through which we perceive and encounter the world, all the while negotiating given images of the old (cf. 2014, 4). We are therefore required to build a psychological bridge across different ages and between inner and outer, as "on the one hand it can seem as though the self never ages; on the other we are forced to register our bodies and minds in constant transformation, especially by the impact we make upon others" (2014, 5). Bringing Segal's work to bear on *Ghost Light*, it is possible to explore how the text reflects upon the complexity of ageing. When readers meet Molly she is in her older years, poor and starving. Thinking back on her illustrious if quarrelsome past, recalling scenes in the Abbey and with Synge, she makes her way across war-torn, wintery London to act in a radio play in the BBC studios. While O'Connor illustrates Molly's outward deterioration, the meandering form and second-person narrative perspective provide insight into her inner life. On her journey, Molly is met with negative stereotypes of ageing that perhaps apprehend the reader, familiar with Molly's past selves, as much as they do Molly. In this manner, the disorientation of ageing emanates out from the text, shedding light on the distinctions and structures that produce the ageing subject.

In his "Acknowledgements and Caveat" to *Ghost Light*, O'Connor notes that "*Ghost Light* is a work of fiction, frequently taking immense liberties with fact" and "Molly's circumstances, although difficult in her later years, were not as depicted here" (O'Connor, 244). However, in bringing to life Molly as an older woman, *Ghost Light* serves to remember and account for this overlooked figure in the Irish historical archive. Ireland is often figured as a woman in Irish literature; she may be young and beautiful or old and in mourning, calling men to fight for her or lamenting their death. Typically, this stereotype serves *as* a figure of loss—lost land, lost culture, lost youth. Opposing this maternal figure, in "the cultural context of ageing," "the personifications of old age almost invariably take a monstrous feminine form, whether gorgon, witch, hag, or crone" (Segal 2008, 314; 315). Each side of this young/old binary sets out laws situating the female body in terms of social roles and expectations. In *Ghost Light*, side-stepping this symbolisation, Molly draws

[5] Segal draws upon psychoanalyst Donald Winnicott, who uses this expression to describe the multiple ages found in patients' psychic lives.

attention *to* lost histories informed by hierarchies of gender and class. This effect is achieved in part through the social and cultural contextualisation against which Molly negotiates her declining circumstances, which draw attention to how inequalities affect an individual's experiences of ageing into old age. In contrast to the situation of Synge's mother in Kingstown, the prosperous suburb of Dublin, for example, Molly's identity in her later years is constructed against a backdrop of 1950s London, in which she is part of an underprivileged stratum. As Toni Calasanti and Neal King illustrate, relations of inequality between groups intersect in a complex way with age. While age "is a source of disparity in its own right, in that those deemed 'not old' benefit from the ageism and maintain control of valued resources," inequalities in the distribution of resources also vary according to the distances and differences between various groups and the most privileged group of any Western society—elite white men (2015, 195; 198). In this light, her precarious position is illustrative of how Molly has travelled as she has aged; from her proximity to Synge, the central figure of privilege in the story, from a theatre culture in which she was celebrated for a time, and from her homeland, to a life on the margins of London society. In this manner, *Ghost Light* creates an alternative to the symbolic language systems of Irish womanhood and old age, drawing attention to other possibilities outside dominant psychical, social and political constructions.

Molly's position as an Irish woman in 1950s Britain further compounds her marginalised status. Notably, women made up the majority of Irish emigrants in the twentieth century (cf. Lennon et al. 1988, 23). In this period, despite women's work in the fight to achieve Irish independence, governments would actively legislate against their rights, particularly around reproduction, employment and benefits, for the next fifty years. The resulting social and sexual confinement created pressure to emigrate. When Britain was rebuilding its economy in the wake of the Second World War, there was a great wave of emigration, with hundreds of thousands of Irish people leaving for Britain and "the numbers of women over men emigrating reaching its highest point" (Lennon et al. 1988, 24; 25). This is the point in history at which we meet Molly. An Irish emigrant in London, her experience of social deprivation is not an unusual one. Gerard Leavey, Sati Sembhi and Gill Livingston note "high levels of social deprivation and poor health" among the Irish in Britain, "some of which has been attributed to prejudice and discrimination, the legacy of a colonial relationship" (2004, 763). Historically, the figure of the Irish Catholic brought together the colonial subject and the Catholic Other against which British National identity created itself. As Mary Hickman explains, despite assumptions of Irish assimilation in Britain, "both the colonial racism stemming from Anglo-Irish relations and the construction of the Irish (Catholic) as a historically significant Other of the English/British (Protestant) have framed the experience of the Irish in Britain" (1996, 5). In the twentieth century, this representation continued to be reproduced, though with specific differences, with the Irish perceived "as a social problem in their own right or as responsible for a wide range of social problems" (Hickman 1996, 208). Given this social and political history, we might observe that the outer world Molly encounters in London represents a continuum of the anti-Catholic discourse that constructed her as inferior in her relationship with Synge. In one respect, it is as though Molly hasn't aged—much of the discrimination that she faces is continuous. To return to Segal, however, as we age into old age we negotiate given images of the old as well as a layering of previous self-states. Older Molly is compelled to register the visual force of her ageing body as it intersects with class and race-based prejudice, and react to her encounters accordingly.

As an actress, Molly has the ability to perform the cultural markers that distinguish between groups, drawing attention to their constructed nature. For example, when a police constable approaches her and says, "Local are you, ma'am?," she states: "'I reside here, yes.' *Give him your genteel accent, Molly. It could do with a rehearsal!*" (O'Connor, 25, original emphasis). In this scene, it is apparent that Molly's old and destitute appearance has drawn the man's attention, though not out of sympathy. He is on the lookout for an elderly woman who is Irish, poor and a drunk:

> He comes closer, sucking his upper lip in a portentous manner. 'Lots of Irish, so I'm told. We've had numerous complaints. Apparently there's some female there too, old tramp sort of thing. Down on her luck I shouldn't wonder. Been seen begging now and again, bothering passers-by for pennies. Makes a nuisance of herself when she's drunk.' (O'Connor, 26)

The allegations are perhaps not unfounded; indeed, Molly is relieved that he doesn't insist on carrying her carpetbag, which is full of empty bottles that she will try to sell for a few pennies. The rhetoric, however, is sexist, racist and ageist. In this manner, the text highlights how the categorisations that situate us as subjects are further influenced by age. In a similar tone, a letter to *The Times* about the "*indignant persons roaming London*" deplores being "*assailed by the sight of a woman of not inconsiderably advanced years [...] in a condition of quite revolting disarray,*" who we understand to be Molly. On being approached by a police constable, she "*proved herself a native of a neighboring island [...] that has been notably far from friendly to Her Majesty's subjects, whilst continuing to export multitudes of her own. It really is 'a bit Irish'*" (O'Connor, 95, original emphasis). On the one hand, it is the case that "Evidence of heavy alcohol consumption and excessive rates of alcohol-related disease among the Irish in Britain is plentiful." However, research suggests that this is possibly connected to social adversity, migrant stress, or "that ritualistic drinking behaviour emphasises Irish ethnicity" (Leavey et al. 2004, 775). In the case of Molly, *Ghost Light* suggests that her drinking is the result of social isolation and devolving living conditions. The text furthermore demonstrates the incongruities between how Molly sees herself, and how society views Molly; to the police constable she is a "poor old mare. Spins a yarn about how she used to be an actress, needs a bob for the gas" (O'Connor, 26–27). To Molly, however, "*I am walking through London because I am busy, a professional. I have an appointment with people who need me*" (O'Connor, 11, original emphasis). The text thus demonstrates ageing in terms of the clash between the inner world and cultural stereotype; the figure others observe would appear a strange other to Molly. Furthermore, in the narrative style of the text, in which the reader is situated both within and outside Molly's consciousness, we are compelled to recognise and react to society's reflections and refractions, as though we are also ageing into old age. Such an experience can be described as uncanny.

The uncanny sense of something that is at once strangely other and eerily familiar permeates *Ghost Light* on a number of levels. "Ghost light" refers to the superstition of leaving a light burning in a theatre so that ghosts may find their way onstage. Throughout the novel, a ghostly past indeed makes its presence known. The action takes place on a day in London in 1952 as Molly travels across the city to act in what will be her final role. As she journeys, history and memories accumulate so that her past and present are revealed over one day. The novel begins "In the top floor room of the dilapidated townhouse" where "across the Terrace, a light has been on all night" (O'Connor, 1). Eerily, "this morning someone else is come to you again, out of the same light, somehow"

(O'Connor, 2). Throughout the day, Molly converses with Synge's memory, and imagines that she sees his ghostly figure (cf. O'Connor, 146). Such imaginings may be read in view of Freud's *The Uncanny*, in which something that is fearful leads us back to something that is known. Linked to this, both Segal and Woodward have elaborated on Freud's insight into the uncanny otherness of ageing. As Segal states, "a living person can appear uncanny, and weirdly frightening, if they trigger thoughts of extinction, reminding us of our mortality" (2014, 21). In addition, a mirror image can reflect personal and socially imprinted fears back to us (cf. Segal 2014, 23). As Woodward observes, "to see [...] one's own aged body with a shock of recognition is to experience the *uncanny*" (1991, 63, original emphasis). Such work accentuates the significance of the uncanny in *Ghost Light*, in which incidents of the familiar in the strange illuminate the experience of ageing. For instance, looking at an image in the National Portrait Gallery, Molly thinks "Heavens to Betsy, what an ugly old trout" (O'Connor, 59). Then she considers:

> But you're no beauty yourself any more. Be honest – the years aren't kind. And you feel that you have submerged into fretfulness with age, hear yourself murmuring of your anxieties with the troubled watchfulness of a child in an unfathomable world. And your old woman's *voice* – how did that happen? Your wheezing, brittle croakiness, distracted, muted, and you gossiping to the teacups for company. (O'Connor, 59–60, original emphasis)

Seeing uncanny echoes of herself in this image exposes for Molly her own vulnerabilities, reminding her of the transience of life and the reality of the ageing body. We might further extend this exploration of the uncanny to consider the text *Ghost Light* as a cultural object. In fiction, according to Freud, an uncanny feeling is produced "as soon as the writer [of fantasy] pretends to move in the world of common reality [...] he deceives us into thinking that he is giving us the sober truth, and then after all oversteps the bounds of possibility" (1919, 18). O'Connor's text, which draws on historical figures and is described by the author as "a work of fiction, frequently taking immense liberties with fact" (O'Connor, 244), is uncanny in that it "[effaces] the distinction between imagination and reality" (Freud, 1919, 15). Furthermore, we experience the uncanny, Freud argues, "when a symbol takes over the full functions and significance of the thing it symbolizes" (1919, 18). As an aesthetic object, then, *Ghost Light* both symbolises a ghost light and takes over the function of the thing it represents, lighting a stage on which its characters may come to life. On this stage, Molly's return as the leading lady, as uncanny, presses against the boundaries of dominant historical and cultural narratives, as in the nature of the uncanny she cannot be suppressed or concealed, and even in her mortality is bound to recur, in the dim ghost light bringing to life the figure of the ageing woman in all her many facets.

The visit from Synge's ghost sets Molly's path in motion. Her journey may fruitfully be read in light of Woodward's work on the role of mourning for stimulating creativity in old age. Attending to Freud, Woodward's focus is not on his seminal *Mourning and Melancholia*, in which it is desirous for the ego to detach its energies from the lost loved one so that it may invest its emotions elsewhere. Instead, she illuminates elements of Freud's later work that reveal how the impossibility of adequately representing loss and psychic pain informs creativity (cf. 1993, 89). Rather than successful mourning signalling the end of grief and pain, in his old age Freud reflected on the power accompanying these emotions and keeping them alive in memory. Thus, Woodward compellingly illustrates that loss in old age stimulates imagination. In this light, if Synge's ghost signifies a return of grief and pain, we might read this as a generative return, recognising the possibility for ghosts that haunt the conscious mind to be transformed as a means of enriching reality. Indeed, the trope of return is central to the novel. For instance, Molly recalls "the picture they made of the Daphne du Maurier novel [...] About the woman and the chap and the house and the drowned wife and the dreaming you went to Manderley again" (O'Connor, 9). The famous opening line of this gothic novel, *Rebecca*, "Last night I dreamt I went to Manderley again," serves to recall for Molly the tempestuous love affair between a wealthy landowner and an inner city Catholic girl. As past and present, reality and narrative merge, "You pout haughtily in the mirror. Fiercely narrow your eyes. '*I* am Mrs de Winter now,' you murmur" (O'Connor, 9, original emphasis). When, in the scene mentioned earlier, the policeman stops her suspiciously to ask her about an old tramp seen begging, making a nuisance of herself when she's drunk, Molly gives him the name "Mrs de Winter. Rebecca" (O'Connor, 25). As she recalls "the poor, brave bride and the sea and the shadows and the ghosts in the windblown curtains" (O'Connor, 21), Molly is at once both the *new* Mrs de Winter and her predecessor Rebecca, Maxim de Winter's first wife. In this, she represents both the uncanny repetition of the past and hope for regeneration. Recognising the creation of meaning as coming from within and from without, Molly's psychic reality merges with and enriches her external reality in the creation of a sense of self. In this manner, *Ghost Light* acknowledges the creative potential of mourning in old age and illustrates that while we understand ourselves through cultural constructions, drawing on personal experience also provides for a significant element of self-creation.

Ghost Light, then, reveals the richness of this ageing woman's inner life. The novel itself, as mentioned, represents a "ghost light," an aesthetic object reminding us why we should remember Molly, beyond what captures our romantic attention. It is possible to further consider the text, in light of the work of Christopher Bollas, as a potentially transformational object, that is, as a process that alters self-experience. To elaborate, a transformational object is an identification that emerges from the symbiotic relationship between a child and a caregiver; the transformational experience of being and becoming, as the mother facilitates the metamorphosis of the self and the environment (cf. Bollas 1987, 14). In adult life, the search for a moment that recalls this transformative experience might be realised in the encounter with an aesthetic object such as, for example, "a painting, a poem, an aria or symphony." Transformational objects are notable for their "uncanny quality"; they represent that which is known but not known (Bollas 1987, 16). Toward the end of *Ghost Light*, the eerie light of the unknown neighbour is still glowing, providing solace for Molly. As the narrator states, "One lamp must always be left burning when the theatre is dark, so the ghosts can perform their own plays" (O'Connor, 206). It is clear that Molly wants to be remembered. In one touching scene, she passes on her last letter from Synge to a girl of about seventeen, a hopeful actress, as a gift for the start of her career. Recalling Yeats' poem to Maud Gonne, Molly says to the girl, "Put that in some old book and take it down from time to time. And say a prayer for me when you do. Have we a bargain?" (O'Connor, 203). It might be argued that as the text functions to light the stage for Molly in the manner of a ghost light, it also works to transform dominant perceptions of the figure of the ageing woman, long perceived, in stage representations at least, as "A jealous auld hag. An irrepressible washerwoman. Some bitch to be bested in a pantomime" (O'Connor, 30). It is worth considering, at this point, that through the second-person "you" narration, the reader might be Molly, or Molly the author. This raises the question, what can the transference of Molly's experience, albeit imaginary, through *Ghost Light* as an aesthetic object, tell us about our own presence? Ultimately, however, and importantly, as the third-person narrator intervenes to remind us that what we are reading is a work of fiction, this also draws our attention to the question of the power and role of art.

In her reflections, which are expressive of the widespread cultural invisibility and alienation of the ageing woman, the reader learns from Molly that:

> It is not easy for an actress once she has passed a certain age to secure a role commensurate with her training. The parts are too few. It is that simple and inescapable. Not in Shakespeare, not in Ibsen, not in Shaw, nor in Chekhov. She wonders, recrossing Queensway, if any of the blockheads had mothers. Did they never once glance up from their inks and their parchments, their grubby little fingerprints besmirching the margins, seagulls of their own inadequacy flitting madly in the rafters, and notice there was an elderly woman moving about in the room, probably preparing their lunch? (O'Connor, 30)

Beyond this bleak outlook, damning of the blinkered view of dominant cultural narratives, we are introduced to a strong-willed woman and talented actress, with grace and self-possession that her colleagues still hold in high esteem. One of the greatest tragedies of this story—all the more because it is drawn from historical account (cf. Lunney, n.p.)—is that Molly meets such a harrowing end, as she dies from burns received on falling into the fire in her London lodgings. In a fictional newspaper clip entitled "Woman Unconscious," we find that police and firemen broke into a boarding house. The language describing the event is stark and unfeeling: "A severely burned elderly woman was found unconscious on the floor, having collapsed into the fireplace where she had evidently been burning books, having no other fuel at hand [...] A number of empty bottles were in evidence [...] It is thought that she was originally from Ireland and may have worked for a time in the theatre" (O'Connor, 207–208). From a cultural gerontological perspective, the power of *Ghost Light* lies in the challenge that it poses to real social issues. The text speaks of women who are ageing into old age and may be marginalised and fighting for representation. It also draws attention to the Irish women who emigrated to Britain in such large numbers in the early decades of the twentieth century. Doing so, *Ghost Light* challenges our ways of thinking about age, highlighting the relationship between age and creativity and embracing cultural complexity. It may be argued that, as with Molly, power relations of race and class have restricted social development for many women in old age. This lends weight to the importance of representation in helping to combat an ageist society. As Helene Moglen asserts, "Understanding how political and cultural forces shape the social relations and the psychology of ageing, we make resistance and innovation possible" (2008, 325). It is only through acknowledging past lives, and articulating anger at present constructions, that we can hope to promote social change. Culture, as it shapes how we understand ageing, can contribute to this discourse. In *Ghost Light*, the ghostly haunting of the text summons Molly's longings and losses, her romances and oppressions, thus acknowledging past lives and confronting ageist and social discriminations in a manner that compels recognition.

Works Cited

Bollas, Christopher. 1987. *The Shadow of the Object: Psychoanalysis of the Unthought Known*. London: Free Association Books.

Calasanti, Toni, and Neal King. 2015. Intersectionality and Age. In *Routledge Handbook of Cultural Gerontology*, ed. Julia Twigg, and Wendy Martin, 193–200. London, New York: Routledge.

Drong, Leszek. 2017. Mnemofictions: Rewriting the Past in *Ghost Light* by Joseph O'Connor. *Estudios Irlandeses* 12: 39–49.

Freud, Sigmund. 1919. *The Uncanny*. First published in *Imago*, Bd. V., 1919; reprinted in Sammlung, Fünfte Folge. Translated by Alix Strachey, 1–21. http://web.mit.edu/allanmc/www/freud1.pdf. Accessed 16 Aug 2017.

Hickman, Mary J. 1996. *Religion, Class and Identity: The State, the Catholic Church and the Education of the Irish in Britain*. Aldershot and Brookfield: Ashgate.

Leavey, Gerard, Sati Sembhi, and Gill Livingston. 2004. Older Irish Migrants Living in London: Identity, Loss and Return. *Journal of Ethnic and Migration Studies* 30 (4): 763–779.

Lennon, Mary, Marie McAdam, and Joanne O'Brien. 1988. *Across the Water: Irish Women's Lives in Britain*. London: Virago.

Lunney, Linde. 2009. O'Neill, Máire (Molly). *Dictionary of Irish Biography*, ed. James McGuire, and James Quinn. Cambridge, UK: Cambridge University Press; Royal Irish Academy. http://dib.cambridge.org/. Accessed 13 Apr 2017.

Moglen, Helene. 2008. Feminism, Transageing, and Ageism: A Response to Lynne Segal. *Studies in Gender and Sexuality* 9 (4): 323–327.

O'Connor, Joseph. 2010. *Ghost Light*. London: Vintage.

Pethica, James. 2004. 'A Young Man's Ghost': Lady Gregory and J.M. Synge. *Irish University Review* 34 (1): 1–20.

Pullen, Kirsten. 2006. Actresses. *Encyclopedia of Prostitution and Sex Work*, 2 Volumes, ed. Melissa Hope Ditmore, 9–11. Westport, CT: Greenwood Press.

Segal, Lynne. 2008. All Ages and None: Commentary on Helene Moglen's Ageing and Transageing. *Studies in Gender and Sexuality* 9 (4): 312–322.

Segal, Lynne. 2014. *Out of Time: The Pleasures and the Perils of Ageing*, intro. Elaine Showalter. London and New York: Verso.

Woodward, Kathleen M. 1991. *Ageing and Its Discontents: Freud and Other Fictions*. Bloomington and Indianapolis: Indiana University Press.

Woodward, Kathleen M. 1993. Late Theory, Late Style: Loss and Renewal in Freud and Barthes. *Ageing and Gender in Literature: Studies in Creativity*, ed. Anne M. Wyatt-Brown and Janice Rossen, 82–101. Charlottesville and London: University Press of Virginia.

Woodward, Kathleen M. 1997. *Telling Stories*. Responses by Andrew E. Scharlach and Marilyn Fabe. Occasional papers for the Doreen B. Townsend Center for the Humanities, no. 9.

CHAPTER 18

The Visibility of Women's Ageing and Agency in Suzanne Lacy's *The Crystal Quilt* (1987) and *Silver Action* (2013)

Kate Antosik-Parsons

For nearly half a century, American visual artist Suzanne Lacy (b.1945) has employed a diverse range of media in her artistic practice, including video, installation, photography and performance. Lacy defines her work as "new genre public art," that is, work created in the public realm that is activist in nature, incorporating traditional and non-traditional media alike to address overtly political and social issues relevant to people's lives. Arguably, her most striking works have been the large scale socially engaged, participatory art projects informed by feminism. A key concern in this body of work has been the potential of provocative conversations to activate wider awareness around pressing social, economic and political issues and how these, in turn, intersect with women's everyday lives. In particular, activism and gender politics feature strongly throughout her work.

This chapter examines two major participatory works, *The Crystal Quilt* (1987) and the more recent *Silver Action* (2013), as they relate to

K. Antosik-Parsons PhD (✉)
Humanities Institute, University College Dublin, Dublin, Ireland
e-mail: kate.antosikparsons@ucd.ie

C. McGlynn et al. (eds.), *Ageing Women in Literature and Visual Culture*,
DOI 10.1007/978-3-319-63609-2_18

women's ageing and agency. Each is unique and distinctive in its aims, framing, location and execution; for example, *The Crystal Quilt* was held on Mother's Day in a busy shopping centre in Minnesota, while *Silver Action* was staged within the museum setting at the Tate Modern, London. However, though separated by a quarter of a century, there is clearly a relationship between these two works, as both engaged approximately 400 women from different racial, class and social backgrounds over the age of 60 in structured conversations. Lacy's approach draws together oral and recorded histories, consciousness-raising discussions, women's community activism and participation, and individual experiences of ageing. Each utilised broadcast media and technologies, analogue and digital, relevant to the era in which they were created, adding to the nuanced layering of the works. This chapter considers *The Crystal Quilt* and *Silver Action* in terms of the visibility of women's ageing and agency and it analyses the possibilities that cultural representations of ageing women hold with regards to the production of knowledge and potential for social change.

Visual representations and media narratives of older age and ageing are often constituted, in part, by ageism; that is, the negative or positive stereotypes, or discrimination or preferential treatment of older people based on their chronological age (Iversen et al. 2009, 4). Although ageism is "most vicious toward the most vulnerable," it also affects younger people, "on how they anticipate their own life course and judge the value of older people" (Gillette 2015, 22). Linn Sandberg identifies two competing discourses of older age, one that characterises old age in terms of decline and the other which focuses on successful ageing. Successful ageing discourses are framed in terms of autonomy, activity and productivity, while decline discourses focus on frailty, illness, reliance on relatives and elder abuse (Sandberg 2013, 13). Successful ageing infers a level of choice; that older people can choose a healthy lifestyle, or to remain in control of their mental faculties, but this proves problematic because these assumptions often do not account for the structural supports necessary to enable this outcome (cf. O'Neil and Haydon 2015, 3). Although the commonly circulated stereotypes may be both positive and negative, it is typically the negative ones that prevail. These include poor health, declining mental ability, the perception that older people are more conservative, unhappy, lonely and undervalued (cf. Lyons 2009, 21).

These problematic representations often shape the public's perceptions of older age and contribute to the discrimination faced by older people.

However, there are specific gendered challenges that older women experience. A woman's social worth is often based on traditional patriarchal, heteronormative ideals of youth, beauty and the ability to bear children. There is a widespread view that "old age for women starts earlier than for men and lasts for many more years" and this perception is "socially defined, constructed, maintained and legitimised" (Victor 2004, 136). Furthermore, the societal expectation that older women must continue to conform to essentialist ideals of womanhood means that those who do not are often devalued. Sally Chivers asserts that for women "being old is an intimate but very public experience" (2003, 11). Ageing is also a highly embodied experience because the physical changes women encounter lead to perceptions of older women as physically vulnerable, asexual and defeminised, rendering them invisible and, simultaneously, hypervisible (cf. Woodward 2006, 163). Martha Holstein reflects: "I think it is safe to say that we are very aware of how we are changing and how these changes are rarely socially valued" (2015, 39). Women who manifest the physical changes of age more profoundly are more likely to be considered helpless and passive, leading them to be viewed as "cognitively incompetent" (Schafer and Shippee 2010, 92). These narratives of ageing and stereotypes of older women frame the analysis of *The Crystal Quilt* and *Silver Action* throughout this chapter.

The Crystal Quilt

The Crystal Quilt (1987) was staged on Mother's Day at the Crystal Court, also known as the IDS Center, a seven-storey shopping centre designed by architect Philip Johnson in downtown Minneapolis. A diverse group of 430 women aged 60 and over, dressed in black, entered the performance space, designated by a giant carpet on the ground floor of the centre, and sat at square card tables covered with black fabric. They folded back the fabric to reveal the red and yellow tablecloths beneath. The women performed choreographed arm and hand movements against the backdrop of a recorded soundscape, composed by Susan Stone, that featured women drawn from throughout the State of Minnesota conversing about their experiences of ageing and reflecting

Fig. 18.1 Suzanne Lacy, *The Crystal Quilt*, 1985–1987. © Suzanne Lacy

on fears and memories. Their discussion was framed by questions such as "What are the positive things about being old?" and "Is being older what you expected?" (Dopson 2012). The viewers, members of the public who happened across the performance either by intent or chance, observed the performance from several floors above as it unfolded below, the women's bodily gestures appearing like changing stitches on a gigantic quilt (Fig. 18.1).[1]

[1]A precursor to *The Crystal Quilt* was the earlier, *Whisper, the Waves, the Wind* (1983–1984). Lacy staged conversations between women aged 65 and over on the beach in La Jolla, California. The 154 women sat at tables covered with white cloths and engaged in conversations around different aspects of their lives. Audiences observed the tableaux from the cliffs above, listening to a recorded soundtrack, before descending to the beach below to experience the space.

In advance of the actual staging of the work, Lacy carried out a two-and-a-half-year research phase that built up a network of individuals from different communities and enlisted the assistance of 500 volunteers, 20 staff members and a team of 15 collaborating artists[2] (cf. Garoian 1999, 27). The research into the politics of ageing was gathered under the Whisper Minnesota project that incorporated different educational aspects, community building functions and artistic outputs with older women from different socio-economic backgrounds in community leadership roles across Minnesota (cf. Basting 1996, 59). As this was a live performance, the remaining traces that document the work's existence include video documentation, photographs, as well as written accounts by those who witnessed the performance. A time-lapse video filmed at a vantage point above the ground floor captured the set-up, performance and cessation of the work. This gave an understanding as to the sheer scale and the coordination of the work, as well as visualising the "life-cycle" of the work as it evolved over the space of several minutes. The concept of the evolution of the artwork, from research phase through to its completion, is intriguing to think about in terms of its relationship to ageing because it suggests that process is at the heart of Lacy's investigations into women and ageing. Furthermore, it is crucial to consider the politics of ageing as it relates to the cultural context of this work. The political climate of the United States in the 1980s was characterised by the conservative economic and fiscal policies driven by President Ronald Reagan. The Republican party aimed to increase defence spending as it sought to cut federal assistance programs for older people, such as Social Security and Medicare (cf. Novak 2015, 450). Organisations like the Gray Panthers, an advocacy group founded in the early 1970s by Maggie Kuhn after she was forced to retire at age 65, resisted these cuts. The Gray Panthers pressed for political action on specific economic and social issues that directly affected older people. They campaigned against the mandatory retirement age and the increasing privatisation of healthcare. They sought affordable housing and aimed to increase awareness of the negative stereotyping of older people. Lacy's work offered a timely and significant consideration of older women and ageing, particularly

[2] Participating artists include Nancy Dennis, Sharon Anderson, Phyllis Jane Rose, Phyllis Salzberg and Judy Kepes. Miriam Shapiro designed the quilt, while the scarves that were handed to participants as the work concluded were designed by Julie A., and PBS live broadcast produced by Emily Goldberg.

as women's projected life expectancy was nearly eight years longer than men's, meaning that these issues most likely had a substantial impact on women's lives over a greater period of time (CDC 2010).

The aural portion of the performance was powerfully significant in terms of rendering visible older women's private lives because it specifically addressed aspects of ageing related to illness, medical expenses, the women's perceptions of the impact their age might have on their children and, inevitably, death. Furthermore, the women considered their own perceptions of age and what they would like people to ask them about their lives. Perhaps most subversive was when they reflected on more hidden aspects such as their sexuality and how they took ownership of their sexual desires. These fragments of dialogue were intercut with different sounds that set the tone for the work: loon cries; Native American songs; the clanging of church bells and thunder claps. The Common Loon or Gavia Immer, the official state bird of Minnesota, has been dated back to approximately 60 million years, making it one of the oldest living bird species. The use of the loon cries, coupled with the sounds of thunder claps, evoked the wildness of the State of Minnesota. The inclusion of Native American songs highlighted that ageing might be valued differently across diverse cultural backgrounds, particularly as First Nations elders are respected for their knowledge and wisdom. This structure of the sounds focused viewers on specific aspects of the performance by giving time for reflection and audibly signalling a change in conversation. The performance ended with participant Meridel LeSeur (1900–1996), a writer and social activist, exclaiming: "I say I'm not aging, I'm ripening" (Brown 1995, 9).

Until the late 1990s, academic feminism ignored women's ageing because "the threat of dependency, whether by economic vulnerability or physical frailty, veils the later years in fear and shame, in turn commonly regulating older women into an isolated silence" (Basting 1998, 118). *The Crystal Quilt* aimed to counter this silencing by challenging the stereotypes of older women as frail and passive. The unusual audience perspective evoked the social isolation experienced by women as they age, but it bridged this distance by emphasising their personal reminiscences. This play on perspective is interesting in terms of its hierarchal structure: the viewer initially adopted the elevated position; however, nearing the conclusion of the performance, the audience was invited to join the women below. Those who engaged directly with the participants presented them with colourful scarves and this shifted the dynamic created by the elevated perspective. In doing so, it signalled an acknowledgement of the metaphorical distance between participant and viewer.

Visually, the design of the quilt was compelling. It featured a simplified pattern of geometric shapes; diamonds and triangles of bold primary colours, red and yellow, set on a black background. There was a strong graphic aesthetic and its bold compositional elements were reminiscent of modernist compositions, particularly those of Dutch painter Piet Mondrian (1872–1944). However, the most striking aspect was that this was a quilt in progress, a living quilt, stitched together by the life stories of the women who gathered together. This drew powerful parallels with historical quilting bees, where a group of women gathered to create a quilt collectively. These were considered especially important social spaces for rural women in the nineteenth century (Bronner 2015, 1024). There was an heirloom quality to *The Crystal Quilt*, as crystal was traditionally a precious wedding gift, which, like fine china, might be handed down from generation to generation.[3] A quilt held important value, especially as its creation historically marked the birth of a child, celebration of marriage, or a symbol of friendship. And yet, it is relevant that grassroots activism is also associated with quilting, specifically the Freedom Quilting Bee, the Black women's quilting cooperative established in 1965 in Alabama. It enabled Black women to financially support their families and organise for civil rights (cf. Callahan 2005, 3). Furthermore, as Kirsty Robertson contends, "across lines of age, class and race, quilting has been interpreted by many scholars, writers and quilters as emancipatory, creating important opportunities and spaces for women and the marginalized" (2014, 201). Although the activist element of the women of *The Crystal Quilt* is not overtly apparent, it is certainly present, as many of those who participated in this work were known for leadership within their respective communities. These

[3] *The Crystal Quilt* also drew a connection to Judy Chicago's seminal work, *The Dinner Party* (1979), as both were feminist installations that elevated craft to the level of fine art and addressed women's legacies.

women included Avis Foley, a human rights activist who was a founding member of the Minnesota Political Congress of Black Women, and Bea Swanson, an Ojibway from Minnesota's White Earth reservation, who founded a "grandmother's circle" to support grandmothers raising young children in the Minneapolis-St. Paul metro area[4] (McNally 2009, 305). Furthermore, the visual aesthetic of *The Crystal Quilt* evoked community building and collaboration in the moments of interconnection between the women when they gently touched hands as they spread out their fingers in different positions. These simple yet knowing gestures communicated support and solidarity. The women of *The Crystal Quilt* spoke of the significance of hands, as a symbol of hard work, as an intergenerational connection between mothers and daughters and powerfully, as one woman explained, "an indication of how much I have learned." In the composition of this work, Lacy deftly bound together the historical connotations of crystal and quilting with the sound installation and live broadcast on public access television. When these elements were juxtaposed with the varying representations of ageing women, it indicated that the work operated at a complex level to generate ideas on the politics of ageing in the late 1980s.

Silver Action

Silver Action (2013) was a five-hour long participatory event in which over 400 women from all over the United Kingdom, aged 60 and older, gathered to discuss their histories of activism. They were seated in groups of four at tables covered with yellow cloths, reminiscent of *The Crystal Quilt*, while their conversations were witnessed by live audiences in situ. The event was documented by 20 social media volunteers who live-tweeted using the hashtag #silveraction. Throughout the course of their discussions, the women self-selected who among their table went to a separate area where stenographers with laptops recorded and projected their stories and reflections onto the concrete walls of the performance space. In another spatially related area, three kitchen-table-style discussions engaged twenty-four older women, while at a fourth table women

[4]Other women in the performance included Margaret Pederson, Edna Schwartz, Muriel Vaughn, a former Irish Catholic nun; Agnes Reick, a white woman raised in a rural area outside of Eau Claire, Wisconsin; and Etta Furlow, an African-American woman whose careers included nursing, factory work and community activism.

Fig. 18.2 Suzanne Lacy, *Silver Action*, 2013. As part of BMW Tate Live, Tate Modern. Photo: © Gabrielle Fonseca Johnson for Tate Photography, 2013

of mixed ages held an intergenerational conversation. Throughout the duration of the event, their discussions were shaped by specific questions such as: "What is different for you now, with age?; What can older women contribute?; What are the challenges we face?"; "Describe something that you witnessed, experienced or read, that might have propelled you to action or activism?" Staging *Silver Action* in the industrial space of the Tanks at the Tate Modern, housed in the former Bankside Power Station located on the Thames river, brought the work into a museum setting, with its connotations of institutional value, yet also evoked the power generated within the former plant. The association with the processing of raw power directly related to the women's activism, suggesting that even as these activists grow older, there remains both the potential and capability to harness their energy and passion for their specific political and social causes (Fig. 18.2).

With *Silver Action,* there were several ways to access and experience the work and this relates specifically to the means through which knowledge in the work was transmitted. Oral history became written history as it was projected onto the wall of the Tanks. As the live audience circulated through the space, they overheard conversations and read the transcribed histories. Their movement through the space allowed for an active engagement with the women's personal histories, because they were actively listening, as opposed to passive engaging, as one often does when gazing at a traditional work of art. The social media element built another layer into the transmission from oral to written histories, as the information was filtered and projected through the lens of the person receiving the information. It was then sent out in real time for those experiencing the artwork remotely and served to disseminate the work to larger audiences. Interestingly, the volunteers were not allowed to engage the women in conversation; their specific remit was quite simply to bear witness by listening and documenting the conversations. The social media team also shared pictures before the work began, and, like the documentations that remain of *The Crystal Quilt*, this sharing of information recorded the set up and, in turn, provided the audience with the insight that the meaning of the work was not generated upon completion but that the process of engagement was responsible for making meaning. The tweets tagged #silveraction were compiled on Storify, a social media platform that allows people to create collections of social media posts. This enabled those who experienced the work in person to return to it via the internet, while those who were not actually present might still access a myriad of different perspectives and information as it unfolded during *Silver Action*.

Silver Action brought together a diverse cross-section of women who participated in, and some of whom remain currently active in, different activist movements. Among the women present were anti-nuclear campaigner Stella Hardiman; Sue Mullan, who worked for the National Council for Civil Liberties during the miner's strike; Ann Rossiter, an Irish woman who, after suffering a botched back-street abortion in the 1960s, became a powerful voice for abortion rights; Paula Kaniuk, a staunch supporter of the Silentnight strike in Lancashire; and Maggie Smith, a founder of the Housewives Register, which led campaigns on many important familial and children's issues (cf. Owen 2013). Pragna Patel and other members of the Southall Black Sisters, a group of Asian women with a long history of fighting racism and organising for human rights, were also participants in the work. One volunteer noted, "Age range at my table is 61 to 75 years, now discussing big differences even between those ages" (Gilheany 2013). In highlighting that these women were on the edges of different generations, it was made clear that they were by no means a homogenous group. This demonstrates that the issues they campaigned for were as diverse as the participants themselves. However, collectivity was also present in *Silver Action*, as there was the possibility for shared participation in specific activism. Additionally, as several social media volunteers commented, collectivity was also physically manifested; the women's voices created a murmur or hum as their stories filled up the space. Another commentator noted, "The silences here are so powerful." This differs from the types of sounds the audience heard in *The Crystal Quilt*, for in *Silver Action* when one distanced themselves from the tables of women, it was not possible to discern individual voices unless the viewer actively turned to read the visibly projected wall stories.

The title of the work, *Silver Action,* calls to mind quicksilver, the liquid metal mercury used in older thermometers; it references movement and rapid change, perhaps alluding to the ability to gauge a temperature or climate for something. This appears contrary to the common cultural perception that people slow down, mentally and physically as they age. The title also implies cherished silverware, an heirloom often associated with age. Though it can acquire a tarnished patina, with careful polishing it remains unchanged by time. It is telling that Lacy chose the word "silver" as opposed to "grey"; although both are associated with the colour one's hair turns with age, grey can be perceived as dull while silver holds a more sprightly or lively connotation. The second half of the title, action, recalls the importance of the term "action" within the context of the performance art genre, particularly from the 1960s and 1970s when it was adopted by feminists, where the focus on an action or series of actions was a disruptive strategy that challenged static definitions of art. Therefore, *Silver Action*, rooted in the histories of women's activism, rendered visible older women's agency by subverting dominant narratives about ageing women as passive and helpless. It undercut patriarchal stereotypes that insisted older women's social value be measured by physical appearance. Instead, *Silver Action* revalued these older women for their lasting contributions to improve the lives of women across a diverse number of communities as they individually and collectively demanded a more just and equitable society.

The Visibility of Ageing and Agency

The visibility of older women's ageing and their agency in Lacy's works is closely aligned with the emphasis that the artist places on the subjectivity of the participant. By focusing on the women's own experiences and the discussion points that enabled them to reflect on their own lives, the individual subjectivity of each ageing woman can be equated with agency. Julia Twigg and Wendy Martin assert that cultural production holds the potential to filter and refigure how the process of ageing and the later years are understood, embodied and performed (cf. 2014, 3). They argue that autobiography and narrative can work to recover "the individuality of older lives" by demonstrating that the depth and breadth of older people's experiences, "contrary to the stereotype, are more and not less diverse than the young" (2014, 3). This was evident in *The Crystal Quilt* when a woman desired to express her accomplishments, stating: "I would like persons, young and old, to ask me what I feel my contribution to society is." Meanwhile, another reflected, "I suffer a lot from nobody listening to me," and she explained that to ignore the untapped potential of the wisdom acquired by older women is "a great cultural loss." Similarly, in *Silver Action*, one observer commented, "You never know what people might have achieved in their life #silveraction #dontjudgeabookbyitscover" (Gilheany 2013). In focusing on the subjectivity of the older woman as an individual, *The Crystal Quilt* and *Silver Action* bridge the perceived divide between women's private and public lives, illustrating the relationship between the two. Yet, it is precisely because Lacy works with large numbers of participants that the multitude of individual voices can emerge. This is not to say that works like *The Crystal Quilt* and *Silver Action* permanently transform the lives of these older women. Even Lacy herself cautions: "An artwork is not as effective as a treaty or a law or a budget change [...] I don't think a single artwork transforms society. But what an artwork does is create a cultural milieu within which things will be understood differently" (qtd. in Barnett 2013). In Lacy's work, older women were given a platform for their voices to be heard because the emphasis on subjectivity enabled them to highlight the similarities and, perhaps most importantly, the differences between them.

In terms of the visibility of ageing and agency, while *The Crystal Quilt* touched upon the narratives of presumed decline women experience as they age, *Silver Action* engaged with narratives of women's successful ageing. These narratives draw upon the idea that "individual lifestyle and consumption choices" drive the individual to age positively (O'Neil and Haydon 2015, 3). The unspoken assumption of this narrative is that those who do not choose well are presumed to have failed to have managed their ageing. In addressing women's involvement in activism, *Silver Action* points to collective organising and public actions as key to improving the lives of marginalised men, women and children. This counters the problematic notion of ageing as solely reliant on the individual, because feminist activism forges connections between diverse groups of people and seeks to expose seemingly invisible inequalities. This relationship to feminist activism acknowledges the complexities of structural inequalities that exist, enabling some women to be perceived as ageing in a positive manner, while others do not.

Furthermore, it can be argued that *Silver Action* built upon several of the themes that emerged from the conversations in *The Crystal Quilt*, particularly that older women feel their contributions to society are invisible and their acquired wealth of knowledge remains untapped. In *Silver Action* this was manifested in terms of intergenerational feminism. Kathleen Woodward argues that "ageism is entrenched in feminism itself"; that it should come as no surprise that "as women we have ourselves internalized our culture's prejudices against aging and old age" (1999, xi). This is particularly evident when feminist movements are conceptualised in terms of waves, for example, when differentiating between second-wave and third-wave feminisms or between feminisms and "post" feminisms, there has been a desire to define oneself against the work of the previous generations. Furthermore, Age UK director Michelle Mitchell argues that the invisibility of older women within feminism is due, in part, to:

> the historic preoccupation of feminism with the first forty years of the female life cycle, [which] is perhaps based on a belief that once the social structures tied up with maternity and employment have been passed, inequality is diffused in a post-labour world. But, as we have seen, rather than being dissipated, the inequalities of gender are focused and extended in later life. (2013, 56)

Silver Action insistently returned to this point, as the women discussed the ways in which they remain involved in their activism. One woman questioned, "Do younger women really value all the sacrifices that 3rd wave activists have made? Probably not" (Gilheany 2013). However, Catherine Long noted, "As a helper on that day, the recurrent refrain I heard from older women was 'we still have so much to give,' and from younger women, 'we want to hear and learn from you'" (2013, 33). As this observation demonstrates, older women are not simply static repositories of acquired knowledge; they can continue to make positive contributions to society and the younger generation values this input.

In the present moment, *The Crystal Quilt* and *Silver Action* take on different, and perhaps more critical, meanings when considered against the backdrop of the current political climate amid several years of harsh austerity measures that have pushed ageing populations into precarious positions. Indeed, what relevance might *Silver Action* now hold given the United Kingdom's impending withdrawal from the European Union? In June 2016, the countries that collectively form the United Kingdom voted to withdraw their membership of the EU. "Brexit," a portmanteau of British Exit, won the referendum with 51.9% of the votes cast in favour of leaving the EU. Post-voting polls show that approximately 60% of voters age 65 and over voted to leave the EU, closely followed by voters 55 and over who voted 57% to leave (Hennessy 2016). The ageist rhetoric that was frequently repeated in the wake of the global economic crisis (2008) again re-emerged in force after Brexit result, and reinforced the idea that the baby boomer population, which is the large, now ageing population born in the aftermath of the Second World War, has little or no regard for the future of younger generations (cf. Segal 2013, 116–117). However, Elaine Showalter argues: "While the popular image of political commitment among the old is a move to the right, many people 'sustain their radical outlook to the very end,' continuing to campaign for peace, women's liberation, socialism, and progressive change, and finding that politics still gives 'meaning to their lives'" (2013, 26). During the kitchen table discussion, a woman reminisced, "We were all struggling with how do we make these links around different forms of inequality and between subservience and domination," while another contributed, "the whole intersectional approach to feminism and to political struggles here developed earlier than in other places in Europe [...] and it was also very connected to anti-colonialism."

These reflections are remarkably relevant in a contemporary context. As the different types of intersectional feminist activism embarked upon by the women of *Silver Action* arguably demonstrates, the agency, knowledge and, indeed, experiences of ageing women can be used strategically to combat the rise of gendered, xenophobic, racially motivated hate crimes. By enabling women to mutually reflect on their participation in different areas of activism, *Silver Action* acknowledges, reaffirms and, importantly, revalues their contributions to the social movements that shaped the face of British society over the last 50 years. The potential for contemporary community organisations and activist movements to mobilise the agency of their older counterparts and allies holds enormous possibilities.

To conclude, *The Crystal Quilt* and *Silver Action* are separate yet related large-scale works that provoke careful consideration of the politics of ageing. It is relevant to the examination of older women and ageing in the context of this chapter to mention that Lacy herself is of the baby boomer generation. This allows for the distinct possibility that the artist's own perceptions of older age, as well as the challenges ageing women face, have changed in the time between the creation of *The Crystal Quilt* and *Silver Action*. In relation to her interest in ageing in the 1980s, Lacy remarked:

> It grew to take on social and political ramifications – older women's cultural invisibility, the potential loss of dignity and respect we face as we age, and the resources that this society shuts off in its flight from death. These are all important aspects of the performance, but as the work progressed I've delved deeper into my own experience, and fear, of approaching death. (2010, 154)

Lacy's work is structured on an aesthetic that advocates rendering visible the political, economic and social conditions that impact deeply on women's lives. In exploring the subject of ageing and the experiences of older women, these works directly challenge viewers to confront their own fears and misconceptions about ageing and reveal the need to approach ageing from multiple points of analyses, accounting for gender, sexuality, race, class and abilities. Throughout these works are woven individual and collective stories of ageing, agency and visibility. Older women are given opportunities to reflect on their own lives as well as to find solidarity and strength in the voices of others. It is most telling that in the artworks examined, a woman from each work expressed, nearly word for word, "I hope for as long as I live, I will retain my curiosity" (Gilheany 2013). The desire of many older women to continue to mentally challenge themselves, to maintain involvement in their communities, and to remain visible, suggests that these women seek to actively subvert the stereotypes of the ageing woman as frail and burdensome. This is strongly brought into focus when a woman from *Silver Action* declared, "We tried to do it all. We did it all! We all had tremendous energy. I think we still have tremendous energy now [...] I'm still very active. I'm still fighting" (Gilheany 2013).

Works Cited

Barnett, Laura. 2013. Tate Modern's Women's Liberation Army. *The Guardian*, Jan 29. Accessed 22 Nov 2016. https://www.theguardian.com/artanddesign/2013/jan/29/tate-modern-womens-liberation-army.

Basting, Anne Davis. 1996. Amnesia Interrupted: Re-Membering the Living Past in Feminist Theory and Suzanne Lacy's *Crystal Quilt*. *Journal of Dramatic Theory and Criticism*. 11 (1): 55–80.

Basting, Anne Davis. 1998. *The States of Age: Performing Age in Contemporary American Culture*. Ann Arbor: University of Michigan Press.

Bronner, Simon. 2015. *Encyclopedia of American Folklife*. London: Routledge.

Brown, Betty Ann. 1995. Some Thoughts on the History of Community Building as an Art Form. *Community Properties*, 6–12. Huntington Beach: Huntington Beach Art Center.

Callahan, Nancy. 2005. *Freedom Quilting Bee: Folk Art and the Civil Rights Movement in Alabama*. Tuscaloosa: The University of Alabama Press.

CDC/NCHS. 2010. Life Expectancy at Birth, at 65 Years of Age, and at 75 Years of Age, by Race and Sex: United States, Selected Years 1900–2007. CDC/NCHS, National Vital Statistics System; Grove RD, Hetzel AM. Accessed 23 Feb 2017. https://www.cdc.gov/nchs/data/hus/2010/022.pdf.

Chivers, Sally. 2003. *From Old Woman to Older Women: Contemporary Culture and Women's Narratives*. Columbus: Ohio State Press.

Dopson, Harriet. 2012. Suzanne Lacy: The Crystal Quilt. *One Stop Arts*, Aug 20. Accessed 28 Nov 2016. http://onestoparts.com/review-suzanne-lacy-crystal-quilt.

Forster Communications. 2013. Loud and Proud, Feb 13. Accessed 28 Nov 2016. http://www.forster.co.uk/insight/loud-and-proud/#.UR0nWQzU-GM.twitter.

Garoian, Charles R. 1999. *Performing Pedagogy: Toward an Art of Politics*. New York: SUNY Press.

Gilheaney, Peter. 2013. Silver Action—The Social Media Story of an Event. Accessed 8 Nov 2016. https://storify.com/petergilheany/silver-action-the-social-media-story-of-an-event.

Gullette, Margaret Morganroth. 2015. Aged by Culture. *Routledge Handbook of Cultural Gerontology*, eds. Julia Twigg and Wendy Morgan, 21–28. London: Routledge.

Hayward-Tapp, Caitlin. 2013. Ripening, Not Aging. *The F Word*. Accessed 10 Nov 2016. https://www.thefword.org.uk/2012/07/suzanne_lacy_interview/.

Hennessy, Mark. 2016. Post-Brexit Poll Shows Gulf between Young and Old Voters. *Irish Times,* June 27. Accessed 23 Nov 2016. http://www.irishtimes.com/news/ireland/irish-news/post-brexit-poll-shows-gulf-between-young-and-old-voters-1.2701611.

Holstein, Martha. 2015. *Women in Late Life: Critical Perspectives on Gender and Age*. Lanham: Rowman & Littlefield.

Iversen, Thomas Nicolaj, Lars Larsen, and Per Erik Solem. 2009. A Conceptual Analysis of Ageism. *Nordic Psychology*. 61: 4–22.

Lacy, Suzanne. 1987. The Crystal Quilt. Accessed 8 Nov 2016. http://www.suzannelacy.com/early-works/#/the-crystal-quilt/.

Lacy, Suzanne. 2010. *Leaving Art: Writings on Performance, Politics, and Publics, 1974–2007*. Durham: Duke University Press.

Lacy, Suzanne. 2013. Silver Action. Accessed 8 Nov 2016. http://www.suzannelacy.com/recent-works/#/silver-action-2013/.

Long, Catherine. 2013. Silver Action—Talking Across the Generations. In *A Compendium of Essays: Has the Sisterhood Forgotten Older Women?*, eds. Sally-Marie Bamford and Jessica Watson, 31–33. London: International Longevity Centre—UK.

Lyons, Imogen. 2009. *Public Perceptions of Older People and Ageing: A Literature Review*. Dublin: National Centre for the Protection of Older People and Health Services Executive. http://www.ncpop.ie/Year%201%20Reports/Microsoft%20Word%20-%20NCPOP%20Lit%20Rev%201%20IL%2001_12_09Cover%20inc22_01_10.pdf.

McNally, Michael David. 2009. *Honoring Elders: Aging, Authority, and Ojibwe Religion*. New York: Columbia University Press.

Mitchell, Michelle. 2013. Older Women and Care: Are They Invisible to the Sisterhood? In *A Compendium of Essays: Has the Sisterhood Forgotten Older Women?* eds. Sally-Marie Bamford and Jessica Watson, 55–58. London: International Longevity Centre—UK.

Novak, Mark. 2015. *Issues in Aging*. London: Routledge.

Avis F. Foley: Obituary. 2002. Accessed 28 Nov 2016. http://www.legacy.com/obituaries/twincities/obituary.aspx?n=avis-f-foley&pid=219642.

O'Neil, Moira, and Abigail Haydon. 2015. *Aging, Agency and Attribution of Responsibility: Shifting Public Discourse about Older Adults*. Washington, DC: FrameWorks Institute.

Owen, Jonathan. 2013. The Women who Changed Britain Forever. *Independent*, Feb 3. Accessed 31 Dec 2016. http://www.independent.co.uk/news/uk/politics/the-women-who-changed-britain-forever-8478498.html.

Robertson, Kirsty. 2014. Quilts for the Twenty-First Century: Activism in the Expanding Field of Quilting. In *Handbook of Textiles*, eds. Janis Jefferies, Hazel Clark, and Diana Wood Conroy, 197–210. London: Bloomsbury Press.
Sandberg, Linn. 2013. Affirmative Old Age: The Ageing Body and Feminist Theories on Difference. *International Journal of Ageing and Later Life* 8 (1): 11–40.
Schafer, Markus, and Tetyana P. Shippee. 2010. Age Identity, Gender, and Perceptions of Decline: Does Feeling Older Lead to Pessimistic Dispositions About Cognitive Aging? *The Journal of Gerontology* 65B (1): 91–96.
Segal, Lynne. 2013. *Out of Time: The Pleasures and Perils of Ageing*. London: Verso Books.
Showalter, Elaine. 2013. Introduction. In *Out of Time: The Pleasures and the Perils of Ageing*, ed. Lynne Segal, 15–29. London: Verso Books.
State of Minnesota. State Bird. Accessed 27 Dec 2016. https://mn.gov/portal/about-minnesota/state-symbols/bird.jsp.
Twigg, Julia, and Wendy Martin. 2014. The Challenge of Cultural Gerontology. *The Gerontologist*, 00.00: 1–7. Accessed 23 April 2017. https://www.researchgate.net/profile/Julia_Twigg/publication/263474947_The_Challenge_of_Cultural_Gerontology/links/53e7292e0cf2fb7487218706/The-Challenge-of-Cultural-Gerontology.pdf.
Victor, Christina. 2004. *The Social Context of Ageing: A Textbook of Gerontology*. London: Routledge.
Woodward, Kathleen. 1999. Introduction. *Figuring Age: Women, Bodies, Generations*, ed. Kathleen Woodward, ix–xxx. Indiana: Indiana University Press.
Woodward, Kathleen. 2006. Performing Age, Performing Gender. *NWSA Journal* 18 (1): 162–189.

CHAPTER 19

Afterword

Germaine Greer

Middle-aged women have hardly to stir from their own sofas to be confronted with an entirely negative vision of the second half of their long lives. As they are innocently enjoying their favourite mid-afternoon TV quiz shows, they are regularly regaled in the commercial breaks with imagery of women rather younger than they, who are delighted to be able to laugh without wetting themselves. They are sufferers, we are told, from "weak bladder" that would have them leaking copiously up hill and down dale, if it weren't for their having spent money on pads and pants that can be relied upon to absorb and store immense amounts of bodily leakage. These rejoice in names like "Always Discreet" and cost significant amounts of money even without the Value Added Tax that is applied to them because the taxman classes them as luxury products.

There is no disease or deformity called "weak bladder." There is stress incontinence, which can be dealt with by pelvic floor exercises, and by medical and surgical interventions (these last being so dodgy that in the UK they are now the subject of agitation for a ban). The TV commercials offer no alternatives and thus both reinforce women's reluctance to seek help and exacerbate their anxiety.

G. Greer (✉)

C. McGlynn et al. (eds.), *Ageing Women in Literature and Visual Culture*,
DOI 10.1007/978-3-319-63609-2_19

Incontinence is mentioned whenever old women are mentioned. Care homes are said to smell of pee, which may or may not be true. What is true is that the old people in them are locked up, imprisoned without charge. Where old women are concerned, Habeas Corpus can be defied with impunity. Occasionally old women break out of their prisons; often CCTV footage can show a last image of an old lady picking her way past the shops only for the track to end there. Some time later, a column inch or so in the local paper will tell us that a body has been found in a ditch. (She made her bolt for freedom, and she found it.)

Advertising is the most pervasive and persuasive form of visual culture. It is based in a thorough understanding of its target audience, arrived at by constant assessment of the effectiveness of its messages. One truth that it has established is that older women will not respond positively to advertising that is addressed to women of their age. This fact should concern us, because it may mean that when it comes to age women are in denial. Age brings real challenges; denial is no way to cope with them. As far as visual culture is concerned, clothing designed for the over fifties must be modelled by women under fifty; a car designed for one careful lady driver will be presented as coveted by boy racers. Older women have greater buying power than younger women, but no one wants to sell to them. When an elderly woman plucks up the courage to cross the threshold of a fashion boutique, she is likely to find either that none of the sales staff is interested in helping her or that they assume she is shopping for somebody else. It is as if they dread the thought that a woman past her sell-by date might be seen out and about wearing their garments. The time is not long past when old women were routinely guyed by TV advertising. The magical effects of a particular lager would become manifest when, as young men supped it, the old women in the pub faded into nothingness. Older women were the people too stupid to understand that new detergents could get clothes clean in cold water. Now they are the people who can't laugh without wetting themselves. Hardly a change for the better.

By middle age, most women have realised that the account of their lives that is peddled by the mass media is not something they can recognise or tolerate. The websites that offer to tell us how to be fabulous at 60 assume that we want to be cover girls when what we would dearly like is well-cut, elegant, comfortable clothes that will outlast the season, shopping being the nightmare that it is. Shopping would be less of a nightmare if the muzak could be turned off so that we could hear what was being said to us. To present us with the phenomenon of Carmen dell'Orefice still strutting the catwalks with the help of two replacement knees at 86 is of no help whatsoever. Most of us have no desire to out-glitter Baddie Winkle or Iman or Iris Apfel or Kris Jenner. Though Joni Mitchell (born 1943) and Joan Didion (born 1934) may have been used as models for leading cosmetic brands in 2015, the campaigns relied on the surprisingness of the choice. There was never any possibility that the images of these female celebrities created by an army of stylists plus lighting designers and leading glamour photographers would increase the visibility of lesser female mortals.

The subject of the present collection is given as "women and ageing in literature and visual culture"; this does not refer to older women who are active in literature and visual culture but to "ageing women as depicted in literature and visual culture." Yet I, who am seventy-eight, have been invited to write an afterword to the volume. In a true spirit of aged cantankerousness, then, I propose to remind readers that aged women themselves have been explicit and eloquent in memoir and in fiction about their condition. In far too many cases, though their works have been successful in their time, they are now forgotten. How could we have forgotten the unforgettable Ivy Compton-Burnett, who produced a masterpiece every two years of her writing life, and was made a Dame two years before her death in 1969 at the age of 85? Her work is still admired by some of the most discerning readers on earth but attempts to get her books back in the bookstores have largely failed. She doesn't even make it as a Virago Modern Classic. There are old women who have continued to achieve great things well into their eighties and nineties, who should not be forgotten. They were lucky, surely, but they did not waste their luck in futile repining about the things they could no longer do or what they looked like in the mirror, as de Beauvoir does, not in *La Vieillesse*, which is here cited repeatedly, but in the third instalment of her biography, *La Force des Choses*, published when she was a spring chicken of 55. De Beauvoir never became reconciled to her own healthy, active, celebrated and extraordinarily privileged old age. Indeed it interests her rather less than the old age of Jean Paul Sartre, her relationship with whom she regarded as the crowning achievement of her life. We now know more about that unequal and in many ways repellent relationship than we would have wanted to know, but there has been little in the way of readjustment of de Beauvoir's credentials as a feminist. Far more courageous is Colette, whose heroine in *Chéri* (1920) and the

The Last of Chéri goes through menopause and beyond; Colette is not mentioned in this book at all, which is a shame. Colette met her last husband in 1925 when she was 52; the couple would stay together until her death in 1954 at the age of 81. More important than any of her novels in its understanding of ageing is *La Naissance du Jour*, a loving and lyrical reminiscence of her mother, Sido.

One of the most assured and rewarding elderly writers to grapple with her own situation, living as she has been for ten years in an old people's home, is 99-year-old Diana Athill. After 50 years in publishing as an editor with André Deutsch, she retired in 1993. Her memoir comes in seven instalments published over thirty years. Athill writes with wit and compassion, and deep acceptance of her condition and her circumstances. She undertook her memoir because, she said, "book after book has been written about being young, and even more of them about the elaborate and testing experiences that cluster round procreation, but there is not much on record about falling away."

There is more written by women about their "falling away" than one might infer from the remark by a reviewer in the *Washington Post* that the subject is no more popular "than a colostomy bag." Leaving aside the classic contributions of Vita Sackville-West, Muriel Spark and Elizabeth Taylor, to name but three, we have Booker Prize winner Penelope Lively's *Ammonites and Leaping Fish: A Life in Time* published in 2013. A.S. Byatt, another Booker Prize winner, has written movingly about older women as her younger sister, Dame Margaret Drabble, does in her latest novel, *The Dark Flood Rises.* Old women are a sizable demographic; even so, *Mad about The Boy*, the third book in the Bridget Jones series, in which the heroine has become a widow in her fifties, is the least popular. Helen Fielding recently positioned the fourth book in the series between the second and third, rather than follow her heroine into her sixties. Fielding herself is pushing sixty, still bubbly, still blonde. As 73-year-old Lynne Segal points out in *Out of Time: The Pleasures and the Perils of Ageing*, published in 2013, the principal peril of ageing is ageism—other people's and one's own.

There is no shortage of women looking for ideas about how to manage their own ageing, but not enough apparently to keep women's own accounts of their *Reifung* on the shelves of the bookstores. It would be good to know whether the foregrounding of Joan Didion by the fashion industry in 2015 made any difference to the sales of *Blue Nights*, her own account of her ageing, published in 2011 when she was 77. The hype that surrounded the advertising campaign made more of her lipstick than her writing. We might wonder too whether anyone is still reading Nora Ephron's account, called *I Remember Nothing*, published in 2010, four years after she was diagnosed with acute myeloid leukemia, and 2 years before her death in 2012 at the age of 71. In Carolyn G. Heilbrun's *The Last Gift of Time: Life Beyond Sixty* published in 1997, she announced her intention of ending her life at 70; in fact she delayed her suicide until 2003, when she was 77. Does anyone now read *The Last Gift of Time*? Betty Friedan began working on *The Fountain of Age* at the age of 60, hoping that she would find an antidote to what she called "the dreariness of old age"; by the time it was finished, she was 72 and had come to the conclusion that there has never been a better time for "older" people. She would publish an autobiography, *Life So Far*, in 2000 when she was almost 80. Ursula Le Guin (born 1929) has written wonderfully in both prose, in *The Wave in the Mind*, and poetry, in *Late in the Day*, on her own ageing. May Sarton kept on writing—actually dictating—almost until the very last minute; 1992 brought us *Endgame: A Journal of the Seventy-Ninth Year*, 1993 brought *Encore: A Journal of the Eightieth Year*, and 1996, *At Eighty-Two: A Journal*. During these years, Sarton was terminally ill and very frail, but undaunted.

So much (but nowhere near enough) about old women in literature. If we were to attempt a discussion of old women in the visual arts, we would find ourselves trying to give a sensible account in a few words of the achievement of, for example, Louise Bourgeois, who worked up to the last weeks of her long life, dying six months short of her hundredth birthday in 2010, when major galleries all over the world were still vying to acquire versions of her famous bronze, "Maman." Louise Nevelson too worked as a sculptor well into her seventies and left an estate worth $100,000,000 when she died in 1988 at the age of 89. Magdalena Abakanowicz is still working on monumental sculptures at the age of 86. Still producing work in an astonishing variety of visual media are Yayoi Kusama (born 1929), Gillian Ayres (born 1930), Audrey Flack (born 1931), Rose Wylie (born 1934), Paula Rego (born 1935), Judy Chicago (born 1939), Jennifer Bartlett (born 1941) and Annette Messager (born 1943). Every one of these women could give an account of her own strategy for coping with old age; we can only hope that some publishers somewhere will give them the opportunity, before it is too late.

Index

C. McGlynn et al. (eds.), *Ageing Women in Literature and Visual Culture*,
DOI 10.1007/978-3-319-63609-2